Business Ethics and Values

Pearson
Education

We work with leading authors to develop the strongest
educational materials in business, bringing cutting-edge
thinking and best learning practice to a global market.

Under a range of well-known imprints, including
Financial Times Prentice Hall, we craft high quality
print and electronic publications which help readers
to understand and apply their content, whether
studying or at work.

To find out more about the complete range of our
publishing, please visit us on the World Wide Web at:
www.pearsoneduc.com

Business Ethics and Values

Colin Fisher and Alan Lovell

Nottingham Business School, Nottingham Trent University

 **FT** Prentice Hall

FINANCIAL TIMES

An imprint of **Pearson Education**

Harlow, England • London • New York • Boston • San Francisco • Toronto • Sydney • Singapore • Hong Kong
Tokyo • Seoul • Taipei • New Delhi • Cape Town • Madrid • Mexico City • Amsterdam • Munich • Paris • Milan

Pearson Education Limited
Edinburgh Gate
Harlow
Essex CM20 2JE
England
and Associated Companies throughout the world

Visit us on the World Wide Web at:
www.pearsoned.co.uk

First published in 2003

ISBN 0 273 65194 3

British Library Cataloguing-in-Publication Data
A catalogue record for this book is available from the British Library

Library of Congress Cataloging-in-Publication Data
A catalog record for this book is available from the Library of Congress

10 9 8 7 6 5 4 3 2
07 06 05 04 03

Typeset in 9.5/12.5 pt Stone Serif by 69.
Printed and bound in China
SWTC/02

Contents

Introduction

Business ethics is an important subject because organisations and corporations sometimes do bad things and the people within them, on occasion, behave improperly. In practice it may not always be clear whether an action is wrong, illegal or both or neither. Many business ethics issues present themselves as dilemmas in which all the options have good and bad aspects.

As we write this introduction, the bankruptcy of Enron, the international energy company, is exercising the business pages of the newspapers. It provides an example of corporate badness or, at the least, an illustration of the arguments that can arise over the morality of corporations' actions. Allegations have emerged that top executives secured their own financial position before the collapse but allowed employees' pension funds to be wiped away. Enron has been accused of using political donations to governments worldwide to ensure that the regulatory constraints on its businesses were not onerous and to secure government support (Cohen, 2002). Amnesty International (1997) reported that the government of Maharashtra in western India used its police forces to suppress peaceful protest against the environmental impact of the 'Enron project' to build a power plant.

If corporations can act badly, in their own right, so can the individuals who work within them. In a survey, conducted by KPMG in America (KPMG, 2002), three-quarters of respondents reported that they had seen violations of the law, or of their organisations' ethical standards, at work in the previous year. The most common infractions were sexual harassment, employment discrimination and deceptive sales practices. Cynicism and low morale were most frequently cited as the cause of employee misconduct.

How should these matters be studied?

We believe that developing rhetorical skills of debate should be the primary focus of a textbook on a subject, such as business ethics, that deals with controversial issues. We do not advocate a particular ethical position in the book, nor indeed do we necessarily provide definitive solutions to the problems raised, because you ought to come to your own conclusions after participating in the arguments and reflecting on your own values and beliefs. Neither are we particularly optimistic or pessimistic, although one of us leans towards the former position and the other towards the latter. We do not assume that the world of organisations and business is the best of all possible worlds, nor do we assume that this world is irredeemably corrupt and selfish.

We are not advocating that business ethics should simply be about debate and not about action to put wrong things right. Only that it is not our responsibility to provide packaged solutions to the ethical problems of organisations. Action is necessary but it is the responsibility of shareholders, directors, managers, employees and stakeholders to act according to their values and their best judgement.

This view does not prevent us taking determined positions on some issues. In much of the book we try to analyse and explain how things are rather than prescribe how they should be. Sometimes the one of us who is the pessimist argues that something is wrong and should be stopped; and the other one, the optimist, argues that an example of good practice should be spread more widely. When we do this you should always bear in mind that for every argument there are counter-arguments (albeit not necessarily convincing ones) that may be put against our positions.

Our emphasis on argument justifies another feature of the book. As well as providing you with the basic material you would expect to find in a textbook on business ethics we also develop new arguments that are subject to challenge and dispute. Consequently the book is not designed as a definitive work of reference (although where the material is standard we have treated it as authoritatively as we can). Instead the book is intended to provide thoughts, ideas and provocations to stimulate your own thinking.

The book is designed for both undergraduate and postgraduate students; each may take from it what they need. The materials on ethical theory and ethical reasoning should be of use to both undergraduates and postgraduates. These theoretical materials are provided to give you resources for developing arguments for and against particular positions on issues in business ethics. Case studies are provided so that undergraduate students, mostly without organisational experience, have ethical matters to debate. Postgraduate students, especially part-time students who are often practising managers and professionals, may apply the theories to their own experience; but they may also find the case studies helpful. Concrete illustrations of moral issues are a more assured route to ethical awareness than mental abstractions divorced from substance. As the medieval historian Gervase of Canterbury wrote in the twelfth century,

> There are many people whose minds are induced to avoid evil and to do good more easily by example than by prohibition and precepts.
>
> (Bartlett, 2000: 629)

The book provides more material than can be covered in either an undergraduate or postgraduate course so the book can also be used as additional reading in support of the lectures. This feature allows the interested student to explore the subject beyond the constraints of lecture and seminar time. You should follow your tutor's guidance on which parts of it are critical to your course. The wider material, and the exercises, in the book should help postgraduate students and practising managers to reflect upon their own organisational experience and managerial practice.

The benefits offered by the study of this book are:

- a comprehensive review of existing material combined with new perspectives equip you for the challenges in the work environment;
- a wealth of diagrams and charts present overviews and contexts of the subject and act as useful revision aids;
- 'definitions boxes' highlight and explain key terms;
- real-life case studies contextualise the theory and provide a springboard for debate;

- simulations and exercises encourage you to reflect upon your own values and ethical standards;
- activities for group and seminar work enliven study;
- the blend of academic theory and concrete issues reflects the challenge and excitement of the subject.

The structure of the book

The first two chapters of the book identify the ethical issues in business and organisational life. Chapters 3 and 4 deal with ways of thinking about ethical issues. The next four chapters focus on the actions of individuals and organisations in response to ethical demands and problems.

Chapter 1: Perspectives on business ethics and values. In this chapter we ask some of the big questions such as 'Can business be ethical?' and 'What are my assumptions about the role of values in business, organisation and management?' We have not provided any straightforward answers, and these questions will reverberate through the rest of the book.

Chapter 2: Ethical issues in business. The purpose of this chapter is to move from the big questions to the particular issues. A 'map' is used to identify the range of ethical and moral issues to be found in business, organisations and management. Detailed case studies are provided to give you a clear understanding of the issues. They will be referred to throughout the book.

Chapter 3: Ethical theories and how to use them. Having presented you in Chapter 2 with the range of ethical problems this chapter describes the formal ethical theories and principles that are available for use in analysing them. The theories are largely drawn from the history of western philosophy (other philosophies are considered in Chapter 8). Few of the theories were developed with reference to business and so the chapter draws out the implications of the theories for organisations and the people within them.

Chapter 4: Values and heuristics. The theories discussed in Chapter 3 are taken from the formal, academic, approach to thinking ethically. This chapter explores how people actually think about ethical issues. It suggests that values are an important component in our day-to-day ethical thinking at work. It is suggested that heuristics, cognitive tricks of the trade, are the mechanism through which values inform our ethical thinking.

Chapter 5: Individuals' responses to ethical issues. The previous chapter considered how people think about ethical issues. This chapter looks at how those thinking processes lead to responses to ethical issues. It proposes a classification of ethical stances people may take in an organisational context and investigates the factors that lead people to make one type of response rather than another.

Chapter 6: Whistleblowing. This chapter follows on from the previous one by dealing with one very important response that a person can make when they discover organisational wrongdoing – blowing the whistle. It considers the arguments for and against whistleblowing and discusses the legal position following the implementation of the Public Interest Disclosure Act 1998 in the United Kingdom.

Chapter 7: Organisational responses to ethical issues. So far the chapters have dealt with individuals' responses to ethical issues at work. In this chapter a wider viewpoint is taken and organisations' responses are dealt with. The chapter is concerned with the role of codes of ethics in organisations and with organisations' attempts to create ethical cultures.

Chapter 8: Ethics and values in international business. This chapter considers how organisations respond to the ethical issues that arise from international business operations and globalisation. In philosophical terms it raises the problem of universalism and relativism by asking to what extent international differences in business values and ethics are valid. It also considers how organisations should respond to the social, economic and ethical differences that exist between countries and societies.

Chapter 9: Corporate citizenship and social responsibility. This chapter returns to the issues raised at the start of the book by asking what the ethical role of organisations and businesses should be in the wider world. It considers what responsibilities businesses have beyond their financial duty toward their shareholders and as good corporate citizens. It also considers how well organisations have met these obligations.

Chapter 10: Review. This is a short concluding chapter that brings together many of the themes that have been raised in the book.

A range of support materials is available to lecturers and students on the website for this book at *www.booksites.net/lovellfisher.*

To Elaine and Sheila

Acknowledgements

We are grateful to the following for permission to reproduce copyright material:

Extract on p. 10 reprinted with the permission of The Free Press, an imprint of Simon & Schuster Adult Publishing Group, from *The Moral Dimension: Toward a New Economics*, p. 5, by Amitai Etzioni. Copyright © 1988 by Amitai Etzioni; Case study 2.8 from 'The mob should never rule' in *The Observer*, 17 September 2000, © Guardian Newspapers Ltd, 2000; Table 4.1 from *Simple Heuristics That Make Us Smart* by Gerd Gigerenzer & Peter Todd, copyright © 1999 by Oxford University Press, Inc. Used by permission of Oxford University Press, Inc.; Table 4.2 reprinted with the permission of The Free Press, an imprint of Simon & Schuster Adult Publishing Group, from *The Nature of Human Values,* p. 58 by Milton Rokeach. Copyright © 1973 by The Free Press; Table 8.1 from 'The 2001 Corruption Perceptions Index', www.gwdg.de/~uwvw/2001Data.html and Table 8.2 from 'The 1999 Bribe Payers Index' www.transparency.de/documents/cpi/index.html reprinted with permission from Transparency International; letter from Anita Roddick to *The Guardian*, 13 July 2001, reprinted by permission of Anita Roddick; extract from Pilger, J., *Guardian Weekend,* 14 July 2001 and Table 9.1 from *The Guardian*, (G2), 27 April 2001, © Guardian Newspapers Ltd, 2001; Figure 5.1 from Fisher, C. and Rice, C. in J. Leopold, L. Harry and T. Watson (eds) (1999) *Strategic Human Resources: Principles, Perspectives and Practices,* © Pearson Education Limited 1999; Figure 5.6 from Fisher, C. and Lovell, A. (2000) *Accountants' Responses to Ethical Issues at Work*, reproduced by permission of CIMA, London; Activity 4.1 from Addendum to Chapter 2 'Monksbane and feverfew' in Fisher, C.M. (1998) *Resource Allocation in the Public Sector: values, priorities and markets in the management of public services,* pp. 64–72, published by Routledge, reproduced with permission of Thomson Publishing Services; Figure 8.1 from Hofstede, G. (2000) *Culture's Consequences*, p. 377, © Geert Hofstede, reprinted with permission; Texas Instruments Incorporated for the TI Ethics Quick Test from TI's website http://www.ti.com/corp/docs/company/citizen/ethics/quicktest.shtml. © TI 2002, used by permission; Activity 3.10 from Figure 2: Ranking Ethical Principles, from Carroll, A.B. 'Principles of Business Ethics: their role in decision making', in *Management Education*, Vol. 28 (8), p. 21, by permission of MCB University Press and Table 8.5 from Figure III: Cultural similarities and differences between Chinese, India and Japanese, from Haley, G.T. and Haley, U.C.V. (1998) 'Boxing with Shadows: Competing Effectively with the Overseas Chinese and the Overseas Indian Business Networks in the Asian Arena', *Journal of Organisational Change Management*, Vol. 11, No. 4, p. 308, by permission of MCB University Press.

We are grateful to the Financial Times Limited for permission to reprint the following material:

Case 2.3 Inside Track: Big pharma and the golden goose, © *Financial Times*, 26 April 2001; Case 2.5 Spy trap, © *Financial Times*, 22 August 2000; Case 2.7 Michael Skapinker examines the issues raised by Luc Vandevelde's recent decision to turn down a generous pay bonus, from FT.com, © *Financial Times*, 4 May 2001; Case 2.9 Medicines arbiter delays decision on beta-interferon clinical excellence, © *Financial Times*, 23 December 2000; Case 2.10 Racism 'remains rife' in the Met, © *Financial Times*, 14 December 2000; Case 2.11 Changing track, © *Financial Times*, 9 May 2001; Case 2.20 Supermarkets facing more scrutiny after election, © *Financial Times*, 11 April 2001; Case 2.23 Hit squad to tackle animal rights activists, from FT.com, © *Financial Times*, 27 April 2001; and 'Brands feel the impact as activists target customers', © *Financial Times*, 18 July 2001.

While every effort has been made to trace the owners of copyright material, we take this opportunity to offer our apologies to any copyright holders whose rights we may have unwittingly infringed.

1 Perspectives on business ethics and values

OBJECTIVES

Having completed this chapter and its associated activities, readers should be able to:

- Give an account of the various arguments about the moral status of business, organisations and management.

- Distinguish between values and ethics.

- Define traditional, modernist, neo-traditional, postmodern and pragmatic perspectives on values.

Introduction

This chapter sets the scene for the rest of the book by dealing with some of the big issues of business ethics. The first question it addresses is whether the activities of businesses are good, as some argue, because the free market is the foundation of an ethical existence. An additional question is whether the use of private corporations (organisations with their own legal existence) to provide public and private goods and services has a sound ethical and moral foundation. The danger is that private bodies might, by the single-minded pursuit of profit, put their own selfish interests before those of society as a whole. However, public and voluntary organisations are not necessarily more ethical than private bodies. By growing larger to meet the ambitions of the organisation's members, they may also act selfishly and not in the public interest. These are matters of ethical debate. By ethics is meant the study of the means by which the morality of human actions can be appraised or evaluated.

The relationship between ethics and values, the twin themes of the book, will be explored in this chapter. We will suggest that people in organisations may take a number of perspectives on the nature and role of values in organisational and managerial life. Each of these views presupposes a different relationship between values and actions.

Business and organisational ethics

In this opening section we consider the contexts in which organisations operate. Four broad theories of the firm, and the assumptions and implications of these perspectives for the exercise of moral agency, are considered. Organisations, in the sense we are using the term here, refers to any configuration of people and other resources that has been created to co-ordinate a series of work activities, with a view to achieving stated outcomes, or objectives. At this stage we make no distinction as to whether an organisation is profit seeking, located within the public sector, or is a charitable/voluntary organisation. The issues we discuss are largely, but not exclusively, sector-blind, although the intensity with which the issues are experienced may vary significantly between organisational types.

As will become evident as we progress through the chapters, the location of an organisation within the public sector does not make it immune from economic constraints, even economic objectives. Likewise, there is a growing body of opinion that argues forcibly that profit-seeking organisations should be more accountable to a body of citizens that extends considerably beyond shareholder-defined boundaries. Whilst the distinctions between private sector and public sector, profit seeking and non-profit seeking, have become less clear-cut in recent years, we do not argue that all organisations are equivalent, and that the sector of the economy in which an organisation is located is irrelevant to understanding the ethical, political, economic and social constraints within which it operates. Penalties or sanctions for poor performance are possibly more obvious and severe in the profit-seeking sectors, but it can be argued that the multiplicity and complexity of the objectives managers are required to achieve in certain parts of the public sector make managing in such a context a far more demanding and ethically fraught role. Although each perspective assumes that organisational relationships are largely, if not exclusively, mediated by market dynamics, the extent to which 'the market' is relied upon as an exclusive mediating mechanism does vary.

However, before we move on we must define what we mean by moral agency.

Definition	**Moral agency** within organisations is the ability of individuals to exercise moral judgement *and behaviour* in an autonomous fashion, unfettered by fear for their employment and/or promotional prospects. The issues relating to calls for business organisations to act in more ethically and socially responsible ways by becoming 'corporate citizens' are considered in Chapter 9.

Table 1.1 presents the schema of four perspectives to highlight the point that different imperatives and assumptions may underpin market-based, capitalist economies.

Within the four categories in Table 1.1 different assumptions are made about the relationships between:

- organisations and the state;
- organisations and their employees;
- organisations and their various stakeholder groups (i.e. beyond the employee group).

We need to understand these perspectives because they are helpful in appreciating the potential for, and the constraints we each face in exercising, moral agency within business contexts.

With the exception of the 'classical-liberal' category, each of the categories is an amalgam of a variety of theories, ideas and practices. The corporatist approach is referred to by Crouch and Marquand (1993) as 'Rhenish'. This latter term refers to a particular (German) approach to a market-based, capitalist-oriented economy, although the writers broaden their consideration beyond Germany to take in a wider group of non-Anglo-American market-based economies. Whilst the German approach displays important differences from the Japanese and the Swedish approaches, they have, for our purposes, been grouped together as representing a more corporatist approach, where the overt involvement of the state and employees in the running of individual organisations is an accepted practice.

This is not to say that the Anglo-American approach to economic development can be simply categorised within the 'classical-liberal-economic' group. Notwithstanding the rhetoric of various UK and US governments, state involvement has been required and forthcoming on many occasions in these two countries, often to overcome what is known as market failure. However, the common belief in the UK and America leans towards the need for less, or minimal, government interference in business, and a drive towards market dynamics to facilitate organisational co-ordination.

The following is a closer examination of the four theories of the firm and their implications for moral behaviour within, and of, organisations.

The classical-liberal-economic approach

A classical-liberal theory of the firm places the organisation within an economic system that is made up of a myriad of interconnecting but legally separate parts, and where relationships between these many parts are defined in terms of free exchange. Money acts as the facilitator of exchange, thus performing the role of the oil that greases the economic system's wheels. The 'invisible hand' that Adam Smith spoke of is the force that drives the mass of individual transactions. The argument is that with no individual person or company able to affect price, the resulting transactions, and the prices that draw both suppliers and customers into the marketplace, reflect people's wishes. This is the strength of the claims for the ethicality of 'free' markets as espoused by writers such as Milton Friedman, Friedrick von Hayek and Ayn Rand. Individual choice, free of government coercion, is seen as the only ethical influence in shaping economic and social development.

Rand is probably the least well known of the three advocates of free markets mentioned above, although her advocacy appears to have been influential. She is reputed to be a favourite writer of Alan Greenspan, the Chairman of the American Federal Reserve at the time of writing. Friedman's arguments in defence of a business world free of government or social obligations beyond those defined in law, are considered in more depth in Chapter 9, so a little more time will be given here to consider some of the key thoughts of Rand on the subject of markets as the basis of economic and social co-ordination.

Table 1.1 Theories of the firm and their ethical implications

Issue	Classical liberal economic	Pluralist (A and B)	Corporatist	Critical
Status of the category	1. For its advocates it is the only game in town, not merely the most efficient, but the most ethically justifiable. 2. For others the 'pure' model must be tempered by interventions to (a) minimise problems of short-termism, or (b) correct power imbalances. 3. Whilst for others the neo-classical model is a corrupting chimera that acts as a cover to camouflage the interests of the powerful.	1. Type A. A stakeholder perspective is advocated in corporate decision making, with key interest groups physically represented on decision-making boards. 2. Type B. Individual managers weigh the full ethical and social considerations of their actions and decisions. Stakeholder groups would not necessarily be present at decisions.	Refers to the business relationships in countries such as Germany, Sweden and Japan (although the approaches adopted are not identical). The interests of employee groups, non-equity finance, and sometimes the state, are represented alongside the interests of equity shareholders, on senior decision-making boards.	Ranging from descriptive theories of the firm that portray how organisations appear to be (or are), rather than how they should be, to critical theorists who portray an organisational world beholden to the demands of capitalism or managerialism (these terms are not the same). Both approaches reflect messier and more ethically fraught worlds than tend to be suggested in the other 3 categories
Number of objectives recognised	One – meeting the demands of equity shareholders.	Multiple, reflecting an array of stakeholder perspectives, although the actual mechanics remain problematic.	A mix of equity share-holder, employee and non-equity finance perspectives, although long-term economic interests of the firm are dominant.	Multiple, reflected by the various coalitions and power groups within an organisation, particularly economic interests.
Status of financial targets	Regarded as the organisation's primary or sole objective, because they will reflect the efficiency with which resources are being employed.	Important, but not to the domination of all other considerations. Ethical as well as multiple stakeholder perspectives are weighed in decision making.	Important, but greater attention paid to the medium to longer-term financial implications of decisions than appears to be the general case in Anglo-American corporations.	In highly competitive markets, or during periods of crisis, likely to be the dominant, although not the exclusive, organisational consideration. During periods of relative stability, other considerations will gain in significance and could dominate.
Significance of ethical behaviour (both individual and corporate)	Defined by national and international laws, which are seen as both the minimum and maximum of required ethicality. The neo-classical model is argued to be the	At the heart of the debate for those who bemoan what is seen as the exclusive, or overly dominant, economic orientation of organisations.	No clear evidence that ethical considerations feature more strongly in corporate decision making, although the lack of an exclusive	An important, but variable, element in defining the reputation of the organisation. Will be shaped by the power of influential individuals and

only approach that allows the primacy of individual interests to be reflected in economic and social co-ordination.		shareholder perspective might offer greater potential for a broader societal perspective.	groups within and external to the organisation.
Role of managers — Portrayed as functionalist, technicist and value neutral.	Type A. Managers come into direct contact with specific sectional interest groups, which should affect decision making. Type B. Individual managers are required to have internalised a societal ethic into their decision making.	The structures of organisations reflect a formal involvement of employee representatives, non-equity financiers, and sometimes state representatives, alongside shareholder interests, on corporate decision-making boards.	Complex, with competing and sometimes/often mutually exclusive interests and demands being required to be satisfied, including the managers' own agendas.
Status of employees — Resources to be used by the organisation in its quest to satisfy shareholder interests.	Employees represent an important interest/stakeholder group within the organisation, although economic considerations are not ignored.	Employee representation is guaranteed on some of the organisation's senior decision-making boards, e.g. supervisory boards in Germany.	Operating within a capitalist mode of production, employee interests will vary between organisations, depending upon the power of individuals and groups of individuals.
Values — Competition seen as the bulwark against power imbalances. Efficient resource allocation facilitated by profit-maximising behaviour.	Inherently societal in orientation, but the views of those actually making decisions will be important.	Those of the shareholders, employees, non-equity financiers (possibly the state) are likely to dominate.	A complex interaction of multiple individual and corporate values. Critical theorists would single out the values that underpin capitalism.
The possibilities for moral agency in organisations — The individual as consumer, as chooser, is the personification of moral agency, but the individual as moral agent when selling his or her labour is troublesome. The atomisation of society, which appears to be an inevitability of this form of individualism, is seen by many as leading to feelings of alienation and anomie.	Type A. Multiple perspectives offer heightened possibilities, but medium to long-term organisational survival will dominate concerns. Type B. Very similar to Type A, but the confidence and integrity of individual managers becomes a critical issue.	With employee representatives on the supervisory boards of organisations (as in Germany), the possibilities again appear stronger than with the liberal-economic perspective. However, economic considerations will remain dominant.	Empirical evidence indicates that the suppression of moral agency might be more than minor and isolated aberrations in an otherwise satisfactory state of organisational affairs. Critical theorists would see these problems as an inevitable consequence of the demands of capitalism.

Ayn Rand was born in Russia in 1905, but she emigrated to America when she was twenty-one, nine years after the 1917 Bolshevik uprising in Russia and four years after the civil war that followed the uprising. On arriving in America Rand took a variety of low-paid, menial jobs. She is quoted as saying; 'I had a difficult struggle, earning my living at odd jobs, until I could make a financial success of my writing. No one helped me, nor did I think at any time that it was anyone's duty to help me.' Rand depicted man as 'a heroic being, with his own happiness as the moral purpose of his life, with productive achievement as his noblest activity, and reason as his only attribute'.

Such snippets of historical context are helpful in understanding some of the factors that might explain an individual's philosophical position on key issues. Randianism (the term used by followers of Rand) rejects government in anything other than its minimalist form, i.e. that which can be justified to protect individual rights, such as the police, the law courts and national defence forces. All other functions can and should be operated by 'the people', preferably via market mediation, and paid for (or not) by choice.

CASE STUDY 1.1	**Biography and philosophy**

Bauman (1994) contrasts two philosophers, Knud Logstrup and Leon Shestov. Logstrop lived a tranquil and civilised life in Copenhagen. He wrote of human nature, 'It is characteristic of human life that we mutually trust each other . . . Only because of some special circumstance do we ever distrust a stranger in advance . . . initially we believe one another's word; initially we trust one another' (Bauman, 1994: 1). Shestov, on the other hand, experienced great persecution during his life, under both the tsarist and anti-tsarist regimes and as a consequence had a far more pessimistic view of human nature, portraying the individual as one who is vulnerable and must be at all times be ready to be betrayed. 'In each of our neighbours we fear a wolf . . . we are so poor, so weak, so easily ruined and destroyed! How can we help being afraid?' (Bauman, 1994: 2).

Rand is credited with developing the philosophical position that is known as objectivism. Objectivism has three key elements:

1 '*Reason* is man's [*sic*] only means of knowledge', i.e. the facts of reality are only knowable through a process of objective reason that begins with sensory perception and follows the laws of logic. Objectivism rejects the existence of a God, because it lacks (to date) empirical support. However, in America, some of the most strident advocates of free markets come from politically powerful religious groups.

2 *Rational self-interest* is the objective moral code. Objectivism rejects altruism (i.e. the greatest good is service to others) as an unhelpful and illogical human attribute. Individuals are required to pursue their own happiness, so long as it does not negatively affect anyone else's. This is compatible with negative freedom, one of Isaiah Berlin's two forms of freedom. It relates to a 'freedom from' approach that grants people a right to be free from interference by others, including, and in particular, government.

3 *Laissez-faire capitalism* is the objective social system. It is important to recognise that laissez-faire capitalism is referred to by its advocates as a social system, and not just an economic system. This is an important issue and one towards which critics of the approach feel unified in their opposition, although such opponents share differing views on how to respond. Some would argue for an overthrow of the capitalist ethic and practice, whilst others would retain a market-based framework, but define boundaries of relevance and ethical justification for markets. The latter is exemplified by writers such as Walzer (1983) and is discussed below.

Definition

> **Laissez-faire** means unrestricted. So laissez-faire capitalism refers to a preparedness to let markets 'sort themselves out', even during periods of disequilibrium and apparent malfunctioning. The belief is that a 'market' will self-correct in time (a natural law, or Darwinist view within economics). Self-correction rather than external intervention is deemed infinitely preferable in the long run for all concerned.

The attachment of modern-day libertarian-economists to a myopic focus upon competition can be criticised for ignoring two other significant elements of economic systems, which are:

- *Command* (the extent to which power, coercion and hierarchy affect economic relationships), and
- *Change* (the way that capitalism effects change and is itself affected by change).

These three central elements of capitalism, competition, command and change, have ethical and moral implications and it is argued here that they are interconnected, not subject to easy and simplistic separation. However, the classical-liberal perspective eschews these arguments and presents a schema in which the operations of the firm, both those within the firm and how it interacts with its external environment, are treated as if they are value neutral.

Within the simple competitive model of economic behaviour managers are expected to behave in ways that reflect what is known as economic rationality. This normative theory is open to challenge in terms of its descriptive rigour, hence the existence of alternative theories of the firm. Supporters of the neo-classical-economic perspective would accept that actual practice is likely to be variable around the preferred norm, but it is argued that economic rationality is the goal towards which organisations should strive. They argue that those organisations that get closest to the normative position will prosper, with competitors having to respond in a similar fashion, or, wither on the economic vine.

The corporatist approach

The corporatist approach does not deny the primacy of competitive market forces, but an exclusive equity shareholder perspective is eschewed in favour of a broader-based set of perspectives in some of the organisation's decision making. These additional perspectives are those of employee representatives, debt financiers, and in some cases, state interests. This broadening of the decision-making base is claimed, and appears to offer, a longer-term view to certain aspects of corporate decision making. For Crouch and Marquand (1993: 3).

The system as a whole trades-off losses in the short-term efficiency on which the Anglo-American tradition focuses against gains in consensual adaptation and social peace. It owes its extraordinary success to its capacity to make that trade-off . . . In a high skilled – or would be high skilled – economy, consensual adaptation and social peace are public goods, for which it is worth paying a price in strict allocative efficiency.

The sphere of inclusion reflected in this approach goes beyond the exclusivity of the shareholder orientation of the classical-liberal perspective espoused by most Anglo-American corporations. Evidence suggests that the corporatist-type approach has avoided, or minimised, many of the worst effects of short-term economic 'adjustments' in world trade that have been experienced since about 1960. This is not to say that countries such as Germany, Sweden and Japan (examples of the corporatist perspective) can be immune from significant movements in world economic activity, but it is argued that significant economic lurches have been avoided in these countries, thus minimising significant rises in unemployment levels, with the attendant impacts upon social cohesion. The significant economic downturns experienced by a number of Asian economies in the late 1990s, including Japan, were associated more with structural factors within these economies, than with inherent weaknesses in Japan's more corporatist approach to market co-ordination.

Whether the corporatist approach is preferred by some because it offers a greater likelihood of economic, and thus political stability, with the greater apparent value placed upon the interests of individual citizens/employees merely an ancillary benefit, or whether the rationale for employing this approach is reversed (i.e. the ethics of the corporatist approach are argued to be the main reasons for its adoption), is not critical for our discussion. What is relevant is that both the 'classical-liberal-economic' and the 'corporatist' approaches can cite ethical justifications for their superiority as economic and social systems. The former can do so because of the primacy attaching to the notion of individual choice, the latter because of its attachment to social cohesion and the desire to avoid, or minimise, what might be deemed unnecessary social disruption and distress to individual lives during periods of economic correction or recession.

■ The pluralist perspectives

There are two main pluralist perspectives. The first (referred to as Type A pluralism) sees broad stakeholder interests being represented (as far as this is possible) by elected or appointed members of corporate boards. This is a development of the corporatist perspective, but with the stakeholder groups being drawn more widely. The corporatist approach is evident in the countries cited above on a reasonable scale, whereas the two pluralist perspectives currently exist as arguments and debates, rather than as practice. Companies such as The Body Shop are very much the exceptions that prove the rule.

In Type A pluralism stakeholder groups are required to do more than argue their particular, vested-interest, case. They are expected to be representative of societal interests. Clearly the extent to which the latter are adequately represented will depend upon the composition of the stakeholder groups. Thus, as compared to the classical-libertarian-economic perspective, where the unconscious forces of individual decisions are deemed to give expression to society's preferences, within Type A pluralism societal preferences are given voice by the presence (or not) of stakeholder groups on company boards or committees.

The second pluralist perspective (referred to as Type B pluralism) does not dispute the possibility of stakeholder groups being physically represented within corporate decision-making processes, but this is neither a prerequisite, nor part of the basic arguments. This second variant of pluralism sees economic rationality being moderated by concerns for, and recognition of, wider social implications of corporate decisions, with these factors being weighed by individual decision makers. Type B perspectives can be presented as a continuum, with writers such as Casson (1991) at one pole, and Maclagan (1998), Maclagan and Snell (1992) and Snell (1993) at the other.

The perspective argued by writers such as Casson is that competition via market-based economies is the preferred economic system, but that reliance upon unadulterated economic rationality as the sole explanation of individual behaviour is both naive and unhelpful. For the discipline of economics to retain relevance Casson argued that it must recognise behaviours that are explained by drives other than, or in addition to, economic rationality.

> These professional prejudices must be overcome if economics is to handle cultural factors successfully. They are the main reasons why, in spite of its technical advantages . . . economics has not contributed more to the analysis of social issues.
>
> (Casson, 1991: 21–2)

Classical-libertarian economics retains a view of human behaviour that sociologists would describe as 'under-socialised' (i.e. unrepresentative of the complexity and variability of actual human behaviour). Type B pluralism argues for a recognition of the realities of everyday market conditions, but also a more socialised set of assumptions of human behaviour. Whilst a market-based economy is seen as the foundation upon which organisational co-ordination takes place, structural issues and problems within markets are recognised, e.g. power imbalances between competitors; information asymmetry between producers and customers; and the capricious nature of (the owners of) capital. Greater responsibility, ethicality and humanity are required of corporate decision makers.

In a similar vein, but with less of Casson's implicit instrumentalism, Etzioni (1988) employed a moral justification for an overt recognition of broader perspectives beyond short-term profit motives. In the following quotation Etzioni used the term 'deontological'. This is an important word in any consideration of business ethics and it is considered in more depth in Chapter 3. However, we offer a brief definition of the term here to allow you to understand the argument that Etzioni was making.

Definition

> A **deontological** approach to moral behaviour is one that believes that moral reasoning and action should be guided by universal principles that hold irrespective of the context in which an ethical dilemma might exist.

Instead of assuming that the economy is basically competitive, and hence that economic actors (mainly firms) are basically subject to 'the market' possessing no power over it (monopolies are regarded as exceptions and aberrations), the deontological 'I & We' paradigm evolved here assumes that power differences among the actors are congenital, are built into the structure, and deeply affect their relationships. We shall see that power differentials are gained both by applying economic power (the power that some actors have over others, directly, within the economy) and by exercising political power (the power that some actors have over others, indirectly, by guiding the government to intervene on their behalf within the economy). These fundamentally different assumptions make up what is referred to here as the I & We paradigm (one of the larger possible set of deontological paradigms). The term [I & We] highlights the assumption that individuals act within a social context, that this context is not reducible to individual acts, and most significantly, that the social context is not necessarily wholly imposed. Instead the social context is, to a significant extent, perceived as a legitimate and integral part of one's existence, a whole of which the individuals are constituent elements . . . The deontological paradigm evolved here assumes that people have at least some significant involvement in the community (neo-classicists would say 'surrender of sovereignty'), a sense of shared identity, and commitment to values, a sense that 'We are members of one another'.

(Etzioni, 1988: 5)

Etzioni continued:

The issues explored here range way beyond the technical, conceptual matters of what constitutes a workable theory of decision-making in economic and other matters. At issue is human nature: How wise are we, and what is the role of morality, emotions and social bonds in our personal and collective behaviour.

(Etzioni, 1988: xii)

Progressing along the continuum, past Etzioni's position, one moves towards those who argue for Type B pluralism on the grounds that a broader ethic than that required by classical-liberal economics is desirable, even essential, on the grounds that society as a whole needs organisational decision makers who understand and can exercise moral judgement in complex situations (Maclagan, 1996, 1998; and Snell, 1993). These writers see management practice as essentially a moral practice, set in a complex and challenging arena (business organisations), for individual moral development.

Thus, our pluralist continuum moves from writers, such as Casson, who argued for theories of decision making to recognise actual human behaviour and instincts in order to make economic theorising more relevant and realistic, to the arguments of writers such Maclagan and Snell, who justify the inclusion of the moral dimensions within business decision making on the grounds of the ethical demands of society as a whole.

▓ The critical perspective

The critical perspective is composed of many different theories about human and collective behaviour, including the politics of organisations (Simon, 1952, 1953 and 1955); expectation theory (Vroom, 1964); the use of ambiguity and hypocrisy as managerial tools (Brunsson, 1986 and 1989); the theory of coalitions (Cyert and March, 1992); the exploitation of people (Marcuse, 1991); the benefits that people seek at work and the importance of these benefits (Maslow, 1987); power and identity in organisations (Knights and Willmott, 1999); and the range of strategic resources that individual managers draw upon to allow them to cope with managerial life (Watson, 1994). This is far from an exhaustive list, but it gives a flavour of the range of research and theories that have been developed to explain actual behaviour within organisations. What these works share is a picture of organisational life that is far more complex and messy than classical-liberal economics would prefer to work with. The behavioural and critical theories are not normative theories (i.e. theories of how things should be, such as the classical-libertarian-economics perspective), but what are referred to as descriptive theories, i.e. theories of how things actually appear to be. However, behavioural theorists and critical theorists do vary in terms of the intentions of their respective arguments.

Behavioural theories are amoral in their stance in that, unlike the liberal-economic, corporatist and pluralist perspectives, they do not put forward a preferred ethical foundation for their theorising. They might however highlight examples of laudable, contentious or downright immoral behaviour. They do so by acting as organisational windows through which we can observe the ways in which employees at all levels in organisations appear to react, and behave, when faced with ethically complex situations. For example, you become aware that a friend and work colleague, who you know has a very difficult financial situation at home, unlawfully takes a small toy (a company product) home to one of their children. Such situations could involve divided loyalties between either colleagues or concepts, where the ethics of a situation are not clear-cut or neat; or where moral agency is compromised by power imbalances that jeopardise future employment and promotional prospects.

Critical theorists, however, have an avowed commitment to societal change, for the emancipation of employees from the shackles of capitalism. However critical theorists make different analyses (for example Foucaudian perspectives, e.g. McKinley and Starkey, 1998, and neo-Marxist perspectives, e.g. Alvesson and Willmott, 1996) and there is no consensus on the preferred replacement for market-based societies. Habermas (whose ideas are discussed in Chapter 3) does, however, outline the necessary conditions for a societally acceptable economic set of relationships to develop.

Boundaries of jurisdiction or spheres of justice

The fear of market-based relationships as the bedrock upon which all societal and interpersonal relationships are based is articulated by a number of writers. Walzer (1983), for example, wrote:

> One can conceive of the market as a sphere without boundaries, an unzoned city – for money is insidious, and market relations are expansive. A radically laissez-faire economy would be like a totalitarian state, invading every other sphere, dominating every other distributive process. It would transform every social good into a commodity. This is market imperialism.
>
> (Walzer, 1983: 119–20)

Taking his cue from Walzer, Keats (1993) argued that:

> It is as if their [liberal economists'] theoretical energy has been so fully utilised in demonstrating the virtues of the market that little has been left to deal with the arguably prior question of what it is that defines the nature – and hence limits – of that 'economic' domain with respect to which market and state are seen as the chief rival contenders.
>
> (Keats, 1993: 7)

As a way of handling this problem Walzer argued that societal life should be seen as a series of spheres, which contain and constrain differing elements of societal existence. One of these spheres is the economic, in which markets are recognised as the most effective mediating mechanism, and competition the most defensible form of organisational co-ordination. Whilst markets, contract and competition are seen as appropriate mediating elements, their relevance is largely constrained within this sphere. Within the spheres representing non-economic interpersonal relationships we find notions of trust, care, welfare, sharing, friendship, leisure and possibly even altruism (although this is not high-lighted by Walzer). There is some similarity between Walzer and the earlier work of the German philosopher Hegel (1770–1831) who also used the notion of spheres to conceptualise the social world (Singer, 1983). Hegel spoke of the spheres of state, family and civil society, and to these Walzer adds the economic as worthy of consideration.

McMylor comments upon the development of market-based capitalism from feudal societies. He presented the development from non-market societies as a process whereby the economic moved from being enmeshed 'within other dom-inating frameworks' to a situation in market societies when

> the economy, with a capital 'E' is no longer so embedded. The market means that there is in some sense, a differentiation of economic activity into a separate institutional sphere, no longer regulated by norms that have their origin elsewhere. The individual economic agent is free then to pursue economic self-interest, with-out 'non-economic' hindrance.
>
> (McMylor, 1994: 100)

From a moral perspective one of the problems with dividing the human world into separate spheres is that it might suggest the spheres are independent to the point of allowing differing forms of behaviour to prevail within each. Behaviour might be accepted, or at least tolerated, in one sphere that would not be accept-able in another. It has been argued that this is a recognition that people some-times act (or feel they need to act), when in 'business mode', in ways which they would not employ within their private, domestic lives. Walzer recognised this and argued that the spheres should not be seen as totally autonomous and inde-pendent. Rather, he portrayed a dynamic set of relationships between the spheres in which shifts between spheres of particular facets of societal life do happen, and that a sphere's scope and importance may wax and wane. Boundary conflict thus becomes endemic:

> The principles appropriate to the different spheres are not harmonious with one another, nor are the patterns of conduct and feeling they generate. Welfare systems

and markets, offices and families, schools and states are run on different principles: so they should be.

(Walzer, 1983: 318)

However, Walzer went on to say that 'the principles must fit within a single culture' (1983: 318). This is highly problematic, unless the single culture is one that recognises difference, a multiplicity of cultures. Within such a complexity of perspectives, the notion of wisdom becomes an important mediating factor, but this has to be an active wisdom, i.e. it is always in a state of emerging through dialogue and debate. Within this perspective the dynamic of change is recognised, is debated and matures through processes that are demanding but which, it must be stressed, are subject to 'social capture' by active groups and voices if participation is shirked by the general polity.

Definition

> **Social capture** is a term used to describe a mechanism, e.g. a committee, a regulatory body or a political process, which is established to oversee a particular facet of social life, but which becomes dominated by, or heavily influenced by, the very sectional interests the mechanism was intended to monitor or control. The original intentions behind the creation of the mechanism thus become at best neutralised, and at worst subverted.

To minimise the risk of social capture and other such distorting influences within political, economic and social systems requires an active citizenry, prepared to be interested in, even involved in, micro- and macro-level debates about equity and justice – the very morality of life's various spheres. Hegel spoke of the dialectic, the processes of debate and argument that are required to surface and (possibly) resolve differences of view and contradictions. The dialectical approach is to be found in the teachings of Socrates, certainly in the way that Plato presents the work of his master. Billig (1996), makes a plea for a resurgence of the practice of rhetoric, not in the pejorative sense in which the term tends to be viewed in contemporary society, but as a return to an engagement in debate and argument, for these are the mechanisms and processes by which civilised societies develop and progress.

Defining the boundaries of the economic sphere

One of the principal virtues of competitive markets, as the mechanisms by which business and social interaction is mediated, is that the 'invisible hand' of the market is amoral, i.e. value neutral. Although some may suffer as a result of market-based outcomes, through unemployment or loss of capital, the outcomes are not intended from the start. They are simply the unintended consequences of the multitude of transactions that comprise a free market. Sir Keith Joseph, a notable politician of the 1970s and 1980s and an architect of the political period and philosophy referred to as Thatcherism, was a devotee of Hayek and Friedman. As Heelas and Morris (1992: 19) observed:

> Policies designed to effect more equal distribution of resources, Joseph claims, are not only coercive and threaten individual liberty but are counter-productive and give rise to a series of negative consequences (economic, psychological, moral and

political) . . . Liberty is primarily to be exercised by the self-interested consumer in the market place, including the political, educational and medical 'markets'.

Plant (1992), taking up the theme of markets being the most appropriate mediating mechanism for medical services, explored the possibilities for a free market in body parts (human organs), as well as the justification for a market-based ethos replacing a service ethic in non-voluntary, public service organisations. With regard to a market for human body parts Plant (1992: 91) observed:

> On a strictly capitalist view of market principles, it is very difficult to see why there should not be such a market. The scope for a market is clearly quite wide. There could be a market in blood and blood products; in kidneys; in sperm; in renting out a uterus for surrogate pregnancy; and so forth.

Plant argued that, from a market perspective, at least three principles would favour a market in these areas:

1 There is a clear demand.
2 The current donor system is failing to meet demand.
3 Ownership of the human organs is clear and would not be undertaken by the donor if it were not in their personal interest.

Despite strong advocacy for such markets, broad public support was (and appears to continue to be) lacking. Plant argued that this reluctance reflected a boundary being drawn by society, with human organs currently residing outside the boundary that defines the limits of market application.

Titmuss (1970), in a seminal work on the marketisation/commercialisation of blood donor services, observed, when responding to arguments that blood should be seen as a commodity and thus private blood banks should be introduced to improve the productivity of the blood giving process:

> In essence, these writers,[ ] are making an economic case against a monopoly of altruism in blood and other human tissues. They wish to set people free from the conscience of obligation. Although their arguments are couched in the language of price elasticity and profit maximisation they have far-reaching implications for human values and all 'social service' institutions . . . The moral issues that are raised extend beyond theories of pricing and the operations of the marketplace.
>
> (Titmuss, 1970: 159)

Titmuss worried about the wider implications of commercialising the blood donor service in the UK. If the altruism that, it is argued, is reflected in the voluntary and unpaid giving of blood is replaced by a commercial relationship, what, asked Titmuss, fills the space that used to be occupied by the sense of community inherent within the existing system?

> There is nothing permanent about the expression of reciprocity. If the bonds of community giving are broken the result is not a state of value neutralism. The vacuum is likely to be filled by hostility and social conflict, a consequence discussed in another context . . . the myth of maximising growth can supplant the growth of social relations.
>
> (Titmuss, 1970: 199)

Titmuss discussed four economic and financial criteria, excluding the much wider and unquantifiable social, ethical and philosophical aspects to concentrate upon those aspects that economists (the focus of his criticism) would recognise. These were:

1 economic efficiency,
2 administrative efficiency,
3 price – the cost per unit to the patient,
4 purity, potency and safety – or quality per unit.

> On all four criteria the commercialised blood market fails. However, paradoxically . . . the more commercialised a blood distribution system becomes (and hence more wasteful, inefficient and dangerous) the more will the GNP be inflated. In part, . . . this is the consequence of statistically 'transferring' an unpaid service (voluntary blood donors, voluntary workers in the service, unpaid time) with much lower external costs to a monetary and measurable paid activity involving costlier externalities.
>
> (Titmuss, 1970: 205)

The discussion so far in this chapter has laid out the arguments for claiming that the market system is:

■ the only defensible economic and social system for protecting the freedom of the individual to exercise personal choice, which allows the development of economic and societal relationships that are free from government coercion and intervention. This is the liberal-economic perspective.

■ something that is preferable to competing economic systems, but which needs to be carefully watched and, if necessary, modified from time to time to ensure that the economic system is compatible with broader societal aims. This incorporates the corporatist and pluralist perspectives.

■ an intrinsically corrupting system that pits human beings against each other, with only an elite few dictating the life chances of the many. This is the critical perspective.

The argument has been about the place of ethics in business life, and the place of business in the ethics of life. To complete this opening consideration of the broad canvas upon which the subject of business ethics and values is displayed, we will move to consider the place of values in the lives of managers and other employees.

Business and organisational values

It is difficult to discuss ethics in a business and organisational context without talking about values. As both are central themes in the book it is necessary to distinguish one from the other.

The broad distinction we wish to make is that ethics is a branch of philosophy and is therefore concerned with formal academic reasoning about right and wrong, but values are the commonsense, often taken-for-granted, beliefs about right and wrong that guide us in our daily lives. Imagine a situation at work where you have to decide whether to take action against a manager who you know to be fiddling their expenses. Ethics provides principles and arguments, drawn from ethical theory, for thinking about the issue. The emotional force of your values in contrast would lead you to an intuitive feel for the right thing to do. Of course how much weight you give to your analysis and your emotions is another matter.

Ethics and values have different sources. Ethics are drawn from the books and debates in which philosophical theories about right and wrong are proposed and tested. Ethics have to be studied. Values are acquired informally through processes of socialisation. We acquire values from our interactions with our friends, family and colleagues and, most importantly for our purpose, from the organisations we work for or belong to. Values are learned, not studied. It is true that our employing organisations may make formal attempts, through induction courses and corporate videos, to inculcate their formal values. We are not required to study them, which would involve a critical engagement with them, we are simply required to 'buy into them', to 'mark, learn and inwardly digest' them. If values are learned rather than studied they must be few and simply expressed so that all in a society can understand them. Ethics in contrast need to be studied, not simply learned, because they are more complicated.

There are overlaps between ethics and values. The processes through which values are formed, adopted and modified within groups and societies may be influenced by debates between philosophers. Equally the rational discourses of ethics may be swayed by the emotional undertow beneath the participants' arguments. Within a group of philosophers social learning, conforming to the group's norms, may be more emotionally comfortable than challenging it. Conversely, critical study and the reading of books may challenge the values people have acquired through life. Nevertheless the distinction between learned values and studied ethics is still a useful one.

It follows from the above argument that values are social. They exist and are communicated through social connections. Rokeach defined values as:

> a small number of core ideas or cognitions present in every society about desirable end-states.
>
> (Rokeach, 1973: 49)

Different organisations, different groups, different cultures and different countries may have different values. Ethical theories, however, are disdainful of societies. It does not matter to the validity of a theory if it is not accepted by the generality of people. The truth of an ethical theory cannot be judged by an opinion poll. It will be a constant theme of this book that in business and organisation there can be great tensions between how an ethical theory says people should behave and how their social values incline them to behave.

Perceptions of values

Just as, in the first section of this chapter, we discussed different views on whether there is a normative ethical order that applies to business so we can ask similar questions about the nature and role of values. It is convenient to do this by using the notion of fragmentation to explain the nature of values. Fragmentation is the idea that things in the social world are disordered and disconnected. A fragmented view of values would see them as diverse, various and expressed through conflict between different views and opinions. There are no wholes in a fragmented social and ethical world, only discordant parts that clash against each other. The philosopher Thomas Hobbes expressed this view in the seventeenth century. He argued that even a single person's view could be fragmented.

> Nay, the same man, in divers times, differs from himself; and one time praiseth, that is, calleth good, what another time he dispraiseth, and calleth evil: from whence arise disputes, controversies, and at last war.
>
> (Hobbes, n.d: 104)

The contrary view is the one we have already noted that Rokeach expressed. He claimed that values, far from being fragmented, are simple and whole. Billig (1996: 240) agreed that the values of a group or society are simple and whole. But he pointed out that this makes them difficult to apply to particular situations. A society may have clear views on the importance of telling the truth and on loyalty. But there may be situations in which such simple nostrums do not help much. There are two reasons for this.

1 The demands of truth telling and loyalty may conflict in a particular case. Should a government spokesman tell the truth about a military operation if it would cause danger to the soldiers who might expect him to show them loyalty? In such cases the simplicity and wholeness of values is broken by not knowing which value should be applied.
2 Simple and whole values can only provide general guidance. When it comes to dealing with specific situations values need interpretation. Can there be situations, as the behaviour of politicians often implies, when truthfulness can be interpreted as not telling lies but equally as not telling the whole truth? Once interpretation is necessary values that were simple and whole become fragmented.

Values express a potential tension then between wholeness and fragmentation. People's responses to this tension can be classified under five headings:

- Traditionalist
- Modernist
- Neo-traditionalist
- Postmodernist
- Pragmatist.

The traditional view of values

From the traditional viewpoint a group – whether a work group, an organisation, a profession or a country – is defined by its possession of shared values. The idea of value fragmentation therefore is considered anathema, a contradiction in terms. A group's values either derive from the ancient traditions of the group or are presented as if they did. In organisations these traditional values are often presented as those of the firm's founder. In companies that were not blessed with a charismatic founder a mythical one is sometimes created for public relations and advertising purposes and to act as a fount for the values the company wishes to present (Mr Kipling of Kipling's Cakes is an example). A group based on traditional values sees them as a whole. By turning their gaze inward and not outwards to other groups and societies, they fail to recognise the fragmentation and diversity of values that surrounds them.

The modernist view of values

The modernist position is that the twentieth and, so far, the twenty-first century have been characterised by value fragmentation. However this is seen as a transitory phase and it is thought that, through rationality, the pieces can be put back together and true values defined. Those who take this position believe that values are tangible, and can be unambiguously stated and defined through formal and rational debate. They accept deductive reasoning that allows truths to be logically developed from first principles. The modernist believes that values can be determined by ethical study. Jürgen Habermas, for example (Pusey 1987: 78ff.), constructed a complex theory of communicative action that defines how the validity of spoken understandings between people can be tested. At the least other modernists believe that values can be defined and clarified (Kirchenbaum, 1977; Smith, 1977) as a preliminary to rational discussion about an organisation's mission and core values.

The rationality that Habermas talks about is not the same as that spoken of by many managers. The former can be labelled as critical and emancipatory whereas the latter is instrumental rationality. Instrumental rationality is focused on achieving a set of given aims. Much managerial effort, for example, goes into maximising return on capital or increasing the number of hospital beds without giving much thought to whether these ends are in themselves the right ones. Questions about whether growth at all costs is a good thing, or whether, for example, a focus on preventive health measures might not be better than simply building bigger hospitals, are forgotten. Emancipatory or critical rationality (Legge 1995: 288) asks these deeper questions. It challenges the conventional wisdoms of modern life so that people become aware of the constraints that deform their lives. Both forms of rationality have a place in the modernist perspective. They develop the 'cognitive adequacy' (Giddens, 1985: 100–1) that organisations and societies might use to improve and unify their values.

The neo-traditional view of values

The neo-traditional approach emphasises the function of culture as a device for mediating the tensions between fragmented values and the need of societies and organisations for a common purpose and mutual understanding. Neo-traditionalists see values in the context of organisational and social cultures; indeed cultures are defined by the values that characterise them. They argue that the fragmentation of values can be overcome and that organisations and societies can have unified values. But such an end cannot be achieved by rational analysis, which sees values as objects for analysis and not as shared myths, which is how neo-traditionalists view them. Myths can act as the glue that holds an organisation or society in unity because of their simplicity (which needs no sophisticated explanation) and because of their ability to finesse dilemmas. Sometimes the glue is weak and sometimes strong. But there is agreement amongst neo-traditionalists that values, presented as vision and myth and not as cold rationality, are the keys to overcoming fragmentation.

Those who take this approach stress that organisations are culture-creating mechanisms and that cultures can change. This thought leads to the notion that culture may be a critical lever or variable with which managers can lead or direct their organisations. As Smircich put it,

> Overall the research agenda arising from the view that culture is an organisational variable is how to shape and mould the internal culture in particular ways and how to change culture, consistent with managerial purpose.
>
> (Smircich, 1983: 346)

Values, from this view, can be deliberately used as a means of overcoming fragmentation and improving organisational effectiveness. As Smircich also pointed out there is an alternative view that cultures are too complex for managers to be able to mould them into a desired form.

The postmodern view of values

The postmodern stance sees nothing in the social and intellectual world as tangible or fixed. At this vantage point fragmentation is accepted as part of the human condition. In Lyotard's (1988: 46) famous phrase there is 'incredulity towards metanarratives'. This means that the large ideological schemes, such as capitalism and communism that used to dominate people's lives, no longer have credibility. In the postmodern view there are no eternal truths or values. What we think of as objectively true emerges through discourses that are embedded in power and knowledge relationships where some have more influence on the outcomes of the discourses than others. But what emerges is in any case uncertain because the language we use is opaque and carries no single, clear messages (Legge, 1995: 306).

The words we use to express our values have no fixed meaning. Statements of value have to be treated as texts and deconstructed. *Différance* is Derrida's device for exploring the limitless instability of language. One aspect of *différance* is that no word has a positive meaning attributed to it; it only has meaning to the extent that it is different from other words. Another aspect is deferral because the meaning of one word is always explained by reference to another and the search for meaning can involve a complex chain of cross-references as one chases a word through a vast thesaurus. Let us take an innocuous statement about public management:

> The first steps to achieving accountability for performance must be to clarify objectives and develop a recognised approach to measuring and reporting performance.
>
> (Dallas, 1996: 13)

This is enough to cause a deconstructionist to salivate. Most of the words in the sentence do not have an unambiguous or uncontested meaning.

Accountability, for example, can only be defined by relating it to other words such as hierarchy, responsiveness, transparency and so on. Accountability may be viewed from different discourses such as political accountability, audit and accounting, consumer rights and investigative journalism. If we had the time to explore this sentence in detail and to plot its webs of signification we would find that the sentence could mean almost anything.

The search for meaning may not be endless; but the end will be terminal confusion rather than clear understanding. The function of deconstruction is to reach a final impasse or aporia. Aporia is well defined by an illustrative quotation from 1657 given in the *Oxford English Dictionary*.

> Aporia is a figure whereby the speaker showeth that he doubteth either where to begin for the multitude of matters or what to do or say in some strange and ambiguous thing.

Deconstruction is not intended to overcome fragmentation but simply to map the instabilities, paradoxes and aporetic states that define it. From this position there is no hope that the fragmented values can be put back together again. As Harvey (1989: 45) expressed it, disapprovingly, postmodernism

> swims and even wallows in the fragmentary and chaotic current of change as if that was all there was.

The political passivity of postmodernism annoyed him:

> The rhetoric of postmodernism is dangerous for it avoids confronting the realities of political economy and the circumstances of global power . . . meta-theory cannot be dispensed with.
>
> (Harvey, 1989: 116)

But, as Derrida (Derrida with Bennington, 1989: 221) said, to deconstruct the enlightenment project (which seeks to raise humanity's moral status through the application of reason) is not necessarily to criticise it. Just because someone may pick holes in the language used when people attempt to analyse the realities of global power does not mean the task is unworthy.

The pragmatic view of values

The pragmatism of this stance is that of the American philosopher Richard Rorty (1990). He shares the postmodernists' scepticism about the possibility of an objective truth and of a fixed hierarchy of values. In this circumstance the issue for Rorty is not how to represent, or mirror, the world in our thinking but how to cope with its ambiguity:

> All descriptions (including one's self description as a pragmatist) are evaluated according to their efficacy as instruments for purposes, rather than their fidelity to the object described.
>
> (Rorty, 1992: 92)

The notion of usefulness is a hermeneutic one. If a belief helps us to interpret our other beliefs and vice versa then it is useful. The justification of belief is therefore conversational. A dialogue between developing beliefs is necessary, not because it will bring us to an ultimate truth, but because it keeps the conversation going (Mounce 1997: 185–9). The line taken by pragmatists is that the inability to ground our values in some grand overarching theory such as Christianity, Marxism, Islam or capitalism does not prevent people making sensible and practical arrangements for living a civil and well-mannered life. As Rorty expressed this view,

> No such metanarrative is needed. What is needed is a sort of intellectual analogue of civic virtue – tolerance, irony and a willingness to let spheres of culture flourish without worrying too much about their 'common ground', their unification, the 'intrinsic ideas' they suggest or what picture of man they presuppose.
>
> (Rorty, 1985: 168)

He argued that the lack of a metanarrative could be overcome by dealing with the concrete and practical concerns of a community and by finding ways of harmonising, but not abolishing, the conflicts of values within the community.

But living in an ungrounded system may call upon people's resources of humour and tolerance. These are needed because value conflict will be endemic in such a situation. Irony is helpful because people's purposes may require them to act in ways that seem naive in the absence of a metanarrative that justifies simple behaviours. Let us explain this point by quoting Umberto Eco (1985: 67). In his reflections on his best-selling novel, *The Name of the Rose*, he used the example of the pragmatist lover. The lover wishes to say to his partner, 'I love you'. But he cannot do so because everyone is aware that the proliferation of romantic novels has devalued that particular metanarrative. He would feel too naive and unsophisticated if he said that simple sentence even though it is the emotion he wishes to express. Being a pragmatist he does not give up, and stalks away undeclared. Instead he says, 'As Barbara Cartland would say "I love you"'. He has thereby expressed his purpose but in a way which reveals his knowledge that such sentiment can no longer be justified by reference to transcendental values. Irony, by which an apparently straightforward statement is undermined by its context, is essential to the pragmatists' stance.

From a pragmatic view, in summary, it is recognised that there is confusion and conflict over the ends of a good organisation or society and that the meanings people ascribe to values change and develop as they debate and discuss issues with others. Nevertheless the pragmatist believes that by maintaining the conversation with good humour and irony it is possible to make organisations and societies more bearable.

The following exercise is designed to test your understanding of the five stances. Read Case study 1.2. Although it is an invented case study many of the incidents have been taken from interviews with managers. Then answer the questions in Activity 1.1.

Chris's managerial development: A fable

Chris is a newly qualified social worker. She didn't start training until she was in her late twenties but she had much previous experience of acting as an unpaid worker with a voluntary agency. In her first role as a field social worker she brought much of the enthusiasm and motivation that she developed during her early experience and training. She liked to see her clients as whole persons and she tried to spend as much time with them as possible so that she could come to a proper understanding of their situation from their point of view. It is important, she believed, not to take action without the full and active consent of the client.

After some years the pressure of Chris's caseload made it difficult to find the time she needed to spend with clients. She often felt frustrated that she had to foreshorten important discussions with them. On occasions this frustration caused her to be short and less than helpful with those clients who seemed to enjoy creating their own misfortune and yet were ungrateful for any help she provided. Although some of her clients were often short-changed on the service they received because of this reaction it did not undermine her essential belief in the need to work with her clients in a way that maintained and developed their dignity.

After a few years Chris was promoted to team leader and she became responsible for the management and professional supervision of a team of workers. In a small way her attitude towards the clients changed. She no longer spent the bulk of her time working face to face with them. She also had the managerial responsibility of dividing her staff resources between all the clamouring demands for service. Her attitude towards clients was more objective. She made sure that careful, measured and objective assessments were made of all clients so that those with the greatest needs received priority.

A few years later Chris was appointed as a Services Manager for a particular category of clients in the northern area of the county. Two important themes within her new job were service quality (as expressed by performance indicators) and budgets. Cost effectiveness became a worrying issue. She had to convince her managers that she was providing value for money and this caused her to question whether the range of services wasn't too wide and whether some of them could be ended or reduced. There was talk within the department about only providing the high 'value added' services. She came to the view that better IT, better information and more rational decision-making processes would improve the service's effectiveness. She was studying for an MBA and its heavy emphasis on IT and management science convinced her that the department needed to put more effort into producing a computer-based needs profiling and resource allocation system. She started, in a small way, to produce such a system for use within her own locality.

A few years later Chris was still a services manager; but she had moved sideways and was now working with a different client group. The move made her realise the differences in professional values between people who worked with different client groups. It was the failure to address these differences, she thought, that was at the root of organisational conflict within the department.

Case study 1.2 continued

She came to believe that it was very important that everyone in her area sub-
scribed to a central vision and mission that would motivate and inspire all staff.
To this end she organised a couple of away-day sessions at which she and her
fellow managers tried to hammer out some key goals and core values for the
service as a whole. The software she had developed in her previous job had
proved very valuable but it had failed to deliver easy solutions to the resource
allocation problems. As a result of this experience Chris thought that focusing
the department on some basic core values was a better way of managing than
relying too much on IT systems.

After a few years in this job Chris was more aware of its political dimension.
Managers seemed to spend their time fighting their corner and the person who
shouted loudest got the most. For example, whilst the IT system optimised the
allocation of staff to clients it caused as many problems as it solved. It gave
some groups of clients a very low priority ranking. Some managers felt that this
was correct ('it would be more effective to pay for them all to go to Lourdes', as
one senior manager put it) but there was a powerful and critical lobby from the
relatives of the clients.

When she was trying to develop core values she began to see it as a game.
People were trying to control the language that was to be used in framing the
values. It was also clear that when they wrote a core value everybody bought
into it whilst retaining the right to define it in their own way. Everyone was
smart enough to play the language games of anti-oppressive practice but there
was no consensus about its meaning. Indeed at meetings Chris thought they
were playing a circular word game in which *client focus* was identified with
quality of service, which in turn was defined as providing equal opportunities,
which in its turn was seen as responding to the diversity of clients. The debates'
ends were their beginnings. The inconclusive debates over policy documents
often led to a point where everything seemed ineluctably confused.

Some years later Chris was a senior manager. Her enthusiasm for the importance of social services was undimmed but her expectations were less ambi-
tious. She was aware that things in organisations do not always work as
planned. She no longer believed that the answer to organisational management was more and better computers; nor did she think that the publication
of a nicely printed and laminated card proclaiming the Mission Statement
actually meant that everyone shared the same values. She saw the organisation as having many stakeholder groups, internal and external, and the task
of managers was to keep them sweet. But this ironic awareness did not mean
that Chris became cynical; although this is precisely what has happened to
some of her colleagues. Chris continued to work for improvement (whatever
that is) but perhaps in a different way. She came to believe in proceeding on
a Ready – Fire – Aim basis. This meant trying things out in a small way, without too much prior planning, and building on them if they worked, and modifying or abandoning them if they didn't. No more rational masterplans. She
no longer believed in acronyms (such as CFI – Clients First Initiative) any

Case study 1.2 continued

more. Truth lay in aphorisms not acronyms. Aphorisms are a statement of a general principle memorably expressed in a condensed form. For example, 'He who is too busy doing good finds no time for being good', (Tagore quoted in Gross, 1987: 197). Aphorisms make you think about fundamental issues, acronyms just require blind acceptance. Chris accepted both the fragmented nature of the managerial role and the plurality of values within the organisation; and she could become a little manic-depressive as a result. But nevertheless Chris tried to maintain manners and tolerance when managing the service. Her attitude was 'pessimistic wishful thinking'.

ACTIVITY 1.1

The fable implies that managers' responses to value issues at work may change as their careers progress. In this fable can you detect the periods when Chris's approach was:

(a) traditional,

(b) modernist,

(c) neo-traditional,

(d) postmodern, and

(e) pragmatic?

◼ Descriptive, normative and reflective approaches

Two ways of discussing ethical matters, normatively and descriptively, are often proposed. Normative discussion is concerned with rules and principles that ought to govern our thoughts and actions. Normative arguments are focused in particular on how such prescriptive claims can be shown to be legitimate or valid. Descriptive discussion focuses on how things **are** rather than how they should be. A descriptive approach to ethics would give an account of the values and ethics of particular groups and try to explain how they have emerged. It would analyse value systems to look for norms and the tensions between them. The word normative is troublesome in a subject, such as business ethics, that spans both philosophy and sociology. In sociology, normative refers to that which is the norm within a group or society. The term is both descriptive, the norms are those of a particular group, but also normative, they define right and wrong within that group. In philosophy normative and descriptive are seen as opposing terms. In this book normative will be used in its philosophical sense.

Many business ethics textbooks take a normative approach. They identify ethical difficulties in business, rehearse the arguments about what should be done about them and then present a resolution or a set of principles. Rather than taking a normative and prescriptive approach this textbook takes a descriptive and analytical approach. It attempts to describe how people in organisations interpret and respond to ethical issues at work. It does not propose solutions to the many ethical dilemmas and problems that face managers and organisations. However, by explaining how others think about and respond to ethical matters, and by providing you with the appropriate tools for thinking, we hope the book will enable you to analyse the issues and to come to your own conclusions.

The intention of the book brings us to a third way of talking about business ethics, the reflective and reflexive approach. Reflection implies careful consideration of ethical issues. Reflexive means to turn back on one's own mind and to consider one's own values and personality. This textbook therefore tries to help you examine your own positions and thoughts. This can be done in part by reflecting on the material in this book and other publications. But this is vicarious learning, piggy-backing on the experiences of others. Reflexive learning occurs when you use your values to challenge your actions and your experiences to challenge your values.

Reflections

One of our concerns in this book is the possibility of the existence of moral agency and ethical practice within organisations. Integrity is one of the concepts that would form part of any definition of business ethics. The importance of integrity within organisational life in general, and executive decision making in particular, is discussed by Srivastva and Cooperrider (1988), although they stress that the way forward is not easily mapped. It can only be navigated and negotiated through dialogue, reflection, learning, tolerance and wisdom.

> Executive integrity is dialogical. Executive integrity is more than the presence of morality or the appropriation of values; integrity involves the process of seeing or creating values. Whereas ethical moralism is blindly obedient, integrity represents the 'insightful assent' to the construction of human values. In this sense, organisation is not viewed as a closed, determined structure but is seen as in a perpetual state of becoming. Dialogue is the transformation of mere interaction into participation, communication, and mutual empathy. Executive integrity is, therefore, a breaking out of a narrow individualism and is based on a fearless trust in what true dialogue and understanding might bring, both new responsibilities and new forms of responsiveness to the other.
>
> (Srivastva and Cooperrider, 1988: 7)

The big weakness of a heavy reliance upon the notion of a dialectic transformation of society is that the associated processes are subject to the risk of social capture. The best chance of minimising this possibility is for all of us to take ourselves seriously and to believe that our individual voices count in shaping the societies in which we live.

We end this opening chapter on a qualified, optimistic note. Spaemann (1989) refused to accept that conscience is either purely instinct or exclusively a function of upbringing:

> In every human being there is the predisposition to develop a conscience, a kind of faculty by means of which good and bad are known.
>
> (Spaemann, 1989: 62–3)

However, Spaemann went on to say that conscience has to be nurtured and supported – shown good practice in order for it to flourish and mature. Fail to do this and the development of a strong conscience becomes 'dwarfed'. The term 'dwarfing' is used by Seedhouse (1988) when discussing the growing attention to a 'business mentality' within UK health care, at the expense of a prioritising of the individual. Both Spaemann and Seedhouse saw the individual as central to any challenge to the primacy of business interests, although, as you will see in Chapter 6, conscience is often the victim of the need to maintain organisational and personal relationships.

Hannah Arendt (cited in Bauman, 1994) also placed the individual at the centre of any developments towards making ethics a live and legitimate subject for debate within organisations. Arendt wrote, 'there are no rules to abide by . . . as there are no rules for the unprecedented'. Bauman continued,

> in other words, no one else but the moral person themselves must take responsibility for their own moral responsibility.
>
> (Bauman, 1994: 14)

With this in mind, this book is intended to inform your understanding of some of the key issues that bear upon this critical element of modern society – the possibilities for business ethics.

Summary

In this chapter the following key points have been made:

- Four different perspectives: the classical-liberal, the corporatist, the pluralist and the critical, on the question of whether organisations, and their role within market systems, are ethically proper.

- The doubts about the classical-liberal model place a premium on the role of the moral agency of individuals within organisations. Moral agency involves reflection on what is right and wrong and working for the good within organisations.

- Ethics represent an intellectual approach to matters of morality at work whereas values represent a response based on beliefs that people hold with emotional attachment. Both perspectives need to be considered when dealing with business ethics matters.

- People may take one of five viewpoints on the role of values in business ethics: the traditional, the modernist, the neo-traditional, the postmodernist and the pragmatist. The position they take will influence their reponses to ethical issues at work.

The Rice Orientation Test (ROT)

This test was devised by our colleague Chris Rice. It is designed to alert you to your approach to ethical issues. It uses a distinction between hedonism, moralism and pragmatism. It is not a statistically validated test and so its results must be used as a trigger for reflection and no more.

Think about each of the headings in the boxes below. Decide whether that term causes you to think in terms of:

A – right and wrong
B – pleasure or pain
C – success or failure.

Then decide whether the concept (A, B or C) that you have chosen is of high (Hi), medium (Me) or low (Lo) importance in your thinking about the headword in the box.

Then place a tick in the appropriate cell of the grid within the box. If you think about the lottery in terms of pleasure or pain but that this is only of medium importance in your thinking then place a tick in the central cell in the grid.

Carry on to complete all the boxes.

The National Lottery

	Hi	Me	Lo
A			
B			
C			

Trade Unions

	Hi	Me	Lo
A			
B			
C			

Ian Duncan-Smith

	Hi	Me	Lo
A			
B			
C			

Competition

	Hi	Me	Lo
A			
B			
C			

Richard Branson

	Hi	Me	Lo
A			
B			
C			

Management

	Hi	Me	Lo
A			
B			
C			

Higher education

	Hi	Me	Lo
A			
B			
C			

Manchester United FC

	Hi	Me	Lo
A			
B			
C			

Profit

	Hi	Me	Lo
A			
B			
C			

Tony Blair

	Hi	Me	Lo
A			
B			
C			

The Welfare State

	Hi	Me	Lo
A			
B			
C			

Parliament

	Hi	Me	Lo
A			
B			
C			

Add up the number of ticks placed in each of the cells in the above matrices and transfer the totals into the table below. Calculate the weighted totals, and their percentage of the grand total, for each of the three rows in the table. The percentages show the relative importance to the respondent of moralism, hedonism and pragmatism.

Scoring ROT

	Hi (N × 3)	Me (N × 2)	Lo (N × 1)	Total	%
A = Moralism					
B = Hedonism					
C = Pragmatism					

Discuss your results with your colleagues in the group.

2 Ethical issues in business

OBJECTIVES

Having completed this chapter and its associated activities, readers should be able to:

- Describe the range of ethical and moral issues that arise in management, business and organisations.

- Distinguish between ethical, moral and legal wrongdoing and assess the importance of a particular misdeed.

- Analyse the complex consequences and motives that typically attend ethical and moral issues in management, business and organisations.

Introduction

Identifying the range and variety of ethical issues in business and management is the main focus of this chapter. It includes many case studies and so is longer than the other chapters. The case studies are provided because understanding of theoretical issues, which are not dealt with until the next chapter, is made easier if the reader first has some concrete examples to refer to. They also provide resources that will be referred to in other chapters. When reading this chapter it is not necessary to read all of the case studies. Only read those that have taken your interest or where you feel you need to think some more about the general issues raised.

The range of ethical issues

To help us identify the range of issues in business, management and organisations that can be called ethical a map or grid of such matters is shown in Table 2.1. The grid has two dimensions and these need explanation.

Ethics and morality

The first dimension makes a distinction between ethics and morality. In most of this book the two terms are used interchangeably. Some writers, however

(Vardy and Grosch, 1999 and Taylor, 2001), do distinguish them, and in this chapter the distinction is a useful one. It can be argued that there are proactive and reactive aspects to ethics and morality. The former is focused on doing good whereas the latter emphasises not doing harm. The term ethics will be used to refer to doing good and morality will be used to refer to the avoidance of harm. Ethics deals with the good life for humankind. Morality in contrast is a concern for justice, which is making restitution if wrongs are done. Ethics, in these terms, can be thought of as developmental whereas morality is judgemental. In Christian terms the Ten Commandments represent morality but ethics are represented by the beatitudes. The Ten Commandments specify what it is wrong to do, for example commit murder or adultery (Deuteronomy 6). The beatitudes are the virtues that Jesus commended in a sermon to his followers. They include meekness, mercy, pureness of heart and peacemaking (Matthew 5). In Table 2.1 a range of issues are positioned on a scale that runs from ethical to moral. The positions at the ethical end of the scale are the obverse of those at the equivalent place at the morality end. For example the ethical concern with reciprocity and fair play, in terms of morality, becomes a proscription against cheating and selfishness. Sometimes the case studies represent compliance, and sometimes disregard, of the ethical or moral concern they are illustrating.

▤ Right and wrong and legal and illegal

The second dimension in Table 2.1 is based on the categories – good, bad, illegal and legal – that can be used to judge the rightness of actions. Legality and illegality are defined by the criminal or civil law. A criminal offence is one so grievous that the state takes action to protect the society. Civil law is concerned with the compensation that people, who are damaged by others (by tort or breach of contract), may seek. Four combinations are formed from these four categories.

1 Actions that are good and legal but not a legal obligation

Some actions may raise ethical issues because, although they are good and legal, people do not take them because the law does not require them to do so. The question is whether people, and corporations, should do them even though they are not obliged to do so.

2 Actions that are wrong and illegal

In the next category ethical or moral questions arise because an action is both wrong and illegal. Such actions face the 'double whammy' and so ought to be straightforward to condemn. However, on issues that many would place in this category, others might argue that the action is neither wrong nor illegal.

3 Actions that are legal but bad

Another category includes actions that may be legal but are also, arguably, bad. Many of the moral and ethical issues that affect business and management fall into this category. They are a reflection of the big question, raised in Chapter 1, of whether business has moral obligations beyond the proprietary claims of the shareholders. The claim that there are no ethical obligations on a private company other than to obey the law and meet the demands of their shareholders was most famously articulated by Milton Friedman (1970).

Friedman's position can be criticised from several perspectives. Solomon's (1993) critique is based on the Aristotelian idea of virtue (*see* p. 72). He argued that the belief that business is simply about the financial 'bottom line' is untrue. However, he claimed, this misconception has generated many false metaphors for business that hide the truth from people. The idea of cowboy entrepreneurs who are driven by greed and profit and who see themselves as loners in competition with all others is one such metaphor. Rather, he argued, the purpose of business is to provide for the prosperity and happiness of the community. This cannot be achieved if people make a distinction between their business and their personal lives. People are social animals but their social needs are ignored if their business lives are focused on the individualistic pursuit of profit. The problem is intensified if working lives are associated with necessary drudgery in contrast to the pleasure that can be had from personal and social lives. Virtues, according to Aristotle, are formed from the ability to find a sensible mean between such extremes as dreary work and pleasurable personal lives.

> The bottom line of the Aristotelian approach to business ethics is that we have to get away from the 'bottom line' thinking and conceive of business as an essential part of the good life, living well, getting along with others, having a sense of self respect, and being part of something that one can be proud of.
>
> (Solomon, 1993: 104)

There is a religious objection to the Friedmanite view of business that can be exemplified from the Roman Catholic position as expressed in the encyclical *Centesimus Annus* (John Paul II, 1991). Humans, it argued, have a capacity for transcendence – the ability to give themselves away to others, and to God. The role of capitalism and profit seeking has to be seen within this context.

> The church acknowledges the legitimate role of profit as an indication that a business is functioning well. When a firm makes a profit, this means that productivity factors have been properly employed and the corresponding human needs have been duly satisfied. But profitability is not the only indicator of a firm's condition. It is possible for the financial accounts to be in order and yet for the people, who make up the firm's most valuable asset, to be humiliated and their dignity offended . . . In fact the purpose of a business firm is not simply to make a profit, but it is to be found in its very existence as a community of persons who in various ways seek to satisfy their basic needs and who form a particular group at the service of the whole society.
>
> (John Paul II, 1991: § 35)

Large companies, such as Shell, are adopting forms of accounting that attempt to balance traditional financial accounting with a concern for environmental sustainability and social justice. This is known as triple bottom line accounting, which provides output and performance measures in the, potentially contradictory, fields of financial, social and environmental performance. The idea, similar to that of the balanced scorecard, is to make it obvious if financial success is only being achieved at a social and environmental cost. The technical problem of identifying measures that can illuminate a company's performance on environmental quality and social justice is difficult. Comparing the many possible measures against each other and against financial performance is a matter of judgement rather than of accountancy calculation (Elkington, 1999).

The issues that arise from legal, but unethical, managerial and business actions all reflect one or more of these criticisms of the Friedmanite perspective.

4 Actions that are good but illegal

The final category of the dimension is one that will always generate controversy. It concerns actions that may be illegal but are morally or ethically good. It concerns the perennial question of when a law can be said to be immoral and when it is justifiable to break or defy it. Campaigning against a law one disapproves of is acceptable within a democratic system; the ethical problem only emerges when a person moves from campaigning to disobedience. The dilemma is twofold.

The first problem is defining the conditions or circumstances in which it would be proper to defy the law. In a democratic system does a general acceptance of governmental authority imply that it is never acceptable to disobey a particular law? Political obligation does not exhaust moral obligation. This is the case with conscientious objectors, for example, who refuse to take a combatant role in a war. But before refusing to obey a law the person needs to consider carefully the balance between their political and moral obligations (Raphael, 1970: 115–16). If in general the state seeks to achieve justice and the common good, and if the law has been passed with the assent of the majority and according to the rule of law, then there is a presumption in favour of complying with the law. Conversely where laws are arbitrary and the state is not just, the contrary presumption may hold. Lyons (1984: 214) argued that the presumption should be that a legal system does not automatically deserve respect. Respect has to be earned. Greenawalt (1987: 222), however pointed, out that there are no plain rules available to guide people on when it is proper to disobey a law.

The second problem is the nature of the defiance, which can extend from passive civil disobedience through to violent direct action. Gandhi, in his campaigns against British rule in India, practised passive resistance. His belief was that people should disobey immoral laws but should not resist when the forces of the law took action in response. His concept of *Satyagraha* was based on the Hindu Vaishnavite principle of *ahimsa* (or non-violence) and the importance of suffering (Brown, 1972: 6). He believed that passive resistance would eventually cause the authorities, through shame, to right the injustices. This increasingly appears to be the position of the Catholic Church. The Pope wrote, concerning the fall of the Soviet bloc:

> It seemed that the European order resulting from the Second World War and sanctioned by the Yalta Agreement could only be overturned by another war . . . Instead it has been overcome by non-violent commitment of people who, while refusing to yield to the force of power, succeeded time after time in finding effective ways of bearing witness to the truth.
>
> (John Paul II, 1991: § 23)

At the other extreme some anarchist and other radical groups argue that harming property, and in some cases people, can be justified by the importance of their cause. As will be seen in Case study 2.23 some animal rights activists argue that the evil of vivisection, practised by some pharmaceutical companies, justifies violent action against those companies, their employees and backers. Deciding when, if ever, violence against an organisation is justified is similar to arguing about which conditions can make war just. The concept of the just war has concerned theologians since the time of St Augustine. St Thomas Aquinas set down the main tests of a just war in the thirteenth century. They were:

- The war must be declared by a lawful authority (*auctor principis*).
- The cause must be just (*justa causa*).
- Those going to war must intend to advance the good and avoid evil (*recta intentio*) (D'Entreves, 1965: 159).
- The test of 'proper means' (*debito modo*), which requires that minimum force be used in accordance with the rules of war and that peace should be established at the end of the conflict, was added to the list later.

An additional requirement that all other means should have been exhausted seems to be a twentieth-century addition.

In considering the question of the justness of violent action against organisations, rather than war between states, the first criterion does not apply. If the actions that people condemn as immoral also happen to be legal then the state could not be expected to take action against the company. However the criterion does alert us to the dangers of validating violent action that is not carried out in the name of some legitimate body. Allowing self-legitimating groups the right to define who is evil, and to use force to attack it, could lead to the intolerance displayed by fascism. Sometimes civil associations or non-governmental organisations (NGOs), such as Greenpeace, take this legitimating role upon themselves.

The cause of militant animal rights activism can illustrate the impact of the other criteria. The cause may be just; but its narrow focus on destroying an alleged evil rather than the creation of a peaceful solution, violates the requirement that the violence should serve the establishment of long-term peace. Nor does the movement's tactics meet the requirement for minimum use of force and adherence to the 'rules of war'. Its actions have included intimidating 'civilians' such as investors and bankers who had only an indirect connection with vivisection. These also violate one of Greenawalt's (1987: 235) considerations for disobeying a law: whether the law objected to and the laws being broken are closely connected. The final criterion has not been met in the case of violent actions in support of animal rights because, in a democratic society, there are always non-violent means of protest that can be adopted. Pacifists of course object to the notion of a just war and would claim that, as violence begets violence, its use to stop evil is never justified.

Table 2.1 plots some recent issues in business against the two dimensions just discussed. The cases (presented later in this chapter) are located in positions on the grid because they illustrate the debates about the legality, ethics and morality of the main themes shown at the heads of the columns. The positions on the grids are not indictments of the people and organisations discussed in the cases. The cases are located at certain coordinates in the grid and these coordinates act as pegs on which to hang arguments and debates. These arguments include whether the location is correct. The case studies have been chosen because they force us to ask questions about legality, morality and ethicality, not because they are definitive illustrations of good or bad behaviour.

Table 2.1 Illustrative cases of the major issues in business ethics

Ethics
The good life
Doing good ⟶ Morality / Justice / Avoiding doing harm

An ethical issue can emerge from actions that are arguably	Corporate citizenship		Equity		Honesty		Avoiding the doing of harm	
	Social development and Caring	Social responsibility and Supporting	Reciprocity and Fair play	Fairness	Truthfulness	Cheating and Selfishness	Bullying and Social irresponsibility	Harming and Social disengagement
Good and legal, but not a legal obligation	*The Nationwide Foundation.* Case study 2.1, p. 36.	*AIDS drugs and patent rights in South Africa.* Case study 2.3, p. 38.	*Paying for staff's professional training.* Case study 2.6, p. 44.	*Providing new drugs for MS sufferers.* Case study 2.9, p. 49.	*BAT and the honorary professor.* Case study 2.12, p. 54.			
Wrong and illegal				*Discriminating against employees.* Case study 2.10, p. 50.	*Jonathan Aitken.* Case study 2.14, p. 55.	*BAT and cigarette smuggling.* Case study 2.16, p. 57.	*British Airways and Virgin Atlantic.* Case study 2.18, p. 60.	*Sexual harassment.* Case study 2.21, p. 63.
Wrong but legal	*British Sugar and Sunday trucking.* Case study 2.2, p. 37.	*Child labour in developing countries.* Case study 2.4, p. 40.	*Executive fat cats.* Case study 2.7, p. 45. *The oil companies and the 2000 fuel crisis.* Case study 2.8, p. 47.	*Railtrack, profits and public safety.* Case study 2.11, p. 51.	*Being truthful with the revenue.* Case study 2.15, p. 56. *McDonald's fries.* Case study 2.13, p. 55.	*Storing of dead babies' organs in hospitals.* Case study 2.17, p. 58.	*The hospital consultants.* Case study 2.19, p. 61. *Supermarkets' supply chains.* Case study 2.20, p. 62.	*The Firestone Tire recall issue.* Case study 2.22, p. 64.
Good but illegal	*David Shayler and MI5.* Case study 2.5, p. 41.							*Huntingdon Labs.* Case study 2.23, p. 65.

Good and bad actions in business, management and organisations

In the rest of this chapter the different types of ethical issues, based on the categories shown in the horizontal axis of Table 2.1, are discussed. Each section begins with a general discussion of the ethical issue. This is followed by a series of case studies that illustrate the impact of these issues on organisational and business life.

▨ Social development

Ethics ⬅————————————————————————➡ Morality

Social development

Social development is defined as actions taken by an organisation or company that are undertaken to improve the social, economic, cultural or environmental conditions of a society. In an earlier period such actions as these would have been termed philanthropy. Andrew Carnegie, who was a poor Scottish immigrant to the USA in the nineteenth century, provides a classic example. He built an industrial empire and when he sold his business he was thought to be the richest man in the world. He disposed of his wealth philanthropically. A particular interest was the founding of public libraries, of which he founded 2,509 throughout the English-speaking world. He thought libraries important because of the role they could play in helping the poor to participate in what he saw as a meritocratic society in which people could become successful through learning. He also saw libraries as a means by which immigrants such as he could learn about the countries in which they had chosen to live.

Social development needs no direct connection with an organisation's business activities, although it may be argued that organisations are hoping indirectly to improve the standing of their business as a result of their good works. Motives, corporate and philanthropic, are nearly always mixed and this should not detract from the value of development activities. Other organisations, such as non-governmental organisations (NGOs) have social development as their prime purpose.

Corporate citizenship is sometimes used as an alternative term for social development. British Airways for example define their citizenship objective as 'To succeed in partnership with the communities in which we work, not at their expense' (British Airways 2000: 26). Amongst its activities, which focus on education, it provides training for school governors and provides a Community Learning Centre at Heathrow. It sponsors the British Olympic and Paralympic teams. It has provided high-profile sponsorship, in the tourism field, for the Millennium Dome (which probably did little for BA's reputation) and the British Airways London Eye (which probably did much for the company's reputation). The company's report also commends the initiative of its staff who have carried out charitable work for children in Africa and the Indian subcontinent.

The first case study reports on an organisation that is seeking to respond to social problems and raises the question of whether philanthropy necessarily must arise from altruism or whether the point is to bring social good from strategic necessity.

The Nationwide Foundation

Building societies are mutual organisations. Their customers own them. This reflects their origins as self-help organisations designed to help people buy their own homes. In the 1990s, and into the twenty-first century, there was a move to demutualise building societies. This process involved converting a society into a public limited company (plc). The new plc would give the previous owners (the customers) shares in the new company to compensate them for their loss of ownership. The new owners could either keep or sell these new shares. If they sold them they would make a windfall profit. They would receive a cash sum for a property that had cost them nothing except the constraint of saving with, or accepting a mortgage from, that particular building society. Some building societies wish to remain as such. The pressure to demutualise is more keenly expressed by their customers.

The Nationwide Building Society wishes to remain mutual. In 1997 it created the Nationwide Foundation to become the channel for its charitable giving. Everyone who became a member of the society from November 1997 onward also became a member of the foundation and agreed to assign to the foundation their rights to any future conversion payments. This meant that should the society demutualise or be taken over in the future then any connected payment of any sort which would otherwise be received by the society members would be passed to the foundation to create a fund for charitable giving. Bluntly, there would be no windfall payments. A number of the society's members who had been members since before 1997 also agreed to become members of the foundation.

The foundation supports schemes throughout the United Kingdom using money donated by the society, its staff and its members. These include a Time Bank scheme in London. In this scheme people give of their time and skills and receive credits that they can use when they need help. It also supports schemes in the areas of adventure training, support for people with hearing difficulties, sport in disadvantaged areas and providing community information services. Its priority in 2001 was a project called the New Generation Initiative that was designed to help parents face the problems of bringing up children.

(Source for further information: www.nationwidefoundation.org.uk)

DISCUSSION ACTIVITY 2.1

Does the use of the fund as a means of meeting the society's own purpose of remaining a mutual institution detract from the worth of its activities?

Case study 2.2 is about a company that was accused of disengaging from the largely rural community within which it operated. Although its plans were legal it drew back from implementing them because people objected to the disruption they would cause to the pattern of weekend life in East Anglian villages.

CASE STUDY 2.2

British Sugar and Sunday trucking

East Anglia is sugar beet territory. There is an annual sugar beet campaign that lasts for five months when the crop has to be taken to British Sugar's factories for processing. For many years there had been an agreement between British Sugar and the National Farmers Union (NFU) that deliveries would take place for five and a half days each week with no lorries on Saturday afternoons or Sundays. Most residents in the villages through which the large and heavy beet lorries rumble accept the beet campaign as part of country life. In 2000 British Sugar, in an attempt to diminish the queues of lorries that formed during the mornings at the factories, decided to switch to seven-day-a-week deliveries and they came to an agreement with the NFU to do so. There was immediate outcry. As a resident in one of the affected villages said, 'We do appreciate that they have a job to do. The noise of these lorries is quite considerable. All we want is for them to leave us in peace for one day of the week.' The hauliers who delivered the beet met at Peterborough and came out against seven-day deliveries. As one of them said, 'Imagine big sugar beet lorries driving past country churches on a Sunday morning while people are trying to worship. It simply won't work – we won't do it.' The campaign against the additional deliveries carried on and within a few weeks British Sugar announced that it was suspending its agreement with the NFU to deliver beet for seven days each week.

(*Sources*: Moore, 2000; Bradley, 2000; Pollitt and Ashworth, 2000)

DISCUSSION ACTIVITY 2.2

Was British Sugar right to forgo the efficiency and cost benefits that could have been gained from a seven-day working week?

■ Social responsibility

Ethics ←――――――――――――――――――――――――→ Morality

Social
responsibility

Social responsibility, in the way the term is used in this chapter, covers a narrower canvas than social development. (A more general treatment of it is given in Chapter 9.) It can be defined as conducting the business of an organisation in a manner that meets high social and environmental standards. It differs from social development in not requiring organisations to do good works beyond the commercial purposes of the organisation. Also social responsibility affects fewer arenas than social development. Social responsibility excludes social and cultural good works that are appropriate to social development. Social responsibility is important to organisations 'not least because of the devastating impact that even isolated acts of wrong doing can have on an organisation's reputation among its stakeholders' (Arthur Anderson and London Business School, 1999). Many large companies report their performance as socially responsible organisations; for an example see British Petroleum's social and environmental report (BP, 2001).

The nature of a socially responsible approach to redundancy illustrates some of the factors that distinguish social responsibility from social development. It is possible to argue that redundancies, especially on a large scale, are morally wrong because they harm individuals, families and communities. The counterargument is that the welfare of families and communities is not the concern of a company or organisation. Another possible defence is that the loss of some jobs protects the jobs and livelihoods of many more. Social responsibility would suggest a middle position. It would argue that redundancy may be justified but that a responsible organisation will take trouble to help those affected. This might involve using outsourcing consultants to provide counselling and career advice to those losing their jobs. It could involve setting up agencies or funds to encourage the introduction of new businesses in affected localities, or to help those made redundant to start their own companies. Social responsibility is an obligation to minimise the collateral harm caused by the organisation's actions and decisions.

The first case study in this section provides an example of assertive public and governmental opinion which judged companies' protection of their patent rights as socially irresponsible. The pressure of global media scrutiny became such that the threat to the companies' reputations became greater than the economic loss caused by the challenge to their patents.

CASE STUDY 2.3

AIDS drugs and patent rights in South Africa

There is an epidemic of AIDS in southern Africa. There is therefore a great need for drugs with which to treat the disease. One of the drugs, Ciprofloxican, cost South Africa's public health sector 52p for each pill when bought from the company that had developed it and that held the patent. A generic version of the drug could be imported from India for 4p a pill. The cost of these drugs was a heavy burden on the health services and the South African government proposed a new law that would allow the cheaper generic drug to be imported. The world's largest pharmaceutical companies opened a lawsuit against the South African government to claim that their property and patent rights were thereby put at risk. However in May 2001, as the case was about to commence in the South African High Court, the pharmaceutical companies withdrew the claim.

The following article from the *Financial Times*, which includes an interview with the chief executive of one of the major pharmaceutical companies, rehearses the arguments.

FT Very sick people need drugs. The world's largest pharmaceutical companies charge plenty for them but they channel that money into research to find new medicines. The companies, now suffering an unprecedented onslaught over the prices they charge and lack of access to their medicines, want to refocus public attention on what they see as the main issue. 'You can kill the golden goose,' says Hank McKinnell, chief executive of Pfizer, of demands for lower prices. 'You'll eat well today but the cupboard will be bare in future.'

Mr McKinnell is a staunch defender of the prices that his company, the world's largest drugs group, charges. He is also very aware that a humanitarian and economic disaster is unfolding in Africa, where 27m Africans are now HIV-positive and only a fraction of them have access to or can afford even deeply discounted western Aids medicines. But in an interview he points out that Aids was first identified by medical researchers in the early 1980s. By 1987, he says, there was one treatment. Now, 64 Aids drugs are available and more than 100 are in development. What was the right thing to do in 1981? asks Mr McKinnell. 'Say the prices are too high and take away the incentives for the research? That doesn't help patients or their families.'

Case study 2.3 continued

But many believe this is an argument the drugs industry will never win. Companies are supplying Aids drugs in Africa at up to 90 per cent discounts but they face demands for larger cuts. This is on the grounds that the products are still unaffordable for almost all HIV-positive patients or their governments. Meanwhile, companies in countries such as India and Thailand are making cheap, often illegal, copies of western drugs and promising to save thousands of lives at a fraction of the cost. And in the US there is speculation that it will not be long before patients lose patience and refuse to pay up to 10 times the price for treatments. Whichever way they turn, Mr McKinnell and his peers will be accused of placing a different value on the lives of people on different continents.

Pfizer's chief executive concedes the industry appears to have lost its way trying to formulate a response to the unprecedented wave of bad publicity. Changing that is one of his new responsibilities. This month he became chairman of the Pharmaceutical Research and Manufacturers of America, the industry's most powerful lobby group. Drugs companies have been caught off-guard by the sheer size of the attack. As well as being criticised for their drugs pricing policy in sub-Saharan Africa, they have endured closer scrutiny of pricing and patent regimes worldwide.

Federal and state regulators in the US have been investigating abuses of marketing to physicians and consumers. Influential Washington politicians have proposed revisions to US patent law that make it easier for cheap copies of drugs to come on the market. Meanwhile, Mr McKinnell says, Indian companies have been lobbying the World Trade Organisation to preserve their ability to break patent laws being ushered in as part of the WTO's Agreement on Trade Related Intellectual Property. He has little sympathy: 'The Indian companies have been making billions of dollars stealing our technology and selling it, not only in India but any place around the world they can get away with it.'

He believes the pharmaceutical industry has convinced people it genuinely wants to help, particularly in Africa. Last week, in a high-profile dispute, 39 pharmaceutical companies abandoned their case against the South African government in which they had said their patent rights were in danger. Bad publicity was an important factor behind the decision to drop the case and the companies have escaped a disastrous legal situation. Mr McKinnell says the companies have also been increasing their efforts to work with aid agencies, non-governmental organisations and local governments to improve distribution.

'Unfortunately, we haven't expanded them rapidly enough,' he says. 'But there is now a realisation that if we don't provide access, we're going to stay as part of the problem . . . I think we've been pretty successful in becoming part of the solution.'

But prices are still too high in countries where any price is unaffordable. The answer, says Mr McKinnell, is to forge partnerships with agencies and governments to bring in more resources. 'If the sole problem is the high price of drugs, you give up. But the industry has been smart enough to take that off the table. When the drug is free or at cost, now what's the problem? It's national will, it's distribution, and it's medical treatment.' In other words, drugs companies have knocked 90 per cent off the price but it is up to someone else to find the rest and to help deliver the drugs.

(*Sources*: A. Michaels, *Financial Times*, 26 April 2001. Copyright © The Financial Times Limited. Reproduced with permission; McGreal, 2001; Clark and Borger, 2001)

DISCUSSION ACTIVITY 2.3

What are the arguments for saying that knowledge that is medically beneficial to humanity should not be private property?

The next case study raises similar issues to those in Case study 2.3 as it reviews why a company acted more responsibly than was required by law.

CASE STUDY
2.4

Child labour in developing countries

The use of child labour by multinational companies, in their factories in the third world, to produce cheaply the products they sell in western markets become an international issue in the 1990s and the first decade of the new millennium. The United Nations' Convention on the Rights of the Child, and the International Labour Organisation's Declaration on Fundamental Principles and Rights at Work (United Nations 1989), condemn the use of child labour. NIKE in particular has been the subject of public campaigns against its labour practices in South East Asia.

The Adidas-Salomon group is a sportswear retailer and manufacturer. Many of its shoes are made in six factories in Vietnam. The factories are not directly owned. They are owned by Taiwanese businesses. The factories are all modern, light, spacious and equipped with the basic facilities that people need at work.

Adidas became aware of child labour issues during the 1998 football World Cup when it was alleged that its footballs were stitched by child labourers in Sialkot, Pakistan. In response it set up a department of social and environmental affairs and developed a code of conduct known as SOE (Standards of Engagement). On child labour the SOE states:

> Business partners shall not employ children who are less than 15 years (or 14 years old where the law of the country of manufacture allows), or who are younger than the age for completing compulsory education in the country of manufacture where such age is higher than 15.

In Vietnam the local managers made a decision that they would introduce a minimum age for employment of 18 years. This was not only a more stringent policy than the company required globally, it was also tougher than Vietnamese law that specified that children should not be in full-time employment until they finished their compulsory education at 15 or 16.

The reasons for adopting a more demanding ethical stance were not necessarily entirely altruistic. The local managers were anxious to avoid bad publicity and the two-year margin of safety made it less likely they would unintentionally employ child labourers because of difficulty in establishing their ages. The local managers also argued that the rigours of the footwear production line were inappropriate to people less then 18 years old.

An audit of labour practices was carried out in the Vietnamese factories. In one particular factory it was found that, out of 3,500 employees, there were 12 girls aged 14 and 15 years. Most of these had already worked in the factory for between one and three years. They had obtained the jobs by presenting false documents that belonged to aunts or sisters. In addition there were 130 staff of 16 and 17 years. The employment of this latter group was of course legal.

The local management decided that the children in the younger age group would be provided with a full-time, two-year, education programme but would continue to be paid a basic wage. The older group of child workers would be provided with some part-time educational input. The company was keen to adhere to the SOE requirements because it valued the contract with Adidas for which 80 per cent of

Case study 2.4 continued

their output was made. The educational programme was being delivered by the USA-based NGO that had carried out the initial labour practice audit although the cost was borne by the local factory management. The visibility caused by the NGO's presence may have encouraged the company to pay the cost of educating the 12 employees. They would have been entitled to dismiss the children and free them to attend school in the normal way.

A Vietnamese teacher in a well-equipped classroom next to the factory floor taught the 12 children. There was formal tuition in the morning. The children were expected to return to the classroom in the afternoon for private study. This expectation did not become practice and the children disappeared after lunch. The factory had decided to teach the children in the factory because it was feared that, if they were sent to normal school, they would truant and find employment in another factory. The children believed they were in 'paradise'. The notion of being paid to be educated was almost impossible to believe. What the other workers thought was not recorded.

(*Source*: based on Winstanley, Clark and Leeson, 2001)

DISCUSSION ACTIVITY 2.4

What action do you think companies should take when they find their suppliers use child labour contrary to their company policy?

The next case introduces a new aspect of social responsibility that considers when it is proper for a person to break their duty of confidentiality to their employer if they know that their employer is acting irresponsibly. This issue, also known as whistleblowing, is discussed in detail in Chapter 6.

CASE STUDY 2.5 David Shayler and whistleblowing on MI5

David Shayler is an ex-employee of MI5. He alleged that the service had plotted to kill the President of Libya. Having made the allegation he fled to France where attempts by the British government to extradite him were unsuccessful. However he decided to return to Britain where he was arrested and charged. As a member of MI5 he had signed the Official Secrets Act 1920 that banned him from revealing official secrets for life. The Public Interest Disclosure Act (*see* p. 199), that gives some limited protection to whistleblowers, does not apply to the security services. Shayler's intention was to use the Human Rights Act 1998, which incorporated the European Convention on Human Rights into English law, in his defence. The Act provides a right to freedom of expression and if a court makes a declaration of incompatibility between the Human Rights Act and a particular piece of legislation, such as the Official Secrets Act, the government would have to consider amending the law. Some of the issues are raised in the following leading article from the *Financial Times*.

Case study 2.5 continued

FT

Here's a paradox for Britain's spymasters. Three years ago, David Shayler, the former secret agent, fled to Paris after claiming that the security service had tried to kill President Muammar Gadaffi of Libya. Robin Cook, the foreign secretary, said the allegation was 'pure fantasy'. Yesterday on his return to Britain, Mr Shayler was arrested. But he would only be guilty in relation to the Gadaffi affair under the Official Secrets Act if what he said about his former employment was fact, not fiction.

The authorities seem to have avoided this difficulty by charging him with unauthorised disclosure related to his other allegations of mess-ups and impropriety in the service. Even so, the case shows up a huge problem for spymasters in dealing with former agents who talk too much. In James Bond's world, the solution was easy – perhaps something nasty with an exploding cigar, or a shark.

Outside spy fiction, the authorities face harder options. They may dismiss mud-slinging agents as mercenary fantasists. But then some of the mud may stick. If the authorities prosecute the agent for a serious disclosure, they risk giving credence to his allegations. If they bring charges for a technical breach, they look heavy handed. If they mount a full investigation into the agent's allegations, they risk further embarrassing revelations –

even if the allegations prove false. If true, the agent faces huge difficulties in proving them in court.

Clearly the secret services must be allowed to keep their secrets. But such secrecy is only tenable in peaceful democracies if the agencies are seen to act within the law and the principles of civil liberty. This requires a good deal more openness than they have shown in recent decades – and more vigorous scrutiny by the parliamentary committee set up to watch over them 11 years ago.

In the present case, the authorities must show that they have not done a shabby deal by promising to soft-pedal charges in exchange for silence. If Mr Shayler has revealed important secrets – as the authorities appear to believe – he must be prosecuted vigorously, however embarrassing his defence might prove.

Equally, the police, who are now investigating his charges against the service, must find ways to demonstrate that they are doing the job properly. Mr Shayler's accusations may be found eventually to be insubstantial or wildly exaggerated. But if the authorities take Mr Shayler seriously enough to prosecute him, there must be a presumption that his allegations against the service deserve, at the least, serious investigation.

(*Source*: Leader article, *Financial Times*, 22 August 2000. Copyright © The Financial Times Limited. Reproduced with permission)

DISCUSSION ACTIVITY 2.5

1 Was David Shayler's whistleblowing justified?

2 Were the British authorities acting in a socially responsible way in choosing the offence David Shayler was charged with?

▨ Reciprocity

Ethics ◄───────────────────────────────► Morality

Reciprocity

If the avoidance of doing good and behaving well is irresponsibility, then selfishness is doing harm through a pursuit of self-interest. This section discusses human beings' inclinations to act selfishly or altruistically. The assumption that selfishness is the norm in the behaviour of human beings may be unsafe. Research into the evolution of insects and animals suggests that altruism, sacrificing oneself to benefit others, may be the result of evolutionary selection. Reciprocity is perhaps a more appropriate term than altruism because such behaviour anticipates a future benefit for the individual's near relatives, if not for the individual. One form of reciprocity is called kin selection. It accounts for the altruistic behaviours found amongst ants, bees and wasps. Individuals in these species, it is suggested, forgo their own opportunity to breed in order to support the queen, their sister, in rearing large numbers of offspring. By doing this they will increase the total number of offspring that are born bearing genes similar to their own. This characteristic is particularly noticeable amongst bees, ants and wasps because their odd genetic system means that they are more closely related to their sisters than they are to their offspring. Reciprocity can also be a successful evolutionary allele (genetic trait) in animal evolution. Some writers, such as Dugatkin (2000), argued, controversially, that studies of altruism in animals and insects can provide clues for improving human co-operation. Of course this behaviour will only develop if in the long run 'cheats' (individuals who accept but do not return the favour) are 'punished'. This issue is most often studied through the medium of a games theory scenario known as the Prisoners' Dilemma.

Definition	The **Prisoners' Dilemma** involves two imaginary prisoners who have jointly committed a murder. They have been arrested by the police and put in separate cells. They have not been able to talk to each other since the murder and the police make sure that they cannot communicate in the police station. The police have inadequate information to charge them with murder but they could charge both of them with possessing illegal weapons. The two prisoners are interrogated separately. They have a choice of two options, to confess or to keep silence. The consequences of each option, in terms of number of years in gaol, are shown in the pay-off figure (Figure 2.1).

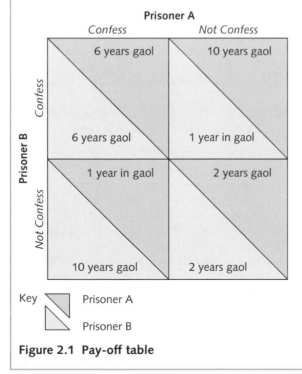

Figure 2.1 Pay-off table

If both prisoners confess they will each receive the normal sentence for murder of six years' imprisonment. If they both keep silent the police have insufficient evidence and they will be charged for the weapons offence for which the sentence is two years in prison each. This is the best option for both of them. However if one confesses after doing a deal with the police, he will only get one year in prison but the one who kept silent will have the book thrown at him and will receive the maximum penalty of ten years. Neither prisoner knows what the other will do because they cannot communicate. If each prisoner feels they can trust the other then neither will confess and both will receive a relatively light tariff of two years' prison each. However if one keeps silent, but the other 'cheats' and confesses, the silent one will receive a harsh ten years. If a prisoner feels he cannot trust the other then the best bet is to confess. The worst that can happen is six years in prison but the worst that can happen if he does not confess is ten years. This is the Prisoners' Dilemma, whether they can trust each other enough to achieve the best outcome for both of them by both not confessing.

The Prisoners' Dilemma can only be avoided if the players exist in a continuing community in which cheats are punished. In these circumstances the players have to continue to meet, which enables trust to develop. Selfishness will occur, on this analysis, where there is a lack of trust or where people do not see themselves as being in the same community as those whom they harm by their selfishness.

These issues can be seen in the following case studies. In Case study 2.6 altruism was present because all the players were part of the same community and there were opportunities for the altruism to be reciprocated. But even in this situation the person explaining the situation found it hard to decide whether the recipients were good bets who were likely to reciprocate his altruism.

CASE STUDY 2.6 Paying for staff's professional training

The case study is an extract from an interview with a partner in an accounting firm who was responsible for the professional training of new staff.

Well, treating people properly and fairly is always an interesting one; it is a very subjective area. In my role as training partner there are undoubtedly incidents every time anybody doesn't pass an exam, we have to decide what to do about it. Whether to terminate their contract, or whether to pay for absolutely everything. There is a whole spectrum of solutions. Yes, and there is never, I don't think, a right or wrong answer. Well, we had a situation a few weeks ago where we had two students, sat the same exams, got very similar results, both marginally failed.

One of them had cruised through the year, not really done enough, but was a bright lad. The other, a girl, had sweated blood throughout the year and still wasn't quite good enough. Then you get a situation where, some people would think, well, Claire deserves another chance because she worked so hard, some people think you should treat Chris better, he is the brighter one, he will be the more marketable one, he will be more use to us. Some people think you should treat them the same. Some people

Case study 2.6 continued

think that people should be allowed to keep sitting exams at our expense for as long as it takes. Some people think we should just terminate people's contracts for failure.

So, I suppose, I take a business decision basically, rather than a moral judgement when anyone fails. I would say that in practically no instance would more than a small minority agree with my decision, some people think they should be treated harsher, some people think they should be treated more leniently. I gave them both a week's study leave and I paid for their exams, so it gave them both another week and a half to find out of their holiday and about £200 to find for the course. It was a close call, it was a difficult call.

But what you have to do as well, is consider the impact on the other students, what message it sends to them. I will have a dilemma within the next year, because I have only been training partner for just over a year. The exam results here; I don't believe they are good enough. I don't think they have been good enough basically because there has been tolerance of failure in the past and I have said repeatedly that in certain circumstances I will terminate people's contracts for failing. That has not happened here for about five years. Sooner or later I am going to have to do it, otherwise people won't believe me. I will only have to do it once. The difficulty is, one person has got to pay the price.

Everyone knows the rules but no one will believe the rules. Now the brighter one of those two, the one who had cruised, the Monday when I spoke to them about it, I was in a foul mood. I didn't terminate his contract – the only reason I didn't – I was sorely tempted to, because (a) I think he deserved it and (b) it would have made an example of him – the reason I didn't was because I was in a bad mood and I thought, there is a risk that I could let my mood take my decision. Had I been in a good mood, I think I would have terminated his contract.

(*Source*: Research interview conducted by the authors)

DISCUSSION ACTIVITY 2.6

Why do you think the training partner acted altruistically when, by not supporting the trainees, he might have better met the (selfish) needs of the firm?

In the next case study it is clear that the highly paid executives do not feel they need to act altruistically towards the generality of employees because they see themselves as belonging to a small elite group of world-class CEOs.

CASE STUDY 2.7

Executive fat cats

An article from the *Financial Times*:

FT

Rough justice in the talent market

Luc Vandevelde, the Marks and Spencer executive chairman who last week turned down an £816,000 ($1.2m) bonus, is unlikely to inspire many imitators. While his gesture was not unprecedented, it is extremely unusual. With thousands of staff being made redundant in the US and Europe in response to the recent market downturn, chief executives

Case study 2.7 continued

have shown little inclination to share their pain. It is not just greed that prevents them from doing so. Those who turn down money risk giving the lie to one of the central tenets of chief executive lore: that their pay is set by forces beyond their control and that they are merely the grateful recipients.

Most chief executives react angrily to news reports that a particular corporate leader has 'paid himself' an impressive-sounding sum. Senior executives do not set their own pay, they point out. The job is done by a remuneration or compensation committee, which carefully examines the market for chief executives' services, researches the going rate and approves a bonus only if the chief executive meets exacting targets. For a chief executive to refuse to accept any of this money would be to sweep aside the committee's careful deliberations.

Gerald Corbett, former chief executive of Railtrack, the UK railway organisation, and one of the few other company heads to have waived a bonus, did so in extreme circumstances. Mr Corbett gave up a bonus of £100,000 after the 1999 Paddington rail crash in which 31 people died. Even Mr Vandevelde's sacrifice was not all it seemed. M&S announced he was giving up his bonus after critical press comment and anger from shareholders and staff that the bonus came at a time when the retailer was doing so badly. But Mr Vandevelde will not go hungry. When he was recruited last year from Promodes, the French retailer, M&S awarded him nearly £2m in shares. And this year's bonus is not so much cancelled as postponed. M&S said it would grant him £352,000 in shares next year, and an equivalent cash sum if he meets specific targets.

Charles Morgan, head of Acxiom, a data management company based in Little Rock, Arkansas, recently made a more substantial gesture. Mr Morgan decided he did not want to lose employees that he would find hard to rehire when the economy recovered. Instead, he imposed a 5 per cent mandatory pay cut on all staff earning more than $25,000 a year and gave them share options in return. He then offered staff the option of taking a further 15 per cent voluntary pay cut in exchange for options. Mr Morgan led the way by cutting his own pay by 20 per cent. 'Acxiom has a shared-fate culture,' the company said. 'Just as the successes of the company have been shared broadly, so are the sacrifices.' Mr Morgan's US colleagues, however, show little appetite for shared sacrifice. Chief executive remuneration climbed 16 per cent last year, giving the average company head total pay of $10.9m, a new record, according to Pearl Meyer & Partners, the consulting firm. The highest-paid US chief executive last year was John Reed, who stepped down as chairman and co-chief executive of Citigroup. Mr Reed gained $293m, followed by Sandy Weill, now Citigroup's sole chief executive, on $224.9m, according to Standard & Poor's and Business Week. Third place was held by Gerald Levin of AOL Time Warner on $163.8m, followed by John Chambers of Cisco with $157.3m. In the UK, the highest-paid company head last year was Martin Read, chief executive of Logica, the information technology group, who gained £27.4m, according to data collected by the Monks Partnership.

Do these pay packages really reflect the demand for executive talent or do they result from remuneration committees looking after their own? The committees are, after all, usually made up of serving or retired senior executives from other companies. By approving large salaries, are they not simply looking after friends and improving the chances that their own pay committees will offer similar sums? Chief executives, particularly in the UK, argue, usually privately, that such questions reflect a culture of envy and a bias against business. They point out that far fewer questions are asked about the huge sums paid to footballers and pop stars.

There is one difference, however. In the case of David Beckham, the Manchester United star, for example, the best clubs in Europe would pay high sums to attract him. Manchester United has to pay him enough to persuade him to stay. The workings of an international market for talent are clear to see. Mr Beckham's salary is not determined by a committee made up of Gary Lineker, Michael Owen and Zinedine Zidane.

Case study 2.7 continued

Pay specialists argue that competition for chief executives' services, particularly in the US, is just as efficient. 'We still have a tight labour market for senior executives that can manage business of the scope of today's global companies,' says Yale Tauber, senior compensation consultant at William Mercer. Mr Tauber argues that trends in executive pay do partly track company performance. His firm examined 350 companies which had a median increase in net income of 8.9 per cent.

The increase in chief executive total compensation in those companies was 10 per cent. The bottom 25 per cent of companies saw net income fall 22 per cent; their chief executives' compensation fell 3.2 per cent. Pay does not track performance precisely, Mr Tauber concedes. 'But there's a rough justice in all of this,' he argues. Employees losing their jobs might not feel that way but, Mr Vandevelde aside, there is little chance they will embarrass their bosses into giving up much more.

(*Source*: M. Skapinker, *www.FT.com*, 4 May 2001.
Copyright © Financial Times Limited. Reproduced with permission)

DISCUSSION ACTIVITY 2.7

Are chief executives inclined to selfishness?

Case study 2.8 raises questions about the obligation on companies to avoid selfishness in times of national crisis.

CASE STUDY 2.8 The oil companies and the 2000 fuel crisis

The UK experienced an oil crisis in July 2000. A combination of self-employed lorry drivers, owners of small haulage companies and farmers took objection to the high price of petrol (the bulk of the price of which in the UK is determined by the excise duty). In a Poujadist protest they used their mobile phones to create a network of supporters who blockaded the country's oil storage depots and led slow-moving convoys up and down motorways causing traffic queues. Any modern country depends on the internal combustion engine and the shortage of fuel caused by the action soon threatened chaos. The National Health Service was put on Red alert and businesses could not carry out their normal business. There were fears that food would not be delivered to the supermarkets.

The government was caught unawares. The prime minister declared that the situation would be back to normal within 24 hours; but it was not. It looked for scapegoats and blamed the international oil companies for selfishness. The government argued that the oil companies should take strong action to break the blockades and ensure that oil was delivered to the nation's petrol station forecourts. The oil companies argued that it was not their responsibility to take risks with the safety of their employees. They would not order their drivers to drive through the pickets if there was a danger that they might be hurt. They were suspected by some politicians of secretly agreeing with the protestors. They claimed to make only small profits of a penny a litre on retailing petrol, and if the protest led to a reduction in excise duties it could only be of benefit to the industry. Oil transport was outsourced to small independent companies and self-employed drivers (some of whom had been sacked by the companies only to be re-employed as independents for less pay) who did

Case study 2.8 continued

have real complaints about the cost of the diesel that fuelled their lorries. The oil companies had little leverage to force these drivers to break the blockade.

The *Observer*, in a leading article published when the blockade had melted away as quickly as it had formed, picked up the theme of the selfishness of the oil companies and their fixation with shareholder value.

> The Government needs to ensure that there is no repeat, and especially to ensure that the fuel delivery system is more robust than at the moment. The oil companies, bent on profit maximisation, now run the system with too few reserves and stocks – the just-in-time delivery system – and have contracted out too much delivery to independent road hauliers who owe them no loyalty, one of the reasons they would not cross the protestors' picket lines. The Government must instruct the companies to hold more fuel stocks at every point in the delivery chain, and to deliver them through in-house tanker fleets. The business contention that their sole duty is to make profit for their shareholders with no thought to their wider obligation to the wider community, the proposition that the Government has been anxious to endorse to prove its business friendliness, now need to be challenged.

(*Source*: Leader article, *Observer*, 17 September 2000. © Guardian Newspapers Ltd, 2000.)

Definition

Poujadism is a set of political beliefs named after Pierre Poujade, a small-town shopkeeper in France in the 1950s. It objects to state interference such as taxation, the investigation of tax evasion and any regulation of small businesses. It also opposes big corporations and large-scale labour organisation.

DISCUSSION ACTIVITY 2.8

Do the oil companies have a moral obligation to maintain fuel supplies in a country?

◼ Fairness

Ethics ◀─────────────────────────────────▶ Morality

Fairness

Fairness concerns the proportions in which resources are distributed between people or causes. The resources can be money, respect or any possession that a community can allocate between its members. Aristotle expressed the central concern, about the appropriateness of the proportions, in a system of distributive justice. He saw it as a matter of algebra in which there are at least four terms: two persons and two shares. A just distribution is one in which the ratio between the first person and the first share is equal to the ratio between the second person and the second share. If Fred is twice as worthy as Jane then Jane's portion should be half of Fred's. In this case the two ratios will be the same. The arithmetic is fine but the question is how the two people involved are to be assessed. Aristotle said it should be done by assessing their merit. But he admitted that people define merit in different ways.

> People of democratic sympathies measure degrees of merit by degrees of freedom, oligarchs by degrees of wealth, others judge by good birth, those who believe in the rule of the 'best' go by moral and intellectual qualifications.
>
> (Aristotle, 1976: 146)

This does not exhaust the possibilities. Marx measured it according to need, 'From each according to his ability, to each according to his needs' (in Marx and Engels, 1962: 24). Others might measure merit by personhood and insist that, since all are equal in this particular aspect, then everyone should receive equal shares.

The debates under the ethical heading of fairness concern the appropriate measure of a person's merit and the fairness of the ratios between one person's merit and share and those of others. The case studies in this section give examples of these debates. Case study 2.9 focuses on need, 2.10 on personhood and 2.11 contrasts the property rights of shareholders with the needs of customers.

CASE STUDY 2.9 | **Providing new drugs on the NHS to people with multiple sclerosis**

Multiple sclerosis is a debilitating and incurable disease. A new drug, with the generic name of beta interferon, has been shown to alleviate the effects of the disease but it costs £10,000 per patient per year. The National Institute for Clinical Excellence (NICE) in the UK investigated the drug to see whether, on clinical and economic grounds, it should be made freely available on the NHS. The belief of those who suffer from the disease, and of those who support them through membership of lobby groups, is that it would be unfair to deny this drug to sufferers. The following article from the *Financial Times* identifies some of the politics and anger that surround the issue.

FT

The National Institute for Clinical Excellence has put off a decision on the use of beta-interferon, the drug for multiple sclerosis sufferers, until at least July next year. The decision to delay has been taken to allow a publicly available economic model of the costs and benefits of the drug to be built. The delay brought a furious reaction from the Multiple Sclerosis Society that accused the institute of putting back the decision to ensure that it came after the likely date of the general election. Peter Cardy, the society's chief executive, described the decision to delay as 'astonishing' and 'breathtaking bungling' given that beta-interferon and glatiramer, another MS drug, have been reviewed by the institute for almost a year.

Mike Wallace, a former managing director of Schering which manufacturers beta-interferon, said: 'I find it appalling. You have to wonder what these guys are playing at. I feel desperately sorry for the people with MS who have had their hopes raised and dashed and raised and dashed again by the NICE process.'

The institute initially judged that MS drugs were not cost effective and should be supplied only to patients already receiving them. Appeals led to that decision being reconsidered, but the institute is unhappy with the economic models that Schering and Biogen have supplied. The appeals committee described as 'flawed' a model built by Biogen that claimed the drug might save money when the cost of working days lost by patients and carers was taken into account. Schering has submitted a new model, but has told the institute that it is commercially sensitive – a stance which appraisal committee members say makes it difficult for the institute to explain its objections to the model's conclusions.

The committee has, therefore, decided to build its own model – an approach that may force manufacturers to reveal more of the

Case study 2.9 continued

assumptions behind their results. Mr Cardy said it was 'impossible to understand why NICE has only now decided to look at the cost effectiveness of these drugs in a different way'. He demanded that Alan Milburn, the health secretary, 'sort NICE's ineptitude out'. Andrew Dillon, the institute's chief executive, said: 'The evidence relating to the cost effectiveness of these medicines is critically important in this appraisal.' It was 'of the utmost importance that the institute's guid-ance is both evidence-based and seen to be fair', and the delay to achieve that was in the best interest of those with MS. The appraisal committee originally said that a big price reduction would be needed before the drugs became cost effective. The process of deciding what would go into the institute's model, and the commissioning and evaluation of its results would be transparent, said Mr Dillon. The results would be published in full, with interested parties free to comment on it.

(*Source*: D. Pilling and N. Timmins, *Financial Times*, 23 December 2000. Copyright © The Financial Times Limited. Reproduced with permission. Additional material from Barlow, 2001; NICE, 2001 and 2002)

In 2002 NICE decided it would not recommend beta interferon or glatimirer for the treatment of MS.

DISCUSSION ACTIVITY 2.9

Should the decision whether or not to provide these drugs to MS sufferers be based solely on clinical grounds or should cost effectiveness criteria also be considered? What influence should powerful lobby groups have on such decisions?

The next case study raises the issue of unfair discrimination at work. In the last three decades of the twentieth century this was one of the major areas of ethical concern in business and organisational life. In the UK discrimination on grounds of race has been illegal since the Race Relations Act 1975 was passed. The Sex Discrimination Act came into force in 1975; it was amended and broadened in 1986. The Equal Pay Act took effect in 1975 and was amended in 1984. In 1995 an Act of Parliament made discrimination on the grounds of disability illegal. There is currently much debate about discrimination on the grounds of age but at the time of writing this was not illegal.

CASE STUDY 2.10

Discriminating against employees – the Metropolitan Police Service

One of the most high-profile cases of race discrimination involves the Metropolitan Police. It was accused of institutional racism by the McPherson report into the police's investigation of the murder of Stephen Lawrence. The following article from the *Financial Times* reports on discrimination against staff from ethnic groups within the Metropolitan Police.

FT Racism remains rife in the Metropolitan Police, according to an internal report by Sir Herman Ouseley, former chairman of the Commission for Racial Equality who is now a senior lay adviser to the force. Details of the report emerged last night on the eve of a speech by William Hague, the Conservative leader, in which he will attack the climate of 'political correctness' created by last year's McPherson report into the investigation of the murder of black teenager Stephen Lawrence. In the toughest Tory response to

Case study 2.10 continued

the report, Mr Hague will say it is now preventing the police from doing their job.

Sir Herman's report, the result of a four-month investigation, says that white officers claim government oversensitivity on the race issue is undermining their ability to fight crime. But it also says that black, Asian and other ethnic minority officers complained of discrimination at all levels of the organisation.

'A vast majority of staff appear to regard the racism issue as overplayed and overemphasised unnecessarily,' it says. But evidence taken from non-white police officers 'strongly confirmed the existence and reality of institutionalised racism'.

As a result, potential black recruits were discouraged from applying, contributing to a recruitment crisis, and government targets of recruiting 6,500 black and other minority ethnic officers by 2009 were unrealistic. 'This is very unlikely to be achieved for another 50 years at the present rate of [ethnic] recruitment,' Sir Herman says.

Non-white police officers regarded the Met as 'an organisation in denial, still wanting, too often, to pretend that there is not a problem of racism and other forms of exclusion. They (ethnic minority officers) see the closed networks, personal relationships and social interactions in self-selected groupings as perpetuating the exclusive inclusion of like-minded people to appointments panels and assessment and review boards which work against equality and fair treatment.'

Mr Hague, speaking to a Tory think tank today, will talk of a 'post McPherson crisis' in the Metropolitan police caused by attitudes of the 'condescending liberal elite that has never trusted the police and now wants us to believe they are all racist'. He will pledge a future Tory government to restoring police morale, which he says has 'collapsed', and will say that he would order police to use their full powers of stop and search 'rigorously', putting the demands of the law-abiding citizen first. Senior Conservative party officials are understood to have been briefed by senior Met officers who claim the morale of their members and their ability to tackle crime effectively has been seriously dented by the McPherson report.

(*Source*: J. Burns and R. Shrimsley, *Financial Times*, 14 December 2000.
Copyright © The Financial Times Limited. Reproduced with permission)

DISCUSSION ACTIVITY 2.10

Should efforts to eliminate discrimination be given priority even if they were leading to a reduction in the morale and effectiveness of the police service?

Case study 2.11 considers whether Railtrack was fair in its treatment of its stakeholders, in particular the travelling public, in relation to its solicitude towards shareholders.

CASE STUDY 2.11

Railtrack, profits and public safety

In May 2001 Railtrack, the company responsible for running the infrastructure of Britain's rail system, published its financial results. It made a worse than expected loss of £534m. This was largely due to the cost of renewing the permanent way after the Hatfield crash in 2000. Despite a disastrous year the company maintained the dividend payment to its shareholders. It was argued that it had to keep the confidence of the financial markets because it would need to borrow millions of pounds in the future to invest in the rail system.

The following leading article was published in the *Financial Times*.

Case study 2.11 continued

FT

That profits conflict with safety on the railways can no longer be in doubt. The draft report of the official inquiry into the Hatfield derailment reveals a catalogue of management and engineering failures.

After privatisation in 1996, the top executives of Railtrack, the infrastructure company, focused too much on immediate value for shareholders and too little on maintenance of the track. This might have been predicted; for although the rail regulator set targets for infrastructure improvement, every pound saved on maintenance helped to increase dividends.

Railtrack would have been entitled to keep such savings if they had resulted from extra efficiency. But the inquiry shows that it lacked managerial and technical skills, was slack in its maintenance discipline and communicated poorly with subcontractors. New management brought in after the fatal crash has admitted past failings and has made some progress towards putting them right. But broader remedies are needed. The company must be subject to a new set of incentives that more explicitly recognises its status as a public service utility in receipt of large government subsidies.

At the time of privatisation, it was decided to adapt the regulatory model used in the gas, electricity and telecommunications industries. This sets a price that the utility may charge, leaving an incentive to make extra profits from greater efficiency.

It is now obvious that this was a bad model for the railways – partly because of the importance and unpredictable costs of safety and partly because the fragmented structure of the industry creates perverse incentives. If Railtrack closes a line for unexpected safety work, for example, it must pay penalty charges to train operating companies.

Regulation should move closer to the US model. That would involve tighter supervision and replace the profit motive with the guarantee of a 'fair' rate of return – provided the company does its job properly. There are disadvantages: the spur to efficiency is blunted and, when the return is assured, managers may try to overinvest.

But since Railtrack has failed to convince its shareholders, the markets and the general public that it can find the right balance between profit and maintenance expenditures, stronger regulation must be the way ahead.

(*Source*: Leader article, *Financial Times*, 9 May 2001. Copyright © The Financial Times Limited. Reproduced with permission)

The case raises the question of whether public utilities, which are necessaries of a civilised life, are ethically different to other products and services. The chairmen of UK regulated utilities, according to a survey (Brigley and Vass 1997: 164), thought they were not, and that the ethical obligations on a private utility company should be no different to those placed on any private company.

In 2001 Railtrack plc was declared insolvent and put into administration. The shareholders demanded that they should be compensated by being paid the value of the Railtrack shares when the company was floated on the stock exchange. The government retorted that taxpayers' money would not be used to spare shareholders the consequences of their poor investment.

DISCUSSION ACTIVITY 2.11

What is a fair balance between interests of the owners of a company that provides a public utility and the interests of the customers? Was Railtrack right in its approach?

▦ Lying

Lying is wrong; except that in everyday usage it is not always so. The acceptability of a lie partly depends on the context in which it is made. Perjury, lying under oath in a court of law, is not acceptable, indeed it is a crime that carries heavy punishment. In the context of business negotiations lying, in the form of bluffing, may be acceptable as Carr argued (1968) in a classic article. Lies, in such a context, may be no more than putting a spin on an unpalatable truth.

Definition	Winston Churchill used the phrase **terminological inexactitude** in a speech on Chinese labour in South Africa. The phrase was not actually used as a euphemism for a lie. He argued that although the labourers' contracts might not be proper or healthy they could not be classified as slavery without 'some risk of terminological inexactitude'. However Alexander Haig, the American politician, is credited with saying, 'It is not a lie, it's a terminological inexactitude'.

The reprehensibility of a lie may also depend upon its nature. Telling an absolute untruth is often worse than failing to tell the whole truth. A cabinet secretary to a British government famously objected to a suggestion that he had lied. He had, he claimed, merely been 'economical with the truth'. Managers often find difficulty when they have to keep silent about privileged or confidential information, as when they know there are proposals to make people redundant but have been required to say nothing until the plans are finalised and can be announced. Their loyalty to their staff conflicts with their commitment to their company's needs. Conflicts of interest are a particular problem for professionals and public officials whose judgement should be seen to be free of private or opposing interests. They should be open about any such conflicts. Recruitment consultants finding new jobs for staff being made redundant would be regarded with suspicion if they received fees from both the organisation buying the out-placement service and the company in which they placed the redundant staff. The Nolan Committee's (1995) seven principles for public life are all focused on ensuring that private or sectional interests do not prejudice people's decisions on matters of public interest.

Another test of the dishonesty of a lie is its purpose. There is a range of names for acceptable lies including fibs and white lies that are intended to avoid giving offence or causing distress to individuals. Not all managers see such lying as acceptable, as one told us in a research interview.

I think for me the most important thing is honesty and what I find difficult is when managers maybe are doing something for one reason but are telling staff it's for another reason. Something like that I would find, and do find, quite difficult. Rather than actually saying to staff, you didn't get the job because your performance isn't as accurate or whatever else; what they give is fairly obscure reasons rather than actually facing the real reason.

A lie involves intent to deceive; if there is no such intent there is no lie. We fill our conversations with figures of speech such as hyperbole ('I'm so hungry I could eat a horse') and metaphor ('That man is a pig') that do not lead people to accept the literal truth of what we are saying. Advertising is a common area in which companies may seek to deceive their customers. The Advertising Standards Authority, in a typical example, criticised Virgin Trains for claiming in their advertisements that all fares were half-price when conditions meant that many were not (Milmo, 2001).

Refusing to be true to one's own beliefs can be a form of self-deception. This can happen when a person justifies continuing their connection to an organisation even though they object on ethical grounds to the organisation's behaviour.

CASE STUDY 2.12

BAT, Nottingham University and the honorary professor

Nottingham University accepted £3.8m from British American Tobacco (BAT), the world's second biggest tobacco company, towards setting up an international Centre for Corporate Responsibility. There was of course nothing illegal about the gift but many individuals and groups thought it was wrong. The problem was that Nottingham University carried out medical research into cancer and its treatment, some of it funded by medical charities. This was thought to fit ill with accepting money from a company that sells products known to cause cancer.

Richard Smith was editor of the *British Medical Journal* (BMJ) and an unpaid honorary professor of medical journalism at Nottingham University. He believed the university's acceptance of BAT's money was a 'serious mistake'. He polled readers of the BMJ to discover their views on whether he should resign from his post at Nottingham University. Of the 1,075 votes cast 84 per cent said the university should return the money and 54 per cent said that Professor Smith should resign if the university did not do so. The latter vote was closer than had been anticipated and this was because some argued that the professor should stay within the university and argue his case internally. The professor did resign, both because he said he would abide by the result of the poll and because he firmly believed the university was wrong in its actions.

(*Source*: Meikle, 2001)

DISCUSSION ACTIVITY 2.12

Is it better to retreat and live to fight another day or to take a stand on a matter one sees as an injustice?

A company's deception of its customers, whether by intention or mistake, is discussed in Case study 2.13.

CASE STUDY
2.13

McDonald's fries

The original McDonald's fries were cooked in beef fat. This of course made them objectionable to vegetarians and to Hindus for whom the cow is sacred. In 1990 McDonald's announced that in future all its fries would be cooked in vegetable oil. It emerged in 2001 however that this was only part of the story. In North America the fries were first cooked in centralised plants using beef fat. They were then frozen and transported to the restaurants for further frying in vegetable oil. McDonald's announced that it was 'not too big to apologise' and that it had given incomplete information to its customers. American Hindus have started seeking damages. Other customers have no problem with the use of beef fat and may even think that it improves the taste of the fries. McDonald's has nearly thirty restaurants in India, where its burgers are made from lamb rather than beef. It assured its Indian customers that its cooking methods were strictly vegetarian.

(*Source*: Evans, 2001)

DISCUSSION ACTIVITY 2.13

When do companies' excessive claims about their products become a lie?

The next case study in this section has the character of an ancient Greek tragedy. Jonathan Aitken, who had publicly defended the freedom of the press in his early career, committed hubris over a weekend spent in the Paris Ritz, received his nemesis and was reported to be looking for catharsis.

Definitions

Hubris, nemesis and catharsis

The first two terms represent the themes of Greek tragedy and the third is the experience of the audience watching the play. **Hubris** is a great pride and belief in one's own importance. **Nemesis** is a deserved punishment that cannot be avoided; and **catharsis** is the release of strong emotion caused by the experience of fear, albeit only expressed on the stage.

CASE STUDY
2.14

The Jonathan Aitken story

Johnathan Aitken is a great-nephew of Lord Beaverbrook, the 1950s newspaper magnate. He was at one time a journalist and in 1992 he became a member of John Major's cabinet. In 1993 he stayed at the Paris Ritz. The *Guardian* newspaper took an interest in this visit and inquired why a cabinet minister was staying at a very expensive hotel at someone else's expense. Aitken said he had paid for the stay himself. He lied. But at the time there was no proof he had. The *Guardian* kept running the story and Aitken, saying that he was going to fight 'the cancer of bent and twisted journalism . . . with the simple sword of truth', sued the newspaper for libel. He persuaded his wife and his daughter to lie in support of the claim that he had paid for the stay himself. When documents were presented

Case study 2.14 continued

that showed that he had lied on oath in the court the libel case collapsed. He was charged with perverting the course of justice and perjury in 1998 and sent to prison in 1999.

Why had he lied over such an apparently trivial issue? Aitken had long had contacts with the Saudi royal family and had been involved in the arms trade with Saudi Arabia. The *Guardian* reported that:

> We know that Mr. Aitken's business in Paris that weekend was closely tied up with multi-million pound arms deals involving his close friend, Said Ayas, and the Saudi royal family. For that to have become public would have been devastating for Mr. Aitken, for the Saudis and the government.

Lying to protect business confidentiality led to perjury. Rumours that Aitken was planning to become a priest after finishing his 18-month sentence were denied by him.

(*Sources*: Harding, 1999; *Guardian*, 1999; Wilson, 1999)

DISCUSSION ACTIVITY 2.14

What would you have done in Aitken's position?

Many of the issues related to lying, as in the following case study, concern the failure to tell the whole truth rather that the telling of falsehoods.

CASE STUDY 2.15 — Economy with the truth when dealing with the tax authorities

This is an extract from an interview with the finance director of a private company.

> Most of the ethical issues revolve around disclosure to the revenue and tax authority. The issues are whether we should disclose all the material facts and secondly when arguing a case with the revenue, whether we should make a case even when we know it is weak. The rule is 'we will make a case as long as we have one argument – however obtuse'. As long as we have an arguable position and we won't be embarrassed.
>
> I have just had a conversation with someone on an issue . . . actually tax again, on whether we give the Inland Revenue a letter or not at this particular point in time. It could be slightly prejudicial, only slightly, to our case, and as we are going to have a meeting and it may settle it, do I need to give it to him [the tax inspector] now? This is a question of timing. If I can settle it without giving it to him I might do.
>
> It's just to do with tax planning and why we actually had done a transaction. It may make the revenue renege on something they have just agreed. Unlikely, but you don't want to raise doubts in somebody's mind who has actually spent some time looking at it. Tax is always slow anyway, so why shouldn't I delay sending the letter? We are likely to have a meeting in July. I would see how that went and if they decide they still want the correspondence – we'll give it to them. It is actually the fact that we know we have got a meeting due that enables us to prevaricate.

(*Source*: Research interview conducted by the authors)

DISCUSSION ACTIVITY 2.15

In what circumstances might it be right not to tell the whole truth?

Cheating

Ethics ⟵——————————————————————⟶ Morality

| Cheating |

This category of ethical issues concerns keeping the rules. However for many in organisations the important question is whether the benefits of bending the rules are high enough, and the chances of being caught low enough, to justify taking a risk. This ethical calculation can be made both at a corporate level and as a matter of individual discretion.

Rules are not always bent to benefit the person doing the bending. In bureaucratic systems rules are often bent to protect people who would otherwise be harshly treated by the system. One example we came across during our research concerned a production line worker in a factory that made prepared foods for supermarkets. The employee was diabetic and, on the day of the incident, had been careless of his diet. Consequently at work he felt the start of a hypoglaecemic attack and took, and ate, one of the products from the production line. This prevented him from collapsing. But he was threatened with dismissal because company rules made theft of company property punishable by instant dismissal. The personnel officer thought the man had been foolish but thought it unjust to sack him. The rules were ignored. Case 2.16 looks at a corporate level issue.

CASE STUDY 2.16

BAT and allegations of cigarette smuggling

An oddity in the world market for cigarettes was discovered in 1997. When global exports were compared with global imports one-third of the total inventory was unaccounted for. The reason was not hard to find. Up to one-third of cigarettes sold are smuggled. The charge made by investigators and journalists against British American Tobacco (BAT) was that it colluded with tobacco smuggling and factored the sales of smuggled cigarettes into its strategic planning. The charge was not that BAT employees actually took cigarettes across borders without paying the excise duties. It was that they sold cigarettes to distributors whom they knew would avoid paying tax. This conclusion was drawn from a study of BAT's internal documents that were made public as a result of legal cases in the USA and in the UK.

BAT used a series of euphemisms for smuggling in its documentation. They included DNP (duty not paid), GT (general trade) and transit goods. Legal goods were known as DP – duty paid. One extract from the documentation illustrates the process. It concerns a 1995 dispute in Colombia between BAT and Philip Morris over the ownership of a cigarette brand called Belmont. One memorandum proposed a contingency plan to be used in the event that BAT lost the case. The plan was 'to launch a new brand in DP and maintain Belmont in a GT channel'. One

Case study 2.16 continued

problem with selling Belmont through GT was that the 'company could not support Belmont in GT through advertising'. Advertising a product that was not officially imported might have caused the revenue authorities to ask questions.

Kenneth Clarke, the deputy chairman of BAT, and a one-time Chancellor of the Exchequer who had been responsible for UK duties on tobacco, responded to these criticisms when they were published in the *Guardian*. He pointed out that smuggling was a major problem in the tobacco business. Cigarettes are easily transportable and of high value. These factors, combined with the high rates of duty and the high differentials between the taxes of neighbouring countries, provide incentives for smuggling. He pointed out that BAT was always willing to co-operate with governments who wished to crack down on smuggling. He added:

> However, where governments are not prepared to address the underlying causes of the problem, businesses such as ours who are engaged in international trade are faced with a dilemma. If the demand for our brands is not met, consumers will either switch to our competitors' brands or there will be the kind of dramatic growth in counterfeit products that we have recently seen in our Asian markets. Where any government is unwilling to act or their efforts are unsuccessful, we act, completely within the law, on the basis that our brands will be available alongside those of our competitors in the smuggled as well as the legitimate market.

Audrey Wise, a Member of Parliament and a member of the House of Commons Health Committee, said of BAT's policy:

> If there was ever a case of being within the letter of the law but clearly outside the spirit of the law then this is a gem. Smuggled goods are illegal goods, so if you're deliberately making your goods available for smuggling knowingly and deliberately you are an accessory to the fact.

(*Sources*: Center for Public Enquiry, 2000; Clarke, 2000; Maguire, 2000)

DISCUSSION ACTIVITY 2.16

Should companies accept being placed at a competitive disadvantage by following the spirit as well as the letter of the law?

The next case study raises a large number of ethical issues. One is whether doctors used people's ignorance of the law and the regulations to 'cheat' parents grieving for their dead children.

CASE STUDY 2.17 The retention of dead babies' organs in hospitals

In the UK, when a child died, the coroner could order a post-mortem examination to discover the cause of death. A hospital could also order a post-mortem with the parents' consent to study the disease that had killed the child. After post-mortems organs from the child were often retained for research or educational purposes. Doctors assumed, wrongly, that a coroner's request for a post-mortem allowed them to retain organs. In other cases the law merely required that the parents should not object. Over a period of years a collection of 50,000 organs from dead children was

Case study 2.17 continued

established in a number of English hospitals. The general public were unaware of these collections; more importantly the parents of the children were not aware the organs had been retained. Even where parents had given consent to post-mortems they were not necessarily aware that the hospital could remove and retain the organs. The parents had not been given the opportunity to give full and informed consent. This is a form of cheating that arose, as Professor Kennedy argued, 'from a type of professional arrogance that ignored – indeed did not acknowledge, the views and voices of parents'.

The issue exploded into the public's consciousness because of the Alder Hey hospital case. Professor van Velzen at that hospital had developed an obsession with organ retention. The Redfern report into Alder Hey found that van Velzen had ordered illegal retention of children's organs, had falsified records and had failed to catalogue the specimens. The identification of this particular example of illegal activity triggered the investigations that revealed a culture of mendacity over organ retention in many hospitals. The issue released raw emotions as parents who believed they had buried their dead child requested that they be allowed to bury their child's retained remains.

The impact of these new stories was a tightening-up of rules for organ retention and an unwillingness of the public to allow organs to be retained. Researchers began to complain that research into cancers was being prevented because of the difficulty of obtaining human material for use in trials and experiments. The pharmaceutical companies were removing clinical development from UK to Europe because of the difficulties in obtaining materials for work on breast and prostate cancers.

(*Sources*: Anon, 2001; Boseley, 2001a; Boseley, 2001b; Redfern Report, 2001)

DISCUSSION ACTIVITY 2.17

Was the general practice (rather than the particular practice of Dr van Velzen) of retaining organs without proper consent a case of acts being ethical but illegal?

Bullying

Ethics ←————————————————————————→ Morality

Bullying

In organisations bullying is the misuse of power to abuse, humiliate or cajole others. Unlike bullying in the school playground, which may also involve physical harm, organisational bullying is more likely to be social. Some bullying may be too insignificant or transient to be turned into an issue. But where should the line between the insignificant and the significant be drawn? At what point does proper assertion within a negotiation, for example, become an improper use of aggression? The problem is made worse by people's differing perceptions of acceptable, and unacceptable, behaviour. What may be harassment from a supervisor, from a subordinate's point of view, may be an effective example of leadership from the team leader's point of view.

One answer to the problem of bullying is to allow the victim to define it. This empowers the weak against the strong by accepting that if someone says they are being bullied then they are. If a legal perspective were to be taken this would put the burden of proof on the accused and not on the victim. The accused would have to prove they were innocent. This of course is the opposite of the legal custom that the accused is innocent until proved guilty.

The following case may not look like bullying but it is an example of a company using its dominant position to control the actions of its agents. It raises the question of when assertive marketing and selling practices cross the line and become illegal.

CASE STUDY 2.18

British Airways and Virgin Atlantic

British Airways and Virgin Atlantic have for many years been in intense competition. In 1993 Virgin had accused British Airways (BA) of 'dirty tricks' that discouraged customers from buying tickets from Virgin. In the subsequent libel proceedings BA paid Richard Branson, the chairman of Virgin, £610,000 to settle the case. Virgin started proceedings in the United States courts seeking damages for BA's unfair and illegal marketing practices.

The core of Virgin's complaints was that BA, by far the larger of the two airlines, was using its dominant position in the market to coerce travel agents to sell its flights. This was done by only paying agents certain commissions when they had sold a quota of BA flights, and by packaging discounts on flights. People who travelled to destinations where BA had little competition were offered additional discounts if they bought BA connecting flights in areas where there were many alternative carriers. In November 1997 Virgin formally complained to the European Commission that these 'illegal' practices were in breach of Article 86 of the Treaty of Rome, which covers abuse of dominant market position.

In 1998 BA accused Virgin Atlantic, in its in-house magazine *BA News*, of using similar marketing techniques to those that BA was accused of using. In November of that year Sir Colin Marshall, chairman of BA, apologised to Richard Branson for the accusations and destroyed all copies of the magazine.

In 1999 the European Commission fined BA £4.5m for operating an anti-competitive loyalty scheme with travel agents. The Competition Commissioner said, 'It is well established in community law that a dominant supplier cannot give incentives to its customers and distributors to be loyal to it, so foreclosing the market from the dominant firm's competitors'. BA announced they would appeal. In October of the same year a New York judge threw out Virgin Atlantic's claim against BA. One lawyer pointed out that the notion of a 'dominant company' did not exist in American law.

At the end of 1999 it appeared that BA's ticketing practices were illegal in the European Union but legal in the United States.

(*Sources*: Anon, 1997; Skapinker, 1998; Anon, 1999a; Anon, 1999b)

DISCUSSION ACTIVITY 2.18

Is corporate bullying as common as personal bullying?

This next case involves powerful individuals within an organisation exploiting their strength.

CASE STUDY
2.19

The hospital consultants

The following is an extract from an interview with an accountant in a hospital.

> You will be aware I am sure, through the media, that the government this year has made available an extra £500 million or £600 million for trying to reduce the waiting lists [of patients awaiting treatment]. What that means with a hospital like this is that suddenly you have got to do an extra lot of work, very quickly over a short period of time and it doesn't really give you time to get additional staff employed. You are really talking about expecting either existing staff to do overtime or to get some agency staff in to help. Also we haven't had confirmation that this money will be recurrent, although it is likely to be. But because we haven't had that specific guarantee hospitals are reluctant to employ people on open-ended contracts.
>
> One of the problems we then face is with consultant surgeons. A lot, if not all of whom have private work as well, and there are some of them who say, 'Right, I will do this extra work, provided I am paid such and such a rate'. The rates that they are inclined to quote will be what they would charge privately. I think they forced the hospital's arm into agreeing to it. They got what they wanted then . . . They will see their job probably in a wider context than just their work in the NHS, because it is regular, their private work. What their stance is of course is, if you are wanting me to do this extra NHS session, in theory I am foregoing doing a private session somewhere else, so I want to be compensated at least somewhere near the level of income that I would have earned.
>
> It causes me some unease. I suppose in terms of unfairness. If we haven't got additional nurses in the hospital prepared to do extra hours, then we won't get the operations done because it needs a team in the operating theatres, both the consultants and the nurses. But of course the nurses haven't got the option of doing private work and being able to earn more money so they haven't got the clout. Yeah, I think, I am sure whoever you speak to, they will see it is the consultants who have got the most clout in the hospital. It is them who can bang the table. Why is it that they can do this? Is it right that they should do this? Don't get me wrong, I am not saying that every surgeon in the hospital has taken a slider, some think the stance taken by most people is totally wrong and unjustified. I know that when there was a meeting of surgeons to discuss it, one particular [consultant] said 'well, he didn't think that any of the surgeons should get additional money for this extra work because they all earned quite enough anyway'. In some ways it can be helpful, because in theory you can maybe marginalise those that have taken a more extreme stance, but that depends really if they are very forceful personalities within the hospital it depends then whether the hospital management wants to stand up to them.

(Source: Research interview conducted by the authors)

DISCUSSION ACTIVITY 2.19

Were the consultants exercising their market power legitimately or were they bullying the hospital management?

The bully in the next case study was an organisation rather than an individual or a group.

<table>
<tr><td>CASE STUDY
2.20</td><td>## Supermarkets' treatment of their supply chains</td></tr>
</table>

In recent years there have been many criticisms of the power that the major supermarket chains exercise in the UK. Amongst these criticisms were the charges that they were using oligarchic power to keep prices to the consumer high and that, by building large out-of-town stores and requiring people to drive to them, they were damaging the environment. The Competition Commission investigated several of these arguments. They found that the market was competitive and that profits were not excessive. However they did uphold the claim that the big supermarkets did bully (to use our word, not theirs) the farmers and smaller companies locked into their supply chains. The following extract from a *Financial Times* article rehearses some of the arguments.

FT The relationship between food suppliers and retailers will again come under the microscope. In the meantime, ministers want to use a new code of practice between supermarkets and suppliers, one of the recommendations of the Competition Commission report, to clamp down on some of the extreme practices, such as retailers imposing retrospective price cuts to contracts.

A draft code has been drawn up by the Office of Fair Trading with the supermarkets. Food suppliers are being consulted on the results and have signalled their dissatisfaction with what they have seen so far. Instead of calling a halt to some of the practices criticised by the Competition Commission, such as asking suppliers to meet the cost of shop refurbishment or staff hospitality, the code suggests retailers should not 'unreasonably' ask suppliers to foot the bill. But Whitehall officials expect the code to be toughened up during the consultation process. 'The code has to be robust. It has to end the practices the Competition Commission criticised, not just say it would rather they didn't happen. If there is no confidence in the new code, a future government may have to consider further legislation,' said one. Colin Breed, Liberal Democrat agriculture spokesman, believes the code will not help suppliers stand up to supermarkets. 'The only sensible way to proceed is to appoint an independent retail regulator who would not be in the pockets of the supermarkets,' he said.

The industry may also come under the scrutiny of the [House of] Commons' trade and industry committee. Members have praised the sector for helping to deliver lower food prices through fierce competition, but say they are aware suppliers further down the chain often pay the price. Martin O'Neill, committee chairman, said there could be room for an inquiry around the time of the planned sweeping review of the farming industry. 'I would hope that review will spark off a broad debate about the future of retail and the protection of consumer choice just as much as consumers' rights,' he said.

Retailers are, of course, keen to avoid any inquiry that focuses directly on their role, although all say they are happy to take part in any wider-ranging review of the supply chain. Inquiries are costly and time consuming. They can also depress share prices across a sector. For many retail analysts, constant carping about supermarket profits risks damaging the industry, leaving it susceptible to overseas predators. 'One day people are weeping and wailing about the fact that Marks and Spencer does not make £1bn profits any more,' said one analyst. 'The next thing, they are complaining that Tesco does just that. Do they want a successful retail industry in this country or not?'

(*Source*: R. Bennett and S. Voyle, *Financial Times*, 11 April 2001. Copyright © The Financial Times Limited. Reproduced with permission)

DISCUSSION ACTIVITY 2.20

How easy is it for supply chain partnerships, that are proposed as a new and better way to manage procurement, to become abusive relationships?

Harming

Ethics	← ─────────────────────────── →	Morality
		Harming

This category involves questions of harm to individuals, animals, institutions, organisations or the environment. One area of controversy is whether a degree of harm is acceptable if the overall results of the harmful action are good. Another concerns the accuracy of the forecasts of the amount of harm and good a particular action will do. An interesting case, which involved such judgements, was that of the Brent Spar oil platform. The issue was whether it was safe to dump the disused platform at sea or whether it would be better to take it ashore and dismantle it. Some time after the issue had been resolved the environmental group Greenpeace admitted that it had exaggerated the amount of environmental harm the sinking of the platform would have done.

Many of the examples of harm being done within or by organisations concern harm to individual employees, as in the following case study.

CASE STUDY 2.21

Sexual harassment

This case study is an extract from a research interview.

> I mean I haven't had it personally but a very close friend of mine was a Secretary in a very large organisation in London and worked for the Assistant Chairman and she felt she was being harassed. Well she was being harassed and when she actually spoke to her personnel department they said, 'Well yes, you're probably right, we've had complaints before but nobody in this organisation will remove the Assistant Chairman. We will help you find another job.' So their compassion went to the individual in getting her another job because their knowledge was, what could they do? The organisation would not support [her], whatever claim she put in, at the end of the day it would not result in his dismissal. It may have resulted in a rap over the knuckles but she could not work for him and . . . sometimes you know that that is the approach you are going to have to take. Fortunately I've never been in that sort of situation of something quite as clearly wrong.

(Source: Research interview conducted by the authors)

DISCUSSION ACTIVITY 2.21

What are the longer-term consequences of not confronting behaviour such as that discussed in the case study?

The next case describes the harm that can be caused by corporate inaction, although in this example there is a dispute as to which of two corporations was culpable. It also raises the question, to be discussed in Chapter 9, of when harm done by corporate indifference can, or should, invite criminal charges as well as civil liabilities.

CASE STUDY
2.22

The Firestone Tire recall issue

In August 2000 Ford and Firestone announced the product recall of 6.5 million tyres used on Ford's sports utility vehicle (SUV), the Explorer. The recall was limited to tyres made at Firestone's plant at Decatur in Illinois. Tyres made at other plants were not recalled. The problem was that the treads on the tyres were prone to separate in hot weather; this could cause a loss of control of the vehicle that could result in a rollover accident. Over 180 people had died in such accidents in the USA and 700 people had been injured.

It was alleged by commentators that Firestone knew the problem was not simply a quality systems fault at Decatur but a general problem that affected all of Firestone's SUV tyres. It was therefore alleged that Firestone, far from putting things right, was replacing the faulty tyres with equally dangerous ones.

The situation was made more complex by the desires of both Ford and Firestone to blame each other for the rollover accidents and the deaths. While Ford blamed Firestone, Firestone partly blamed design faults in the Explorer. In a report on the accidents Firestone identified some problems for which it was responsible, but also claimed that Ford's recommendation that the tyres should be inflated to a pressure significantly below the tyres' maximum capacity (to overcome a design fault in the Explorer) increased the temperature of the tyres and increased the possibility of tread separation. Ford, in its 'root cause' report, claimed that design problems played no role in the crashes and that underinflation was not a contributory factor. The argument continued during 2000 and was the subject of Congressional hearings.

On 22 May Firestone announced that it would no longer be a supply partner of Ford, ending a relationship that had lasted nearly a century. On the same day Ford announced that it was recalling 13 million tyres at a cost of $2.1 billion. On the previous day it had recalled 47,000 of its SUVs because of fears, unconnected with the Firestone issue, that tyres had been damaged on the production line.

The case paralleled that of the Pinto model which exercised Ford in the 1970s (De George 1999: 240–1). The Pinto was a car produced in a hurry. When it was tested for rear-end impact it was found to be below the standard of comparable cars. There was a danger, because of the positioning of the fuel tank, that the tank could be punctured in a crash and the car would explode. Ford undertook a cost–benefit analysis. They estimated that the cost of inserting a protective baffle was greater than the cost of legal claims that might arise from deaths attributable to the design fault. The design of the car was not changed between 1971 and 1978 and the customers were not informed of the potential problem. Between 1976 and 1977 thirteen Pintos exploded after rear-end crashes. The cost of the legal compensation proved to be much greater than the cost of the alteration and in 1978 the cars were recalled and protective baffles were fitted.

(*Sources*: Turner, 2001; Firestone Tire Resource Center, n.d.; Bowe, 2001)

DISCUSSION ACTIVITY 2.22

Had Ford's strategic attitude to safety fears concerning its vehicles changed in over twenty years?

This last case study concerns when it might be right to break the law to prevent an organisation doing harm. It also, as it centres on the issue of the moral status of animals, questions the definition of harm.

CASE STUDY
2.23

Huntingdon Life Sciences

This case raises questions about whether there are situations in which it is appropriate to take illegal action because either the law is immoral or the law has to be broken to prevent some greater harm being done. This case study concerns Huntingdon Life Sciences (HLS), a company that carries out pharmaceutical testing on laboratory animals. The company's activities are highly regulated by government agencies and the testing it does is legal.

Animal rights activists argue that testing drugs on animals is cruel and immoral. The case raises difficult questions about whether animals have rights. The traditional view was that animals are not accorded moral status or rights because they lack the power to reason. The obvious response is that this does not prevent them from suffering. This argument may justify minimising the pain caused during experiments; but it does not necessarily mean that the experiments are bad in themselves, especially if they contribute to a greater benefit for humanity through the development of better drugs and medical treatments. The arguments around this issue, which are not primarily the concern of this text, can be explored in Tester (1991) and Scruton (2000). When people claim the existence of rights they may be exhibiting emotivism. This simply means claiming something is right because it feels right. Moral judgement becomes a subjective emotional reaction to a situation.

Animal rights activists believe they are justified in using violence, or the threat of violence, to stop vivisection. The shareholders of HLS, as well as its managers and employees, have been intimidated. The activists threatened to identify and protest to the shareholders. Various institutional shareholders decided in consequence to cease investing in HLS and a number of brokers advised shareholders to sell after threats from activists. Two of HLS's market-makers had also withdrawn and this made it difficult for investors to trade their shares. The company responded by proposing to set up a rarely used shareholding structure to keep investors' identities anonymous and to protect them from intimidation. The proposed corporate nominee scheme is within the rules set out by the Financial Services Authority.

Case study 2.23 continued

The government felt it had to take action, as described in the following article from the *Financial Times*, to protect a legitimate business.

FT

The authorities on Thursday stepped up their fight against animal rights activists with the launch of a police hit squad and a top-level government committee. The two measures are aimed at preventing violent attacks against companies that carry out medical research, their customers and financial backers. The police announced the creation of a squad 'to target the ringleaders of animal [rights] extremist activity who are organising and taking part in serious criminal offences'.

The group will draw officers from different police forces and will work under the National Crime Squad. It aims to prevent attacks such as those suffered by directors, staff and customers of Huntingdon Life Sciences, the drug-testing group. Over the past year, activists have set fire to Huntingdon workers' cars, sent hate mail to staff and assaulted Brian Cass, its managing director. No one has been arrested in connection with these attacks.

The Association of Chief Police Officers denied that the police had acted slowly in dealing with animal rights extremists. It would 'not say [the squad] was late. We felt this was the right time to act.' The squad will liaise with the new government committee, which includes five ministers and is chaired by Jack Straw [at the time, Home Secretary]. The committee will co-ordinate government action against the activists. The home secretary, who on Thursday visited Huntingdon's laboratories in Cambridgeshire, said: 'We will not tolerate a small number of criminals trying to threaten research organisations and companies.' Some 15 protesters stood outside the gates but were denied a meeting with the home secretary. Greg Avery of Stop Huntingdon Animal Cruelty said the campaign group had no involvement in the violent attacks.

(*Sources*: F. Guerrera, *www.FT.com*, 27 April 2001, *Financial Times*, 12 May 2001. Copyright © Financial Times Limited. Reproduced with permission)

DISCUSSION ACTIVITY 2.23

In what situations do you think it might be justified to break, or defy the law, to end an injustice?

Reflections

This chapter has presented a panorama of the ethical and moral issues that concern managerial and organisational life. Some patterns can be seen to emerge from plotting the case studies on the matrix in Table 2.1. Many of the issues that cause difficulty and controversy in the business and organisational world concern actions that are, arguably, wrong but legal. These cover the range of matters from the ethical to the moral. Issues that centre on actions that are wrong and illegal mainly concern questions of morality rather than ethics. They are about stopping organisations doing harm. Conversely issues arising from actions that are good and legal, but are not legal obligations, rest mostly at the ethical end of the spectrum in Table 2.1. The most contentious issues, and perhaps the least common, are those concerning illegal actions that are ethically and morally justifiable.

All the case studies are matters of controversy, every claim that an act is illegal or wrong can be challenged. As Watson (2002: 455) argued, ethical ambiguity and ethical dilemmas are inevitable in organisational and managerial life.

Summary

In this chapter the following key points have been made:

- The major virtues of corporate and organisational behaviour are:

  - social development
  - social responsibility
  - reciprocity
  - fairness
  - truthfulness
  - fair play
  - supporting
  - caring.

- Under each of these headings issues at work may raise questions about what is right and what is wrong. What is right may in many cases also be legal but not necessarily a legal obligation. In other cases what is right may not be legal. Conversely, things that the law allows might not be right.

- Ethical issues are not easy to categorise. They appear as dilemmas in which arguments can be made for all sides. The protagonists in the cases, however, may see and present only a single point of view.

Suggested further reading

A good review of current issues in business ethics is P.W.F. Davies (ed.) (1997) *Current Issues in Business Ethics*, London: Routledge. D. Winstanley and J. Woodall (2000) *Ethical Issues in Contemporary Human Resource Management*, London: Macmillan is a very useful guide to ethical issues related to human resource management.

GROUP ACTIVITY 2

Locating issues in the grid shown in Table 2.1 is not straightforward. An issue may involve several of the moral and ethical problems identified. It might, for example, exhibit an unfair distribution of resources as well as lying and bullying. It might also be possible to argue about which categories of rightness and legality the issue best fits. Different readings of the facts of the case might lead to different opinions about whether an action was, prima facie, illegal or not.

In class identify current business ethics issues that are being discussed in the media. Identify as best you can the facts of the issue and discuss where, on the grid in Table 2.1, the issue might best be placed. It might be necessary to plot different aspects of the issue in different places on the grid.

3 Ethical theories and how to use them

OBJECTIVES

Having completed this chapter and its associated activities, readers should be able to:

- Compare and contrast four approaches to ethical theory.

- Describe the implications of different ethical theories for businesses, organisations and management.

- Apply the theories to ethical issues in business, organisation and management.

Introduction

In Chapter 2 the range of ethical issues that can affect businesses, organisations and managers was plotted and examples were given that you were invited to think about. This chapter will give you tools for ethical thinking that you can use in analysing such issues. We have called them ethical theories because they are speculations or mental conceptions about how one should think about ethical matters. They should help you to move from an intuitive response to ethical matters to a systematic and analytical approach. However the theories do not provide an easy resolution. One reason for this is that there are many theories and it may not be obvious which should be applied to any particular set of circumstances. A second reason is that the theories are general. It is not always clear how they should be applied or interpreted in specific cases. The fact that some of these theories have been the subject of philosophical debate for many centuries implies that there is no consensus, or final resolution, to be had on these questions. It may be best to consider that the theories provide means of legitimating the stances you take on an issue rather than as sources of definitive or authoritative solutions.

A map of ethical theories

As there are many ethical theories they will be plotted on a map (Figure 3.1) based on that developed by Petrick and Quinn (1997: 48). A note of warning is needed. Figure 3.1, as are all two-by-two matrices, is a work of simplification. It is only intended to give you a broad overview. It does not capture the subtleties

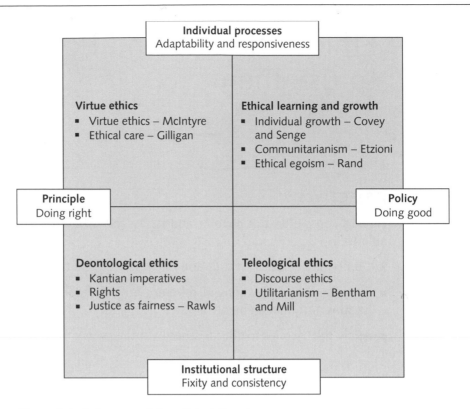

Figure 3.1 A framework for ethical theories

of the writers included in it because to do so would make it impossible to constrain them within any one quadrant of the figure.

The two elements of the horizontal axis of Figure 3.1 are policy and principle. The terms are taken from Dworkin's (1977: 22) work on rights.

Policy is defined as an approach that *sets out a goal to be reached, generally an improvement in some economic, political or social feature.*

Principle, in contrast, *is a standard that is to be observed, not because it will advance an economic, political or social situation, but because it is a requirement of fairness or justice or some other dimension of morality.*

Those ethical theories on the left of this dimension determine what is right and wrong from predetermined principles and standards. They take no regard of the consequences of an action – 'let justice be done though the heavens fall', a maxim of Roman law that was famously used in 1772 by Lord Mansfield during a legal case concerning slavery. Those theories to the right of the dimension measure the rightness of a thing according to whether it brings us to, or closer to, a desired state. The vertical dimension in Figure 3.1 contrasts a focus on ethical individuals with a focus on ethical institutions. The theories in the top half of the framework emphasise individuals' responsibility to develop themselves and the groups they belong to, by acquiring judgement and self-knowledge. The theories in the lower half of the framework are concerned to develop fixed structures, institutions, that are independent of us but which determine our principles and govern our ethical deliberations.

■ Virtue ethics

We will begin our consideration of Figure 3.1 by focusing upon those theories and ethical perspectives shown on the left-hand side, the principle-based perspectives. This does not mean that those ethical positions on the right-hand side of Figure 3.1 are unprincipled, not at all. Principle, in the sense being used here, refers to beliefs that are not affected by, or shaped by, the people involved, or what might result if a particular course of action is followed. This disregard for the consequences, which could result from an undiluted adoption of these

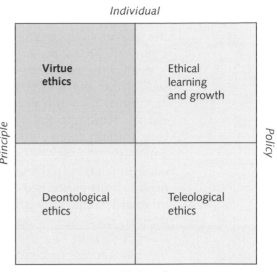

approaches, is why they are sometimes grouped under the broad heading of 'non-consequentialist' positions. This, as you will see, can sometimes lead to awkward and fraught situations.

Virtues are not 'ends'; rather they are 'means'. They are personal qualities that provide the basis for the individual to lead a good, noble, or 'happy' life. Whilst the notion of what is virtuous behaviour has changed over time, the person most associated with virtue ethics is Aristotle, a philosopher of great eminence who lived in Greece between 384 and 322 BC. Not only have the characteristics of a virtuous life undergone significant changes, but the meanings attaching to the terms used to describe particular characteristics are also a source of difference.

The Greek word, εὐδαιμονία (eudemonia), is loosely translated as 'happiness'. However, as MacIntyre (1967) pointed out, in Greek the term actually embraces both the notion of behaving well and faring well. Its use in ancient Greece was not concerned with hedonistic notions of happiness. It concerned itself with the individual's behaviour, and thus the way others perceived the individual. The latter was an essential ingredient to personal happiness. The 'good life' had, and retains, strong connotations of a 'whole' life, and places the individual within a social context. Even though social structures were deeply class-ridden during Aristotle's life, within the social and political elite there was a strong sense of being part of a whole.

Aristotle, reflecting the ideas of his age, placed the 'great-soul-man' on a pedestal. As you will see, the great-soul-man displays those virtues that were regarded as of the highest order. In ancient Greece the views of one's peers were critical to feelings of self-worth. Whilst the individual is the focus of Aristotle's attention, it is an individual within a society. Some social commentators, like MacIntyre (1967, 1987), have argued that since the eighteenth century liberalism has placed the individual outside of society. In this latter context, society is at best the sum of its parts. At worst, in Margaret Thatcher's famous words, 'there is no such thing as society'.

Virtue ethics is not a system of rules, but rather a set of personal characteristics that, if practised, will ensure that the individual is likely to make the 'right' choice in any ethically complex situation. Thus, the question for the individual, caught in the maelstrom of an ethically complex situation and appealing to virtue ethics as a guide for action, would ask, 'What would a virtuous person do in this situation?'

Plato, Aristotle's teacher, had identified four virtues, those of wisdom, courage, self-control and justice. For Aristotle, justice was the dominant virtue, but he expanded upon the number of personal qualities that could be regarded as virtues. Thus, into the frame came qualities such as liberality (the virtuous attitude towards money); patience (the virtuous response to minor provocation); amiability (the virtue of personal persona); magnanimity, truthfulness, indifference (in relation to the seeking of public recognition of achievement), and wittiness. It must be stressed that these virtues were not seen as of equal merit. The original Platonic virtues were seen as central to the attainment of a 'good' life, whereas the other virtues were seen as important for a civilised life. To understand the nature of a virtue we must understand how they are derived, and to do so we introduce the concept of the 'mean'.

For Aristotle, those personal qualities that were regarded as virtues were reflected in behaviours that represented a balance, or mean, in terms of the particular personal quality being considered. Thus, if the response of an individual to the threat of 'danger or significant personal challenge' was being considered, we can envisage a continuum with cowardice at one extreme and recklessness at the other (as in Table 3.1). Neither of these personal qualities (what Aristotle termed 'dispositions') is appealing as they are both likely to lead to detrimental outcomes in the long run. In the face of danger the 'noble' or 'great-soul-man' (and it was always the male that was considered in ancient Greece) would have to overcome his fears (i.e. suppress feelings of cowardice), but avoid acts of rashness, which would be likely to reduce the chances of success. Thus, an intermediate-point is required. This mean, or disposition, in this context is termed 'courage'.

Aristotle also considered modesty (used by Aristotle to mean 'respect', or 'sense of shame') as a possible virtue, but he dismissed it, other than as a virtue in the younger man. In the latter case, Aristotle saw it as a curb on youthful indiscretion, but he considered that the virtuous mature man should not require modesty for he should not commit acts of which he could be ashamed.

For Aristotle, the 'great-soul-man' was magnanimous, which was defined as 'possessing proper pride, or self-control' (Aristotle, 1976: 153). It is not surprising that in the class-ridden society of ancient Greece, the virtues described by Aristotle were only available to the elite of society. McMylor (1994), citing MacIntyre, observed:

> certain virtues are only available to those of great riches and high social status, there are virtues which are unavailable to the poor man, even if he is a free man. And those virtues are in Aristotle's view ones central to human life.
>
> (McMylor, 1994: 103)

Wealth, however, was not a necessary prerequisite of a magnanimous man.

> It is chiefly with honours . . . that the magnanimous man is concerned; but he will also be moderately disposed towards wealth, power, and every kind of good or bad fortune, however it befalls him
>
> (Aristotle, 1976: 155)

Table 3.1 Aristotle's moral virtues

Context	The vice of deficiency	Virtue (mean)	The vice of excess
Danger or a significant personal challenge	Cowardice	Courage	Rashness
Physical pleasures	Indifference (being unable to recognise the joy that physical pleasures can offer)	Self-control (knowing when and where to enjoy oneself)	Greed
Wealth	Meanness	Liberality (discriminating generosity)	Profligacy
Money	Miserliness	Magnificence (knowing when to spend, how much and on what)	Spendthrift
View of self	Meekness	Magnanimity (being able to feel and display personal pride when it is deserved, but without vanity)	Vanity
Personal recognition	False modesty	Indifference (good deeds are done for their own sake and not for personal recognition)	Careerist
Minor irritants	Defeatism	Patience	Irascibility
Personal demeanour	Obsequious (fawning and grovelling)	Amiable	Quarrelsome
Sincerity in expression	Self-deprecating	Truthfulness	Boastfulness
Sociability	Boorishness	Wittiness	Buffoonery

Indeed when discussing the virtuous approach towards wealth Aristotle identified liberality as the virtue (the mean). Illiberality or meanness was one extreme vice, while prodigality or profligacy was the other. However, Aristotle did not regard the two extremes as vices of equal unacceptability, judging profligacy as less objectionable to meanness. This ranking of profligacy over meanness underscores the slightly lower importance attaching to money and wealth, although this is not to say that wealth was unimportant.

Magnanimity was not equated with self-deprecaton or undue humility. These were seen as approximating to vices, but so too were vanity and boastfulness. Being *rightly* proud of who you were, or what you had achieved, was not a vice, only unjustified high self-esteem was unacceptable.

> A person is considered to be magnanimous if he thinks that he is worthy of great things, provided that he is worthy of them; because anyone who esteems his own worth unduly is foolish, and nobody who acts virtuously is foolish or stupid.
>
> (Aristotle, 1976: 153)

The point about this statement is that it is the perception of others that determines whether behaviour is vain or deserving. In one sense a person can be both vain and deserving, but for Aristotle, vanity implied a degree of exhibitionism above that which could be justified by one's achievements or social standing. Thus, vanity becomes a relative term in this context, relative to the state of deservingness attaching to the achievement of the individual or his position in society.

Aristotle gave justice prominent consideration, but the notion of justice in ancient Greece was quite different from that which we articulate today. As is further explored below, the accepted standards of ethical behaviour are a product of their times, notwithstanding that notions of justice feature in most philosophies of ethics. Aristotle, while he spent some time differentiating between differing forms of justice, nonetheless offers a less than precise definition of justice, with the notion of the 'mean' again featuring strongly.

> To do injustice is to have more than one ought, and to suffer it is to have less than one ought and justice is the mean between doing injustice and suffering it.
>
> (Aristotle, 1976: 78)

This concentration upon the notion of justice as the bedrock of ethical behaviour is not universally shared, with the invisibility and muteness of women within such debates a cause for concern.

A challenge to the primacy of justice

The role of women in ancient Athenian society did not register on political and social seismographs. Thus, the virtues as articulated by Aristotle can be said to be virtues from a masculine perspective. This is a relevant observation when we consider, as we do later, the work of psychologists, such as Lawrence Kohlberg, who developed a hierarchy of moral reasoning, based upon the assumption that justice is the ultimate test of the superiority of one form of moral reasoning over another. Within this framework, hard choices can be made between competing claims using justice as the decision criterion. The hypothetical scenarios employed by Kohlberg during his studies presented research subjects with choices to be made, but compromises were not available. Under this approach, one claim could be successful, whilst all others would fail.

Gilligan (1982), a former student of Kohlberg, has taken issue with the use of justice as the pre-eminent determinant of moral reasoning. Within Kohlberg's studies fewer females than males have displayed the form of moral reasoning that has allowed them to be classified as reasoning at the highest levels of Kohlberg's hierarchy. Gilligan has argued that this should not be interpreted as a lower level of reasoning than is possible, rather that the form of reasoning often displayed by women is *different* from that held by men. It is argued that women's early socialisation processes (particularly observing their mothers) encourage them to seek out compromises, not to allocate blame exclusively to one side or another, nor to distribute prizes or plaudits exclusively to only one member of a group. Rather the resolution of competitions, games or arguments is achieved with a sense of 'everyone gets something'. This approach is adopted with one eye on the medium to long term, that is, if a family is to develop cohesively there must be give and take from all sides at one time or another. From Gilligan's perspective the wisdom of Solomon involves more than the simple application of all-or-nothing justice to resolve a family dispute. Gilligan's argument contains a strong sense of the wisdom of the female perspective that she referred to as 'care'.

The need for wisdom to temper justice is possibly best exemplified in recent times by the approach adopted by President Mandela's government in South Africa when, on coming to power, it established the Commission for Truth and Reconciliation. The Commission was charged with investigating the myriad of stories and accusations of atrocities, murder and brutality inflicted upon the black and coloured communities by individuals, the police and the army during the apartheid years. Under the chairmanship of Archbishop Desmond Tutu, the Commission for Truth and Reconciliation continues to investigate a wide range of cases, with the accused giving evidence in the knowledge that they will not be prosecuted for their crimes. It is hoped that the truth relating to each case will thereby emerge (a critical issue for the bereaved), and gradually the nation's shame will be exorcised. In the process a potential bloodbath of retribution will have been avoided. Whether the Commission's work has satisfied everyone is a moot point, but it represents an understanding that justice, if exercised exclusively in the form of retribution ('an eye for an eye'), would be unlikely to serve the longer-term interests of the people of South Africa.

Gilligan argued that the concept of 'care' should be regarded as highly as justice when interpreting responses of research subjects to moral reasoning scenarios. This is not care (which is too often interpreted as compromise) born out of an 'anything-for-a-quiet-life' approach. Rather, care is reflected by an approach that seeks to find a way forward that not only provides some form of equitable resolution to a conflict (although not necessarily reflecting 'full' justice in an Aristotelian or Kohlbergian form), but also holds out the possibilities for maintaining a working relationship between the protagonists, so that future co-operation might be possible. This is not to deny that there are times when guilt or success should be identified with individuals, to the exclusion of all others. Gilligan's argument is that such an approach is undoubtedly appropriate on occasions, but not as a universal maxim.

If we think about this issue from an Aristotelian perspective, we can employ the notion of a mean as in Figure 3.2. You may wish to consider this perspective when you tackle Activity 3.1.

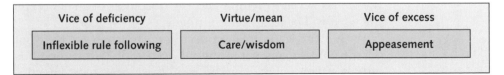

Vice of deficiency	Virtue/mean	Vice of excess
Inflexible rule following	Care/wisdom	Appeasement

Figure 3.2 Care and wisdom as a virtue

Changing perceptions of virtue

The notion of virtue is heavily dependent upon the period in which the concept is being considered. As MacIntyre (1967: 174) observed, it [virtue] always requires for its application the acceptance of some prior account of certain features of social and moral life, in terms of which it has to be defined and explained.

As centuries have passed, so shifts can be detected in what becomes regarded as virtuous behaviour.

■ In the time of Homer (who lived some 400 years before Aristotle and during a period of constant hostilities), the warrior was the model of human excellence and achievement.

■ During the Greece of Aristotle's time, with its relatively stable Athenian city-state, the virtues embodied in the privileged, Athenian gentleman were paramount.

■ From a western perspective, the rise of Christianity, as reflected in the New Testament, brought with it a fundamental shift in the perception of virtuous behaviour. Contra Aristotle, the New Testament presents an image of goodness that is unattainable by the wealthy and the privileged. Only the poorest are deemed worthy, with slaves (the lowest class within Aristotle's Athenian society), more likely to be seen as virtuous than the rich.

■ The coming of the Industrial Revolution, in the eighteenth century, found new personal qualities becoming valued. Benjamin Franklin, for example, espoused the virtues of cleanliness, silence and industry, as well as punctuality, industry, frugality, plus many others, but always with utilitarian motives (McMylor, 1994).

■ Solomon (1993: 207–16) identified honesty, fairness, trust and toughness (having a vision and persevering in its implementation) as the important virtues for managers in modern corporations.

The Aristotelian and Christian perspectives recognise different virtues but both link means and ends. Unethical means cannot be justified by good outcomes. A good deed is not a good deed if it is done with bad motives, e.g. to avoid pain, or to ingratiate oneself with the recipient. In Aristotelian terms, a virtuous life is one that allows individuals to achieve their *telos*, or end, to its full potential. Practice of the virtues makes this potential realisable. The emphasis is thus upon both means (virtues) and ends (*telos*). From this perspective the relationship between means and ends is an internal one, not external. Both are within the control of the individual.

For Franklin however, virtue was dependent upon some specified notion of utility. Achievement of socially acceptable ends (which have increasingly become articulated in material terms), can justify less than virtuous means. Understanding the values, social structures and key discourses of an era is crucial to understanding what will be regarded as virtues.

Within the Franklinian conception of virtues we have some of the seeds of what troubles many people about juxtaposing ethics and business. Some of the virtues articulated by Franklin can be achieved most effectively by the suppression of individual rights, e.g. silence and industry, whilst others, e.g. punctuality and cleanliness, are regarded as virtues, not primarily because they benefit the individual concerned, but because they contribute to the economy and efficiency of business. Thus, whilst the ends (punctuality and cleanliness) can be regarded as beneficial in themselves, they would not be regarded as virtues from an Aristotelian perspective, because they are driven by a concern with ends and not means.

One of the problems with this instrumentality is that it turns people into means rather than ends. This was of considerable concern to another major figure in the development of the philosophy of ethics – Immanuel Kant.

◼ Deontological ethics

Kantian ethics

Kant's ethical philosophy was that actions must be guided by universalisable principles that apply irrespective of the consequences of the actions. In addition an action can only be morally right if it is carried out as a duty, not in expectation of a reward. From a Kantian perspective, principles exist a priori. By this is meant that, knowing what to do in a situation will be determined by a set of principles that have been established by deductive reasoning, independent of, or before, the specifics of the decision in hand have been considered. Indeed, for Kantian ethics the context and consequences of a decision are irrelevant. Lying, for example, is invariably employed to illustrate the inflexibility of Kantian ethics. Lying, irrespective of the context, is wrong. So, for Kant, truth telling, even if the telling of a lie would save a human life, has to be a strictly adhered to – no deviations, no exceptions.

For Kant actions have moral worth only when they spring from recognition of duty, and a choice to discharge it. The 'duties' to which Kant refers were a response to the question, 'What makes a moral act right?' They were formulated around the concept of the 'categorical imperative'.

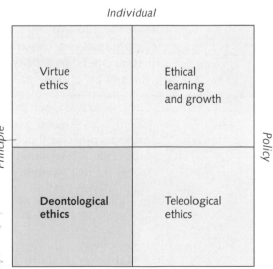

Definition

Categorical imperative

Categorical means unconditional (no exceptions), whilst **imperative** means a command, or in Kantian terms, a principle. Thus a categorical imperative refers to a command/principle that must be obeyed, with no exceptions. If the categorical imperative is conceptually sound we should be able to will all rational people around the world to follow this particular law. This is the concept of universalisability.

The Ten Commandments of The New Testament are written in the form of categorical imperatives, i.e. 'Thou shalt not . . .', although the extent to which they are universalisable is problematic. (The commandment 'thou shalt not kill' is debated below.)

For Kant an act is morally right if it can be judged by all reasoning people to be appropriate as a universal principle of conduct, irrespective of whether they are to be the doers, receivers or mere observers of an act. The issue of putting oneself in a state of ignorance as to one's own position within a situation is an interesting one, and one to which we will return when we discuss the ideas of John Rawls.

The 'Golden Rule', which is normally expressed as 'do unto others as you would have done unto yourself', is an example of a categorical imperative. It is a rule that can be willed as universalisable. Indeed, Shaw and Barry (1998) cited the scriptures of six world religions, that go back over millennia, identifying quotations from each that are examples of the 'Golden Rule'.

Bowie (1999), in his proposal for business organisations built upon Kantian principles, provided three formulations of the categorical imperative.

1 The first is that universalisability provides a theory of moral permissibility for market interactions. Interactions that violate the universalisability formulation of the categorical imperative are morally impermissible. This might appear reasonable, but it must be remembered that under this rule, someone who is prepared to allow others to exploit, harm and cheat him could, within the universalisability principle, proceed to exploit, harm and cheat others. Bowie tackled this issue when he cited Carr (1968), who argued for a different set of rules and morality for business. Carr observed:

> The golden rule for all its value as an ideal for society is simply not feasible as a guide for business. A good part of the time the businessman is trying to do to others as he hopes others will not do unto him . . . The game [poker] calls for distrust of the other fellow. It ignores the claim for friendship. Cunning, deception and concealment of one's strength and intentions, not kindness and open-heartedness, are vital in poker. And no-one should think any worse of the game of business because its standards of right and wrong differ from the prevailing traditions of morality in our society.
>
> (Carr, 1968: 145–6)

A further example of this attitude is provided by Pava (1999) who, drawing upon the work of Badaracco (1997), referred to the case of the pharmaceutical company, Roussel-Uclaf, and its chairman, Edouard Sakiz. The case concerned the abortion drug, RU 486. Sakiz wished to market the drug, but a range of powerful interest groups opposed the drug's sale, including Roussel-Uclaf's majority shareholder, the multinational Hoechst organisation. One of Hoechst's drugs (Zyklon B) had been used by the Nazis in their pogrom against the Jews in the Second World War. Since then the company had committed itself to 'placing our energy, our ideas and our dedication to the service of Life' (Pava, 1999: 82). Sakiz is claimed to have employed a devious and high-risk strategy, in which he forced a vote of the executive committee on the drug's launch, voting against the decision himself. However, in so doing he compromised the French government, which was keen to see the drug launched. The French government threatened to move production of the drug to another company, which forced Roussel-Uclaf to reconsider its decision. This it did, but now 'under the seeming protection of the government' (Pava, 1999: 83). Pava observed:

> Sakiz obtained his ultimate goal and avoided the pitfall of publicly proclaiming his real intentions. Badaracco justifies such seeming hypocrisy by stating that public leaders must follow a 'special ethical code', one that differs from their private morality and from Judeo-Christian ethics. Badaracco elaborates that 'only a naive manager would think otherwise'.
>
> (Pava, 1999: 83)

A Kantian refutation of this argument would avoid a consequentialist assessment, that businesses could not work effectively if lying and deviousness was the universal norm, on the basis that Kant refused to allow considerations of consequences to enter into issues of ethics. Instead a Kantian refutation would take the form of a rebuttal of the logic of the attempted categorical imperative, 'always lie, always be devious'. If everyone always lied or was devious, there would be no point in listening to what anyone had to say. Conversation, language even, would be meaningless and would therefore become redundant. Thus, 'always lie, always be devious' cannot be universalised. Because categorical imperatives are derived deductively, they can be successfully challenged, if flawed.

2 Bowie's second formulation of the categorical imperative is, 'respect for humanity in persons'. This is normally taken to mean treating fellow human beings as ends not means. However, Bowie's formulation is looser than this, and might fail to achieve this objective. Bowie's argument is that this formulation provides the basis for a moral obligation in the employment of people. Employees would cease to be commodities. Everyone involved in market transactions – employees, suppliers, customers and indeed all stakeholders – should be treated with respect. However, this presupposes that it is not possible to treat a commodity with respect. If it is possible to do so, then this formulation fails to achieve its stated aim – to treat people as ends not means. The ultimate test of this formulation would be the reaction of the Kantian organisation to a dramatic fall in demand for its goods or services. If the economics of the situation demanded cost-cutting measures for the firm to survive, with redundancies high on the agenda, the people-as-ends-not-means philosophy is severely tested. It is possible to show respect to those who are being made redundant, for example by providing as generous a financial severance package as is feasible, providing counselling sessions and assistance in interviewing techniques, but, in the end, the redundant employees are redundant because they are judged to be a resource that can no longer be justified (economically) by the firm. They are ultimately a means, not an end.

This particular circle can only be squared if it is acknowledged at the outset that a market-based economy is the backdrop against which the Kantian firm is located. Thus, it is within the actions permitted by market dynamics and economic logic that the Kantian perspective is being argued. In which case, short-term pressures from financial markets to protect the company's share price are likely to take precedence over desires to accept lower profit figures in order to protect employment levels. Any significant deviation from this set of relationships would require a different set of institutional arrangements between a business and its significant investors to that which currently exists. These issues are taken up further when we discuss the stakeholder perspective later in the chapter.

3 The third formulation is an attempt to further minimise or remove the 'people-as-means' accusation. It is an argument for greater democracy in the workplace – the moral community formulation. For example, by involving all employees (or at least their representatives) in corporate decision making, as with the 'Type A' pluralist model discussed in Chapter 1, the Kantian firm will seek out the most equitable solution when faced with a severe downturn in its markets, arriving at a 'way forward' that reflects the views of the employees. Whether this will be the majority view, or some other formulation would presumably be left to the firm to decide.

The criticisms levelled at Kantian ethics, over the rigidity of the categorical imperative, are challenged by both Beck (1959) and Bowie (1999). Kant is partly to blame for the criticism, argued Beck, because of the examples he used to illustrate his principles (Kant actually argued for truth telling in a situation in which a lie would save an innocent life). One possible way out of this cul-de-sac is to create a hierarchy of categorical imperatives. In this way the categorical imperative of 'always tell the truth' would be inferior to the categorical imperative of 'lie if it will save an innocent life'. Whether this form of hierarchical formulation is permissible, within a strictly Kantian categorical imperative perspective, is debatable. The notion of categorical imperatives being ranked contains a logical inconsistency. If categorical imperative 'A' can be overridden on occasions by categorical imperative 'B', then it cannot be a categorical imperative because it is not universalisable. We will return to this issue when we discuss prima facie obligations, but for the moment we will concentrate upon those writers and arguments that have sought to stay true to an undiluted version of the categorical imperative, but have offered ways of overcoming its rigidity.

De George (1999) offers one such resolution. The scenario depicted by De George addresses the truth-telling categorical imperative. It involves the shielding of an escaped slave who is being pursued by his slaveholder. For De George an untruth that might be told to the slaveholder to throw him off the scent would *not* be construed as a lie, on the basis that slavery is immoral, irrespective of what the law of the land might say. The slaveholder is not judged to have a legitimate interest in the information being sought. Under this interpretation the telling of an untruth is not lying if the person seeking information has no legitimate (ethically acceptable) interest in the information.

This approach is arguing that the telling of an untruth to someone who does not possess a morally legitimate interest in the information being sought is not merely acceptable, but accordingly not actually a lie. The enquirer's lack of moral legitimacy does not warrant the same level of truthfulness from the respondent, as would be required if the enquirer had possessed a legitimate interest.

Kant's use of truth telling has created many problems for the principle of categorical imperatives. The above, rather tortuous, attempts to try to overcome them are not altogether convincing. Purposely misconstruing known facts is a lie, to whomever the lie is to be told, and whatever the justification for the lie. By adopting a pure Kantian perspective, the concealer of the slave is left with no option but to reveal the whereabouts of the slave. However, if the protection of an innocent person is judged more important than telling an untruth, at a *universalisable* level, then there is something wrong with making truth telling a categorical imperative.

The critical question with regard to the truth-telling example used by Kant thus becomes: is the flaw within the principle of a categorical imperative, or is the problem the use of truth telling as an example of a categorical imperative? Whilst Kant did indeed cite truth telling as an example of a categorical imperative, this is not to say that the example is an appropriate or helpful one. If the way out of this difficult situation is simply to reject truth telling as an example of a categorical imperative, then further questions arise, namely:

(a) Is it possible to identify a categorical imperative? and/or
(b) Is it not possible to think of at least one exception to every categorical imperative that might be suggested, thereby nullifying its claim to being universalisable?

You might, for example, suggest 'one should not kill another human being' as a categorical imperative. But would a mother be morally wrong to respond to the pleas of her child who was being attacked by someone intent on taking the child's life? The killing of the assailant might be unpremeditated, unintentional even, but in an unequal struggle between mother and crazed assailant, how does the mother defend her child and herself? This is not to say that the killing of the assailant is the only outcome possible from such a scenario, but what is the status of a categorical imperative of 'no-taking-of life', if the mother does ultimately stab or shoot the assailant? This is an extreme example, but a categorical imperative is intended to be universalisable and must therefore be able to withstand such tests.

Writers such as Ross (1930) have felt the need to develop a more flexible form of principled reasoning, but remaining emphatically within a non-consequentialist perspective. Ross employed an approach known as prima facie obligations.

Definition

A literal translation of the Latin term **prima facie** is 'at first sight' or colloquially 'as it seems'. 'Prima facie evidence' is a legal term that refers to evidence that is deemed sufficient to establish a presumption of truth about an incident, unless or until counter-evidence is discovered. Thus, we can define a prima facie obligation as one that should be respected in one's practice, unless and until a different prima facie obligation, with a superior claim for adherence, is presented.

Thus, whilst supporters of prima facie obligations would see truth telling as a prima facie obligation, in a situation where truth telling would lead to the probable death of an innocent human being (e.g. by revealing the whereabouts of an inno-cent fugitive), the prima facie obligation of 'lying to protect a wrongly or unjustly accused person' would override the obligation to tell the truth.

ACTIVITY 3.2

Employing a Kantian perspective, briefly analyse Case study 2.17 (*The retention of dead babies' organs in hospitals*).

1 Can you develop a categorical imperative that would be appropriate for this case?

2 Would prima facie obligations be more helpful? If so, what would they be?

Notwithstanding the above problems, Kant and others who argued for principle-based ethics did so out of a belief that there are certain principles upon which societies need to be based if they are to develop in positive ways. With the emphasis on the atomised individual in modern society, non-consequentionalists feel that principle-based ethics are particularly relevant in the present day. At the root of consequentionalist concerns are the issues of justice and human rights. It is to these issues that we now turn.

Justice and rights

The notion of justice has featured throughout our discussion of non-consequen-tialist ethics, and Aristotle spent much time discussing different aspects of justice. Whilst Aristotle's understanding was a particular one, with the 'great-soul-man' able to benefit from all the splendours that his station in life might afford, the issue of human rights has progressed since the time of Aristotle. The United Nations' Declaration of Human Rights made human rights universal, not limited to the male of the species, let alone a small subset of the male population. Whilst inequality of opportunity could be justified by Aristotle (and was the accepted norm throughout ancient Greece), others have worried more intensely at the issue of inequalities in society. Barry (1989: 3) observed, 'In Plato's time, as in ours, the central issue in any theory of justice is the defensibility of unequal rela-tions between people'.

In the political ferment that existed during much of the eighteenth cen-tury, some significant works were published that had an influential bearing on political matters in France and America. Thomas Paine (1737–1809) and Jean-Jacques Rousseau (1712–78) were two writers whose publications are said to have provided a philosophical justification to those who sought to wrest con-trol from the then ruling authorities in France and America. In England, Mary Wollstonecraft (1759–97), inspired by Rousseau and the revolution in France, wrote what Held (1987: 79) described as 'one of the most remarkable tracts of social and political theory, the *Vindication of the Rights of Women*. Along with Paine and Rousseau, Wollstonecraft argued that liberty and equality were intertwined. She argued that the then debates on 'rights of man' needed to embrace the rights of women, but this was a distinctly minority view. Rousseau was himself dismissive of women's rights. Pateman cites Rousseau's comments in *Emile*:

Woman is made to please and to be in subjection to man, . . . they must be trained to bear [a] yoke from the first . . . and to submit themselves to the will of others.
(Pateman, 1985: 157)

Wollstonecraft's work was published in 1792, but it was not until 1948 that the principle of one person one vote was finally established in the UK, and Swiss women were not fully enfranchised until 1971 (Pateman, 1985: 5). While major developments in human rights legislation have taken place in relatively recent times, justice remains a problematic concept and practice. The debates concerning human rights are ongoing ones, and many of them concern or involve business organisations.

This brief sojourn in a particular field of political philosophy is offered to provide at least a feel for the troubled and protracted history of the notion of rights in human practice and relations. Notions of liberty and equality are central elements of social justice and the philosopher upon whom we will focus (although not exclusively) to explore contemporary thinking is John Rawls. However, we begin with Robert Nozick (1974), a leading advocate of the libertarian position on justice and rights.

The libertarian perspective adopts the notion of negative freedoms. That is, it holds as its primary tenet the individual's right of 'freedoms from'. The most significant of these is freedom from government interference in all but the most critical of property rights protection systems, e.g. police forces for private property and military forces regarding property of the realm. From a libertarian perspective, there is little outside the maintenance of property rights that represents legitimate government activity. Differences in personal wealth, talent, physical attributes and intelligence are seen as being obtained in the 'natural' sense, in that their ownership owes nothing to social or political institutions. If they are obtained in this way, nothing can deny the owner possession of them, or the value that derives from that ownership. Differences caused to the life-chances of individuals by the possession, or not, of these qualities/characteristics are not seen as justifying the meddling of governments in attempts to redistribute some of the associated benefits.

Within the libertarian frame of reference, and as long as what an individual wishes to do is within the law, then nothing should prevent the individual from fulfilling those desires. It is for this reason that taxation (and particularly the taxes levied on inherited assets) is such a vexed subject. From a libertarian perspective, taxation is the forcible, involuntary withdrawal of economic resources from individuals to be spent by governments in ways that might fail to satisfy or be compatible with the desires and values of the taxed individuals.

Nozick coined the term 'entitlement theory' to express the view that what has been acquired legally and fairly (although fairly is an ill-defined concept), cannot be taken away within a libertarian concept of justice. This is despite the fact that practices that are regarded as immoral and illegal today, e.g. slavery, have not always been so, yet they represent an important factor in explaining the present distribution of wealth that shapes so many people's life-chances. Interestingly, in his later works, Nozick recognised the problems associated with resources obtained or lost by dubious methods and modified his views a little with respect to inherited wealth, an example being the plight of the American Indians. However, inherited resources and life-chances remain central issues within this debate.

Entitlement theory attempts to draw a veil over the means by which wealth may have been acquired. The ramifications of being denied an equal opportunity to education, health care, legal justice are seen as irrelevant within a libertarian conception of justice, or at least a greater injustice would be to transfer 'legally' acquired assets from those that have to those that have not. With no limits attached to what individuals can achieve in a liberal society, it is for every individual to improve their own life-chances.

Rawls, justice as fairness

Rawls takes a different view of distributive justice to Nozick. In 1971 Rawls published a book (revised in 1999) that has had a significant impact upon debates about theories of justice. Whilst Rawls does not argue that his theory is a practical one for everyday decision making, it presents a normative approach to deciding what a just society would look like in what he describes as 'the original position'. It offers a reference point against which contemporary social, political and economic systems can be contrasted. We then have to decide, as individuals and as societies, what we want to try and do about the differences between these two states – the should-be and the actual.

The original position is an artifice of Rawls that allows each of us to contemplate a 'just' society without the burden of our life experiences and prejudices tainting our views. We are required to envisage a situation in which we have no knowledge of who we are. The distinctive personal characteristics that we will ultimately possess (assuming we will actually have some bestowed upon us) are unknown within the original position. We have no knowledge of any natural or social advantages, or disadvantages, we might ultimately possess. We do not even know where in the world we would live, and therefore under which type of political system we might be governed. We do not know our ethnic origins; whether we will have a privileged or deprived upbringing; whether we would be intelligent or slow-witted; male or female; be sexually abused or lead an idyllic childhood; be short or tall; born with profound physical disabilities or be an Olympic-grade athlete; or experience a very poor or excellent educational system. We are placed behind what Rawls refers to as a 'veil of ignorance'.

From this position of total ignorance we are then asked a series of questions about the type of society we would like to live in. We are expected to employ actual knowledge of the chances of being placed within a privileged or elite position when answering a series of questions relating to issues such as social, political and economic governance; health care; education; social norms; wealth distribution and hereditary wealth; race, gender and religious equality; and employment opportunities. It must be emphasised again that the world we construct from the original position is a world in which we do not know where we will ultimately fit.

Faced with this challenge, Rawls argued that the rational person would adopt a maximin strategy. This is a risk-averse strategy that works on the basis of studying all the worst-case scenarios that exist within each option before us. Having identified all the worst-case possibilities, we then select the one that is the least worse. Thus, we opt for the option that gives us the greatest possible benefit, assuming we were unfortunate enough to be dealt a position at the bottom of the economic and social ladders in any of the choices with which we are confronted. Case study 3.1 illustrates the approach.

CASE STUDY 3.1

The veil of ignorance

You are in the 'original position' and the choice of political systems in which you will live are feudal, dictatorship, democracy and anarchy. You can imagine a range of outcomes for yourself in each system. In a feudal state, a dictatorship or a centrally controlled state, history has shown that the lives of those in power can be privileged ones, and that such an outcome is a possibility for you. However, maybe only a few can be expected to enjoy such lives. For the rest of the population, life is likely to be miserable. In a democracy the distribution of power will be far greater, going beyond political democracy and taking in workplace democracy. The opportunities to exercise moral agency should be higher than in the other options, although the opportunities to enjoy the sumptuous lifestyle of the elite of the feudal or dictatorship systems would be slight. Anarchy might possess certain attractions, but the uncertainty surrounding the notion of anarchy is likely to prove unappealing to you. Remember, Rawls anticipates that you are a calculating, risk-averse individual. Thus, considering the options before you, Rawls assumes you will judge that if you were to be one of the general members of the public (and there is a 90–99 per cent chance that this will be the case), it would be better for you to live in a full democracy.

A way of rationalising Rawls's original position is to see it as a mechanism to free each of us from our personal prejudices and life experiences. By removing us from the shackles of the inequities of how things are, it can enable us to focus upon what we believe distributive justice would/should look like, without the distortions born of history or fate.

Flowing from the assumption that the individual in the original position will desire not to be dealt a station in life that is unpalatable, Rawls argued that there are two guiding principles that will explain the reason for each choice made. These are:

1 Each member of society would be entitled to the same civil and political rights, and
2 Open competition for occupational positions exists, with attainment being based upon merit, but with economic inequalities being arranged so that 'there is no way in which the least advantaged stratum in the society could as a whole do any better' (Barry, 1989: 184).

The second principle is referred to as Rawls's difference principle. This is because Rawls was not arguing that everyone could be or should be the same. He recognised that differences relating to qualities such as intelligence, acumen, technical skills, physical abilities and so on will exist. However, he viewed the arbitrary and random distribution of social and natural attributes as no justification for the individuals blessed with these attributes prospering to the detriment of others less fortunate. Rawls thus rejected Nozick's entitlement theory. As Shaw and Barry observed,

> Rawls' principles permit economic inequalities only if they do in fact benefit the least advantaged.
>
> (Shaw and Barry, 1998: 114)

In dealing with differences in personal attributes and qualities, Rawls argued that contingencies must be set in place to handle the issues raised by such differences. These contingencies would be mechanisms, established at the original position, built upon co-operation and mutual respect.

> We are led to the difference principle if we wish to set up the social system so that no-one gains or loses from his arbitrary place in the distribution of natural assets or his initial position in society without giving or receiving compensating advantages in return.
>
> (Rawls, 1971: 101–2)

Thus, before you would be asked questions about your preferred political system, education, corporate governance, etc. (and still in a state of ignorance about your personal position), you would have to identify the mechanisms that would need to be in place to minimise the worst effects of the differences that would exist between individual members of society, and between societies, when the final allocation of roles was made.

You may have detected a form of schizophrenia within Rawls's theory, in as much as the first principle has a strong socialist egalitarian moral perspective, whilst the second principle clearly assumes market-based, self-interest-driven behaviour. Rawls has been challenged on this 'inconsistency' from a variety of sources. Meade (1973) observed:

> In my view the ideal society would be one in which each citizen developed a real split personality, acting selfishly in the market place and altruistically at the ballot box . . . [It] is . . . only by such altruistic political action that there can be any alleviation of 'poverty' in a society in which the poor are in the minority.
>
> (Meade, 1973: 52)

Rawls also acknowledged that there have to be limits to what people can reasonably be expected to do on behalf of others less fortunate than themselves. He termed this limit the 'strains of commitment'. In doing so Rawls accepted that there would be boundaries to the demands that the least privileged could make of those more fortunate than themselves. However, Rawls's theory does demand far more of individual citizens than that advocated by free market theorists. The 'hidden hand' of Adam Smith delivers an impoverished form of justice from a Rawlsian perspective. Incentives are acknowledged, albeit in a reluctant way. As Barry observed:

> Inequalities are not ideally just, but . . . once we concede the need for incentives, inequalities permitted by the difference principle are the only defensible ones.
>
> (Barry, 1989: 398)

ACTIVITY 3.3

Briefly analyse Case study 2.3 (*AIDS drugs and patent rights in South Africa*) from a Rawlsian perspective.

We will conclude our discussion of non-consequentialist ethical theories by focusing upon the use of child labour in the present day. The use of poorly paid children, often tied, as labourers has a long and troubled history in all parts of the world. Where the children are 'tied' they are the property of adults (slaveholders), with their parents sometimes having received a payment from the slaveholder. Some of the worst examples involve the use of children in prostitution. The practice of child (sometimes slave) labour is still prevalent in certain parts of the world, and a number of western multinational corporations have been heavily criticised for sourcing their supplies (e.g. designer clothes and sportswear) from companies that operate sweatshops involving more than, but including, child labour. How would the respective ethical positions we have considered, i.e. virtue ethics, Kantian and Rawlsian perspectives, perceive this situation?

- A **virtue ethics** approach would reflect the behaviours regarded as virtuous at any given time. In this context, we must remember that child labour has not always been regarded as a social ill. In the UK child labour was a regular feature of Victorian life. For a virtue ethics perspective to be able to reject the use of child labour, there would need to be a high-status virtue that expressly spoke of equality, the preciousness of children and the need to protect them from exploitation and abuse. With virtue ethics being about the personal qualities of individuals, where the perception of one's peers (thereby emphasising the importance of social norms) is of critical importance in judging the 'virtuous person', virtue ethics does not offer an automatic disqualification of child labour as unethical and immoral. A virtue would need to exist that explicitly addressed the relationship between adults and children, and particularly the rights of children.
- A **Kantian** perspective would not be equivocal. Respect for fellow human beings, and the need to treat other people as one would want to be treated oneself, would make exploitation in general, not just against children, immoral. The vulnerability of children would merely emphasise the importance of these categorical imperatives.
- **Rawlsian** notions of justice in the context of child labour will depend upon the parameters established in the original position. Assuming that no adult would volunteer themselves to be subject to exploitation, deprivation and possibly prostitution in childhood, then such acts would be unjust and immoral.

The above analysis has shown a range of non-consequentialist positions with regard to ethical theories. The degree of variation is significant within the non-consequentialist group, but they in turn offer an orientation towards ethical reasoning that is quite distinct from that of consequentialist theories. It is to the consequentialist theories that we now turn.

■ Ethical learning and growth

The ethical theories in the top right quadrant hold that policy ends should be the yardsticks against which the morality of actions should be judged, and that they can only be achieved indirectly. An ethical organisation cannot be achieved by decree. A CEO publishing an ethical code will not of itself bring about its implementation. The end has to be approached obliquely by encouraging processes of learning that enable people to decide for themselves to act ethically.

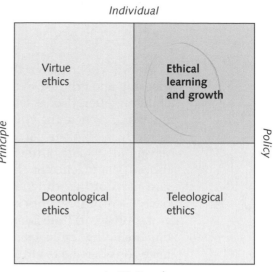

Individual growth and organisational learning

There is a large literature, and indeed an industry, that explains how people can develop and make themselves more effective. Stephen Covey's (1992) *The Seven Habits of Highly Effective People* can stand as an example. He raised two themes that place him firmly in the upper right quadrant of Figure 3.5. He taught that people should 'begin with an end in mind' (Covey, 1992: 97). This is clearly a policy orientation. He also argued that people develop their character ethic through a process of deep self-reflection. He distinguished character ethic from personality ethic (Covey, 1992: 18–21). The character ethic proposes basic principles of effective living, things like integrity, fidelity, humility, courage and so on. These are hard precepts to live by. In contrast the personality ethic proposes 'quick-fix solutions' drawn from a public relations approach that aims to present a good image of oneself and easy behavioural tricks used to manipulate others. It is the character ethic that people should concentrate on.

Covey (1992: 36) adopted the 'principle of process' of personal growth in the spheres of emotion, human relationships and character formation. These processes cannot, he argued, be short-circuited; people have to go through the necessary stages to achieve greater effectiveness. He applied these lessons not only to people's personal lives but also to working lives. His book has become a very popular guide for managers. Senge, in his book *The Fifth Discipline* (1990), also stressed the importance of individuals' learning, which he saw as necessary for the development of learning organisations. These, he argued, were the only kind of organisation that will be successful. For Senge learning is not simply an acquisition of useful information; it is a personal moral development. He used the classical Greek term *metanoia* (Senge 1990: 13–14) to describe the sort of learning that learning organisations should aspire to. It means a shift of mind. The word was used by the Gnostics who, in the early years of Christianity, saw gnosis, or knowledge, as an awareness of a person's relationship with God. Gnosis involves relating to the divine power of creativity by truly learning to know oneself (Pagels, 1982: 133–4). Senge's view of organisational development parallels this view of learning as ethical and spiritual growth.

> Real learning gets to the heart of what it means to be human. Through learning we recreate ourselves. Through learning we reperceive the world and our relationship to it. Through learning we extend our capacity to create, to be part of the generative process of life.
>
> (Senge, 1990: 14)

Individual growth and learning is not simply learning how to use a new leadership or financial appraisal technique. It is a process of becoming aware of one's ethical potential. Learning becomes an ethical end in itself.

ACTIVITY 3.4

Briefly analyse Case study 2.22 (*The Firestone Tire recall issue*) from a learning organisation perspective.

Communitarianism

The communitarian approach to ethics is a reaction to the liberal view that sees the individual as more important than social groups. The communitarian approach argues that people are inherently social and that they can only achieve their moral potential by being part of growing and developing communities. By contributing to the ethical growth of a group people also become ethical individuals. These communities may be based on place, such as a neighbourhood, on shared group memories, such as in immigrant communities, or on a host of voluntary associations such as golf clubs, parent teacher associations, churches and so on. A tenet of the communitarian perspective is that different communities might be expected to develop their own values and moral principles. The universalism of liberalism's claim, that democratic, free market systems are the correct solution for all societies, as argued by Fukuyama (1993) in his book *The End of History*, is false. This acceptance of particularism or relativism will become important when we discuss international business in Chapter 8. Amitai Etzioni (1993) is the most high-profile advocate of a communitarian approach.

It follows from a communitarian point of view that anything that limits the potential for communities to grow and be responsible for themselves is reprehensible. Such threats may come either from the political left, with its concern for creating centralised, bureaucratic welfare structures for dealing with social problems, or from the right, whose protagonists do not see why granting rights such as flexible working hours, parental leave and child care facilities to support families should be tolerated in a free market system.

Communitarian ethics raises a number of questions for businesses and organisations.

■ Should business try to create a homogenous world in which everyone consumes the same products and shares the same values? This would maximise industry's efficiency. Or should business respond to the particularities of different societies and groups by diversifying their products and business models?

■ To what extent should businesses and organisations contribute to the growth and development of local communities? Should they provide resources and managerial expertise to encourage the development of self-help groups in the communities in which they work? Should such support be philanthropic or be part of commercial sponsorship deals? The development of 'family friendly' employment practices (Elshtain *et al.*, n.d.) is important from a communitarian perspective. These matters of corporate citizenship are considered in Chapter 9.

■ Should organisations attempt to create themselves as communities? The Foster architectural partnership has long sought to design office buildings that encourage the development of community bonds, as well as employment relationships, between the staff. Their buildings include 'streets', cafés, restaurants, swimming pools and games areas so that in one building the staff described working in the building as 'homing from work' (Foster, 2001: 206). The commercial pressures on organisations mean that such facilities are often converted to a more directly productive use.

ACTIVITY 3.5

Briefly analyse Case study 2.1 (*The Nationwide Foundation*) from a communitarian perspective.

Ethical egoism

J.S. Mill praised those who would sacrifice their personal happiness to gain a greater happiness for others. Ethical egoists would not understand such an act. They argue that an individual should pursue their own interests by applying their reason to the task of identifying and achieving their own best interests.

Ethical egoism gained popularity in America during the twentieth century through the novels of Ayn Rand (1905–82), who has already been discussed in Chapter 1. Her ethical stance is known as objectivism. It gives primacy to people's capacity for rational thought. This facility, when applied to a knowledge of the world gained through the senses, leads to an objective understanding of the world that leaves no room for the sceptical belief that all knowledge is mere opinion. The theory's ethical position is that each individual should seek their own happiness through a productive independent life in which their own rational judgement is their only guide. The main virtues of objectivist thought are independence, integrity, honesty, productiveness, trade and pride. It encourages a robust belief in self-help and accepts that people who cannot or will not take responsibility for themselves would have to bear the consequences. They should not expect the state or society to bail them out. An individual should not sacrifice themselves to others or expect others to sacrifice themselves for him.

We will illustrate the main themes of objectivism through Kirkpatrick's (1994) defence of advertising. He used objectivism to counter the social criticisms made of advertising, which are that advertising can be manipulative and offensive. His broad argument is that laissez-faire capitalism is good because, according to

Rand, the principle of trade is the 'only system consonant with man's rational nature' (Kirkpatrick, 1994: 28). If capitalism is good then advertising, which is a necessary part of it, must also be good. Kirkpatrick blames Kant for the common mistake of seeing advertising as unethical. He attributed to Kant the ideal that human reason cannot objectively comprehend reality because reason is always affected by the innate structures of a person's mind. If this were so then human reason would not be adequate to cope with the blandishments of advertising. But he argued that Kant is wrong and Rand is right. Objective knowledge is possible and human reason is capable of properly evaluating the advertisers' messages. As to the charge of offensiveness, he argued that values are not intrinsic to objects. So a cigarette for example is not in itself a bad thing; only the way people use it can make it good or bad. If cigarettes are not intrinsically immoral and individuals have free will then 'tobacco advertisers defraud no one' (Kirkpatrick, 1994: 80). The only necessary constraint on advertising is the common law one against fraud. 'Anything less than that turns both marketers and consumers into victims of subjective law, that is, of "rule by men" [*i.e. by bureaucrats*] rather than the "rule of law"' (Kirkpatrick, 1994: 51). The American-ness of the argument was emphasised when he quoted Daniel Boorstin arguing that advertising is the American epistemology – the way in which Americans learn about things. Kirkpatrick's argument for advertising only stands, of course, if objectivism is held to be objectively true.

The difficult question for ethical egoism is how far self-interest would cause individuals to give away some of their independence in order to accommodate others. Kirkpatrick argued that obeying the common law should be the limit of the surrender. Hobbes, who wrote in the seventeenth century, identified the key problem. People are very similar in wit and strength and therefore,

> If two men desire the same thing, which nevertheless they cannot both enjoy, they become enemies; and in the way to their end, which is principally their own con-servation, and sometimes their delectation only, endeavour to destroy, or subdue one another.
>
> (Hobbes, n.d.: 81)

Self-interest, therefore, would cause people to

> be willing, when others are so too, as far-forth, as for peace, and defence of him-self he shall think it necessary to lay down this right to all things; and be contented with so much liberty against other men, as he would allow other men against himself.
>
> (Hobbes, n.d.: 85)

Of course, in modern business terms, it is a matter of dispute as to the degree of liberty a person, or a company, would rationally agree to forgo.

ACTIVITY 3.6

Briefly analyse Case study 2.19 (*The hospital consultants*) from an ethical egoism perspective.

■ Teleological ethics

The theories in the final quadrant of Figure 3.1 combine an
intention to work towards an
end with a particular view of
what institutions are necessary
to achieve it. These institutions
govern the way in which the
appropriateness of an act to an
end should be evaluated. These
theories are called teleological.
This term means that the rightness or goodness of an action is
not intrinsic to that action but
can only be judged by its consequences. These theories are
sometimes therefore called consequentialist.

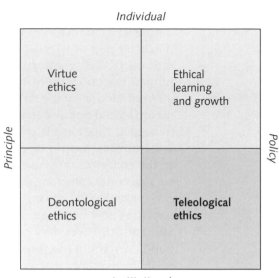

Discourse ethics

Discourse ethics is a normative approach that deals with the proper processes
of rational debate that are necessary to arrive at a resolution of ethical questions. It does not lay down what is right and wrong but it does distinguish right
and wrong ways of arguing about right and wrong. It is an ancient idea that the
process of argument, or rhetoric, is key to discovering the truth. Some, such as
Protagoras, argued that there are always two sides to any argument (Billig,
1996: 72). This implies that dialogue cannot lead to a definitive truth because
there are always arguments to be made for or against any proposition. However
Protagoras was prepared to argue, as reported by Socrates, that although opposing arguments could be presented some were more useful than others. Whether
or not argument and debate can lead to true or useful statements about what is
right and wrong, these classical concerns established an importance for forensic debate, and the classification of rhetorical techniques, that has remained in
western culture.

The approach in modern times is most closely associated with Jürgen
Habermas, of the Frankfurt school of critical theorists (Pusey, 1987). Habermas
built upon the philosophical heritage of Kant; and so perhaps should not be
included in the lower right quadrant of Figure 3.6. However he breaks with Kant
in his belief that knowledge develops through social interaction and discourse.
Knowledge is not, as Kant argued, a matter unaffected by social and cultural
processes. Habermas holds that disagreement can be resolved rationally through
debate which is free of compulsion, in which no disputant applies pressure to
another, and in which only the strength of the arguments matters. This calls for
linguistic skill but it also requires a critical self-reflection in which those involved
in a debate challenge their own arguments at:

- The objective level – at which a statement is tested against an observed state, checking for example whether the statement that 'the balance sheet does not add up' is true.
- The inter-subjective level – when a statement is made and heard it creates a social relationship between the hearer and the speaker. At the inter-subjective level it has to be questioned whether this relationship is legitimate. If the statement that the balance sheet doesn't add up implies, without evidence, that the listener is accused of cooking the books the relationship may be unfair; especially if the speaker is the listener's boss.
- The intra-subjective level – at which a speaker has to consider whether their speech sincerely or authentically mirrors their internal thoughts and values.

It is these processes of validation that Habermas refers to as discourse. The application of these in organisations would be very difficult. However writers have attempted to put these ideas into operation. Some have focused on the skills of debate. Schreier and Groeben (1996) looked at the advice, given in popular books on how to persuade and influence people, about which tricks of presentation were unfair. They asked a panel of experts to categorise 84 of the rhetorical tricks against four ethical categories that are used to assess whether an argument in a debate was proper. Using the results they were able to identify some possible rules or tests for assessing the ethical integrity of any debate. A few examples follow.

- **Formal validity** – are the arguments logically rigorous?
  e.g. do not select only those cases to use in your argument that support your point of view.

- **Sincerity/Truth** – are the arguments intentionally misleading, inconsistent or economical with the truth?
  e.g. misrepresenting an opponent's position or exaggerating a point.

- **Content justice** – treating your opponents unfairly or imposing impossible requirements on them.
  e.g. ad hominem *attacks on an opponent in which the opponent is vilified rather than his or her arguments criticised. Making mutually exclusive demands on an opponent.*

- **Procedural justice** – preventing an opponent from fully and freely participating in the debate.
  e.g. unnecessary use of technical jargon in a way intended to confuse the opponent.

Others have proposed rules and procedures for debate. This has been particularly common in the field of public policy making. Fischer (1983) made a case for forensic skills to be applied to the process of evaluating public policy options through ethical discourse. He drew upon a method he called normative logic. This was based on studies of how people discuss and decide normative issues in everyday speech and life. He concluded that despite the lack of final ethical truths, people resolved value matters by combining questioning based on empirical knowledge with a lawyer-like process of marshalling a supportable case, by drawing upon their knowledge of:

- the consequences of the different positions or actions they may take;
- the alternative positions and actions open to them;
- established norms, values and laws;
- the facts of the situation;
- the network of circumstances that preceded the situation;
- the 'fundamental needs of humankind'.

People can construct defensible cases for taking particular actions or positions. According to some philosophers this process is untenable because it requires decisions, about what ought to be, to be derived from descriptions of how things actually are, and this they claim is illogical. Fischer's response was to say that the purpose of drawing up guidelines for debate is not to establish ultimate values but to arrive at pragmatic resolutions through a rigorous, if ungrounded, process that is not anchored in immutable values.

So far the discussion has focused on fair and open debate of ethical matters. But the question of who should have a voice in the debate is also an important ethical matter. This question can best be considered by looking at the application of stakeholder theory to ethical matters. This theory proposes that, for every organisation, stakeholder groups can be identified:

- who are affected by,
- who can affect, or
- whose welfare is tied into

the actions of a corporation. It may be necessary to add a criterion of legitimacy to the identification of stakeholders. As Whysall (2000) pointed out, a shoplifter's welfare may be affected by a retailer's actions but that does not make them a legitimate stakeholder.

Donaldson and Preston (1995) presented four perspectives on the roles of stakeholder management.

- *Descriptive* – that the stakeholder theory describes what corporations are, i.e. constellations of interconnected interest groups.
- *Instrumental* – that if corporations adopt stakeholder management they will, all other things being equal, be more successful than those organisations that do not.
- *Managerial* – that the theory enables managers to identify options and solution to problems

But underpinning each of these roles was the fourth *normative* one; stakeholder theory can be used to develop moral or philosophical guidelines for the operations of corporations. In particular it forces corporations to make a broad ethical appreciation of its actions that considers its impact on communities as well as on the profit and loss account. Whysall used the case of companies that retail goods, at premium prices to affluent consumers, which were manufactured in sweatshop conditions in third world countries. A traditional management approach would only consider the benefits of the business model to the corporation and its customers. A stakeholder approach would also involve consideration of the impact upon the workforces, the communities and governments of the countries involved as well as activists and lobbyists.

ACTIVITY 3.7

Briefly analyse Case study 2.11 (*Railtrack, profits and public safety*) from a stakeholder perspective.

Utilitarianism

The utilitarianism theory accepts utility, or the greatest happiness principle, as the foundation of morals. It holds that actions are right in proportion, as they tend to promote happiness, wrong, as they tend to promote the opposite of happiness. Or as Jeremy Bentham, the eighteenth-century philosopher who proposed the principle, put it:

> The greatest happiness of the greatest number is the foundation of morals and legislation.
>
> (Bentham, 1994: 142)

The term utilitarianism, however, was coined by John Stuart Mill, a nineteenth-century writer, and not by Bentham. One interesting question that arises from utilitarianism is, 'What is happiness?' Most philosophers were at pains to suggest that it is not simply sensual pleasure. As J.S. Mill argued, 'It is better to be a human being dissatisfied than a pig satisfied' (Mill, 1998: 140). The importance of the higher pleasures over the lower has long been a theme in western ethics. St Augustine recognised that worldly pleasures were not of themselves bad but that they were insufficient to achieve an admirable life. He saw the sensual, material world as but part of human experience that has to be understood within the wider context of the intelligible world, which is one of clear and enduring ideas. Utilitarianism, according to Mill, who took a similar view, is not concerned only with material and sensual pleasures.

Utilitarianism is a calculating approach to ethics. It assumes the quantity and quality of happiness can be weighed. Bentham (1982) identified the following features of happiness that ought to be considered when measuring it:

- Intensity.
- Duration.
- Certainty – the probability that happiness or pain will result.
- Extent – the number of people affected.
- Closeness (propinquity) – pleasure or pain now or deferred in time.
- Richness (fecundity) – will the act lead to further pleasure?
- Purity – is the pleasure unalloyed or is it mixed with pain?

It is often assumed, in a business context, that maximising happiness is the same as maximising profit or return on capital invested. Plainly, improved profitability will generate happiness for some. But to apply the utilitarian principle properly one must consider the possibility that the pleasure derived from increased profitability has been achieved at the cost of a greater pain to other people. Mill (1998: 151) pointed out that most of the time someone applying the utilitarian principle need only concern themselves with their private interest. This is not necessarily so when the 'person' in question is a corporation.

Cost–benefit analysis is a natural tool of a utilitarian approach because it measures not only the direct costs and benefits to an organisation but also externalities. Externalities are defined in economics as social costs and benefits that are not reflected in the price of a product because they do not accrue directly to the organisation concerned. When people smoke the cigarettes produced by a tobacco company they are more likely to fall ill and so create costs for health care systems. But the costs of that health care are not reflected in the costs of the cigarettes because the medical bills are not the tobacco company's responsibility. In the USA however, the claim that tobacco companies misled their customers as to the harmful effects of smoking led the courts to require the companies to reimburse states with the cost of the medical treatment of smoking-related diseases. In this case externality was converted into a private cost of the companies.

Definition	**Cost–benefit analysis** is a form of project appraisal. The costs and outputs of the project are identified and priced. If the outputs will arise over an extended period of time, and inputs are needed over a similar time span, the benefits and costs are discounted. If the benefits are greater than the costs then investment in the project would be sensible. If the project were, for example, a malaria control programme in a poor country, it is clear that the benefits would be widespread. Many lives would be saved; the health of the population would be improved. But these benefits are intangible and difficult to measure in financial terms. It might be thought that the costs of such a project would be easier to identify. Some, such as the cost of the labour and the insecticide, would be. But there may be wider, and less easy to measure, costs such as increased costs of education because more children survive and are fit enough to attend school.

One danger of utilitarianism, which cost–benefit analysis is designed to address, is that organisations seek to maximise *a good* rather than *the good*. In the British National Health Service, for example, the government set a target for reducing the size of the waiting lists for treatment, maximising a good – the number of patients treated. However many hospitals achieved this by treating patients with minor problems that could be quickly and cheaply resolved and leaving those who needed lengthy and difficult treatment at the back of the queue, and so they failed to maximise the overall good.

In the case of public policy, public, and not simply private, utility has clearly to be taken into account. Kemm (1985) used a utilitarian approach in a discussion of the ethics of food policy. He was interested in the ethical issues involved in modifying the eating habits of the population through regulation, facilitating measures (such as differentially taxing foods) and education. He argued that a policy is ethical if it produces more beneficial outcomes than harmful ones. But his suggestions about how policy makers might analyse issues sheds light on the limitations of technical means such as cost–benefit analysis.

Kemm stressed the interconnections between subjective and objective thinking in assessing the outcomes of policies. The three stages in this process are:

1 Determining the inherent goodness or badness of an outcome. This is a subjective value decision such as that involved in stating that dental mottling is less bad than carcinoma of the colon.
2 Measuring the probability that the desired outcome will be achieved. This is a scientific and objective activity.
3 Assessing the degree of certainty with which the probability of the outcomes has been estimated. This is a matter of judgement rather than measurement.

The subjective element can be illustrated by an example from the first item in the above list. Utility's concern for populations makes these subjective judgements difficult. How, for example, should moderate good for the majority be weighed against great harm to the minority? Fortifying chapatti flour would provide some health benefit for most chapatti eaters; but for the rare individual with vitamin D sensitivity it might cause serious vitamin D toxicity. The ethical problem can be exacerbated by the fact that the majority may not be aware that they have received benefits from the fortified flour. To give another example, if food policies increase the amount of fibre in the diet this will benefit people by protecting them from diverticulitis. But they will not be aware of this. But those who suffer from flatulence as a result will be in no doubt that they have suffered, albeit the pain is not critical.

> Most would take the view that a very small harm to a very few individuals could be outweighed by a sufficiently large benefit to a sufficiently large number of individuals.
>
> (Kemm, 1985: 291)

One of the criticisms of utilitarianism is that it is unconcerned with equity. As Sen said:

> The trouble with [utilitarianism] is that the maximising the sum of individual utilities is supremely unconcerned with the interpersonal distribution of that sum.
>
> (Sen quoted in Barr, 1985: 177)

The problem of forecasting future consequences, as identified in the last two items of Kemm's list, is a general difficulty with utilitarianism. If people cannot make accurate predictions about the consequences of particular actions then it is hardly worth the bother of weighing the anticipated pleasures and pains. Common experience, as expressed in Murphy's Law (if it can go wrong it will), suggests that people's forecasting skills are not to be overestimated. There is psychological evidence that people are overconfident when they make predictions. Fischoff, Slovic and Lichtenstein (1977) asked people a series of general knowledge questions (e.g., is absinthe (a) a liqueur or (b) a precious stone?) and found that when people said they were 100 per cent certain they had given the right answer they had in fact only done so on 80 per cent of occasions.

The form of utilitarianism that has been discussed so far is known as act utilitarianism, which calculates the net pleasure to be obtained from a particular act. One of the practical problems with it is that the calculations it would require are too many and too complex. Others have tried to overcome this difficulty by proposing rule utilitarianism. This approach looks at the general consequences, in terms of pleasure and pain, of particular rules of conduct. The rule, the following of which produces the best results, is the best rule to follow. This approach does not, however, necessarily make matters simpler. A rule such as 'you should always keep your promises' would probably have to be followed by so many exceptions that it would be no simpler than act utilitarianism.

A further criticism of utilitarianism is that it is implicitly authoritarian. This tendency can be illustrated by the public debate, in the early part of the nineteenth century, over the sources and mechanisms of revenue collection in the Indian provinces ruled by the East India Company. James Mill, the father of John Stuart Mill, was at the centre of this debate and through him the utilitarian philosophy of Bentham became a dominant theme in the argument. The utilitarians argued that the company had a duty to decide how best to spend the tax revenue of the country. As Holt Mackenzie argued in 1820

> Holding 9/10ths of the clear rent [revenue] of the country as a fund to be administered for the public good, the government may, I think, justly be regarded as under a very solemn obligation to consider more fully than has hitherto been usual, how it can dispose of that fund so as to produce *the greatest sum of happiness.*
>
> (Stokes, 1959: 113, emphasis added)

There was a clear authoritarian and paternalistic strand in the thinking of these utilitarians. They believed they had a mission to transform India; but this mission could only be achieved by strong government. They would decide how the revenue should be spent. Utilitarianism requires the presence of a powerful figure who can calculate where the happiness of the country lies and then take the necessary action to bring it about. This strain of thought can be found in Bentham's own writings in which he argued that the will of the executive should not be checked by constitutional or popular devices (Stokes 1959: 72, 79). It can also easily take root in companies and organisations where management become the judges of utility.

Despite the criticisms that can be made of utilitarianism its core ideas are commonly expressed by managers when they talk of 'business cases'. These are arguments that a thing should be done because it would be good for the business; the good of the wider society is not always considered.

ACTIVITY 3.8

Briefly analyse Case study 2.9 (*Providing new drugs for MS sufferers*) from a utilitarian perspective.

Applying ethical theories

There are many ethical theories. Even if you find it easy to discount some of them, because you think them trivial or ill-founded, several will remain. This raises a question for someone who wishes to think ethically. Should all or several theories be applied when thinking about an issue or should one approach be adopted that seems best suited to the matter in hand? Petrick and Quinn (1997:

55–6, 63) argued that those managers who are temperamentally attached to one of the theoretical perspectives on ethics 'fanatically rush to judgement'. They claimed that there can be no 'quick fixes' when dealing with matters of managerial integrity and that managers ought to use the ethical insights from all four quadrants of Figure 3.1 to make balanced ethical decisions.

The matrix in Activity 3.9 is a way of evaluating options, for responding to an ethical issue, that considers a wide range of ethical perspectives. The criteria in the matrix are based on the ethical perspectives that have been discussed in this chapter. The fairness/Golden Rule and universality tests are Kantian, the enduring values and disclosure tests draw on some of the themes of virtue ethics and the consequential test is utilitarian. The self-interest test draws upon ethical egoism and the remaining tests are aspects of discourse ethics.

There are many ways of constructing such mechanisms. This is a simple one because it is based on a series of yes/no questions about the importance to be given to the various ethical principles and about the principles' implications. The matrix allows four levels of weighting or importance to be given to each of the criteria.

1 **The 'trigger' level.** A criterion is of such importance that a position or action can be chosen because it meets this criterion alone, irrespective of how it fares on the other criteria.
2 **The 'veto' level.** A veto criterion can veto a particular position or decision that negatively affects the criterion, no matter how well the action or decision does on all the other criteria. However it is not important enough to be the single trigger for an action. For example someone might reject an option because it does not meet his or her self-interest criterion but would not be prepared to choose an option simply because it met his or her self-interest needs.
3 **The ordinary level.** A criterion that deserves to be considered but carries no more weight than the other criteria.
4 **Reject level.** A criterion that you feel should not be considered.

The scoring part of the framework encourages you to assess whether each criterion would positively suggest acceptance of the option or negatively suggest rejection.

ACTIVITY 3.9

An ethical evaluation framework

The issue

For example – Bribery and corruption in international business deals.

Your proposed decision/position on the issue and the action you will take

For example – to pay a large commission to an intermediary to obtain his influence to secure a large overseas deal.

Activity 3.9 continued

Instructions

1 Identify any criterion you see as a veto item. Circle Y. Otherwise N.
2 Identify any item you see as a trigger item. Circle Y. Otherwise N.
3 Identify any criterion you see as a reject item. Circle Y. Otherwise N.
4 Answer each question. Circle + for a positive answer or − for a negative answer.
5 Ignore any criterion you have rejected.
6 Total the number of circles in the positive and negative columns.

A veto item is any criterion that is so important to you that if your decision and plan score negatively on it you will reject the proposal even if, overall, it scores more positives than negatives.

A trigger item is any criterion that is so important to you that if your decision scores positively on it you will accept the proposal even if, overall, it scores more negatives than positives.

Ask the following questions of your proposed decision and plan of action	Reject	Veto	Trigger	Positive	Negative
1 **Involvement test.** Are those who have a right to be involved in this decision broadly for or against my position?	Y/N	Y/N	Y/N	+	−
2 **Consequential test.** Are the anticipated consequences of my decision and plan positive or negative?	Y/N	Y/N	Y/N	+	−
3 **Fairness test/Golden Rule.** If I were to take the place of one of those affected by my decision and plan would I regard them positively or negatively?	Y/N	Y/N	Y/N	+	−
4 **Enduring values test.** Do my decision and plan positively support my core values or does it negate them?	Y/N	Y/N	Y/N	+	−
5 **Universality test.** Would it be a good thing or a bad thing if my decision and plan were to become a universal principle applicable to all in similar situations, even to myself?	Y/N	Y/N	Y/N	+	−

Ask the following questions of your proposed decision and plan of action	Reject	Veto	Trigger	Positive	Negative
6 Light-of-day test. Would I feel good or bad if others (friends, family, colleagues) were to know of my decision and action?	Y/N	Y/N	Y/N	+	–
7 Self-interest test. Do the decision and plan meet or defeat my own best interests?	Y/N	Y/N	Y/N	+	–
8 The discourse test. Have the debates about my decision and plan been well or badly conducted?	Y/N	Y/N	Y/N	+	–
9 The communitarian test. Would my action and plan affect the community positively or negatively?	Y/N	Y/N	Y/N	+	–

If any trigger item scores positive – **accept the decision and action**.

If any veto item scores negatively – **reject the decision and action**.

Otherwise **accept the decision and plan** if there are more positives than negatives or **reject the decision and plan** if there are more negatives than positives.

Although we claimed that this evaluation framework was a way of integrating many ethical perspectives it will have occurred to you that, through the use of the 'reject', 'trigger' and 'veto' options as trump cards that can rule out some ethical tests, the framework allows the rejection or prioritisation of ethical positions. This thought leads us to an alternative approach – to choose one ethical approach and to ignore others, or at least to put the approaches into rank order of preference. Carroll (1990) proposed a simple exercise (Activity 3.10) for people who wish to reflect on the relative importance they give to a range of ethical perspectives. The list of principles he proposed included both normative approaches, methods for thinking about the right response, and norm approaches, which invite a person to accept the values and standards of a particular group. The categorical imperative, the Golden Rule and the utilitarian principle are all methods for normative thinking whereas the disclosure rule, the organisation ethic and the professional ethic concern decisions about which social group one wishes to belong to. These norm-based questions could be seen as an application of a stakeholder analysis.

ACTIVITY 3.10

Prioritising your ethical principles

Here are a number of 'principles'. Identify your top three and rank them 1, 2, 3 in order of importance/relevance to you and your decision making. Then mark your least relevant 9, 10 and 11.

Principle	Description	Rank
Categorical imperative	You should not adopt principles of action unless they can, without inconsistency, be adopted by everyone else	
Conventionist ethic	Individuals should act to further their self-interest so long as they do not violate the law	
Golden Rule	Do unto others as you would have them do unto you	
Hedonistic ethic	If it feels good, do it	
Disclosure rule	If you are comfortable with an action or decision after asking yourself whether you would mind if all your associates, friends and family were aware of it, then you should act or decide	
Intuition ethic	You do what your 'gut feeling' tells you to do	
Means-ends ethic	If the end justifies the means, then you should act	
Might equals right ethic	You should take whatever advantage you are strong enough and powerful enough to take without respect for ordinary social conventions and laws	
Organisation ethic	This is an age of large-scale organisations – be loyal to the organisation	
Professional ethic	You should only do that which can be explained before a committee of your professional peers	
Utilitarian ethic	You should follow the principle of 'the greatest good for the greatest number'	

Carroll used the list in Activity 3.10 as the basis of a research project and found that the Golden Rule was given the highest ranking by his respondents. The disclosure rule came second in the study.

Some ethical checklists, such as the Texas Instruments Ethics Quick Test, emphasise the social acceptability of an ethical decision rather than the philosophical correctness of the mode of thought used to achieve it. Use the questions of the Quick Test to decide whether an action you are planning to take is right.

The TI Ethics Quick Test

- Is the action legal?
- Does it comply with our values?
- If you do it, will you feel bad?
- How will it look in the newspaper?
- If you know it's wrong, don't do it!
- If you're not sure, ask.
- Keep asking until you get an answer.

(*Source*: Texas Instruments, 2001)

Reflections

This chapter has provided the formal, philosophical, tools that can be used when you have to think about an ethical problem. These tools are not, however, easy to handle. There is first the problem of which theories you are going to use. If all the theories were to give the same answer to a problem then admittedly there would be no problem. But this is not always the case and then you have the difficulty of choosing which theories to ignore or deciding how much weight to give to the various theories. Once you have chosen a theory there remains the difficulty of applying it to the particular circumstances of the issue confronting you. It may be these problems that make the TI Ethics Quick Test (Activity 3.11) look so attractive. The 'quick and dirty' approach it uses leads us into the matter of how people actually decide about ethical issues – which is the subject of the next chapter.

Summary

In this chapter the following key points have been made:

- Ethical issues at work might be best approached by concentrating on developing people who are virtuous and have the judgement to be able to make moral decisions and act upon them when faced with ethical problems.
- Ethical issues at work might best be approached by seeing organisations as networks of individuals who learn personally and collectively through experience, reflection and the sharing of that learning. Learning about learning, learning how to deal with ethical issues, is more important than learning prepackaged solutions.
- Ethical issues at work might best be tackled by applying sound moral principles that should guide our actions.
- Ethical issues at work might best be tackled by forecasting which actions will bring about the greatest amount of good.

Suggested further reading

P. Vardy and P. Grosch (1999) *The Puzzle of Ethics*, London: Fount, is a good introduction to the main ethical theories. Simon Blackburn's (2001) *Being Good. A Short Introduction to Ethics*, Oxford: Oxford University Press, is an elegant reflection on the main issues in ethics. Anne Thomson's (1999) *Critical Reasoning in Ethics*, London: Routledge, is a good guide to the application of theories to issues.

GROUP ACTIVITY 3

Form into groups. As a group, choose one of the case studies from Chapter 2. Each member of the group should then choose a different ethical perspective, utilitarian, fairness, ethics of care and so on, and individually produce an analysis of the case from that perspective. Come back together as a group and debate the issue.

4 Values and heuristics

OBJECTIVES

Having completed this chapter and its associated activities, readers should be able to:

- Explain the role of heuristics in decision making.

- Explain the concept of values and their role in thinking about ethical issues.

- Reflect upon how individuals' values may impact on their thinking about ethical issues.

Introduction

This chapter considers how people think about and make ethical decisions in practice. It is in contrast to the previous chapter that considered how philosophers and writers on ethics argued people should think about ethical matters. The central theme of the chapter is the role of heuristics in human thinking. The argument is that people do not use a comprehensively rational process when they come to a view on moral matters. Rather, it will be argued, people use heuristics, to ease the process of arriving at a view or taking a decision, and to simplify the mass of competing views and information that surround any issue.

The account of ethical thinking provided in this chapter is to some extent speculative. It presents an argument about how people might make up their minds on ethical matters. The argument is based on well-established ideas as well as on newly emerging theories; but their application to thinking on ethical matters is incomplete. Unusually for a textbook therefore it remains for you to make up your mind on the arguments presented.

Definition

> **Heuristics** are a means of discovering or finding out something. They are mental tricks of the trade or rules of thumb that are used, almost unconsciously, to simplify the process of decision making. They are cognitive devices that limit the need to search for, and evaluate, further options. The term also carries with it the idea of discovering things by trial and error rather than by systematic analysis of all appropriate information.

Heuristic thinking

The idea of heuristic thinking can be illustrated by contrasting it with a rational approach to making a non-ethical decision such as choosing a car to buy. If this decision were to be approached from an analytical and rational position you would have to go through the following stages.

- Identify all the cars available on the market.
- Identify all the factors that are important to you in a car, such as cost, reliability, acceleration, colour and so on.
- Decide on the relative importance to you of the above criteria by either putting them into rank order or assigning weights to them.
- Research each car on the market and decide how they score against each of the criteria.
- Calculate the degree to which each car would satisfy your wishes by combining the cars' performances against each criterion with the criterion's importance, so that cars that do well against the more important criteria will have the higher scores.
- Choose the car which scores highest in these calculations.

The process just described is called subjective expected utility. This is because the decision maker makes a personal (subjective) assessment of both what is important to them about a car (utility) and the chances (expected) that any particular car would actually provide that value.

This is obviously a time-consuming process. A heuristic approach would simplify it. A large number of heuristics could be involved in deciding which car to buy. Here are just a few. To begin with you would probably not evaluate every car available on the market but simply focus on those you have been made aware of by advertising. This is the availability heuristic. The recency heuristic might mean that a pleasurable trip last weekend in a friend's new car weighs heavily in your preference for that model. Your dislike of the colour purple might mean that the purple car you have been considering seems to have a lot of factors that turn you against it. This is an example of the halo and horns heuristic that is explained on p. 108. The application of one or more of these heuristics will leave you with a narrow range of cars to choose from and an intuitive inclination to buy one particular car.

Let us move on to consider decision making about ethical matters. Benjamin Franklin proposed, in the eighteenth century, the use of a moral algebra to resolve such issues (Gigerenzer *et al.*, 1999: 76). This was similar to the rational and analytical model, described above, for choosing a car. He would divide a sheet of paper into two columns and head one 'Pros' and the other 'Cons'. He would then identify the factors for or against a particular course of action. On further consideration he would strike out some pros and cons because they cancelled each other out. If two cons were, in his view, equal to one pro he would strike out all three. As a result of this process he would come to a balanced view about the right thing to do.

If we applied moral algebra to an ethical question we might find, but not necessarily, deontological pros ranged against consequentialist cons. Rights would have to be weighed against justice and equity and the virtuous mean might be hard to find. Giving equal consideration to potentially mutually exclusive ways of thinking about ethical questions may lead to confusion. Some writers (Kaler, 1999) suggest that the way business schools teach business ethics ('well, you could look at it from a deontological viewpoint or alternatively from a consequentialist position') encourages such confusion. It will be argued, contrarily, that people tend not to combine all the ethical perspectives on an issue but choose one and use it in a heuristic manner.

It is further argued in this chapter that values and emotions can perform the role of decision-making heuristics. Two examples of the role of values as heuristics in ethical decision making are provided to illustrate the process.

- The first example focuses on priority setting and uses the case of resource allocation in health care management.
- The second example concerns ideas of integrity and loyalty as decision-making heuristics.

Each of these is explained, and illustrated by an Activity.

Decision-making heuristics

The idea has long been recognised that people do not possess the capacity to obtain and process the amounts of information necessary in order to take a rational approach to decision making. Herbert Simon's (1983) concept of bounded rationality is the classic formulation of this viewpoint. Search behaviour is the process of looking for the information and options necessary to make a decision. Bounded rationality sets limits on the extent of such searches. He introduced the concept of satisficing, which is the process of searching for and evaluating options until one finds one that is good enough. He recognised that this solution may not be the best or optimal one. If the decision maker had continued to identify and assess options better ones might have been found. But, he argued, once a solution has been found that will do, the psychological and practical costs to the decision maker of looking for the best solution outweigh the additional benefits of a best solution that may not, in any case, be found. Simon's work emphasised that fully rational decision making was at best an aspiration and that the way people actually made up their minds about things was less analytical and was based more on trial and error – which is one definition of a heuristic.

Base-rate neglect

In the 1970s psychologists, among them Kahneman, Tversky and Slovic (1982) studied the exercise of judgement. In particular they investigated how people made estimates about the probability or likelihood of situations and events. The research was done using questionnaires. Case study 4.1 presents an example of the questions they asked.

Blue taxi or green taxi?

A taxi was involved in a hit and run accident at night. Two taxi companies, the green and the blue, operate in the city. You are given the following data:

(a) 85 per cent of the taxis in the city are green and 15 per cent blue.
(b) A witness identified the cab as blue. The court tested the reliability of the witness under the same circumstances that existed on the night of the accident and concluded that the witness correctly identified each of the two colours 80 per cent of the time and failed 20 per cent of the time.

What is the probability that the cab involved in the accident was blue rather than green?

(*Source*: Kahneman *et al.*, 1982: 156–7)

This example identifies a heuristic (known as base-rate neglect) that leads people to pay more attention to immediate sources of information (the witness's statement) and to ignore background information (such as the relative frequency of the two types of cabs). The correct answer, derived from Bayes' theorem (which takes both items of data into account), is 0.41. Most people, when asked to answer this question however, ignored the data in point (a) because they were considered too general and distant from the event, and produced an answer around 80 per cent, which was based on the information given in point (b) alone.

The research questions were constructed so that if a heuristic were present respondents would misuse or neglect important information and give incorrect answers. The inference was then drawn that heuristics were a source of bias and prejudice in judgement. In hindsight it can be objected that the questions were so deviously constructed that they did not represent the kinds of judgement people have to make in real life. If so the possibility remains that in everyday situations the heuristics might not be a cause of error.

■ Other heuristics

A large number of heuristics are identified in Hogarth (1980). Just a few will be mentioned here. The recency effect was mentioned in the example of the car buying decision mentioned above. This heuristic causes people to put more weight on information they have collected recently and to undervalue things they may have learned in the past. The halo and horns heuristic has long been known to selection and recruitment specialists. This heuristic leads people to latch on to one aspect of an interviewee to which they have a strong like or dislike. It may be the fact that the interviewee has a moustache or is wearing blue suede shoes. This one feature then dominates the recruiter's whole assessment of the individual. They might think that a man with a moustache cannot really be trusted; or that anyone who wears blue suede shoes must be just the sort of creative person the company needs. The heuristics-and-biases programme of research established the existence of heuristics in judgement but suggested that they were a problem.

A current programme of research led by the ABC research group, based in Berlin, has revisited heuristics and come to the conclusion that far from being a distortion of decision making they are both necessary and effective. The programme is intended to 'capture how real minds make decisions under constraints of limited time and knowledge' (Gigerenzer *et al.*, 1999: 5). They reject the rational, subjective, expected utility model as a description of decision making and instead propose the idea of fast and frugal heuristics. These are rules for limiting the search for information and options, and for making choices, that employ a minimum of time, knowledge and computation. They argue that fast and frugal heuristics are bounded rationality in its purest form.

The working of fast and frugal heuristics can best be explained by an example. One of the heuristics is the recognition heuristic that applies to situations where a person has to decide which of two objects has a higher value on a particular criterion. The heuristic is defined as follows; 'If one of the two objects is recognised and the other is not, then infer that the recognised object has the higher value' (Gigerenzer *et al.*, 1999: 41). In an experiment they asked students at the University of Chicago and the University of Munich the question, 'Which city has more inhabitants: San Diego or San Antonio?' Sixty-four per cent of the Chicago students got the answer right, but 100 per cent of the Munich students gave the correct answer. Why did the German students do better? They had heard of San Diego but not of San Antonio. They applied the recognition heuristic and got it right. The American students recognised both cities and could not apply the recognition heuristic. They had to search their memories for further clues as to the right answer. The additional information merely confused them. There is of course logic to the recognition heuristic; cities of which you have heard are more likely to be bigger than those that are unknown to you. The heuristic uses this logic as the basis of a very simple decision rule. But because of the logic the heuristic is not only simple, it is effective.

Of course there are many situations in which the recognition heuristic cannot be used because both of the options are recognised. Gigernezer *et al.* (1999: ch. 4) used a computer simulation to evaluate some simple heuristics for searching through data for solutions in such circumstances. As in their work reported above the simulation was based on the task of deciding which, of pairs of cities, was the larger. They built into the simulation a series of ten cues or clues about each of the cities. Whether a city was a capital or not was one clue. In the database of information, which was to be searched in the simulation, the cue was recorded as positive (if it was a capital city) because a capital city was likely to be larger than a city that was not, as negative (if it was not) or as a 'don't know'. Some additional information was included about the reliability of each cue (how often its use could give the right answer) and how often it would prove useful (as only one city can be a capital city you will not often have an opportunity to use it to discriminate between pairs of cities). In the simulation six search strategies were tested. The first three were based on heuristic principles.

1 *Minimalist.* Choose one of the ten cues at random. If one of the pair of cities you have to decide between scores a positive on this cue and the other a negative then choose the positive city as the larger one. If not go on trying cues randomly in turn until one provides an answer.

2 *Take the last.* Choose whichever cue worked well last time this kind of decision had to be made.

3 *Take the best.* In this strategy some of the information about the reliability and usefulness of the cues is used to decide which cue is likely to provide the most accurate answer.

The other three search strategies were all based on the rational model. They were:

- Franklin's rule
- Dawe's rule
- Multiple regression.

We will not explain each of these in detail. It is sufficient to point out that they all shared one common feature, that, when choosing between two cities, they aggregated all ten cues about each city in order to decide which was likely to be bigger. The heuristic strategies, in contrast, only used cues one at a time and when a decision had been reached ignored all the other cues.

The results from the simulation are shown in Table 4.1. The results suggest that not only are heuristics efficient because they give answers by using less information than the rational strategies; but they are also as accurate as the rational techniques. The fast and frugal researchers see heuristics as (generally) effective strategies for making decisions. This leaves open the possibility that ethical thinking, as well as judgement, might be heuristic processes.

Table 4.1 The results of the simulation comparing heuristic and rational research strategies

Type of strategy	Strategy	Frugality (no. of cues looked up)	Accuracy (% of correct answers)
Heuristic	Take the last	2.6	64.5
	Minimalist	2.8	64.7
	Take the best	3.0	65.8
Rational	Franklin's rule	10.0	62.1
	Dawe's rule	10.0	62.3
	Multiple regression	10.0	65.7

(*Source:* Gigerenzer *et al.*, 1999: 87)

Values as heuristics in ethical reasoning

In this section we want to move away from what is established in the literature and to speculate about how the fast and frugal heuristics may apply to ethical decision making. The argument is that heuristics operate in ethical decision making and that values are the basis of these heuristics.

Gigerenzer *et al.* (1999: 30) pointed out that, while most of the fast and frugal research concerns cognitive heuristics, emotions and social norms can also act as heuristics. For example a social norm such as 'copy the choices made by your social peers' acts as an efficient heuristic for stopping further searching for other options. This heuristic might be particularly powerful in academic recruitment procedures in which academics apparently appoint those whom they think their colleagues would approve of. Emotions, such as love for one's child, prevent wasteful ethical dithering. If a child screams in the night the emotional response forces the parent to get out of bed and comfort the child. Such parents do not calculate whether the greatest utility is achieved by this action or whether staying in bed so that they might be fresher for work the next day might do greater good. If emotions and social norms can act as heuristics then it is possible that values can also do so. This is because values are closely related to emotions and social norms. Values are like emotions because people find it hard to give a rational account of why their values are important to them; they just are (Eden *et al.*, 1979). The same thought can be expressed using the psychoanalytical term cathexis. Cathexis is a strong sense of attachment that people have towards their values and it is this commitment that drives people to act in the world (Young, 1977). The link with social norms derives from the fact that values are acquired as part of the process of growing up and becoming socialised in a society. It is this early acquisition of values, according to Rokeach (1973: 17–18) that makes values simpler and more robust than attitudes.

Definitions

> **Values** are core ideas about how people should live and the ends they should seek. They are shared by a majority of people within a community or society. They are simply expressed generalities, often no more than single words such as peace and honesty. As they are very broad they do not give guidance on how particular things should be evaluated.
>
> **Attitudes**, like values, are evaluations of whether something is good or bad. But unlike values they are evaluations of particular things, issues, people, places or whatever. Attitudes, because they relate to specific circumstances, are more changeable than values.
>
> A **belief** is an acceptance that something is true or not. This acceptance does not imply any judgement about whether that thing is good or bad.

Rokeach's work is helpful because it distinguishes between different types of values that might affect thinking about ethical issues.

- *Moral values* – concern interpersonal behaviour, e.g. being honest is desirable.
- *Competence values* – concern one's own valuation of one's behaviour, e.g. behaving imaginatively is desirable.
- *Personal values* – concern the ends, or terminal states, that are desirable for the self, e.g. peace of mind.
- *Social values* – concern the ends that one would desire for society, e.g. world peace is desirable.

The first two items in this list concern instrumental values that are about how a person should live and behave. The second two items are terminal values that concern the ends or purposes that we should be striving for. Table 4.2 lists the instrumental and terminal values identified by Rokeach's survey of a sample of Americans.

Table 4.2 The instrumental and terminal values of Americans

Terminal values	Rank order (females)	Rank order (males)	Instrumental values	Rank order (females)	Rank order (males)
A comfortable life	13	4	Ambitious	4	2
An exciting life	18	18	Broadminded	5	4
A sense of accomplishment	10	7	Capable	12	8
A world at peace	1	1	Cheerful	10	12
A world of beauty	15	15	Clean	8	9
Equality	8	9	Courageous	6	5
Family security	2	2	Forgiving	2	6
Freedom	3	3	Helpful	7	7
Happiness	5	5	Honest	1	1
Inner harmony	12	13	Imaginative	18	18
Mature love	14	14	Independent	14	11
National security	11	10	Intellectual	16	15
Pleasure	16	17	Logical	17	16
Salvation	4	12	Loving	9	14
Self-respect	6	6	Obedient	15	17
Social recognition	17	16	Polite	13	13
True friendship	9	11	Responsible	3	3
Wisdom	7	8	Self-controlled	11	10

Note: 1 = the top rank.
(*Source*: Reprinted with the permission of the Free Press, an imprint of Simon and Schuster Adult Publishing Group, from *The Nature of Human Values* by Milton Rokeach, p. 58, Copyright © 1973 by The Free Press.)

▦ Illustration of values acting as heuristics

The ways in which values may act as heuristics can be illustrated by considering a well-known management development exercise called *Cave Rescue* (Woodcock, 1979, 1989: 81). In this exercise groups have to decide how to allocate scarce resources between people who are described in thumbnail sketches which are deliberately brief and partisan. *Cave Rescue* concerns six volunteers in a psychological experiment that requires them to be in a pothole. The cave is flooding and the research committee in charge of the experiment have called for a rescue team. When the team arrive they will only be able to rescue one person at a time because of the narrowness of the cave's entrance. The committee have to decide the order in which the volunteers will be saved from the cave when the rescue party arrive. The exercise provides a good opportunity to study the values that are articulated in such debates.

Observations of people doing the exercise suggest that they used their preferred values to select the information from the thumbnail sketches that they consider useful. Each of the characters in the *Cave Rescue* exercise has positive and negative aspects included in their thumbnail sketches. Some material about each of the characters has to be edited out for other information to become useful in making the necessary ranking decisions. A number of different values are used that include:

- Maximising the number of people who are saved by rescuing first those likely to panic, and hamper the rescuers.
- Maximising the happiness of society by rescuing first those who can make the greatest contribution to society (utilitarianism).
- Rescuing first those who have the most family or other dependants.

- Rescuing the youngest first because the oldest have already had their opportunity for life.
- Rescuing the morally worthy before the morally unworthy.

The heuristic use of values can be explained by reference to volunteer Paul who, according to the information given to the participants, has been convicted of indecent assault. But he also has, in his working notes, details of a cheap cure for rabies. People who used the morality criterion to choose whom to rescue assumed that the cure could be understood from the working notes (and that in any case he was bound to have a research assistant who understood and could continue the work) and that there was, consequently, no barrier to using his behaviour to decide his order of rescue. Other people, using a utilitarian value, assumed that it was impossible to make sense of the working notes. This allowed them, when making their decision, to ignore Paul's criminal activities and concentrate on his potential contribution to society. People edited out, or rationalised into insignificance, that information which inhibited the application of their preferred values.

How values are used as heuristics

So far, the argument seems straightforward. Values are simple but strongly held beliefs such as the importance of honesty. People, it is suggested, use values as filters to reduce the amount of information they take into account when making a decision. Values may act as a fast and frugal heuristic for limiting the amount of search behaviour. To the three heuristic search strategies proposed by Gigerenzer *et al.*, 1999 – see p. 109 – might be added another one: choose a cue that you like because it fits with your values.

If people do not change their values ethical decisions ought to be easy. But it is not. Ethical issues are often seen as dilemmas that are not easily resolved. According to Billig (1996: 238–47) values may be simple in themselves but in at least two ways they are complex matters of controversy.

- The first concerns the interpretations of the values. Their very simplicity makes them banal. This in turn means that they have to be interpreted before they can be of use in making decisions. An example can be taken from health care management. Everyone in the field would agree that patients come first. But different health care professionals may make sense of this value in different ways. For some it would mean improving the patients' clinical condition. Others might say it is empowering the patients to take control of their treatment and their condition. Yet others might claim it means making the patient physically comfortable and at psychological ease.
- The second source of argument and conflict over values is the multiplicity of conflicting values in any given society. This can be illustrated by referring to Table 4.2. Ambition, for example, may clash with honesty. Ethical issues are often difficult because it may not be certain which value, from a variety of contradictory values, should be applied in any given situation.

The problem for someone faced with an ethical matter is to choose which of many values to apply to the situation. This brings us back to a feature of fast and frugal heuristics as described by Gigerenzer *et al.* (1999: 30). They proposed that people are equipped with a psychological adaptive toolbox that is filled with a jumbled collection of one-function tools. Just as a mechanic manages to choose the right tool to repair a car so people choose the best heuristic to hand to help them make their mind up or take a decision.

In the next two sections we explore the ways in which particular values might be used.

■ Value heuristics and priority setting

Resource allocation is a particular form of priority setting. It involves deciding which things are more important and which less. In this section it is argued that right answers to problems of priority setting cannot be found by technical means. Priority setting is a matter of values. The person setting the priorities has to decide which values they will use to determine relative importance. Whether a particular set of priorities is right or wrong depends upon the values used to judge it. This makes that priority setting an ethical matter.

This section explores the use of values as heuristics for making decisions in ethical matters, using a simulation exercise called *Monksbane and feverfew*. The exercise is based on a problem in health care management. A limited budget has to be divided between two health care programmes, one aimed at the diagnosis and treatment of monksbane and the other at the diagnosis and treatment of feverfew, both dangerous diseases. The problem is to decide which programme should be given priority. Fisher (1998) identified six values concerning priority setting in the allocation of resources. They are listed here but will be defined later in the chapter:

1 utility
2 individual need
3 deservingness
4 ecology
5 fairness
6 personal competence and gain.

In *Monksbane and feverfew* there are opportunities to apply each of these values in setting your priorities between the two programmes. Whichever you choose will lead to a different allocation of resources. It may be that you will change your mind as you work through the simulation. Do Activity 4.1 now and then the different values will be explained.

ACTIVITY 4.1

Monksbane and feverfew: A diagnostic instrument about values in public sector resource allocation

Introduction

In this questionnaire you imagine yourself to be a manager responsible for screening programmes for two diseases; feverfew and monksbane.

Activity 4.1 continued

You have a total budget of £70,000 (£70k) to spend on these two programmes. In this questionnaire you will be presented with some initial information and asked to say how you would divide up the budget between the two diseases. In the subsequent sections you will be given additional information, and for each additional piece of information you will be asked to review the use of the budget available to you.

- All the information you will be given is mutually consistent, i.e. information at the end of the questionnaire will not invalidate earlier information.
- Answer the questions in order. Do not look ahead.
- Once you have answered a section please do not return to it later and change it.
- There are no 'right' answers to the questions in this questionnaire. It's all a matter of your own values.
- Please make your allocations of the budget between monksbane and feverfew in units of £5,000 (£5k), i.e. £0, £5k, £10k and so on.

(*Source*: Fisher, 1998)

Section 1

The graph below tells you the number of lives that will be saved as a consequence of different levels of expenditure on the two diseases. The graph is based upon sound research conducted by the Paracelsus Epidemiological Institute. You need have no doubt about its accuracy.

The result of splitting the £70k equally between the two diseases would be:

No. of lives saved as a result of spending £35k on monksbane	7
No. of lives saved as a result of spending £35k on feverfew	59
Total no. of lives saved	66

Feverfew and monksbane affect men and women equally and also affect the same age group and social classes.

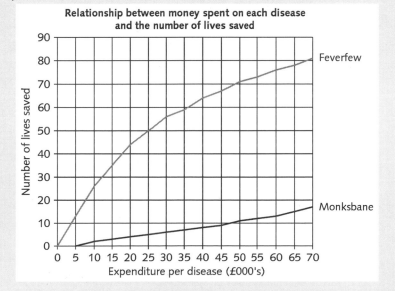

Relationship between money spent on each disease and the number of lives saved

Activity 4.1 continued

How much of the £70k do you think ought to be spent on monksbane?

£

When you have written your decision in the box please go to Section 2.

Section 2

Monksbane is a much more dangerous disease than feverfew. If people with early signs of the disease are not identified through screening and treated there is a certain (100 per cent) chance they will die of the disease. Feverfew on the other hand can be fatal but the chances are smaller. If sufferers with feverfew are not identified and treated there is only a 57 per cent chance that they will die of the disease.

There have been great advances in the medical understanding of monksbane and only 5 per cent of people treated die from the disease. The death rate amongst patients treated for feverfew is 38 per cent.

Assume that currently no money at all is being spent on monksbane. How much of the £70k do you think ought to be spent on monksbane and how much on feverfew, as a result of the information given on this page?

Monksbane	£
Feverfew	£

If the figure you have put in the monksbane box is £10k or less please go to Section 3b. If it is more than £10k please go to Section 3a.

Section 3a

Feverfew is a disease that can be caught by anybody. Monksbane, however, is much more likely to be contracted by people with certain habits and lifestyles which they have chosen to adopt.

Another characteristic of monksbane is the tendency for sufferers to be of a particular personality type. They are of a choleric disposition: aggressive, demanding and ungrateful. This relationship has been well researched by the eminent group of scientists from St Barty's who have recently published their work on personality and disease. This relationship has always been well known in popular folklore. It is the origin of the disease's name since sufferers were the bane in the life of monk almoners and hospitalers in medieval monasteries.*

Bearing in mind this information how much do you now think ought to be spent on monksbane?

£

Please go to Section 4 when you have put your decisions in the box.

*Adam of Barnsley (1372) *De Naturae et Nomine Opus Malleficarum.*

Activity 4.1 continued

Section 3b

Monksbane is a disease that can be caught by anybody. Feverfew, however, is much more likely to be contracted by people with certain habits and lifestyles which they have chosen to adopt. Another characteristic of feverfew is the tendency for sufferers to be of a particular personality type. They are of a choleric disposition: aggressive, demanding and ungrateful. This relationship has been well researched by an eminent group of scientists from St Barty's who have recently published their work on personality and disease. However this relationship has always been known in popular folklore. As Victorian doggerel had it,

'e's a gringer and as poisonous as yew is the man whats got feverfew.'[*]

Bearing in mind this information how much do you now think ought to be spent on feverfew?

Please go to Section 4 when you have put your decision in the box above.

[*]F. Smith Jnr. (1978) *Semiotics and Ethnomethodology of Disease in Victorian England*, California: Albertus Publishers.

Section 4

A recent television programme in the 'Medicine and Society' series has highlighted the problems of monksbane sufferers and it has caused a tremendous increase in the donations received by the M.R.C. (Monksbane Research Society). This money is only available for research and cannot be used for screening or treatment. There is a very powerful national pressure group representing the needs of monksbane victims and they have the ear of several key members of your health consumer watchdog body. In addition your organisation employs a number of consultant medical staff who have made their reputations developing treatments for monksbane.

There is pressure from these groups to spend *more* on monksbane than you are currently spending, i.e. more than you have agreed to spend on monksbane in any of the previous sections.

Bearing in mind this new information how much of the £70k do you now think ought to be spent on monksbane?

£ [   ]

When you have entered your decision in the box please go to Section 5.

Section 5

Your research indicates that the percentage of the population that can be screened for each disease, and therefore the proportion of sufferers from each disease that can be identified and treated, is as shown in the following table.

Activity 4.1 continued

Identifying and treating sufferers

Amount spent on screening £K	Percentage of feverfew sufferers identified	Percentage of monksbane sufferers identified
10	30	5
20	51	10
30	63	15
40	72	20
50	79	25
60	86	30
70	92	40

This means that an expenditure of £10k on feverfew and £60k on monksbane will enable you to treat 30 per cent of the sufferers from both diseases. To put it in other words, people with the two diseases will have an equal chance of being identified and treated.

Assume that at present the £70k available is split between the two diseases as follows:

feverfew   £40k

monksbane   £30k

Bearing in mind this new information how much of the £70k do you now think ought to be spent on monksbane?

£

Please go to Section 6 when you have written your decision in the box.

Section 6

It would be possible to treat the £70k budget for feverfew and monksbane as a combined budget and not allocate it between the two diseases. That means you would treat feverfew and monksbane sufferers as they presented themselves through their GPs until the budget ran out (if it did).

Would you take up this option to run a combined budget and work on a first come/first served basis?

Please tick the appropriate box and then go to Section 7.

YES	
NO	

Section 7

What is your current allocation of the £70k between the two diseases?

Monksbane £   Feverfew £

Activity 4.1 continued

If you are planning to spend most of the £70k on feverfew complete this section.

> You have just been told that someone very close to you is suffering from monksbane. How would you now allocate the budget between the two diseases?
>
> Monksbane £ _____   Feverfew £ _____

If you are planning to spend most of the £70k on monksbane complete this section.

> You have just been told that someone very close to you is suffering from feverfew. How would you now allocate the budget between the two diseases?
>
> Monksbane £ _____   Feverfew £ _____

Now proceed to the scoring and interpretation information.

Scoring and interpretation of monksbane and feverfew

Evaluate your answers by working through the boxes below.

> **Section 1**
>
> How much did you decide to spend on monksbane? £ _____
>
> – If it is zero (£0) then you score HIGH on UTILITY.
> – If it is £20k or less then you score MEDIUM on UTILITY.
> – If it is more than £20k you score LOW on UTILITY.

> **Section 2**
>
> How much did you decide to spend on monksbane? £ _____
>
> – If it is £15k or less you score LOW on INDIVIDUAL NEED.
> – If it is more than £15k but less than £35k you score MEDIUM on INDIVIDUAL NEED.
> – If it is £35k or more you score HIGH on INDIVIDUAL NEED.

Activity 4.1 continued

If you answered Section 3b ignore this box.

Section 3a

How much did you decide to spend on monksbane?　£ _____

- If this is the same amount as you decided in Section 2 you score LOW on DESERVINGNESS.
- If you have reduced the amount spent on monksbane by a third or less compared with the amount in Section 2 you score MEDIUM on DESERVINGNESS.
- If you have reduced the amount spent on monksbane by more than a third compared with the amount you spent in Section 2 then you score HIGH on DESERVINGNESS.

If you answered Section 3a ignore this box.

Section 3b

How much did you decide to spend on feverfew in Section 2?　£ _____

How much did you decide to spend on feverfew in Section 3b?　£ _____

- If the two amounts are the same you score LOW on DESERVINGNESS.
- If you have reduced the amount spent on feverfew by a third or less compared with the amount in Section 2 you score MEDIUM on DESERVINGNESS.
- If you have reduced the amount spent on feverfew by more than a third compared with the amount in Section 2 then you score HIGH on DESERVINGNESS.

Section 4

How much did you decide to spend on monksbane?　£ _____

- If this is the same as you spent on monksbane in Sections 3a or 3b you score LOW on ECOLOGY.
- If the amount is £5k more than you spent in Sections 3a or 3b you score MEDIUM on ECOLOGY.
- If the amount is £10k or more than you spent in Sections 3a or 3b you score HIGH on ECOLOGY.

Activity 4.1 continued

Sections 5 and 6

How much did you decide to spend on monksbane in Section 5?   £ ☐

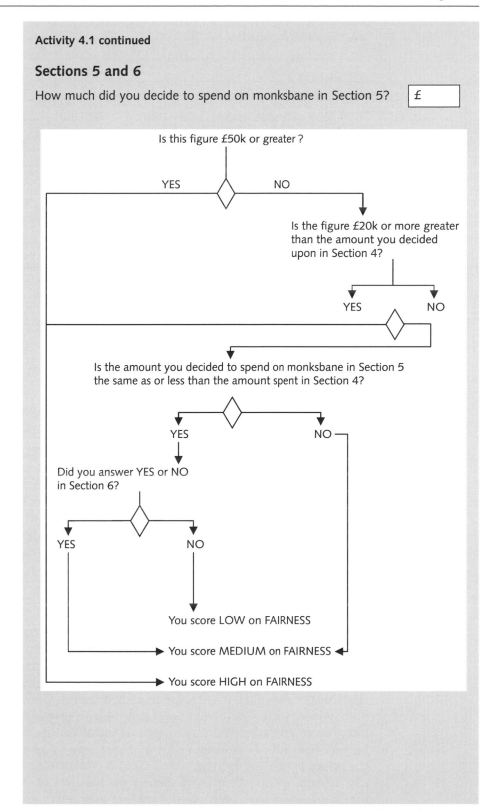

Activity 4.1 continued

Section 7

- If you increased the sum spent on the disease which affects you personally, then you score HIGH on PERSONAL COMPETENCE AND GAIN.
- If you kept the allocation the same you are LOW on PERSONAL COMPETENCE AND GAIN.
- If you decreased the allocation you are VERY LOW on PERSONAL COMPETENCE AND GAIN.

Transfer your score to the grid in the table below by placing ticks in the appropriate cells.

Heuristic	Low	Medium	High
Utility			
Individual need			
Deservingness			
Ecology			
Fairness			
Personal competence and gain			

■ The value heuristics of resource allocation

Each of the six value heuristics for resource allocation will be explained by reference to the information provided to the decision maker in *Monksbane and feverfew*.

Utility

Utility is a value concerned with allocating resources in a way that maximises the common good (or the beneficial impact of services). Utility values the maximisation of the quantity of good done. It is a form of utilitarianism.

In Section 1 of *Monksbane and feverfew* you are given enough information to apply utility as a value. If the graph is studied carefully it is clear that at any point money spent on feverfew will always save more lives than will be saved by spending it on monksbane. The way to save the most lives is to spend all the money on feverfew and none on monksbane. Those who make this decision are using the utility value. Not everyone can bear to do this. Those who know that rationally any money spent on monksbane costs the lives of feverfew sufferers, who might otherwise have been saved, may find themselves unable to spend nothing on monksbane at all. They therefore decide to spend a small amount on its treatment. This suggests that they are not entirely at ease with the utility value.

Utility is the heuristic that underwrites much management theory, and management science in particular. The development of QALYs, in health policy studies, provides an illustration of this approach. QALY stands for quality-adjusted life years (Gudex, 1986) and it is a measure of the benefit, to the average patient, of a medical treatment in terms of additional years of life and of the quality of life. Once the benefit of a medical intervention is measured its cost can be calculated to produce a ranking of treatments in cost effectiveness terms. Haemodialysis produced a cost per QALY of £9,075 whilst for scoliosis surgery the cost was £194. The latter treatment will therefore produce more benefit for any given sum of money than the former. There have been many criticisms of the utilitarian QALY approach, as reported in Pereira (1989) and Baldwin *et al.* (1990); but it is still persuasive to many.

Individual need

Individual need is the value that can be triggered by the cues and information given in Section 2 of *Monksbane and feverfew*. This value holds that resources should be allocated in proportion to people's needs. Needs can of course be attributed to groups of people but those who adopt this value prefer to consider people as individuals. Needs are not the same as wants or demands, however. A need can only be defined by an expert in the field, in the cases of monksbane and feverfew by a doctor. Needs have two further characteristics: they can be objectively described, which means that it is possible for someone to have a need they do not know about, and secondly, they can be ranked so that some are seen as more pressing than others.

The information provided in Section 2 of *Monksbane and feverfew* suggests that people who suffer from monksbane have greater need than those ill with feverfew. Monksbane patients are much more likely to die if not treated than feverfew patients. The information in Section 2 also highlights another aspect of individual need. It is the belief that if there are the means and the technology to improve people's lot then we are obliged to use them. In a medical setting it is the belief that everything that can be done, that has some chance of providing some benefit to the patient, should be done. It is to be noted that more can be done to treat people with monksbane than can be done for those with feverfew. If someone adopts the individual need value therefore, they will decide to spend significant sums of money on the treatment of monksbane.

The problem with individual need as a value is that it wills the expenditure of money without any regard for the availability of that money.

Deservingness

The deservingness heuristic, which is made available in Sections 3a and 3b of Activity 4.1, divides people into two moral classes, the deserving and the undeserving. When resources are being distributed according to the deservingness heuristic the favourable allocation is given to the former and the unfavourable portion to the latter. Deservingness is an Edwardian concept. This traditional view saw the provenance of all poverty and need in individual moral failure and indolence. The growing depersonalisation and alienation of social life, caused by nineteenth century industrialisation, made this view untenable; and a distinction was drawn between the deserving poor, brought low by social and economic factors beyond their control, and the undeserving poor, whose failure was of their own doing. New possibilities for morally classifying people have emerged since Edwardian times. People can be allocated to moral categories according to whether they are, on the one hand, greedy, truculent and ungrateful or, on the other, meek, humble and full of gratitude. The final moral criterion is group membership. The deserving person is one of us; the undeserving person is an outsider.

In more recent times the debate about the funding of treatment for sufferers from AIDS suggests that the distinction between the morally deserving and the undeserving is still current. Academic writing on the subject has been concerned with whether the treatment of AID sufferers is cost effective (Eastwood and Maynard, 1990). But there were arguments put forward, particularly in the press, which suggested that AIDS patients should be seen as 'less eligible' for treatment because they had visited the illness upon themselves through homosexual behaviour or drug abuse. It is, perhaps, the effect of deservingness that accounts for the different public perceptions of the plights of haemophiliacs, who acquired the disease through the necessary treatment of their primary illness, and that of homosexuals who, more likely, acquired it as a result of chosen behaviours. Whilst the UK government was initially curmudgeonly in the question of compensation for haemophiliacs, who had become HIV positive from being treated with infected blood products, public opinion clearly thought they should be compensated quickly (Mihil, 1990). There was a popular temptation to see haemophiliacs as deserving, and homosexuals as undeserving, and to fund their programmes accordingly.

In *Monksbane and feverfew* you are informed that people with the disease to which you have given the biggest share of the budget are ungrateful and truculent and that their behaviour has contributed towards their condition. If you are attracted to the value of deservingness you will have little patience with these people and decide to spend less on their treatment. However if you do not hold this value you will probably regard all the information given in this section as irrelevant to the problem and decide to leave the budget allocation unaltered.

Ecology

The apologists for the ecology heuristic take a very different approach. They see clients as morally autonomous agents who are not passive recipients of services but actors within the resource-allocation process. Put simply the ecology value states that the voices of all the parties interested in a decision should be heard. Those who value this perspective are pluralists who assume there will be many different points of view that have to be accommodated.

The ecology heuristic is concerned with identifying the different perceptions of the many groups involved with a service and trying to create a consistent policy from that variety. Ultimately this concatenation is achieved by giving more weight to the views of those who are most closely involved with the service. Some groups, particularly the most powerful in respect to the decision makers, will be listened to more intently than others. In other words an ecological resource allocation is one that meets the expectations and aspirations of the most significant interest groups. But such allocations also have to meet the minimum requirements of all the interest groups. If they do not then those disregarded groups will seek to make themselves more significant to the organisation and so reach a condition in which the decision makers have to listen to them.

Section 4 of *Monksbane and feverfew* provides enough clues for people who adopt this value to act upon it. Some very powerful interest groups are pressing for more money to be spent on the monksbane programme. People who accept ecology respond by putting another five or ten thousand pounds into the programme. Most of those who reject ecology as a value simply ignore the demands of the pressure groups. Some respondents however are so incensed, by what they see as bullying by the pressure groups, that they reduce the expenditure on monksbane to punish those who would seek to bring pressure to bear.

Fairness

Fairness is concerned with impartiality between individuals. Fairness emphasises the importance of giving everyone equal access to services or at least an equal chance of access. This makes the use of arbitrary mechanisms for allocating scarce resources possible. Some managers, for example, when faced with too many job candidates, all of whom fit the employee specification, believe the only fair way of choosing the successful candidate is to draw lots. People who apply the fairness heuristic are interested in the standardisation and consistency of services to customers and clients. One of the clearest definitions of fairness, as it is defined here, can be found in a medieval Islamic story.

> A child and an adult both of the True Faith are in Heaven, but the adult occupies a higher place. God explains that the man has done many good works whereupon the child asks why God allowed him to die before he could do good. God answers that he knew the child would grow up to be a sinner and so it was better that he die young. A cry rises up from the depths of Hell: 'Why O Lord did you not let us die before we became sinners?'
>
> (Russell, 1985: 85)

The Lord was obviously working on an ad hoc basis; dealing with individuals as they appeared before him for judgement. For some reason this child was noticed and saved whilst many others were not, a lapse on God's part that those in hell naturally thought unfair. Fairness therefore must operate according to universally applied rules. Either all potential sinners die young or none.

Fairness is only concerned with equality of access and opportunity, not with equality of outcomes. In Section 5 of *Monksbane and feverfew* the table shows that if £10,000 is spent on feverfew and £60,000 on monksbane then 30 per cent of sufferers from feverfew and 30 per cent of sufferers from monksbane would be identified and treated. This would be fair because, irrespective of which disease a person had, their chances of treatment would be the same. This does not of course mean that they would all have the same chances of being made well. Some people favour the value of fairness but would not wish to impose it by dividing up the budget 10 : 60. Section 6 of *Monksbane and feverfew* therefore provides another option for applying the fairness heuristic. In this section you are given the opportunity to leave the allocation of resources between the two treatment programmes to chance. This is done by treating patients as they present themselves, irrespective of their diagnosis, and by stopping all treatments when the budget is spent. This alternative puts everyone in a queue and so everyone is dealt with in the same way – fairly.

Personal competence and gain

Personal gain and competence is a heuristic which, when applied to the allocation of resources, causes decisions to be made to the decision maker's benefit. The benefit can be of two different kinds. The first is the sense of worth and self-esteem that can come from having done a job properly. This implies that the decision has been made using appropriate methods and that no short cuts, which offend against the decision maker's beliefs, have been used. The second sense relates to personal advantage. In this sense the decision makers allocate resources in a way that brings some material or personal benefit to them – this may be an increase in organisational influence, professional satisfaction, something which eases the burden of daily life, cash or a bottle of whisky. Personal gain does not necessarily imply gain for the decision maker because they may value being able to help their friends or family, but it does imply that decisions are made according to private rather than public considerations.

In *Monksbane and feverfew* respondents are invited to respond to this value in Section 7. It suggests that someone very dear to the respondent is suffering from the disease that is being given the smaller amount of money. Clearly that person's chances of recovery would be better if more money were spent on the screening and treatment for that disease. If the respondent increases the money allocated to the disease of the person close to them they are using the personal gain value. A range of other factors could of course trigger this value. The person making the decision might, for example, have a research or clinical interest in the treatment of one of the two diseases. We do not necessarily think people will answer this part of the simulation honestly. We suspect people do not know how they would behave in such a situation until they are in it. However Section 7 does illustrate how this value could be used as a heuristic for making the decision.

Values as heuristics in *Monksbane and fewerfew*

We are suggesting that *Monksbane and feverfew* illustrates how values can operate heuristically in the way that people search for solutions to a priority-setting problem. Although it does not prove that people use values heuristically when making real-life decisions it does provide some interesting issues for you to think about.

When completing *Monksbane and feverfew* some people apply a range of values and change their minds as they work through the exercise. Some use only one. These people might, for example, adopt the utility value and decide in Section 1 to spend nothing on monksbane. They do not veer from this decision as they work through the simulation. In either case the use of a particular value causes them to look for some kinds of information and to ignore others. A person who has the deservingness value will look for and respond to information about people's moral failings. A person who favours the utility value will be much taken by the graph in Section 1 (Activity 4.1) that offers the prospect of the information necessary to calculate cost–benefit figures for the two diseases. Someone who favours individual need will tend to reject the information in Section 1 because it is 'just statistics' and provides no information about the needs of the people behind the statistics. Values act heuristically by allowing people to select the information they believe is important to making the decision. Once this has been done the process of making a decision is relatively straightforward. If someone accepts the ecology heuristic, and they know what the demands of the most powerful interest groups are, then they know immediately what has to be done to please those groups.

The complexity of *Monksbane and feverfew* arises from the fact that the application of different values leads to very different conclusions. Utility would lead to nothing being spent on monksbane. Individual need would lead to a large amount being spent on it. These kinds of dilemmas are of course very common in health management (*see* Case study 2.9). However, it is suggested that the six value heuristics identified in this chapter can be seen in any priority-setting or resource-allocation decision. They can be seen, for example, in decisions about the allocation of budget cuts or increases between departments, in deciding whom to make redundant in a round of downsizing and in decisions about responding to different market segments.

Integrity and loyalty as value heuristics

There are two other values that, it will be argued, play an important role as heuristics for deciding what to think, say or do in an ethical matter. They are integrity and loyalty. A commitment to either loyalty or integrity can act as a heuristic for deciding what should be done in a situation. The process may be complicated, however, by the extent of a person's ethical horizon, the breadth of the arena in which they wish to exercise their loyalty or integrity. This will also influence their decisions. All of these issues need to be explained in more detail.

Defining integrity and loyalty

Integrity is defined as basing action on sound judgement and seeking a unity or wholeness of thought and action. The medieval scholar Aquinas, after Aristotle, argued that the practice of virtue requires people to act knowingly, voluntarily and according to a fixed principle or habit (D'Entreves, 1965: 147–8). Winstanley and Woodall reflected these ideas when they argued that

> The development of integrity [is] based upon ethical judgement and a sense of responsibility, the development of appropriate virtues.
>
> (Winstanley and Woodall, 2000: 285)

Integrity therefore is defined by its possessor's self-reflection and awareness. As C.P. Snow, quoted by Adair (1980: 171), epigrammatically expressed it:

> Give me a man who knows something of himself and is appalled.

A sense of self-doubt, as well as the tension between integrity and loyalty, can be illustrated by an account of an incident given during a research interview we conducted. The interviewee was a senior manager. His company required all managers to attend a series of development workshops that were designed to apply the precepts of an eastern mystical tradition to modern management practice. The respondent was a man of strong Christian belief who believed the philosophy of the seminars was contrary to his Christian principles. He felt that he should not in conscience attend the seminars. He was aware that taking this stance to maintain his integrity was at odds with his sense of loyalty. His loyalty was not particularly directed at the company but was focused on the rest of the management team who would be going to the seminars. The other team members told him that they thought him an important team member and they wished him to attend the seminars. The respondent reported that the issue caused him to think deeply about his beliefs and his responsibilities to others. His final position on the issue spoke of a self-conscious attempt to meet the demands of both integrity and loyalty. He attended the seminars but made a personal statement at the commencement in which he stated his personal objections to the values that informed them.

In contrast to integrity loyalty is an unthinking faithfulness to a person, group or purpose. If a loyal person were to reflect on their actions they would have to question whether they were being loyal to the right thing. As Snell (1993: 82) characterised it, loyalty can range between a high commitment, analogous to a marriage, and a low level, which requires only the performance of actions contractually agreed. In a situation where high loyalty is demanded, but there is no opportunity for developmental openness (which would allow an individual to develop their own values and ethical reasoning),

> Unquestioning conformity is expected of members: one must suppress individuality, ignore one's own arguments and perspectives and accept what one has to do.
>
> (Snell, 1993: 82)

The unreflective nature of loyalty can be illustrated by another account of an ethical issue given by a manager in a finance department. When he moved to a new job he asked a colleague with whom he had previously worked to move with him and to support him in his new role. The manager was aware that the colleague was a discharged bankrupt who had invested unwisely when he had worked in the City. The financial accountant, who also reported to the manager, warned him of suspicions about the colleague's use of the credit card that the company had given him for business expenses.

> I had to take a view whether to expose him or to bring him to account, make him pay it back, and to carry on . . . Either to keep it to myself and the financial accountant, or to let other people know. I think there was enough going on that could have cost him his job: and I chose the latter. I had known him for a number of years, he was an extremely hard working individual, played hard as well, and played hard sometimes in my time. But if someone is working for me I take a balanced view. I don't expect them to work like an automaton . . . He was always getting phone calls at home in the early hours of the morning from the department, 'can't do this and can't do that', and he solved it . . . he was also being hounded by the CSA [Child Support Agency] so he wasn't having an easy time. All this encouraged me to take a lenient view. I also knew of his background and he was probably finding life a bit tough.

The colleague had spent £600 improperly using the credit card. The manager challenged him privately and, instead of starting disciplinary proceedings, made him pay the sum back within two weeks. The manager's loyalty towards the employee was at a cost to his honesty and integrity. He thought the colleague reciprocated the feeling of loyalty:

> I believed that he, I felt that as he was working for me he would behave himself and he would not wish to implicate me. I thought I was entitled to more consideration than somebody he didn't know.

However within a short space of time the colleague had found himself a new, better-paid, job with a different company and in his last few weeks of his old employment he again misused his credit card.

> And so I felt as if I had paid my dues . . . I had no loyalty to him then once he had done it twice . . . On many occasions I have gone back and questioned my initial judgement. I find it quite difficult to think of abstract examples and decide what I would do, *because most things are instinct*. I am nearly forty-six years of age and so I have had a fair amount of experience; I am not sure I would do the same thing again.
>
> (Research interview: our emphasis)

Loyalty, in this account, is seen as a matter of instinct and experience and not as a matter of self-reflection. The instinctive wish to act loyally can easily be destroyed, as here, by an act of betrayal by the person to whom loyalty is given.

■ Ethical horizons

People in organisations may experience conflicts of loyalties. There may be situations, concerning whistleblowing for example (De George, 1999: 248, 412–16), in which they have to choose between being loyal to the organisation, to a professional body, to society at large or to themselves and their families. Less obviously conflicts may also emerge within the sphere of integrity. The issue is well illustrated by a conversation imagined by Watson (1998: 266).

> *David*: Alright for the sake of argument, imagine we set up a business to murder people.
>
> *Colin*: Murder Incorporated.
>
> *David*: OK; it's been done. But say we did this and we followed all the culture and empowerment stuff. We could have democratic management, lots of trust and all that. There's good pay for everybody, welfare arrangements, good pensions, and Christmas parties for the kiddies. There's a moral code – just like the Mafia – that holds everything together. Everything we have said so far makes this a moral business. But it is not. Murder isn't moral is it?

Legge expressed the dilemma, raised by this thought experiment, in a more formal way when discussing human resource management (HRM):

> If capitalism is, or has the potential to be viewed as ethical, then HRM similarly has a good chance. If not, it is difficult to imagine how an ethical system for managing people at work can emerge from an essentially unethical economic order.
>
> (Legge, 1998: 166)

Table 4.3 The ethical horizons of loyalty and integrity

The limits of loyalty

The limits of loyalty concerns the breadth of the unit to which a person gives their loyalty. Four levels are identified.

1   Loyalty to self, family. This horizon may be represented by the alleged judgement on many East End gangsters that they were essentially good because they 'were good to their mothers'.

2   Loyalty to the groups and associations a person has chosen to belong to (civil society). This is perhaps exemplified by E.M. Forster's (1975) remark, 'If I had to choose between betraying my country and betraying my friend, I hope I should have the guts to betray my country'.

3   Loyalty to the employing organisation. As the Civil Service code of ethics states, 'Civil servants owe their loyalty to the duly constituted government' (Cabinet Office, n.d.).

4   Loyalty to society at large.

The limits of integrity

The limits of integrity concerns the breadth of the arena in which a person seeks to achieve a unity of their thoughts and actions. Four levels are identified.

1   The personal and private arena.

2   The personal and public arena of associations and networks (civil society).

3   The corporate and organisational arena within which a person is employed.

4   The arena of the wider society, polity and economy.

The dilemmas in the quotations hinge on the question of ethical horizons. A person's assessment of whether the situations in the two quotations given above represent integrity and morality depends on their choice of ethical horizon. The broader the horizon the less likely is a person to see the situations as showing integrity. If their horizon is local, focused within the organisation, then the more likely they are to represent these situations as ones showing morality and integrity. It is argued therefore that perceptions of loyalty and integrity, and the actions that each demands, are affected by the extent of the subject's ethical horizon. A simplified analysis of the range of ethical horizons is shown in Table 4.3.

A preference for either loyalty or integrity, together with a preference for an ethical horizon, can be used to identify someone's likely actions when they find themselves embroiled in an ethical question such as what to do when one's organisation is discovered to be behaving badly. The options are shown in Table 4.4.

The first level in the hierarchy of ethical horizons in Table 4.4 is the broadest one and encompasses a concern for the well-being of society as a whole. At this level people see themselves as parts of the whole, as flakes of rock chipped from the mountain. It is more difficult to say how society might view its members because society has no single view or form of expression. The diversity of society makes it difficult for its members to believe that society could see them as anything more than a small part of the whole. Such a sense of personal inconsequence, yet commitment to society, creates a willingness to sacrifice the self for the greater good. The difference between loyalty and integrity is the amount of personal loss the whistleblower is prepared to risk for the good of society at large. Loyalty to society requires the subject to blow the whistle on the organisation's wrongdoing, but anonymously and secretly. Integrity requires the whistleblower to take a public stand. The loyalist sacrifices openness to minimise loss and

Table 4.4 An analysis of the actions open to an employee, when they discover wrongdoing by their organisation, according to the levels of ethical horizons

Ethical horizon	Loyalty	Integrity
Society	*Sacrifice of self for other's benefit*	
	■ Anonymous whistleblowing	■ Public whistleblowing
Civil associations	*Sacrifice to show membership and commitment*	
	■ Lying to protect the group ■ The group members agree to maintain silence to protect the group	■ The group collectively offer to help management find a way to make things right ■ The group collectively blows the whistle on the organisation – a form of collective civil disobedience
Organisations	*Acting as a scapegoat*	
	■ Offering to keep silent ■ Cover up the wrongdoing	■ Trying to persuade the organisation to reveal its wrongdoing and to put things right
Self	*Sacrifice to maintain or increase personal benefit or status*	
	■ Seek personal advantage from the situation ■ Protect self by lying ■ Protect self by telling lies about others	■ Keeping silent – inaction is believed not to damage integrity ■ Resigning when the organisation will not take the right action ■ Refusing to be bought off by the organisation

retribution; the person exercising integrity does not. The degree of risk also depends on people's circumstances. Some public whistleblowers are at less risk by taking a public stand because they have no dependents and may not be reliant on their salary from their employer.

At the ethical horizon of civil association there is an imbalance in the relationship between a member of a civil group and the group itself. Members of such groups see themselves as a mere part of the associations they belong to; but the associations see them as a metaphor for the whole. Each member stands for the whole group. This can be illustrated by popular attitudes about teamwork. Team members can only see themselves as a part of the whole team. As in Belbin's (1981) analysis of teams the individual team member is less than the whole because they cannot fulfil all roles necessary for effective team functioning. In contrast a team, it is often argued, is only effective because the team subsumes the members in a team unity and sees them as metaphors for itself. These perceptions lead people to wish to protect the group, which values them so highly, whilst minimising the threat to themselves by acting as part of a larger, supportive whole. Loyalty to a civil association, in the scenario, is represented by the subject encouraging the group to protect itself by keeping silent about the organisation's wrongdoing. This has the advantage, to the member who sees their link with the association as only partial, of saving them from an obligation to sacrifice themselves for the group's integrity. The group jointly blowing the whistle on the wrongdoing, on the other hand, represents integrity. This collective responsibility protects the individuals within the group.

The next level in the hierarchy of ethical horizons is the organisation. If employees set their focus on this horizon they believe themselves to be at one with the wider organisation, but the organisation does not reciprocate; it sees them as mere cogs in something bigger. When, out of integrity, an employee seeks to persuade the organisation to do the right thing they are assuming a unity, a metaphorical relationship between themselves and the organisation. But the organisation in this case may see the employee as an irritating and replaceable component. There is a danger that the employee in this situation, by raising their head above the parapet of organisational bad behaviour, will be made into a scapegoat by the organisation and dismissed or by other means punished. Loyalty, at this level of ethical focus, is expressed by the employee offering, because they assume an affinity with the organisation, to protect the organisation by covering up its wrongdoing. The organisation, however, may still feel threatened by such help; the employee may, after all, decide the organisation has done wrong and blow the whistle on both the original wrongdoing and the subsequent cover-up. This fear may cause the organisation to punish the employee even though the employee has shown loyalty (Fisher, 2000a). Within the ethical horizon of the organisation the employee becomes a scapegoat for the wrongs of the organisation. In the biblical origin of the term the scapegoat is not killed but is allowed to escape into the wilderness. This is an appropriate image for the ways in which modern organisations 'let go' those who carry the taint of organisations' bad behaviour.

When the ethical horizon does not extend beyond the self the focus of actions will be on the protection and improvement of the self's position. Protecting the self's integrity can be achieved in two ways. The first involves drawing the ethical horizon so tightly around the self that any wrong action is kept beyond it. In plainer terms the subject claims or feigns ignorance of the wrongdoing. This approach to integrity has similarities with the concepts of ethical closure and ethical bracketing (Jackall, 1988; Kärreman and Alvesson, 1999). If the situation makes this stance untenable then people can maintain their integrity, not by attempting to put things right, but by removing themselves, by resigning from the organisation. When a person acts with integrity, by resigning from an organisation that they cannot prevent from behaving unethically, they sacrifice their material well-being, their job and their salary, to protect their ethical well-being.

Loyalty to the self involves sacrificing integrity for material benefits. In the scenario described in Activity 4.2 it is represented by using knowledge of the organisation's wrongdoing to gain advantages for the self. The subject believes their integrity justifies self-seeking behaviour; and that the self-seeking legitimates their integrity.

In summary, what has been argued is that a preference for integrity or loyalty and a preference for a particular ethical horizon can act in a heuristic manner. The combination of the two values leaves a person with a restricted range of actions to choose from. The values act as a heuristic for closing down and restricting search behaviour and so make coming to a conclusion easier. As has been pointed out earlier the problem for the person facing the situation is to decide what values to apply. Integrity and loyalty are commonplaces in western society; both are regarded as good things. Each of the ethical horizons is valued in society. How then does a person choose between them? You can see which values you favour, at least under simulated conditions, by completing Activity 4.2.

Dilemma: A diagnostic inventory of managers' ethical horizons

Instructions

This inventory is in the form of an action maze. You take the part of a manager and you have to make decisions about how to react to a problem at work. You start the inventory with Section 1. In each section the situation you are facing is explained and a range of possible actions that you can take is presented. *Tick the option that is closest to the one you would take in the circumstances.* Then go to the next section as indicated. When you have finished the inventory please complete the scoring sheet.

Section 1

You are a middle-ranking manager in an organisation. You report to a board level manager and your responsibilities include managing the budgets of several operational areas. As part of your personal development you attended a seminar on tax and VAT liability. You realise from what you learned at the seminar that a practice that had been going on for years in the organisation was liable for VAT but had never been declared for VAT purposes. You have quietly and anonymously checked out your suspicions and confirmed their truth. You do not know whether the undeclared liability is the result of ignorance or an oversight, or whether it is a deliberate attempt to reduce the tax bill. However the amount of unpaid tax is large.

Which of the following actions would you take? Tick the option you choose.

Option	Action	Go to
1 ☐	Keep quiet and say nothing to anybody.	Section 2
2 ☐	Inform senior management about the situation and try to convince them that the situation should be disclosed to the tax authorities.	Section 3
3 ☐	You send a signed letter to the tax authorities informing them of the undeclared liability; and you send a copy with an explanatory covering letter to senior management.	Section 4
4 ☐	You have an informal discussion with the senior managers in which you let them know that you know about the tax liability. You keep them wondering about whether you will report the matter to the tax authorities whilst assuring them of your commitment to achieving success in the organisation.	Section 5
5 ☐	You report the tax liability anonymously and secretly to the tax authorities.	Section 6
6 ☐	You tell senior management about the tax liability and offer your help in keeping the matter quiet.	Section 3

Activity 4.2 continued

Section 2

You are a member of a professional development group. This is a private association of people with an interest in their own professional development, and with improving the public's perception of the profession's integrity. The group was formed when the original members were on a postgraduate management course together. It so happens that many of the group members also work for the same organisation as you do. All members of the group have agreed that its discussions should be kept confidential unless they agree otherwise.

You are attending one of the group's regular six-weekly meetings. As the meeting is coming to an end, under 'any other business', a couple of members say that they have discovered that the organisation has not been declaring its VAT liability for one of its activities. The group is concerned about the organisation's apparent lack of integrity; although they realise that the financial consequences for the organisation of declaring the liability would be heavy. You have good relationships with the group and you are very committed to it. The group ask you for your advice about what to do because of your important role in the organisation.

Which of the following actions would you take? Tick the option you choose.

Option	Action	Go to
1	Tell them to keep quiet about the matter because the organisation can be hard with people, insiders or outsiders, who stir up trouble.	Section 14
2	Inform senior management, on behalf of the group and yourself, of the tax liability issue and try to convince them that the situation should be disclosed to the tax authorities.	Section 3
3	Tell the group to keep quiet about the matter and that you will tell senior management and try to convince them that the situation should be disclosed to the tax authorities. When you have the opportunity you do what you told the group you would do.	Section 3
4	Tell the group to keep quiet. Without telling the group what you are going to do you tell the senior managers about the situation and offer your help in keeping the matter quiet.	Section 3

Activity 4.2 continued

Section 3

You are called to a meeting with the senior management team. The subject of the meeting is the undeclared tax liability. The senior managers tell you that they have decided to stop the activity that caused the tax liability and not to reveal the past liability to the tax authorities. They call upon your loyalty to the organisation, and your obedience as an employee, to support this decision. They ask you to sign a memorandum that disguises the existence of the tax liability.

Which of the following actions would you take? Tick the option you choose. NB. You may visit this section more than once.

Option	Action	Go to
1	Disagree with the senior managers and continue to argue that the organisation should be honest with the tax authorities.	Section 8 (if you tick this box a third time then go to the Scoring Grid on p. 141)
2	You disagree with what the senior managers have decided and after further fruitless discussions with them you offer your resignation.	Section 9
3	You agree with the senior managers and sign the memorandum.	Section 13
4	You hedge a little and point out that you might consider it your duty to inform the tax authorities. You also hint that it might be easier to sign the memorandum if you were certain that your long-term prospects in the organisation were good.	Section 5
5	You tell the senior managers that you cannot agree with their decision. You send a signed letter to the tax authorities informing them of the undeclared liability; and you send a copy with an explanatory covering letter to senior management.	Section 4
6	You play for time in the meeting. As soon as it ends you report the tax liability anonymously and secretly to the tax authorities.	Section 6

Activity 4.2 continued

Section 4

The senior managers meet with you and point out that because they no longer have faith in your commitment to the organisation they wish to end your employment contract with the organisation. They are willing to compensate you for breaking the contract. If you agree to accept the compensation it will avoid the necessity for the disciplinary action they would otherwise have to take against you for breaking your duty of confidentiality to the organisation. However the compensation would be dependent upon your signing a gagging clause, which would prevent you from discussing the organisation's business with any third party.

Which of the following actions would you take? Tick the option you choose.

Option	Action	Go to
1 ☐	Refuse to accept the deal on offer.	Section 10
2 ☐	Accept the deal on offer.	Section 11

Section 5

The senior managers decide to call your bluff on the implied threats you have been making. They demand that you commit to maintaining silence about the tax liability. They insist you sign a memorandum that disguises the existence of the tax liability.

Which of the following actions would you take? Tick the option you choose.

Option	Action	Go to
1 ☐	You agree to keep silence and you sign the memorandum.	Section 13
2 ☐	You cannot agree to the cover-up and you give your resignation.	Section 9
3 ☐	You play for time in the meeting. As soon as it ends you report the tax liability anonymously and secretly to the tax authorities.	Section 6
4 ☐	You tell the senior managers that you cannot agree with their decision. You send a signed letter to the tax authorities informing them of the undeclared liability; and you send a copy with an explanatory covering letter to senior management.	Section 4

Activity 4.2 continued

Section 6

The tax authorities have been asking senior management some difficult questions about the undeclared tax liability. It is clear to senior management that someone must have tipped off the authorities. Senior management confront you and accuse you of being the source of the leak.

Which of the following actions would you take? Tick the option you choose.

Option	Action	Go to
1 ☐	Admit that you informed the tax authorities and offer your resignation.	Section 12
2 ☐	Admit that you informed the tax authorities. You do not offer to resign because, as you argue to the senior managers, you were only doing the right thing when faced with the organisation's unethical and illegal position.	Section 10
3 ☐	Deny that you were the source of the leak.	Section 4
4 ☐	Admit you were the source of the leak. Admit that you were wrong to inform the tax authorities and offer to write a letter to them withdrawing the accusation and claiming it was the result of a misunderstanding.	Section 10

Section 7

You have the prospect of a successful career in the organisation. You anticipate rapid promotion.

End of exercise. Go to the scoring sheet on p. 141.

Section 8

You have had a meeting with senior managers and you have made your best effort to convince them that the organisation should do the honest thing and disclose the past tax liability to the authorities. However, your argument, that the tax liability on the particular activity that is causing the difficulty is an obvious anomaly and that the regulations will be changed as soon as the tax authorities are aware of it, does not suit the cynical mood of the senior managers.

Go to Section 3.

Activity 4.2 continued

Section 9

As you know, you are a member of a professional development group. This is a private association of people with an interest in their own professional development, and with improving the public's perception of the profession's integrity. The group was formed when the original members were on a postgraduate management course together. All members of the group have agreed that its discussions should be kept confidential unless they agree otherwise.

The group know about the undeclared tax liability. This is not surprising as many of the group, as well as you, work in the organisation. They also know that you have resigned over the issue rather than take action to put the situation right. They argue with you that the situation is wrong. They believe that the ethical thing to do is to declare the tax liability to the tax authorities. They believe that, in the period of notice before you leave the organisation, you may be able to help them put the situation right.

Which of the following actions would you take? Tick the option you choose.

Option	Action	Go to
1 ☐	Tell them to keep quiet about the matter because the organisation can be hard with people (insiders or outsiders) who stir up trouble.	Section 12
2 ☐	Support the group in their decision to inform the tax authorities of the tax liability. You agree to sign the letter to the tax authorities along with the rest of the group.	Section 12
3 ☐	Tell the group to keep quiet, and protect their own careers, and that you will send a signed letter to the tax authorities informing them of the undeclared liability; and you will also send a copy, with an explanatory covering letter, to senior management.	Section 12
4 ☐	Tell the group to keep quiet but agree to inform the tax authorities anonymously of the tax issue.	Section 12

Section 10

A few months later you receive notification that you are being made redundant from the organisation. This appears to be part of a general de-layering process designed to reduce the organisation's costs.

Go to Section 12.

Activity 4.2 continued

Section 11

You have been looking for a new job. It is difficult to get interviews for new jobs that are at the same level as your old one. You do wonder whether your old employer has put the word around on the grapevine that you are not a loyal employee. At least you have the substantial pay-off from your old job to keep you going and you are not yet in major financial difficulties.

End of exercise. Go to the scoring sheet on p. 141.

Section 12

You have been looking for a new job. It is difficult to get interviews for new jobs that are at the same level as your old one. You do wonder whether your old employer has put the word around on the grapevine that you are not a loyal employee. Your financial situation is beginning to look desperate.

End of exercise. Go to the scoring sheet on p. 141.

Section 13

As you know, you are a member of a professional development group. This is a private association of people with an interest in their own professional development, and with improving the public's perception of the profession's integrity. The group was formed when the original members were on a postgraduate management course together. All members of the group have agreed that its discussions should be kept confidential unless they agree otherwise.

The group, as you may be aware, know about the undeclared tax liability. You are not the only group member to work for the organisation. The group also know that you have worked with senior management to keep the matter quiet. They argue with you that the situation is wrong. They cannot believe that you are going along with the cover-up. 'We thought you were better than that', they say. They believe that the ethical thing to do is to declare the tax liability to the tax authorities. They believe that you may be able to help them work towards a more honest outcome.

Which of the following actions would you take? Tick the option you choose.

Option	Action	Go to
1 ☐	Tell them to keep quiet about the matter because the organisation can be hard with people (insiders or outsiders) who stir up trouble.	Section 7
2 ☐	Support the group in their decision to inform the tax authorities of the tax liability. You agree to sign the letter to the tax authorities along with the rest of the group.	Section 10
3 ☐	Tell the group to keep quiet, and protect their own careers. You, however, undertake to send a signed letter to the tax authorities informing them of the undeclared liability; and also to send a copy, with an explanatory covering letter, to senior management.	Section 10
4 ☐	Tell the team to keep quiet but agree to inform the tax authorities anonymously of the tax issue.	Section 6

Activity 4.2 continued

Section 14

The tax authorities have been asking senior management some difficult questions about the undeclared tax liability. It is clear to senior management that someone must have tipped off the authorities. The senior managers have come to the conclusion that the professional development group, of which you are a member, must be the source of the leak. Senior managers know that several of their key staff are a members of the group and they are suspicious that membership may conflict with their obligations to the organisation.

The senior managers invite you to a meeting. They tell you about the tax liability problem and that the tax authorities are suspicious. They know you are a member of the group and they ask you to confirm their suspicion that the group is the source of the leak.

Which of the following actions would you take? Tick the option you choose.

Option	Action	Go to
1 ☐	Deny that the group is the source of the leak and claim that, to the best of your knowledge, the group is not aware of the situation.	Section 3
2 ☐	You agree that the group must be the source of the leak.	Section 3
3 ☐	You agree that the group must be the source of the leak. You also offer to help senior management to cover up the problem and you sign a memorandum that disguises the existence of the liability.	Section 7
4 ☐	You say that you do not know how the tax authorities became aware of the possible tax problem; but you are pleased that it is in the open and you recommend that senior managers are open with the tax authorities and negotiate with them to overcome the problem. You point out that the tax liability on the particular activity that is causing the difficulty is an obvious anomaly and that the regulations will be changed as soon as the tax authorities are aware of it.	Section 6
5 ☐	You point out that the discussions of the development group are confidential. The group could not function if it were otherwise. Therefore you are not able to make any comment on the group and its actions.	Section 3
6 ☐	You point out that you cannot discuss the business of the group because of its rule of confidentiality. However you offer to discuss the issue with the group and encourage them to enter into dialogue with the organisation.	Section 3

Activity 4.2 continued

Scoring grid

Instructions

Tick, in the second column of the grid below, those sections of the inventory that you completed. Transfer your decisions from each of the sections you completed by circling the option number of the action you took. If, for example, you took option 2 in Section 3 then circle the number 2 in the sixth column in the second row of the scoring grid. When you have finished this task for all the sections you completed (remembering that you may have visited some sections more than once) add up the number of circles in each column and write them in the 'Total' row.

Section	√if done	L1	In1	L2	In2	L3	In3	L4	In4
1		5	3			6	2	4	1
2				1	2	4	3		
3		6	5			3	1	4	2
4								2	1
5		3	4			1			2
6						4	2	3	1
9		4	3	1	2				
13		4	3	1	2				
14				1	6	3	4	2	5
Totals (row A)									
% of total responses (row B)									

Transfer the figures from row B on to the chart that follows.

Activity 4.2 continued

Interpreting the results

Transfer your scores from the scoring grid into chart below.

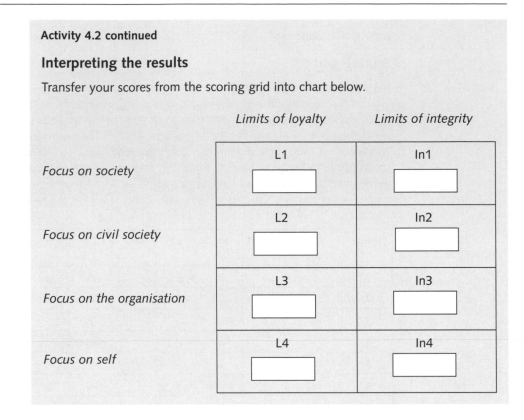

Discussion of the dilemma simulation in Activity 4.2

The exercise you have just done has been tested on a sample of undergraduate business students. Studying the sequence of choices they made as they worked their ways through the action maze can identify their ethical horizons. In the first section of the maze just over half of the respondents chose integrity in the organisational arena and tried to convince the management to admit the tax liability and to regularise the situation. Nearly 30 per cent continued with this position when the management at first refused to concede. A small percentage of respondents (5.8 per cent) found themselves in a closed loop, by continuing to suggest, despite the management's intransigence, that the tax liability should be admitted. But most of the respondents, when rebuffed by the management, chose integrity at the level of self and resigned from the organisation. Twenty-five of the 30 respondents who chose resignation subsequently took a position of integrity at the civil association horizon, by whistleblowing on the organisation, when urged by their professional peers to do so. The most common route through the maze took, at every opportunity, a path of integrity rather than loyalty, but the ethical horizon changed as circumstances changed. Practising managers may not share undergraduates' commitment to integrity.

A minority of respondents took the route of loyalty but changed the focus of their loyalty. Nineteen per cent of the respondents initially opted for loyalty to self, by using their knowledge of the tax liability to gain advantage for themselves. But in Section 5 of the maze most of those who had chosen loyalty to self changed their focus to loyalty to the organisation as they helped in the cover-up.

People's commitments to the sometimes competing demands of loyalty and integrity illustrate the importance of values as heuristics in decision making on ethical questions. The issue of whistleblowing, raised in Activity 4.2, is explored more fully in Chapter 6.

Reflections

Many textbooks on business ethics have relatively little to say about values. When they are discussed it is in the context of corporate codes of ethics or statements of organisational core values. The materials and arguments put forward in this chapter suggest that values may be central to people's thought processes when they are deciding what to say or do in response to an ethical issue. There is a paradox however. Values can be used heuristically to *simplify* the process of making up one's mind; but the problem of which particular value to apply to an issue, when there are many values within organisations and society, all of which are valued but which conflict with one another, is *complex*.

The account of values as heuristics in this chapter may provide a good description of how people make decisions on ethical issues. This does not imply that this is how such decisions should be made. Indeed, if heuristics are more a matter of habit than conscious thought they may merely be ways of avoiding complex value and ethical choices. Choices involve thinking about what we ought to do, not recalling what we normally do. In the next chapter we will explore these tensions between taking habitual stances on ethical issues, bred from our upbringing and experiences, and having to knowingly challenge our habits because the ethical matters we face contain novel circumstances or inconvenient facts.

Summary

In this chapter the following key points have been made:

- Rational and analytic theories explain how decision making ought to be done.
- Heuristic theories probably explain how people make decisions in practice.
- Research into heuristics used to see them as sources of bias and distortion; the fast and frugal research programme sees them as efficient and effective procedures for decision making.
- Values probably act in a heuristic manner in decision making about ethical matters.
- Values can be used to limit and stop decision makers' searches for further information and options.
- In decisions such as setting priorities and deciding how to respond to wrongdoing in an organisation the problem is to choose which of many mutually exclusive values should be applied.

Suggested further reading

If you are interested in the role of heuristics in decision making see G. Gigernzer, P.M. Todd, and the ABC Research Group (1999) *Simple Heuristics That Make us Smart*. Oxford: Oxford University Press. On the topic of the role of values in management see P. Griseri (1998) *Managing Values*, London: Palgrave.

GROUP ACTIVITY 4

Obtain a copy of the *Cave Rescue Exercise*, which can be found in Woodcock (1979, 1989: 81) and in the appendix to Fisher (1998). Another version of this exercise can be found in Francis and Young (1979). Both are variations on a classic management game theme, of which *The Kidney Machine* is another popular version (Jones and Pfeiffer (1974)).

Divide into groups of between six and ten people and do the exercise.

5 Individuals' responses to ethical issues

OBJECTIVES

Having completed this chapter and its associated activities, readers should be able to:

■ Explain the different ways in which people may respond to ethical issues at work.

■ Use this understanding to think about their own reactions to ethical issues.

■ Explain the processes of categorisation and particularisation in ethical thinking.

■ Explain the range of factors that influence how people respond to ethical issues at work.

Introduction

This chapter concerns people's responses to ethical issues at work. The previous chapter dealt only with ethical thinking. Responses to ethical situations obviously involve thinking about the issue but also go beyond it. Responses include what people say, how they say it and how they behave. There are two main cognitive processes involved in choosing responses, categorisation and particularisation (Billig, 1996). The first of these involves putting an issue into a box or category and saying, 'That is the way in which I will deal with this matter'. These categories are often based on values. Someone might decide, for example, that an issue is a matter of following the core values set by an organisation; or that an issue is a question of loyalty. However the particulars of a situation might make someone think that the categorisation is not right. It is the details of a situation that make people debate which value an issue should be categorised under or indeed whether it should be put in a separate category of its own.

The first part of the chapter describes and explains different categories of ethical response. Later the chapter explores the possibility that people do not adopt a single categorisation but debate with themselves and with others about a range of competing possible categorisations. The exercise in Activity 5.1 also raises the possibility that people's categorisations may change over time as they become aware of new information and different perspectives on the issue. The third section of the chapter discusses the range of factors that may influence how someone chooses to categorise an issue. The final section summarises the arguments of the chapter and gives the reader opportunities to reflect upon them.

Categories of response to ethical issues

In this section we will use a matrix to describe the categories, let us call them stances, people at work may use to classify ethical issues. The model is shown in Figure 5.1. Before the eight categories it contains can be described we will explain the two dimensions that form the matrix.

■ Ethical integrity, the horizontal axis in Figure 5.1

The dimension of ethical integrity will be described first. The position at the extreme left of the horizontal axis in Figure 5.1 represents clarity and certainty about values. A person at this point on the scale sees moral issues in a straightforward way, which helps them to know what should be done in a situation or how an issue should be analysed and resolved. A person at the extreme right of the dimension, however, is more likely to be confused or even aporetic (this term is defined in Chapter 1, p. 20). A person in this condition will find the plurality of views on an issue difficult to reconcile and they will often change their minds. If integrity is defined as the congruence, or fit, between a person's thoughts on an issue then the left-hand column in Figure 5.1 represents a high degree of integrity and the right-hand column a low degree of integrity.

■ The dialectic of ethical purpose, the vertical axis in Figure 5.1

The vertical dimension represents stages in the dialectical development of a personal and conscious view of right and wrong. It models a developing personal responsibility for recognising the presence of ethical issues at work and addressing them. In the initial stage, at the origin of the framework – self-consciousness – a person sees their moral universe as a personal one. They accept responsibility for themselves but wish to remain apart from ethical issues in the wider world. They show this unwillingness to accept a moral responsibility by turning a blind eye. But an individual's moral isolation is an ideal; it cannot be sustained, it is contradicted by the clamorous demands from others, bosses, colleagues, customers and so on, that they become involved.

Definition

The *dialectic* is a method of analysis (associated with the German philosopher Hegel (1770–1831)) in which an initial, formal concept (thesis) is challenged by practical contradictions contained within it (antithesis) until a synthesis comes about that overcomes, or transcends, the tensions between thesis and antithesis. The thesis is a blank ideal because it has not been expressed in reality. It is when it confronts social reality that the messy detail of life negates the formal ideal. The synthesis negates this negation and the dialectic moves to a new, positive stage. The synthesis does not abolish the tensions but moves beyond them. The synthesis becomes a thesis and the cycle begins again.

The contradiction at the self-consciousness stage is between a person's sense of their own moral worth and their defensive refusal to take a moral stand on ethical issues. Ethical duty is the synthesis of this contradiction. People at this stage take a stand and, without much critical reflection, do what their backgrounds and their consciences tell them is their duty. However doing one's duty can lead to an awareness that others have contrary conceptions of what their duty is.

> Unreflective duty can take its imperatives from the dooms of Zeus, from priest or parent, from the custom of a tribe or city, and act in peace and faith. But the first conflict unveils an Antigone and the question 'Whose standard?' soon brings down all standards.
>
> (Mabbott, 1967: 44)

Antigone, in Greek myth, followed her conscience by giving a ritual burial, against custom and the decree of King Creon, to her brother Polyneices who had tried to usurp the throne. The formal idea of doing one's duty is undermined by uncertainty about what that duty is in any particular circumstance. This tension causes this stage to be expressed either as sincerely, but uncritically, held principle or its opposite – cynicism.

The lack of grounding, or legitimisation, of the idea of duty leads to the next stage in the dialectic, which is the search for the common good as a basis for moral certainty. In this phase people try to reconcile competing ethical demands by using such notions as organisational values and mission statements, economic utility or the public interest. This stage involves difficult debates about values and priorities. Consequently attempts to create a consensus or a common ethical convention constantly threaten to dissolve into ethical plurality and dilemmas.

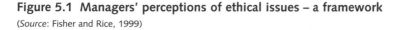

		Personal certainty, fixed priorities and values	Personal aporia, shifting priorities and values
Dialectic of ethical purpose	*Developing principles*	Ethical puzzle	Ethical problem
	Achieving the common good	Ethical convention	Ethical dilemma
	The obligation of duty	Ethical awareness	Ethical cynicism and caprice
	Self-consciousness	Ethical neutrality	Ethical negotiation

Degree of ethical integrity

Figure 5.1 Managers' perceptions of ethical issues – a framework
(*Source*: Fisher and Rice, 1999)

When, and if, attempts at consensus building stumble or fail a person may move into the final phase of the vertical dimension. In this phase, through self-analysis and debate, people create their own set of moral precepts and values. At this level on the dimension people are aware of the plurality and fragmentation of the moral world and make choices about how to respond to it. They may either take a postmodern route, and learn to live with an ungrounded moral plurality, by playing with problems, or they may seek to re-integrate the fragments by reason and categorisation, as if they were doing a jigsaw puzzle.

Now that the dimensions in Figure 5.1 have been described the eight categories of ethical issue can be defined in relation to them. The categories are important because they define the range of possible reactions to a moral issue.

■ The ethical categories

Ethical neutrality

People put ethical issues into the category of ethical neutrality when they argue that nothing should be done about an issue that troubles them. There may be many reasons for this response. People may have applied ethical bracketing (Jackall, 1988) or ethical closure (Kärreman and Alvesson, 1999: 10–11). This causes them to suspend their normal ethical standards when they would obstruct them in getting the job done. This may lead people to argue that an issue, such as redundancy for example, has no moral dimension and should be seen as a practical question. De George (1999: 112) identified the range of excusing conditions people may use to justify their neutrality. These included the arguments of inability (you cannot be expected to save a drowning person if you cannot swim) and ignorance (you cannot be culpable if you were unaware of the consequences of not taking action).

Ethical awareness

Ethical awareness is a category of ethical responses that causes a person to feel uncomfortable because an issue offends against their instinctively held values. At this stage the individual has an intuitive knowledge of what their duty is. As Mabbott (1967: 45) argued,

> everyone knows what in any particular set of circumstances his duty is . . . I know my duty in each particular case and that I can give no reasons, nor are there any, why I should assert this act or that to be my duty, except the self-evidence of every particular instance.

In the stage of duty a person knows what is right but cannot say why. Their reaction to an issue may only involve making their feelings known but it may extend to active opposition to the proposal under consideration. Ethical awareness is the same as emotivism, which is discussed in Chapter 2. A feature of emotivism, which is important in the context of ethical awareness, is the apparent irresolubility of moral disagreements as one person's statements of their values, in relation to an action, person or situation, contradicts others' value statements.

Ethical convention

An issue is allocated to the category of ethical convention when it is thought that it can best be resolved by applying accepted norms to it. They may be social norms, the expectations and standards of professional behaviour or the constraints of organisational cultures and sub-cultures. A feature of conventional ethical norms is that they are informal and unwritten or, if they are written, they are expressed in general terms and not as detailed prescriptions. In one incident that was described to us the respondent, a personnel manager, believed there was a norm in her organisation that one should not turn against people who had come looking for professional advice and assistance. She consequently felt a little guilt when she suspended a manager who had initially come to seek her help in disciplining a member of his staff, but who was later ensnared in the investigations he had initiated.

Ethical puzzle

A puzzle is a conundrum, such as a mathematical teaser or a crossword puzzle, to which there is a technically correct or best answer. Arriving at the correct solution may be no easy matter, involving much hard thought and work, but the effort is justifiable because a best answer can be obtained. A puzzle can only exist in a clear moral context in which there is little argument about the values appropriate to its resolution. The wish to transform ethical difficulties into puzzles can be illustrated by those who argue that if only we had, in the National Health Service in the UK for example, better information (on clinical effectiveness, public views on medical priorities, costs and hospital activity rates) and better decision-making software to process the data, then questions of medical priorities could be settled technically, optimally, without recourse to messy political arguments about competing values in which, quite commonly, the one who argues the loudest gets the most resources (*see* Case study 2.9).

A decision to see an issue as a puzzle requires the puzzle solver to place the issue within a coherent moral framework and to ignore the demands of contrary values and perspectives. This often enables a puzzle solver to construct detailed mechanisms and steps (rules, procedures and techniques) for resolving an issue.

Ethical problems

A problem is a conundrum to which there is no optimum solution. It may be necessary to take action on a problem, but the action will not remove the difficulty. A problem may be ameliorated or modified but it is unlikely to be resolved. Problems are complicated entities that form, develop and disappear according to their own dynamics. An issue is likely to be categorised as a problem because it involves many different values and principles which, when taken in isolation, make perfect sense, but which, when taken together, fall into conflict. In these situations there has to be a debate between the differing conceptions of value; and part of the difficulty, for people who see issues as ethical problems is to ensure that the arguments in the debate are conducted rigorously and fairly. The discussion of discourse ethics in Chapter 3 is relevant to this stance.

Ethical dilemma

A dilemma is a perplexing state involving difficult or unpleasant choices. The options presented by a dilemma are often unpleasant because they demand a choice between conventions. If the person decides to act according to one set of conventional norms or rules then they will break another set of expectations. As conventions are social constructs it follows that dilemmas are essentially social and political issues. Breaking out of a dilemma necessitates choosing to support one group, by accepting their rules and values, but annoying another group by offending against theirs. It is not unsurprising therefore that categorising an issue as a dilemma can lead to indecision and inaction.

Ethical cynicism and caprice

Cynicism emerges when ethical duty turns bitter. In the category of ethical awareness a person tries to do what their conscience tells them is right. The cynical person, however, has given up on this aim and become, as in the original definition of the word, like a surly dog. The cynic believes that all ethical issues will be resolved in ways which primarily meet the personal and private interests of those involved. Sometimes, the cynic thinks, it would be better to leave matters to capricious chance than to try and improve things. The cynics' aim, apart from maintaining their safely detached position, is to cast blame on those who are trying to deal with an issue.

Ethical negotiation

Ethical negotiation is the process followed when someone is seeking to protect their self-interest (keeping their heads down and getting on with their work), by remaining ethically neutral, but find themselves caught between powerful groups with different views and values. Ethical negotiation therefore is a search for consensus or compromise between differing positions. This category is not concerned with the rightness of a decision but with the correctness of the process used to arrive at it. Put another way, the morality of an action is ignored, only a broad acceptability of an action, as determined by voting, opinion polling, consensus seeking, deal cutting and negotiation, is required. Responding to opinion becomes more important than doing the right thing. This was a barb frequently thrown at the Labour Party during the 1997 election campaign as they responded to feedback from focus groups. This category involves defending oneself by responding to the demands of competing interest groups.

▧ The stances in practice

The model presented in Figure 5.1 represents a range of stances or reactions to an ethical issue at work. However the descriptions of them are very general and summary. They would be difficult to identify in everyday life. Table 5.1 identifies the sorts of arguments and values, arising from each of the stances, that people would use in their discussions.

Table 5.1 A summary of the eight categories of ethical response

Stances	Grids	Way of thinking about the issue	Likely actions
Ethical neutrality	Keeping out of trouble/ jobsworth	People decide to ignore what they see as an injustice because to raise the issue would cause them trouble.	Inaction and keeping quiet.
	Getting the job done	For example a team leader might choose not to respond to concerns raised, about the unethical behaviour of some staff working on a contract, because it would have disrupted the staff scheduling that had been planned with much difficulty.	
Ethical awareness	Dignity of persons	A sort of pop Kantianism which is triggered when it is thought that people are used as means and that their proper dignity is not respected.	Assertion of, and acting upon, one's values. Expressing surprise that others may see things differently.
	The importance of truth	The moral imperative of always telling the truth.	
	Just desserts	Rewarding people according to their merits. A form of deservingness. One respondent, working in government, regarded the catering management as feckless and shed no tears when they were threatened by competitive tendering; but he thought it unjust when the laundry, which the respondent believed provided an excellent service, lost out to an external bidder.	
Ethical convention	Professional norms	The argument that people should adhere to professional and organisational norms and standards.	Seeking advice and help from others on what the normal and acceptable response would be. Applying norms and conventions.
	Fairness	Keeping a level playing field and being fair, treating all the same.	
Ethical puzzle	Policies, rules and procedures	The belief that things are best kept ethical and proper by sticking to the rules and regulations and not bending them to allow for special cases.	Applying the rules of an organisation or institution.
	Utility	Belief in the maximisation of an objective or of utility. This is the philosophy of utilitarianism.	Calculating the consequences of an action. Acting to resolve the issue on the basis that they have the correct or best solution. The assumption is that, the correct action having been taken, this will be an end to the matter.
Ethical problem	Moral judgement	The application of moral judgement rather than the moral calculation of utility. Moral judgement, the ability to define the ethical mean proportionately is acquired through the development of virtues. One respondent argued that ethical codes were unnecessary because the organisation's staff were virtuous and honest.	Clarifying how the conflicts between different values would lead to different actions or decisions. Acting upon one's best judgement.
	Learning from moral exemplars	The argument that ethical lapses can be temporarily tolerated if people have the opportunity to learn new and better ways.	

▶

Table 5.1 (Continued)

Stances	Grids	Way of thinking about the issue	Likely actions
Ethical dilemma	Personal relationships	In a wicked world one should concentrate on the development of personal relationships. *See* Case study 5.1 for an example.	The emphasis of action is on maintaining discussion about the issue rather than seeking closure on it. When conflicts about issues are serious it is important to maintain good manners and interpersonal relationships.
	Ironic liberalism and pragmatism	This notion is taken from Rorty (1989). It is a view on how sanity can be maintained in a world where values are ungrounded. The key techniques are the separation of private and public domains and giving priority to 'keeping the conversation going' (Mounce, 1997: 197, 207).	
	Relativism	The argument that different cultures have different moral precepts and that what may be unethical in one culture, or organisation, may not be so in another.	
	Holism	Trying to take the whole position into account. At its most extreme it is like the Buddhist belief that great effort is needed to see beyond the illusion of fragmentation to the unity beyond (Kjonstad and Willmott, 1995: 457).	
Ethical cynicism	Façadism	One person thought others wanted to be seen to follow the proper recruitment procedures even though the person they wanted to have the job had been decided beforehand. This grid includes being economical with the truth and the belief that business involves games playing and bluffing (Carr 1968).	The cynic will withdraw from any action or decision but will snipe from the sidelines at any action or decision that others may have taken.
	Personal gain and selfishness	The argument that people are distorting situations and procedures to their own private advantage.	
Ethical negotiation	Complex politics	'There are high-level politics concerning this issue to which I am not privy—so I keep my own views to myself.' A person working with this perspective tries to steer a compromise route through the competing demands of different groups. The problems of allocating scarce car parking spaces at work are often a good example.	Seeking out others' views and supporting or acquiescing in the wishes of the most powerful.
	'Dodgy deals'	Bending rules, or acquiescing in rule bending, to accommodate the interest of powerful groups.	

Competing stances: the possibility of cognitive dissonance

It would be convenient to claim that people opted for one of the eight categories just described, when dealing with an ethical issue, and kept to it. In practice people may change their categorisation of an ethical issue, indeed they may hold conflicting views in their minds at the same time. This latter possibility will be explained first.

Let us consider how someone might hold conflicting views. When someone is thinking about an ethical issue it can be speculated that there are at least four perspectives from which the issue can be addressed:

- What is it that is ethically or morally wrong about a situation? What has triggered the recognition of the issue as an ethical one? What in other words has triggered their *conscience*?
- What ideally should be done about the situation? When they apply their *ethical reasoning* to the situation what will they think is the proper course of action?
- What do they think all the other interested persons and parties think about the situation? What are the *demands and expectations* that other stakeholders in the situation wish to impose?
- What, in practical terms, should be done about it given all the constraints and complexities of the 'real' world? What are their *options for action*?

The theory of cognitive dissonance claims that people try to make all their perspectives fit neatly together in their own minds. Instead it will be argued that people may hold contradictory views. Each of these perspectives can be discussed in more detail.

Conscience

Aspects of an issue might cause some pain or difficulty because they are thought to be wrong. This feeling may be termed conscience, defined as an anxiety caused by the belief that a thought or act is wrong. Conscience is the starting point for the analysis of people's response to ethical incidents. It is conscience that causes, as one of our interviewees phrased it, 'the ethical twinges' that lead us to identify an issue as an ethical one. Conscience, or the superego to use a psychoanalytic term, is the function that keeps bad impulses in check. It does this by drenching the mind with anxiety whenever temptation is on hand and by creating feelings of remorse and humiliation when bad impulses are succumbed to. Conscience does not, however, tell us what is right; that is more the province of social norms and ethical reasoning.

Ethical reasoning

Ethical reasoning is a person's rational, or rationalised, analysis of what they think should be done in relation to an incident or issue (Snell, 1993). If conscience defines the problem then ethical reasoning identifies the solution. It is the actions (or inactions) that the person thinks, on the basis of their values and analysis, they should take.

The demands and expectations of others

From the perspective of the demands and expectations of others a person undertakes a mini 'stakeholder analysis'. They identify the motives they attribute to the speech and actions of others. It is important to note that this perspective cannot pretend to know what the other's motives actually are. It is focused on what the person thinks the others involved in the story are thinking and why.

■ Options for action

If conscience is the expression of the superego then the perspective of options for action represents the ego. In psychoanalysis the ego is the instinct for self-preservation. It is the aspect of the self that is aware of the external world and rationalises how one should act within it. From this perspective therefore the concern is not what should, in moral terms, be done, but what it is sensible and practical to do.

These four perspectives and the eight categories of ethical response can be used to analyse someone's (or one's own) position on any particular ethical issue. An example of how this might be done is shown in Case study 5.1.

CASE STUDY 5.1	An ethical issue

This case study presents an example of an ethical incident, described by a research interviewee (R), analysed using these four perspectives.

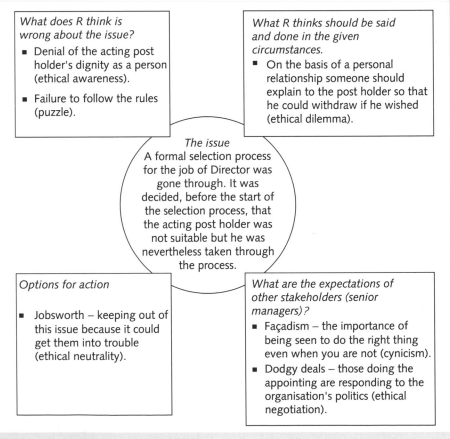

What does R think is wrong about the issue?
- Denial of the acting post holder's dignity as a person (ethical awareness).
- Failure to follow the rules (puzzle).

What R thinks should be said and done in the given circumstances.
- On the basis of a personal relationship someone should explain to the post holder so that he could withdraw if he wished (ethical dilemma).

The issue
A formal selection process for the job of Director was gone through. It was decided, before the start of the selection process, that the acting post holder was not suitable but he was nevertheless taken through the process.

Options for action
- Jobsworth – keeping out of this issue because it could get them into trouble (ethical neutrality).

What are the expectations of other stakeholders (senior managers)?
- Façadism – the importance of being seen to do the right thing even when you are not (cynicism).
- Dodgy deals – those doing the appointing are responding to the organisation's politics (ethical negotiation).

Figure 5.2 Analysis of an ethical issue

◼ Conflicts between perspectives

Case study 5.1 illustrates how a person can hold different views on an issue at the same time. People may think that something is wrong, and suffer pangs of conscience about it, but simultaneously believe that it may not be ethically proper to do anything about it. It is also clear, as Snell (1993) pointed out, that just because someone is capable of thinking at an advanced ethical level it does not mean that this will be reflected in his or her actions. There is no necessary connection between reasoning and action.

When people experience conflict because they adopt contradictory stances at some or all of the four perspective points they may experience a number of states, as shown in Figure 5.3. We argue that if people adopt different stances in the four perspectives, which clash with each other, then certain consequences can be predicted. Six types of conflict have been identified.

- Type 1 conflict occurs when conscience and ethical reasoning are at odds and this produces feelings of anxiety. There was no type 1 conflict in Case study 5.1 because, although there are differences between the respondent's conscience and ethical reasoning (denial of personal dignity and personal relationships), a personal approach would have restored the personal dignity of the acting director.
- A type 2 conflict could be seen in the case study. The respondent took a position of neutrality on an issue her conscience told her was wrong and this might be expected to produce feelings of guilt, shame or remorse.
- The case study also suggests a type 3 conflict because there was disagreement between what the respondent thought should be done and the position of those conducting the selection process. The respondent thought the selection

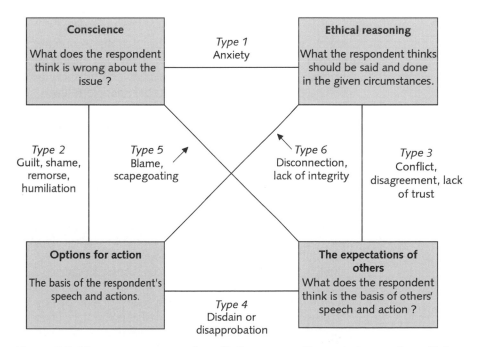

Figure 5.3 The consequences of conflicting perspectives: six types of conflict

procedure should have been properly applied with no prior decision being taken about the suitability of any candidate. The senior managers however were happy to maintain a façade of keeping the rules and spirit of the recruitment policy whilst ensuring that the acting director did not get the job. This conflict might be expected to reduce the respondent's trust of the senior managers. If they were capable of 'shafting' one individual then they might just as easily do it to others.

- The respondent's position, in the case study, of neutrality in the 'action' box prevented a type 4 clash with the views of others.
- There was a type 5 conflict in the case study because the respondent blamed the others for behaving wrongly.
- Type 6 conflict, in which a person acts contrary to their ethical reasoning, will damage people's sense of integrity because they cannot consider their thoughts and actions to be of a piece. This was the situation in the case study because the respondent did not do that which her ethical reasoning told her to do.

Festinger's theory of cognitive dissonance (1957) held that the consequences of holding conflicting ideas in our heads were so unpleasant that we jerk our attitudes and actions into line so that they all fit comfortably together. Billig (1996: 202) pointed out that dissonant thoughts are not in themselves a cognitive problem. They only become an issue if an external opponent makes a public criticism of them. Even in this case, if it can be argued that the dissonances are trivial and not to be taken seriously, then the contradictory thoughts need not be a problem to the possessor of the ambiguity. Many may find little difficulty in taking different stances from each perspective.

ACTIVITY 5.1

Describe, using the categories in Table 5.1, the respondent's view of the problem described, in the interview below, under the headings of conscience, ethical reasoning, the positions of others involved and practical action. The issue concerns making a building appropriate for disabled people to use.

Extract from an interview with a personnel manager

The fact [is] that both sites are not access friendly in a way that they would need to be for a lot of disabled people. So we've had a small audit of access and mobility type issues. You think it's small when you start out and then you get into it and there are major changes that would be required and therefore the money comes into it and how much we should be spending. So there's fairly wide ranging discussions going on at the moment about whether any of those changes should be made up front of employing anybody, or whether we wait to be pushed along that line by the employment of somebody. The law says you can obviously wait for the latter. There's two distinct camps. Those in slightly more senior positions, those with the clout, are favouring small changes now and delaying big spend on bigger changes until there's a need because we already employ a couple of individuals who fall into the definition of disabled; and both are perfectly well able to carry out their jobs with the arrangements that we have currently. But then we do have some people who strongly believe

Activity 5.1 continued

that we should make ourselves more overtly accessible and as a result we would attract a greater range of people.

Well we have a working party set up and there are some people on it who are motivated by different things. Some are not often invited on to a working party and have taken the issue to heart so strongly that they feel that you should do something with it. Others have members of their family, or people that they know, who have disabilities and are therefore fighting from a particular corner for it. You do get into a moral argument with some people about, you know, it's the proper thing to do, we should do it. But there's quite a lot of proper things to do and at some point in time they have to be slotted into some sort of order, to deal with them. I would argue that there are a number of lower cost areas that could be addressed that would make us [more accessible], for instance we do not have ramp access to our reception. Now that wouldn't be a big deal but would be very visible and would then allow those with access problems to get into us. We could then move from there. We tend to have a lot of people that make assumptions about the nature of disabilities of people and assume that anybody with [a] disabled nametag is in a wheelchair and therefore everything should be wheelchair related. When we know it's not like that at all. So I would much rather get into some of the more obvious things like somewhere to park that's not too far away from the front. A ramp so that people can actually get in. Some of the problems we have are huge, like upstairs [you have to go] round goodness knows how many corridors, downstairs and back up again to get to the canteen. And that's the only place where people can buy food. But on the basis that we employ a couple [of] males already who have fairly strong disabilities we can get round it. No I don't think it's easy. It's particularly difficult. I recently popped back from work to attend a conference at which one of the lads, who is disabled, was arguing very, very strongly for spending all this money – big sums of money; and it's a very sensible argument. He delivers it with force. I mean at the end of the day [he was] saying that you have your independence and you should therefore do everything to ensure other people have independence because all a disabled person wants is independence. You should therefore facilitate that however you can. Yes it is hard to argue against but at some point things have to take their place. It's hard to argue against the fact that the best person for the job could cost ten grand a year more than you've actually got available. You know you could get the value for that person but somewhere it's got to stop. It is hard and I don't sit on the working party personally but obviously I've got quite a lot to do with what they're up to. I do know that they go round in circles on that one quite a lot and they will do. We have a policy decided and we don't have a disability budget. Budgets are set for the next twelve months and have been for quite some time so it is a question of saying well if you spend the money on X it doesn't get spent on Y. Or finding it from somewhere else, well we're always looking for money from somewhere else for something.

A suggested analysis is shown in Figure 5.4. In this figure the informant's perspectives on the central issue of access improvements have been shown by quoting her words and then by categorising them using the eight ethical stances and the list of values shown in Table 5.1. The analysis could have been done more simply without recourse to the eight stances, but their use clarifies any conflicts between the four perspectives.

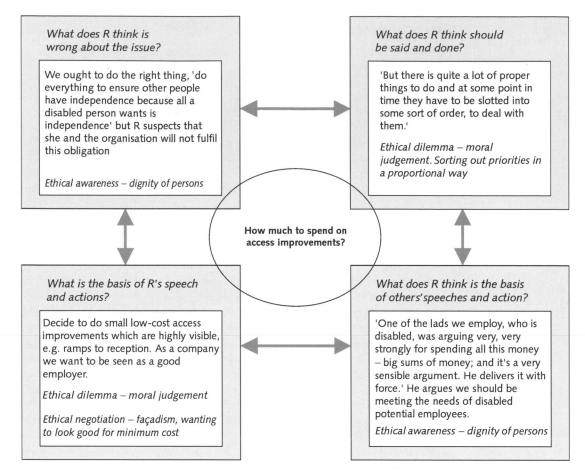

Figure 5.4 A suggested analysis of the case study in Activity 5.1

The contradictions between the respondent's perspectives are indicated by the arrows in Figure 5.4, which shows type 1, 2, 3 and 4 tensions. Her conscience informed her that there was a major wrong that ought to be righted, but her ethical reasoning suggested that it would be wrong to do everything that needed to be done. Her conscience had sympathy for the views expressed by the member of staff but her ethical reasoning did not. So her actions (in sympathy with her reasoning rather than with her conscience) contradicted what she thought the staff were telling her. This pattern of conflicts and congruencies might be described as melancholic acceptance. With regret she thought it wrong to do what her conscience, and the consciences of others, demanded (Fisher, 1999).

■ Shifting stances

The discussion in the previous section and in Activity 5.1 has illustrated how a person might take potentially conflicting perspectives on an ethical issue and hold them simultaneously. In the changing circumstances of a working life it might be that people give emphasis to different perspectives as the situation develops and more particulars become known. Others of course might adopt an initial stance and then keep to it without distraction. This is the issue that is explored in Activity 5.2.

Downsizing: An instrument on perceptions of ethical considerations in human resource management and management accountancy

Instructions

In this questionnaire you are put in the place of a team manager who is facing pressure to make someone in the team redundant. Please work through the various sections of the questionnaire in sequence and please do not flip through the document to see how the storyline develops and ends!

There are a few points you need to bear in mind as you work through the questionnaire.

■ All the information you are given is consistent, i.e. you will not be given information in the latter part of the questionnaire that contradicts information given earlier.

■ There are no right answers to the questions posed in the questionnaire. The purpose of the questionnaire is to research the variety of responses to it and not to find out how many people get it 'right'.

■ Do not backtrack to earlier sections of the questionnaire when you get near the end and change your decisions.

Section 1

You are a human resource management specialist managing a team of four professional staff. A benchmarking exercise, which you have no reason to doubt, has shown that the organisation's unit costs, in the function in which the team works, are much higher than those of similar and competing organisations. The market environment of the organisation is becoming more competitive and market share is showing a marginal decline.

Senior management have announced staff redundancies and the team's share of the overall reduction, which actually is proportionately smaller than that demanded of other teams and departments, is one member of staff. You have been lucky in previous rounds of redundancy and your team has escaped cuts. Whilst you have heard rumours on the grapevine the actual announcement of the latest round, when it came, was unexpected.

The team members are:

Chris who is a willing worker and makes a good contribution to meeting the team's objectives.

Leslie who has long service with the organisation. You have begun to be dissatisfied with the quantity and quality of Leslie's work.

Phil who has joined the organisation in the last few years, and

Nicky who is a good worker but can be uncooperative and curmudgeonly (a curmudgeon is surly and niggardly person).

Activity 5.2 continued

You have had previous experience of making people redundant, in an organisation you worked for earlier in your career, and you found it very difficult. You have no doubt that this round of redundancy will be equally emotionally wearing and it is not an experience you are keen to repeat.

On balance would you:

Adopt a position of grumbling acceptance and argue that, as you were not consulted about the decision, your senior manager should decide who should be made redundant. ☐ (01)

Accept the redundancies as an unfortunate necessity and start thinking about the decision you have to make. ☐ (02)

Lobby and fight to get the redundancy decision reversed and/or argue that redundancy is unethical. ☐ (03)

Please go to the next section.

Section 2

Through your managerial position you have gained inside knowledge about the organisation and there are several things you know which some people might consider as ethical failings. The organisation has been making large profits in recent years but it is clear that it has given more priority to shareholders than to customers and staff in the way its added value has been allocated. The chairman of the organisation might also be branded a 'fat cat' because, through pay increase, bonus payments and share option schemes, his income has increased at a rate many times greater than inflation. The organisation is based in Skegmouth which has one of the highest unemployment rates in the country and there is little chance that those made redundant could obtain new jobs locally.

On balance would you:

Adopt a position of grumbling acceptance and argue that, as you were not consulted about the decision, your senior manager should decide who should be made redundant. ☐ (04)

Accept the redundancies as an unfortunate necessity and start thinking about the decision you have to make. ☐ (05)

Lobby and fight to get the redundancy decision reversed. ☐ (06)

Please go to the next section.

Section 3

You have had discussions with the team, following the announcement of redundancies, and they all agree, and so do you, that in these situations the opportunities for voluntary redundancies and early retirements should be taken up before there is any consideration of compulsory redundancy. This is a strong matter of principle with you. You find it hard to explain why it is so important to you, it just seems the fair and just solution.

Activity 5.2 continued

Chris is in his early sixties and is willing, almost desperate, to take early retirement. He has been talking to you about going early for several years. He is the only man in the team, in an organisation that has appointed more women in recent years. There is some grumbling in the organisation that a policy of accepting voluntary redundancies will discriminate against women. The older staff (who are more likely to want and to get early retirement) are disproportionately male. Therefore more men are likely to benefit from an early retirement policy than women. Whether this issue causes you any concern or not, it is clear that Chris's experience and competence in the job will be hard to replace.

Would you continue to fight against the cuts, probably by ☐ (07)
  using delaying tactics?

If not, would you ☐ (08)
Refuse to give Chris early retirement?

Agree to Chris retiring early because it seems the right thing ☐ (09a)
  to do, and/or

Agree to Chris retiring early because it gets you out of a ☐ (09b)
  tricky decision.

Please go to the next section.

Section 4

Chris has recently come to see you to say that he and his partner have been discussing their retirement plans, and although he has always been keen to go, he now realises that it will not be financially possible to buy his dream retirement home in the Caribbean if he retires now. So, with some regret, he has withdrawn his offer to take early retirement or voluntary redundancy. If you had agreed to accept Chris's offer in the previous section you are no longer able to. As there are no other team members willing to take voluntary redundancy you have accepted that it is up to you to decide which member of the team should be made redundant. All the team are on approximately the same salary so there is no greater cost saving to be had by making a particular team member redundant. You also recognise that you will have to establish some clear guidelines for choosing whom to make redundant so that the process can be made open, transparent and fair.

The organisation has no policy, or joint agreements, or preference for 'last in first out' or any other criterion for choosing which jobs to make redundant. The following seem to be the decision criteria available to you.

- **Contribution** to team and organisational objectives – you make redundant the person who makes least contribution.
- **Last in first out** (LIFO).
- **Deservingness** – the least deserving person, i.e. the one who makes least effort to be a good team player, should be made redundant.

Activity 5.2 continued

- **Career potential** – the young, who have a career ahead of them and perhaps a greater contribution to make in terms of their ability with new technology, should not be made redundant. It is the older members of staff who should bear the brunt of redundancy.

You have thoroughly studied appraisal records, 360° multi-rater returns, attendance records and work records of your team members and constructed Table 5.2 which gives your considered evaluation of each of them against the possible criteria for redundancy.

Table 5.2 Suitability of each team member for redundancy against each criterion

	Career potential	Contribution	LIFO	Deservingness
Chris	1	4	2	3
Leslie	2	1	3	4
Phil	4	2	1	2
Nicky	3	3	4	1

1 = most suitable for redundancy.
4 = least suitable for redundancy.

Who would you make redundant?

        Chris   ☐ (10)

        Leslie   ☐ (11)

        Phil   ☐ (12)

        Nicky   ☐ (13)

Or would you decide you cannot choose someone for redundancy because you:

        Don't know/won't do it   ☐ (14)

If you chose a team member to make redundant go to the next section. If you ticked the 'don't know' box, go to Section 6.

Section 5

You found the decision in Section 4 difficult. If you accepted the 'contribution' criterion then Leslie would have to be made redundant but you do know that her poor performance at work is because her partner is suffering from terminal cancer and she is finding it hard to keep her concentration on her work. If you accept the LIFO criterion then Phil would be the one to go. But Phil has been critical in purchasing and installing the new IT systems that are going to be the bedrock of the organisation's success in the future. The 'deservingness' criterion would lead you to choose Nicky for redundancy but she also makes a valuable contribution and often adds a useful note of scepticism in a group that can otherwise be a little too

Activity 5.2 continued

cohesive, inward looking and blinkered in its approach. On the basis of the 'career potential' criterion then it is Chris who would be the obvious candidate for redundancy but his experience cannot be easily replaced.

The team member you chose to make redundant in Section 4 describes themselves as of an Afro-Caribbean ethnic origin. They had been recruited when the introduction of an equal opportunities policy, and the provision of formal training in selection and recruitment, were beginning to increase the number of people from minorities who were appointed. There was no affirmative action policy, however, and there is no doubt that they were appointed on merit and were the best candidate available. The organisation still does not have a good record on the employment and promotion of people from minority groups, despite the signs of improvement. Because staff from minorities were often recruited after the recent development of equal opportunities polices they generally have short lengths of service with the organisation and the use of LIFO to decide who should be made redundant would discriminate against them. The result for the organisation would be that staff from the minorities would be more likely to be made redundant than other categories of staff and the proportion of staff from minority backgrounds would diminish.

Many people feel that several of the criteria for choosing who to make redundant, and not just LIFO, discriminate against people from the minority groups. Often their contribution, or career potential, is not as great as it could be because they have had less opportunity for staff development. When, as occasionally happens, they are seen by others as not fitting in with their team and being difficult and uncooperative often the failure is as much the result of unconscious racism on the part of their colleagues as their fault.

Taking the above information into consideration whom would you now decide to make redundant?

| Name of person | | (15) |
| Don't know | ☐ | (16) |

Please go to the next section.

Section 6

As you agonise about the decision you talk to more and more people about the situation, and people seek you out and lobby you to make the decision one way or another. The trade union representatives believe that LIFO is the only fair way to make the decision. The equal opportunities office is determined that the redundancy policy should not discriminate against minority groups. The senior management are firmly convinced that in a competitive market it would be folly to choose whom to make redundant on any grounds other than merit – or contribution to the organisation's goals. You find you have sympathy with each of these views when you are talking face to face with their proponents but you find it difficult to square all the conflicting viewpoints.

Activity 5.2 continued

The senior managers are pushing you for a decision. The deadline to inform the HRM director is tomorrow morning. Do you:

Decide to make [   ] redundant.   ☐ (17)

Decide to report that none of the team should be   ☐ (18)
made redundant and let senior management decide.

Decide to choose the person to be made   ☐ (19)
redundant by drawing lots.

Decide to have a very large drink.   ☐ (20)

Please go to the next section.

Section 7

The decision you have to make is so complex that you decide to discuss it, and negotiate, with others and arrive at a compromise. Which of the following groups, if any, would you negotiate, and seek consensus, with?
Tick as many boxes as appropriate, or none.

The team   ☐ (22)

The senior managers   ☐ (23)

The equal opportunities office   ☐ (24)

The trade unions   ☐ (25)

You have had the discussions, and the large drink, you sit down and you feel, in your heart of hearts, that

[   ] should be the person to go.   [   ] (21)

Or you feel that you just cannot make this decision.   ☐ (26)

This is the end of the instrument.

Instructions for scoring *Downsizing*

■ At first sight the scoring matrix for *Downsizing* (Figure 5.5) looks complex. But if you follow these instructions it should not be too difficult

■ First of all note that all the boxes you ticked in the exercise had a field number attached to them in brackets. You will use these to score yourself.

■ Start at the left of the scoring form and work your way across it. In Sections 1 to 4 put a cross in the cell that corresponds to the answer you have in that section, as follows.

■ In sections 5 to 7 it is a little more difficult because you have to apply the decision rules described in the cells to decide which cell is the correct one to describe your decision.

■ Join up all the 'X's in the columns to draw a profile line across the grid that represents the categories of ethical response you chose in the exercise.

Use the decision rules in each box to allocate responses to an ethical category

Forced hard choices: stances and values in practice

	Section 4	Section 5	Section 6	Section 7
Ethical cynicism	If 10 ticked	If 15 is Chris	If 19 ticked	If none or 22, 23, 24 or 25 is ticked & if 26 ticked
Ethical negotiation				If 22, 23, 24 or 25 is ticked & if 26 ticked
Ethical dilemma			If 18 ticked or if 17 is different from 15 or if 20 ticked	If 26 ticked, or if 21 is the same as 17, or different from 15
Ethical problem	If 14 ticked	If 16 ticked, or 15 different from person chosen in Section 4, or if 14 ticked	If 17 is the same as 15, or if a choice is made after choosing 14	If 21 same as 15
Ethical puzzle	If 10 or 11 or 12 or 13 ticked	If 15 is same as person chosen in Section 4	If 17 is same as person chosen in Section 4	If 21 same as person chosen in Section 4
Ethical convention	Name of person chosen:	Name of person chosen:	Name of person chosen:	Name of person chosen:

Espoused stances and values

	Section 1	Section 2	Section 3
Ethical awareness	If 03 ticked	If 06 ticked	If 07 ticked
			If 08 ticked
			If 09a ticked
Ethical neutrality	If 02 ticked	If 05 ticked	
Ethical cynicism	If 01 ticked	If 04 ticked	If 09b ticked

Figure 5.5 Scoring matrix for *Downsizing*

■ Some research findings from the use of *Downsizing*

Downsizing has been completed by a large sample of financial professionals and accountants and by a smaller sample of human resource managers (Fisher and Lovell, 2000). The results are shown in Figure 5.6. You might wish to compare your results with those of these two samples.

The great majority of both accountants and human resource specialists began by taking a neutral position in Section 1. The inference would seem to be that redundancy is a common part of organisational life and there is no reason to suspect there are any particular moral issues arising from the situation. In Section 2 doubts are sown about the ethical status of the organisation in the case study. A narrow majority of the HR specialists changed their view of the case, took a position of ethical awareness, and began to protest against the redundancies. The majority of accountants continued to take a neutral stance although a minority shifted to the ethical awareness position. In Section 3 respondents were given the opportunity to adopt a conventional response to the situation (reducing numbers through voluntary redundancy) and the majority of both accountants and HR specialists took this option.

The opportunity for a conventional response is removed in Section 4 when Chris withdraws his or her offer to take voluntary redundancy. The respondents are given sufficient information to treat the problem as a puzzle. A number of criteria that can be used to select candidates for redundancy are provided and all the team members are ranked against each of the criteria. These can be used to make a rational choice of who should be made redundant. Over 80 per cent of the accountants, and over three-quarters of the HR specialists, took this opportunity and used the information provided to choose the most suitable candidate for redundancy. A small percentage of respondents (although fewer accountants than HR specialists) recognised that it was not possible to identify an optimum candidate for redundancy when all of the proposed criteria were applied. Put simply, there was no candidate who was the best choice on all the criteria. These respondents took an ethical problem stance that recognised the conflicts between the values represented by the different criteria.

Further information is provided in Section 5 of the exercise. This reports a clash between incompatible values. Those respondents who chose a candidate for redundancy on apparently rational grounds are told that the choice raises other problems and ethical difficulties. Some accountants, as a consequence, did move their stance to that of ethical problem but most ignored the new complexities and continued to see the issue as an ethical puzzle. The majority of HR specialists however did take a new, ethical problem, stance. Further complexities are introduced in Section 6. Most of the accountants still saw the issue as a puzzle. A fifth of the HR specialists now saw the issue as a dilemma; a third saw it as a problem but the single biggest group of the HR specialists returned to a puzzle stance. The pattern was the same in the last section of the exercise in which some information was provided that was intended to encourage some to take a position of ethical negotiation. Only a small proportion of respondents did so.

In the latter half of the exercise most accountants stuck with their ethical puzzle stance no matter what ethical difficulties they were presented with. Most of the HR specialists did initially respond to these difficulties but they

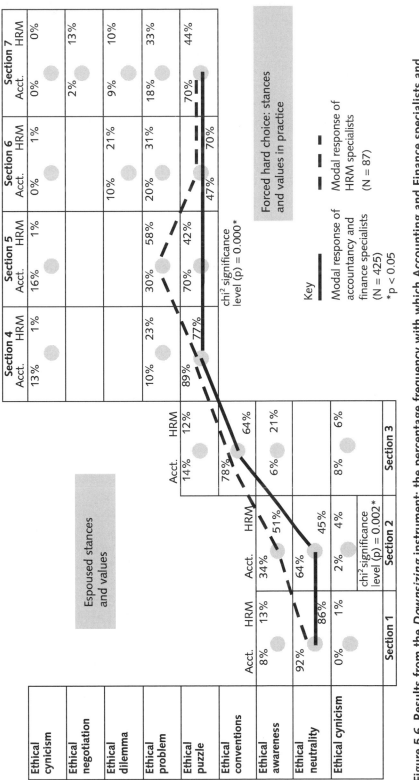

Figure 5.6 Results from the *Downsizing* instrument: the percentage frequency with which Accounting and Finance specialists and HRM specialists chose ethical positions in the seven sections of the instrument

(*Source*: Fisher and Lovell, 2000)

subsequently returned to a pragmatic ethical puzzle stance. You can see from the scoring matrix (Figure 5.5) that the results for the second part of the exercise are labelled 'forced hard choices' whereas those in the first part are termed espoused stances. Espoused values are those that people would wish others to think that they hold. These are often contrasted with those values that people use in practice, especially when under pressure.

■ Categorisation and particularisation and the eight stances

The results from *Downsizing* suggest that some people pigeon-hole an issue under one category, and do not change their minds; other people change their views as the issue unfolds. This phenomenon can be explained by using the concepts of categorisation and particularisation that were mentioned at the start of the chapter. The emphasis in this chapter so far has been on categorisation but the idea of particularisation will be useful in explaining the processes that cause people to take different stances on ethical issues.

Categorisation is the process of placing an object within a general category or schema. Psychologists have claimed it is the fundamental process of thinking. As Cantor *et al.* (1982: 34) claimed:

> Categorisation schemes allow us to structure and give coherence to our general knowledge about people and the social world, providing expectations about typical patterns of behaviour and the range of likely variation between types of people and their characteristic actions and attributes.

The terms category and schema are similar in meaning. However it is generally claimed that schemata are more general and complex than categories. It is possible for example to see schemata as formed from collections of categories.

On its own however, Billig (1996: 154) argued, categorisation can lead to bureaucratic and prejudiced forms of thinking. The story (which may be an urban myth) of the doctor who would not give emergency treatment to a person who had a heart attack on the pavement in front of the hospital, because his employer's liability insurance did not extend beyond the hospital premises, illustrates the typical ethical costs of bureaucracy. The research finding (Galton and Delafield, 1981), that primary school teachers' ways of talking to and questioning pupils they had judged to be low performing led such pupils to do less well than they ought, identified the prejudicial impact of categorisation.

Illustrations of the bureaucracy and prejudice that can emerge from categorisation were found when we interviewed people about ethical incidents they had experienced at work. In some cases the rigidity of bureaucracy was at the organisation's (rather than the employee's or customer's) cost. In one incident a young marketing manager had been partly disabled by a stroke that prevented him from driving. His job required him to work on two widely separated sites and the company paid his taxi fares and overnight costs. In other circumstances a manager of his seniority would have had a company car with free petrol. The week before his summer holiday he asked personnel to hire a car for him so that his wife could drive him about on their continental holiday. He argued that other managers were able to use company cars and petrol on their holidays and that he should be treated the same as them. Most of the personnel department, for they all became involved in discussing the case, tended to the view that the manager was trying it on, manipulating the bureaucratic rules to gain a personal advantage. They thought that the bureaucratic rules were being used to achieve an unfair and undeserved benefit for the marketing manager.

Other interviewees gave accounts of many instances in which an injustice may have resulted from the way in which people were categorised. In one case an employee was appointed to a post but was denied membership of the company pension scheme because he was too fat. In other cases managers refused, illegally, to appoint young women to jobs in case they later caused disruption by becoming pregnant and taking maternity leave.

Billig proposed that categorisation, because it can lead to distorted responses, should be understood in the context of the tension with its opposite – particularisation. Particularisation is the process of recognising the specific and unique features of a situation, which mean that it cannot be categorised. At the least particularisation causes controversy about how an issue should be categorised. It provides a counterweight to categorisation. Those whose powers of particularisation are diminished may become bureaucratic and prejudiced in ways that deny justice, or at the least provide a dulled and mechanical response to ethical issues.

Comparison of the *Downsizing* results of the accountancy and HR specialists (Figure 5.6) suggests that categorisation, evidenced by an unwillingness to change one's categorisation of an issue, need not be the dominant way of thinking about ethical issues in organisations. The HR managers were more likely than the financial specialists to change their categorisation as they worked through the instrument. They were readier to change their categorisation in response to new particulars. The greater proportion of women in the HRM profession could account for the relative strength of particularisation in the HR sample. Some research (Helson and Wink, 1992) has suggested that women have a greater tolerance of ambiguity as they get older. This tendency, if related to a greater ease with particularisation, contrasts with men's inclination to see things in the puzzle mode more often as they get older (Fisher and Lovell, 2000).

The point is not which mode, categorisation or particularisation employees ought to be encouraged to adopt, rather that they should be helped to use both. As Winter puts it (1989: 53) dialectical critique means looking for 'unity concealed behind apparent differentiation and contradiction concealed within apparent unity'. People should be helped to challenge, and argue about, how ethical issues at work should be categorised. Particularisation and categorisation need to be operated in combination because particularisation is the trigger for challenges to habitual categorisation. Billig (1996: 171) discussed

> the rhetorical strategies which turn around our schemata and unpick our categories. It will be seen that these strategies are not based upon a simple process of particularisation. Rather they are located within a continual argumentative momentum, oscillating between particularisation and categorisation.

There are two aspects to this momentum: arguing about which category it is appropriate to use in a particular case; and arguing about what the categories are, or what they mean. An issue from our research interviews can illustrate this. A company that trades with developing countries had relieved its managers of wrestling with the ethical problems associated with accepting gifts from overseas agents. It required that any employees who were offered gifts by an overseas agent should accept them (thereby avoiding giving offence to the agent), but hand them over to the company. During the year such gifts were auctioned and the proceeds donated to charities. Thus, the need to think or worry about how to handle such situations is removed from the individual manager involved by the adoption of an ethical code.

Whilst managers' lives were made easier by the code it also took away from them their personal moral responsibility. For this reason the categorisation of the issue as a matter of rule following should have been challenged. It could, for example, have been recategorised as a matter of ethical awareness, and the view taken that nothing that could be seen as corruption should be tolerated. In this case no gifts should be accepted. Or, by way of redefining the categorisations, it might have been argued that it was a question of following ethical conventions, but not those of the company's home base. Instead the norms of the country in which the business was being conducted (where giving bribes was accepted) should be followed. There is another possibility. Texas Instruments' (1999) code argued that a gift is improper if it is expected to provide the giver with an advantage. The impropriety of a gift is not judged by its scale, which customarily differs between countries, but by the intention of the gift giver. This approach categorises the issue as one of moral judgement within a problem perspective. These possibilities leads to the conclusion that ethical behaviour in organisations requires employees to balance their tendency to categorise or 'label' ethical issues by using the particularity of a situation to challenge their categorisations.

Case study 5.2 shows how particulars can suddenly challenge categorisations as one particular feature of a case acts as an epiphany that causes a major realignment in a person's view of an issue.

Definition	**Epiphany** was originally a Christian term for the manifestation of God's presence in the world. James Joyce took the term over, in his novel *The Portrait of an Artist as a Young Man*, to mean a commonplace object or gesture that provides a sudden insight.

CASE STUDY 5.2	## Particularisation and categorisation

The following incident was recounted by one of our research interviewees, a senior personnel manager in a food processing company. The company had a van sales force that sold and delivered the product to small shops and catering businesses. She became indirectly involved in discussions about the fate of a van salesman who had been accused of theft. She was told that on his rounds the salesman had seen a bike on waste ground outside a shop he was delivering to, and had put it in the van to take it home to give to his son. The police had stopped him and accused him of theft and the question was whether the salesman should be summarily dismissed in line with the company's disciplinary policy. The man's manager, realistically in the personnel manager's view, said that he was loath to dismiss the salesman because he was good at his job and, in any case, 'wouldn't we all take the bike in similar

Case study 5.2 continued

circumstances; pick up an abandoned bike?' The manager also reported that the police had said it would be unfair to dismiss the salesman. Despite this the police had decided to prosecute, which seemed a little odd to the personnel manager.

The personnel manager thought it important to maintain the reputation of the van sales force for trustworthiness.

> They are out on the road on their own and we trust the van sales people. Your sales reps have to be honest because the shopkeepers have a degree of mistrust and it's important that we build up a reputation as an honest company.

This thought inclined her to dismiss the van salesman. However there had been a number of recent cases where staff had been involved in minor theft and had been let off with a caution because they had been good employees. It seemed sensible to show leniency to the salesman especially as there was some doubt about whether it was a case of theft or simply a matter of 'finder's keepers'. On this basis the personnel manager was inclined to accept the manager's wish to retain the salesman.

Out of curiosity she asked:

> 'What sort of shop was it where the bike was taken from?' The manager replied, sheepishly, 'It was a newsagent's early in the morning'. Suspicions aroused she asked, 'Was it a newspaper boy's or girl's bike?' 'Yes it was', came the resigned response. 'It was leaning against the side wall of the newsagents–but it was on waste ground. It was just alongside the newsagents.'

This fact was enough for the personnel manager who insisted that the employee be dismissed. The manager was annoyed because he had lost a good salesman and recruiting new ones was not easy. The sudden revelation of a few particulars about the nature and position of the bike were enough to settle the personnel manager's mind on how the issue should be categorised. It was a clear puzzle, which could be easily resolved by applying company rules, not an ethical problem that called for fine moral judgements. This small example provides an illustration of how particulars may serve to challenge categorisations.

Influences on choice of stance

So far this chapter has concentrated upon identifying the categories people use to label ethical issues. It has also highlighted the importance of allowing categorisations of an issue to be challenged and changed by particulars. It is now necessary to look a little more closely at these particulars. The emphasis in this section will be on the factors and influences that bear upon people's choices of the stance to be taken on an ethical issue. Some of the influences upon these choices have been pre-empted in the description of the two dimensions in Figure 5.1. The vertical axis suggests that the adoption of a stance will depend upon the sophistication of a person's ethical reasoning. The horizontal axis indicates that a person's certainty about their values will also affect their choice of stances.

There are many other factors that have a claim to influence ethical categorisation and decision making. Models of the antecedents influencing ethical decision making often include four broad areas. They are:

1 Cultural factors

The importance of an organisation's ethical culture or ethos is discussed in Chapter 7. Trevino and Youngblood (1990) identified a link between an organisation's culture and the ethical position adopted by organisational members that they called vicarious reward and punishment. They hypothesised that people's actions would be influenced by whether they saw the wrongdoing of others being punished and whether others' ethical actions were praised. The conclusion was that vicarious reward and punishment influenced ethical decisions if they were greater than expected. It was argued that people expected wrongdoing to be punished and ignored this effect unless the punishment was stronger than they had anticipated. Conversely they did not expect good to be praised, and when they saw it was, it did have a positive effect on their assessments of the probability that their own good actions might attract praise and reward.

2 Situational factors

The specifics of a situation can also affect someone's response to an ethical issue. Some people's jobs and organisational positions make it easier for them to take a moral stand than do those of others. The degree of closeness to an ethical problem, or their formal responsibility for resolving it, is an important factor. The closer one is the greater the obligation to act. Stewart (1984) defined this as the Kew Gardens Principle. (The geographical reference is to the public gardens in New York where passive bystanders witnessed a murder, and not to the British botanical gardens.) This principle proposed an obligation to take action against an ethical wrong where:

- there was a clear case of need;
- the agent was close to the situation in terms of 'notice' if not space;
- the agent had the capability to help the one in need; and
- no one else was likely to help.

In our research interviews people often claimed their 'distance' from an issue, in terms of their managerial responsibility, justified taking a position of neutrality on some example of organisational wrongdoing. Equally a person's general situation, in terms of their responsibility for others, for family, or their degree of economic independence, will also affect their willingness to move beyond neutrality. The specific circumstance of the ethical issue will also affect a person's response to it. Most people's response to the theft of a box of paper clips from work will be different from their response to serious misuse of a company credit card.

3 Psychological factors

Trevino (1986) suggested a number of individual variables that could affect a person's response to an ethical issue. They included ego strength, which is the tendency to stick to one's convictions. People with high ego strength are less likely to be swayed by circumstances or impulses into changing their mind. Field dependence was another possible variable. This refers to the degree to which someone depends on information given by others when faced with an ambiguous situation. A person with high field dependence, if asked by their superior to take a possibly unethical action, would be influenced by the superior's assurances that they will not be blamed and that the action is not really improper. A person with low field dependency would wish to make up their own mind independently of the advice from others. Other writers (Verbeke *et al.*, 1996) have suggested that Machiavellianism, as a personality trait, may affect someone's response to an ethical issue.

Definition

Machiavellianism is named after Nicolo Machiavelli (1469–1527), whose name (rightly or wrongly) has become synonymous with cunning, amoral, devious and manipulative behaviour. The reputation is based on his book *The Prince*, in which he gave practical advice on statesmanship. He saw democracy as the best form of government but recognised that it was not always possible to behave in the most virtuous way. The dictum that 'the end justifies the means' is attributed to Machiavelli. By this he meant that there is no moral distinction between ends and means so that any badness in a proposed means can be balanced by the goodness of the outcome. It does not mean that good ends can justify any means no matter how wicked (Mackie, 1990: 159), but, as Machiavelli (1950, ch. XVIII) put it, 'the prince must have a mind disposed to adapt itself, according to the wind, and as the variations of fortune dictate . . . not deviate from what is good, if possible but be able to do evil if constrained'.

Rotter's (1966) internal-external locus of control scale is another psychological construct that may affect ethical choices. It measures an individual's perception of how much control he or she exerts over events in their lives. Some people believe that most things in life are within their control. They do not believe in luck; they believe people make their own luck. Others do not believe they control their own lives. They believe in luck, fate and happenstance. Trevino's analysis found there was a relationship between this factor and people's ethical choices. It showed that people who felt in control of their actions were more likely to make ethical rather than unethical decisions than those who believed themselves influenced by external factors. To some extent this relationship was reinforced by the tendency of people with an internal locus of control to believe that they can bring about the beneficial consequences of their actions that they hoped for.

ACTIVITY 5.3

Scoring the locus of control scale

Versions of the locus of control scale for you to fill in, and obtain your own score from, are to be found in plenty on the World Wide Web. Go to one of the following sites and see how you score.

Locus of control questionnaires on the World Wide Web

http://uhddx01.dt.uh.edu/~avenf/locus.html
http://home.hkstar.com/~ttyu/psytests/loc.htm
www.ballarat.edu.au/bssh/psych/rot.htm

4 Cognitive factors

The seminal work on levels of cognitive development was conducted and published by Lawrence Kohlberg (1969, 1984). His theory was originally developed in the field of developmental psychology. He researched the development of children's capacity for ethical reasoning and it was only later that the model was applied to adults and people in organisations in particular. Whether the focus is on adults or children the key idea is that people pass through an invariant and hierarchical sequence of three stages, the pre-conventional, the conventional and the post-conventional in the development of their ethical cognitive ability. However it is not quite as simple as this. Kohlberg originally proposed that each of the three stages subdivided into two, giving a total of six stages. Subsequent developments have led to this being expanded to eight or possibly nine stages. We will take you through these one at a time.

■ Pre-conventional stages

Stage zero

At this stage a person has no capacity for moral reasoning. They simply act impulsively and respond to any urge no matter what the consequences.

Stage one

People at this stage, and certainly all young children, have no innate sense of morality but they have learned that certain actions bring praise and others bring punishment. They can respond to the carrots and sticks without knowing the rationale for their subsequent behaviour. This stage of development consists of unwitting compliance with the demands of those with the ability to praise and punish. Parents clearly have this power but so do managers and supervisors in organisations.

Stage two

Personal gain, and the wish not to miss out on good things, characterises moral thinking at this stage. People evaluate options according to the benefits that they might gain. This is a selfish stage at which a person cannot, when considering a situation, think beyond what might be in it for them. In an organisational context only the prospect of higher pay, promotion or some other benefit would be of weight.

■ Conventional stages

Stage three

It is at this level of development that a person responds to their social role by thinking about morality in terms of being, to use the phrase always used of this stage, a 'Nice Boy/Good Girl'. At this stage people accept as legitimate the social norms and expectations of the groups they belong to. This stage does not involve ethical thought about the issues. People abide by the social norms not because they have analysed them and concluded they are correct but because they wish to be socially accepted.

One of these social norms is the obligation to be caring towards others; and this lowly positioning of care (level three when eight or nine represents the highest level of morality) has been the source of a major criticism of Kohlberg's model. Gilligan (1982) showed that girls' moral development differs from that of boys (*see* p. 74). Girls place more emphasis on relationships, responsibility and caring for others than boys. Gilligan argued that care is more than a response to social norms, that philosophically it is the equivalent of the cold abstraction of justice that, as we shall see, Kohlberg placed at the apex of his model. Kohlberg responded to this criticism by placing welfare higher in his model, but many argue (Snell, 2000: 274) that this response is inadequate.

Stage four

At this stage the conventions that frame a person's morality are not social but organisational and institutional. Sometimes this stage is further divided into two. At the inferior of these two stages morality is framed within the rules and regulations of a specific organisation such as a company or a professional association that has defined rules of conduct and ethics. At the superior level the adherence is to the wider institutional rules of society. Some people argue that rule utilitarianism (*see* p. 98) is the guiding morality of this stage. The critical factor in both stages, however, is that the commitment to 'law and order' is a knowing one. People have chosen to apply the rules by choice because they believe them to be good for themselves individually as well as for the wider institutions of society.

▧ The post-conventional stages

Stage five

At the post-conventional stages people are capable of questioning and reflecting upon the systems and principles of morality that they follow. At this stage, which is referred to as the social contract stage, people challenge the prevailing morality and seek to change it in accordance with their own reflections. They might, for example, campaign to change the law on cigarette advertising because they think it would advance social justice to do so.

Stage six

At stage six, which in some versions is the final stage of the model, there is an acceptance of the existence of universal principles of justice (and in later versions, *pace* Gilligan) welfare. This knowledge of universal principle is not easily come by but gained through intellectual struggle and practical confrontation with injustice in the world. A person at this level takes risks to bring justice wherever they find injustice. Kohlberg's definition of level six is Kantian (*see* p. 77). It is austere and concerned with abstract principle. Not all of Kohlberg's critics were at ease with this.

The postmodernists in particular had trouble with the notion of justice as a metanarrative. Snell (1993: 20) reported, and to some extent accepted, the arguments of those who see stage six as a capacity for principled relativism rather than irrefragable justice. This mirrors Rorty's views (Mounce, 1997: 185–9) in stressing the need for continuing conversations, a celebration of doubt and paradox and a playful sense of irony when dealing with complex moral matters.

Stage seven

This stage we find hard to define because of its transcendental nature, which means you have to achieve it to know it. It does in general draw themes from many of the world's major religions including Christianity, Buddhism and Judaism. One such is the idea of the unity of all creation; the belief that in some way all things are part of a single whole. The idea of morality at this highest level is linked with the idea of becoming at one with the whole of creation. This is the final stage in the ninefold developmental sequence (remembering that the first phase is called stage zero and that stage four can be subdivided).

There have been many criticisms of Kohlberg's model but it has proved robust and remains a core theory. It has been pointed out that the stages may not be hierarchical. One particularly relevant form of this argument is that even though people may have acquired a capacity to think morally at one of the higher levels there is no guarantee that they will choose to do so. Nor is such a capacity a guarantee that people will act according to the highest level thinking that they are capable of. Nevertheless it is clear that a person's capacity for moral reasoning will have an impact on which of the ethical stances is chosen.

Reflections

This chapter has presented a classification of eight stances that may be taken in response to an ethical issue at work. The question has to be asked whether some stances are more ethical than others. It might be considered in two parts. The first is to consider whether, in Figure 5.1, the stances higher in the matrix are more ethical than those lower on the vertical scale. The second part is whether those stances on the right-hand side of the matrix are more ethical than those on the left-hand side.

Kohlberg has made the case that ethical cognitive development is hierarchical. On this basis it could be argued that the ethical puzzle and problem stances are better than neutrality or negotiation. However such a claim would suggest that people should always aspire to the higher stances. This might lead to some odd consequences. Would it be sensible to apply the relatively complex stances of ethical puzzle or ethical problem to a relatively simple matter such as the casual theft of office stationery? This question implies that a contingency approach might be sensible in which the 'higher' and more complex stances would be more appropriate for major and difficult ethical dilemmas. Snell made a suggestion of this type in relation to Kohlberg's stages of moral development. He argued that an ethical difficulty arises when a level of ethical development creates rather than solves a problem. If someone is thinking at level three (nice boy/good girl) then they will be in a dilemma if the people they want to like them are tugging them in contradictory directions. It is the level of thinking that is causing the difficulty. Snell (1993: 62) recommends overcoming the difficulty by shifting the level of ethical thinking up at least one stage. If the demands of social peers are incompatible then the difficulty can only be overcome by thinking in terms of the rules and regulations of the organisation (stage four). The general principle is that one should use the minimum cognitive level, or stance if we move from cognition to action, that is required to overcome an ethical difficulty.

The second part of the question is whether the left-hand stances are ethically better than the right-hand stances. The two sides of the matrix in Figure 5.1 can be described in terms of categorisation and particularisation. The left-hand stances give priority to categorisation. They all operate by pigeon-holing issues so that their commonalities may be stressed and standard responses applied. The right-hand stances give more emphasis to particularisation. They all emphasise the complexity and ambiguity of issues, which are things that make it difficult to categorise an issue. These stances do not dictate particular solutions to issues though they do suggest ways of dealing with or coping with the uncertainty (debating judgements, keeping the conversation going, cynical withdrawal or negotiation with stakeholders). The trade-offs between the left-hand and right-hand stances are clear. If the left-hand stances are taken actions can be decisively chosen and implemented; but they may be inappropriate or unfair. The right-hand stances might be more responsive to the nuances and complexities of an issue but they may also lead to prevarication and inaction. The results from the *Downsizing* exercise (Activity 5.2) suggest that many managers and professionals were uncomfortable with the right-hand stances (the accountants being more uncomfortable than the HR specialists). This may be dangerous because it is the neglected right-hand stances that provide the critical element necessary to limit the left-hand stances' propensity for inflexibility and unfair discrimination. As has been suggested earlier in the chapter people at work may need to develop a momentum that swings them between the left-hand stances and the right-hand stances – between categorisation and particularisation.

Summary

In this chapter the following key points have been made:

- There are eight stances that people may take in response to an ethical issue at work.
- People may take different stances on an issue, depending on their consciences, ethical reasoning, perceptions of others' views, and in their actions.
- Tensions between a person's conscience, ethical reasoning, perceptions of others' views and their actions can cause psychological discomfort and interpersonal conflicts.
- The particulars of a specific ethical issue will also have an influence on the stance a person chooses and their inclination to change stances.
- Their choice of stances will be affected by a number of factors such as their level of cognitive development and the values they share with a group or society.

Suggested further reading

Many of the key themes and ideas of this chapter are taken from M. Billig (1996) *Arguing and Thinking. A rhetorical approach to social psychology*, 2nd edn, Cambridge: Cambridge University Press. It is not an easy read but it is very rewarding. R. Snell's book provides a good introduction to Kohlberg and has convincing case studies that relate the theory to resolving ethical problems at work: R. Snell (1993) *Developing Skills for Ethical Management*, London: Chapman and Hall.

GROUP ACTIVITY 5

The following is an extract from an interview with a personnel manager. It gives two examples of situations where an organisation's senior managers wanted to dispense with employees whom they thought no longer fitted with the official culture and values of the organisation. The personnel manager, who was an intermediary in both of these situations, took a different stance in each case. In the first case she was in favour of parting with the employee but in the second case she thought it would be wrong to part with the member of staff.

Read the interview and discuss how the respondent might explain why she took different stances on issues that seem to involve the same matter of principle.

1 Should employees be let go if they do not fit with an organisation's official culture?

2 What particulars might have triggered different categorisations in each of the incidents?

The most recent example is a retail business manager who has got a consistently high appraisal rating, high performance rating over the last few years. But what is required over the next three years? Has this person the ability to move forward? Therefore there is a big question mark over where that person goes. Because we're talking about somebody who's perceived by the organisation as a high performer. Yet in terms of everything they do everyday we can see that they have the inability to change, to move forward with the change in an emerging brand.

Well the whole style of the operation is changing. We have a new Director and General Manager and senior management team for a start. They have a different way of working. The emphasis is on empowerment. The emphasis is moving away from control culture, control type management to a more loose management culture and more sales oriented and building on development in sales. This person is not interested in development and growing sales. He's more about the old control culture. Hit them with a big stick and sack them if they don't do what you tell them mentality. But has an excellent performance record, and if you look in terms of actual year on year profit performance he's the best achiever in the company.

Also the difficulty is because he has a reputation throughout the company for that tough management style nobody else wants to face him. So the fact is that we'll end up losing somebody [*said ironically, meaning the manager*] from the organisation. Which will also cause or create a huge employee relations issue. Because he will take us to tribunal. Rightly so in terms of performance.

Well we've decided he's got to go. Well it will be a severance. He'll have to go. We've looked at the other alternatives and there aren't any.

I think in terms of the organisation's culture it's absolutely right but actually this guy has worked for the company for some time and in his own way has been committed. So I think there probably is a view that maybe over the years this person hasn't been managed properly in the past and maybe if he'd been managed better in the past then maybe we wouldn't be at this point now. Yes we've worked on him, we've been working on it for the last six months. It's not even a runner. We're basically saying, up yours, you know, as good as.

Group activity 5 continued

Well I've dealt with so many [severance cases] that I always think that if I go home at night and sleep, my conscience is relatively clear. I have a job to do and I believe when it comes round and it's right for the business, then it's part of the job. I think so, yes.

I quite often won't do something if I don't agree with it being morally right, or I'll look for a compromise. Yes, somebody who works for me who, one of the Directors felt, wasn't committed enough to the organisation because they didn't work seven days a week. He told me that I needed to do something about that person and I refused point blank. I said that they actually worked more effectively than anybody else here and no I don't intend to get rid of him. I refuse to do that. At the end of the day, just because you [the director] believe that we should work seven days a week it doesn't prove that they're not committed. So I actually did dig my heels in and said no I'm not going to do it. I refused and we've worked around that. I did then talk to that person and let that person know how he [the director] felt about it and said you know you just need to think about raising your profile and meeting part way. Well I think I responded as I did because that person is an extremely effective member of the team and actually the output is far higher than the average. And really it was more about profile. In terms of the organisation it's the nature of the business and because our business does operate seven days a week, then it becomes the accepted norm. If you've got pressure from a senior manager then it makes life difficult for you and then ultimately it forces somebody out. The director was being unreasonable, totally un-reasonable, absolutely.

It's settled down again now but it was very difficult at the time. It put me in a difficult position. I'm a great believer in sticking to your guns and I'm a spade or shovel person.

6 Whistleblowing

OBJECTIVES

Having completed this chapter and its associated activities, readers should be able to:

- Review the various issues that relate to the act of whistleblowing.
- Describe the role that whistleblowing potentially has to play within corporate governance processes.
- Explain the whistleblower's plight.
- Describe and critique the legislation, which seeks to protect whistleblowers in the UK.

Introduction

In this chapter we discuss the issue of those employees, who for a variety of reasons, come to a position where they are so uncomfortable with a particular practice or activity within their employing organisation that they feel they have no alternative but to raise the matter with another person. This other person might be a work colleague, a senior member of the organisation, a family member or a non-related third party who is external to the employing organisation. The person to whom the revelation is made can be important because in the UK, for example, it can affect the degree of legal protection that is available to the concerned employee. However, to whomever the concerned employee confides, the act is the same. It is often referred to as whistleblowing and the people who 'blow the whistle' are usually referred to as whistleblowers. However, this can be a pejorative term and some writers prefer other descriptions, e.g. Beardshaw (1981) described such employees as 'conscientious objectors at work', whilst Winfield (1990) preferred 'principled dissenters'.

The words we use to describe people or things are important because they create an initial context and orientate our emotions towards the discussion that might follow. Thus, if the term whistleblower brings to mind the notion of a 'snitch', or a 'grass', then you are more likely to be inclined, initially at least, towards a negative view of a whistleblower with regard to any discussion of a particular whistleblowing case. If, however, you prefer the descriptions proffered by writers such as Winfield and Beardshaw, because that is how you see most whistleblowers, then your interpretation of the 'rights and wrongs' of a particular case is likely to lean towards the position of the whistleblower. Our quest in this chapter is to consider the issue of whistleblowing and whistleblowers, using the terms neither pejoratively nor with praise, but merely descriptively.

In this chapter we will present you with the arguments surrounding whistleblowing, but also with evidence of the pressures within organisations that can constrain potential whistleblowers and the implications of such 'muteness'. We will use actual cases to illustrate the arguments, reflecting the messiness that is often to be found in organisational life, and the organisational impotency that many employees feel, irrespective of their position within the organisation. This is not to justify or to recommend an uncritical acceptance of the messiness and personal impotency that can be experienced in ethical dilemmas. The tools of analysis and the implications of the differing philosophical positions discussed in Chapters 3 and 4 will allow you to form reasoned judgements on the questions, issues and cases relating to whistleblowing that you will now consider.

When is a whistleblowing act performed?

A commonly held understanding of a whistleblowing act is the release of confidential organisational information to an external third party, often, but not exclusively, the media. However, as suggested above, a whistleblowing act can be a conversation, a remark even, to a work colleague, or a family member, in which organisational information, unknown to others participating in the conversation, is revealed. If these concerns are relayed back to 'management' before the employee concerned has raised the issue through the company's formal procedures (assuming they exist), and they are dismissed as a result of the revelation, then, in the UK, they are likely to lose the protection of the law that was introduced to protect whistleblowers. This is the Public Interest Disclosure Act 1998 (PIDA), which is discussed in more detail later in the chapter.

The PIDA was designed to provide protection to those who raise awareness of an act or practice that poses problems for public safety, or threatens other specific areas of public interest. From the above it is clear that whilst whistleblowing is normally a purposeful and intentional act, it might also be unintended and innocent. The law makes little, if any, distinction between intended and unintended whistleblowing.

Reacting to a particular organisational activity or practice in a way that does not comply with the requirements of the PIDA does not mean that legal recourse is not available to a whistleblower, should they wish to bring a case for wrongful dismissal. A civil action will still be possible. It is simply that the protection afforded by the PIDA will not be available.

Why whistleblow?

The personal outcomes experienced by many whistleblowers have been damaging, whether the outcomes are considered at a psychological, financial or social level (*see*, for example, Soeken and Soeken, 1987; Winfield, 1990; Miceli and

Near, 1992; Hunt, 1995, 1998). Loss of employment is common for the whistle-blower, with opportunities to gain alternative employment often limited. Some whistleblowers have become unemployable as their names have been circulated amongst employing organisations as 'troublemakers'. Borrie and Dehn (2002) refer to such an example.

Robert Maxwell was the dominant figure in Maxwell Communications, a conglomerate which included within its empire the *Daily Mirror* group of newspapers, which in turn owned the Scottish newspaper mentioned in the following quotation.

> Two years before Robert Maxwell stole $1m pension funds, he sacked a union official who had challenged what he was doing with the pension money at a Scottish newspaper. Maxwell, a powerful businessman, was able to ensure that the man could not get another job in the industry so destroying his career.
>
> (Borrie and Dehn, 2002: 5)

In addition, both the whistleblower and his or her family often experience great financial and emotional hardship, with break-ups in marriages or partnerships frequently reported. Suicides of whistleblowers have also been attributed to the financial and psychological fallout from their whistleblowing experiences. In the light of this evidence, the question might well be asked, why whistleblow?

The answer to this may be found in a number of tragedies of recent times. In these instances we often find evidence of employees who have raised concerns prior to the occurrence of the final incident. Had these concerns been acted upon the tragedy in question might not have happened. Whether we look at examples such as the Piper-Alpha disaster or the Zeebrugge (*Herald of Free Enterprise*) tragedy, BCCI, Maxwell Communications, Barlow Clowes, the Lyme Bay canoeing tragedy, the Southall rail crash, the Clapham rail crash or the incidence of high fatality rates among operations on young children at Bristol Royal Infirmary, we find evidence of the ignored concerns of employees.

These were tragedies in the Greek sense. They could have been predicted from their specific circumstances yet they also appeared inexorable. The circumstances in question often related to lax controls and practices, and a failure to listen to the concerns of employees. The concerns either had been reported to management, but not acted upon, or had been unreported due to oppressive and authoritarian management practices or misguided feelings of loyalty. For example, the *Herald of Free Enterprise* capsized as it left Zeebrugge harbour because its bow doors had been left open, resulting in the deaths of 192 passengers and crew. The inquiry report into the disaster concluded:

> If this sensible suggestion . . . had received the serious consideration it deserved this disaster might well have been prevented.
>
> (Lewis, 2000: 3)

The suggestion in question was the fitting of lights to the bridge that would have indicated whether or not the bow doors were closed. On five occasions prior to the capsize of the *Herald of Free Enterprise*, P&O staff had expressed their concerns about the risks of ships leaving port with their bow doors open, but these concerns were not acted upon. The concerns expressed on five previous occasions had been reported, but they had not been conveyed to the top management of the company. The concerns had become lost in the middle management tiers of the organisation. Tragedies, such as those mentioned above, created a socio-political climate that was sufficiently supportive to allow the PIDA to be passed as an Act of Parliament in 1998 and to become operative in 1999.

In response to the question, 'why whistleblow?', examples can be cited of situations in which (many) lives might have been saved, had the concerns of employees been listened to and acted upon, or if the concerned, but ignored, employees had taken their worries to a broader public platform and made the general public aware of the practices concerned. So does this type of evidence make the general argument in favour of whistleblowing correct, and is whistleblowing justifiable, and to be encouraged? If so, why is the act of whistleblowing and of a whistleblower so often portrayed and perceived as a negative force within society?

A contributory factor in explaining why one person might choose to whistle-blow in a given situation, whilst another, when faced with the same circumstances, would opt for a different strategy, is associated with the issues we discussed in Chapter 3. Although no substantial evidence exists concerning the ethical orientation of whistleblowers (and more significantly suppressed whistle-blowers), we can employ our understanding of ethical theories to hypothesise about their likely ethical orientation. In terms of the ethical theories represented in the quadrants of Figure 3.1, people who display a predominantly deontological orientation towards ethical issues, whose ethical thinking, and possibly action, reflects principled-based responses, are more likely to feel compelled to whistleblow if resolution of an ethical dilemma proves impossible.

With concepts such as justice, honesty and integrity normally included in any set of virtues, a virtue ethics orientation (the top left-hand section of Figure 3.1) would also suggest that someone possessing such an orientation would be more likely to resist pressure to compromise themselves should an ethical issue prove insoluble. Whistleblowing would again be a likely outcome to an intractable ethical issue.

This contrasts with someone whose ethical orientation reflects consequential-ist thinking, i.e. who thinks through the consequences of the available options before choosing a course of action. With this orientation, the course of action chosen will depend upon the circumstances of each situation. Given the history of whistleblowing cases (and not just the negative outcomes for the whistle-blowers, but also for other employees and the organisation concerned), whistle-blowing becomes a far less likely outcome if the concerned employee applies a consequentialist orientation.

The above discussion assumes, of course, that the individual is free to adopt the ethical reasoning which reflects her or his own orientation. This, however, is often not possible, due to powerful pressures upon individuals to suppress their personal values and compromise their principles. We discuss the implications of these pressures in the case examples that follow.

In terms of the theoretical framework presented in Chapter 3, the organisation that develops and employs a bona fide whistleblowing process can be located in the top right-hand section of Figure 3.1. Such an approach would suggest a reflective, thoughtful orientation towards organisational development, with employees seen as important stakeholders and contributors to that development. Such processes would reflect the best of practices.

When might whistleblowing be justified?

Some writers have set out what, for them, are the essential conditions that make whistleblowing acts justifiable. De George (1999) argued that there are six such conditions. De George's position on whistleblowing is a consequentialist one. Because any whistleblowing act is likely to do harm to the employing organisation, the act can only be justified if the overall effects of the act are likely to be positive. There is no reference to principles or virtues. It is the overall consequences of a whistleblowing act that determine its justification. It is argued that the first three conditions (shown below) make whistleblowing permissible, but not obligatory. If conditions 4 and 5 can be satisfied then whistleblowing becomes a far more persuasive option, in De George's terms, morally obligatory. Another way of interpreting these conditions is to say that without them, an act of whistleblowing cannot be morally justified as the likely outcome will be painful and probably fruitless for the whistleblower, and deleterious to the organisation. The conditions are as follows:

- A product or policy of an organisation needs to possess the potential to do harm to some members of society.
- The concerned employee should first of all report the facts, as far as they are known, to her or his immediate superior.
- If the immediate superior fails to act effectively, the concerned employee should take the matter to more senior managers, exhausting all available internal channels in the process.
- The prospective whistleblower should hold documentary evidence that can be presented to external audiences. In this condition De George argues that the evidence should show that the product or policy 'poses a serious and likely danger to the public or to the user of the product' (De George, 1999: 255).
- The prospective whistleblower must believe that the necessary changes will be implemented as a result of their whistleblowing act.
- The sixth condition is a general one and it is that the whistleblower must be acting in good faith, without malice or vindictiveness

These conditions will now be considered to assess their defensibility, but first we would like you to ponder their appropriateness and helpfulness.

ACTIVITY 6.1

Challenging the conditions for justifiable whistleblowing

The six 'conditions of whistleblowing' suggest that if they cannot be fulfilled, then a whistleblowing act cannot be justified. Develop arguments against as many of the six conditions as possible so that whistleblowing could still be justified.

■ A consideration of the conditions

1 *A product or policy of an organisation needs to possess the potential to do harm to some members of society.*

At first sight it might seem difficult to find fault with this requirement, because if no public safety or public concern issue exists, where is the public interest in the 'problem'? What can be the justification for any revelation? An important caveat would be that harm must be interpreted widely and not confined to physical harm. Economic harm, as in the cases of BCCI and Maxwell Communications, or psychological harm in the form of race or gender discrimination can be just as damaging as physical harm.

2 *The concerned employee should first of all report the facts, as far as they are known, to her/his immediate superior, and*

3 *If the immediate superior fails to act effectively, the concerned employee should take the matter to more senior managers, exhausting all available internal channels in the process.*

These two conditions are considered together because of their obvious linkage. Some would argue that organisations should view internal whistleblowing procedures as important mechanisms within their corporate governance processes. It might seem commonsense that organisations would wish to be informed about practices that threaten the well-being of their customers, or the public at large. After all, reputations and brands can take years and considerable expenditures to build, but be destroyed in a very short time by adverse publicity. Thus, enlightened self-interest would seem to dictate an interest in encouraging internal whistleblowing. So why are some organisations not more receptive to the concerns and criticisms of their employees?

The roots of the explanation are complex, but they have to include personal reputations and relationships. Suggesting that 'organisations' would wish to be informed about unsafe practices or products gives a physical status to the term 'organisation' which is, in this context, inappropriate and unhelpful. Criticisms made of products and practices will invariably be criticisms of people, usually more senior than oneself. Condition 2 implies that one's immediate superior within the organisation should be consulted; even if they are part of the problem, hence condition 3. The PIDA also recognises this potential problem and allows the whistleblower to bypass their immediate supervisor if this can be shown to be warranted.

Condition 3 assumes that some form of internal whistleblowing process exists and is operated with integrity. A good example is Carmarthenshire County Council's (2000) whistleblowing policy, which is available for inspection on the World Wide Web. Yet it is quite possible that the cause of one's concerns lie with the policies or practices of the senior management. For example, budgetary pressures to achieve improved output targets within existing or reduced resources might compromise quality, including safety checks. Alternatively, managers at differing levels within their organisation may each, unknown to the others, impose planned efficiency savings on budgetary forecasts in order to impress senior management (De George, 1999: 244, cites such a scenario). In the process a final budget is created that might involve production outputs and cost levels that are wholly unrealistic. As a consequence corners are subsequently cut to try and approach the agreed output or cost budgets. Any expression of concern by an employee may become 'lost' within the management hierarchy. Finding out where the blockage exists might be a far from simple task. Expecting employees who are employed 'at the coal face' to have the awareness or confidence to express their concerns higher up the management tree (assuming one can identify how far one needs to go to escape the vicious circle of partially implicated managers) could be an unrealistic assumption. In real life, raising one's concerns internally can simply mean that management can identify which employees are likely to reveal problems which are of the managers' making.

Thus, conditions 2 and 3, whilst initially suggesting a way for concerned employees and enlightened organisations to operate open channels of communication, might in fact be more reflective of a desire to keep the problem within the organisation. This implies an emphasis upon loyalty to the organisation, loyalty which history would question in terms of reciprocated loyalty and commitment.

So far we have shown that a number of circumstances can exist which make conditions 1, 2 and 3 problematic. Yet these are only considered to be conditions that would make a whistleblowing act permissible. They are argued to be insufficient on their own to constitute the necessary conditions for an act of whistleblowing to be morally obligatory. To achieve this, De George argued that conditions 4 and 5 need to be satisfied.

4 *The prospective whistleblower should hold documentary evidence that can be presented to external audiences.*

Here it is being argued that without hard evidence of your concerns, you are not obliged to reveal them to an external (or internal) audience. The rationale is that without strong evidence you may risk the negative outcomes experienced by many whistleblowers, without being able to expose the bad practices that concern you. This has to be a sensible, cautionary note for any potential whistleblowers to weigh in their deliberations about expressing their concerns, but it does not address the moral dilemma that the concerned employee faces.

Obtaining the evidence one requires to substantiate one's concerns can be extremely difficult. First, there is the problem that ownership of the information is likely to rest with the organisation. The law of property rights would make the photocopying of such evidence a criminal offence. However, to blow the whistle without such evidence would be naive in the extreme. Most whistleblowers obtain as much evidence as they can and let the courts decide whether accusations of stealing company property are an adequate defence by the employing organisation.

The other major problem is that sometimes incriminating evidence is either too difficult to obtain or simply not available. In the example of the misappropriation of pension fund monies by Robert Maxwell, the case was so complex, due to the interlocking nature of so many of the subsidiary companies within the Maxwell Communications empire that the task for one, or a few, employees, of obtaining sufficient corroborating evidence to support their concerns, was simply impossible. It took accountants nearly two calendar years, and many more person years, to unravel the web that Maxwell had woven.

So if one has deep concerns about a particular issue (say, the use of pension funds as in the Maxwell case), but a lack of hard evidence, is one absolved from one's civic responsibilities? The financial loss suffered by the pensioners of the Maxwell companies was significant. This was not a minor financial scam. Whilst it is wise to counsel caution to prospective whistleblowers if their corroborating information is not strong, society as a whole might be the lesser if this condition was used as an ethical loophole, through which individuals could escape their personal dilemma, i.e. to divulge or not to divulge. It is unlikely that sufficient corroborating evidence will be gathered in many cases to prove irrefutably that a particular revelation is watertight. This is why the PIDA uses phrases such as that the whistleblower should 'reasonably believe' and should believe the accusation to be 'substantially true'. UK law does not require that the accusation be 'true', only that it was reasonable to believe that it was true.

5 *The prospective whistleblower must believe that the necessary changes will be implemented as a result of their whistleblowing act.*
The emphasis here is again on the protection of the whistleblower. Given the negative personal outcomes that the majority of whistleblowers have experienced, this condition is merely saying, 'If the probabilities are that nothing will change as a result of your action, you are not duty bound to make your revelation'. Although the condition is expressed in a positive sense, i.e. 'if conditions 1–5 exist and you are of the view that your revelation will cause the offending or dangerous practice to cease, then you are morally obliged to make your revelation', the condition can be reinterpreted as possessing a negative slant. In its negative form the condition is effectively offering an escape route to the uncertain whistleblower.

6 *The whistleblower must be acting in good faith, without malice or vindictiveness.*
This is a contentious condition. It begs the question, 'Why are the motives of the whistleblower important or relevant?' If the whistleblower can be shown to have grounds for harbouring resentment at being passed over for promotion at some time in the past, or for being disciplined for an organisational infraction, why should this invalidate or undermine any revelation that they might make about an organisational malpractice? One reason might be, as some managers claimed in our research interviews, that the disgruntled employee was lying, out of spite, about the alleged wrongdoing.

We might prefer that those revealing organisational malpractices do so for honourable reasons, and the purity of the whistleblower's position is an oft-cited requirement for acceptable whistleblowing, but it is a doubtful argument. As you will see when we discuss the PIDA, one of the requirements of the Act is that for a whistleblower to gain the protection of the Act, they must not profit from the whistleblowing, e.g. from publishing their revelations in a newspaper or book. Whilst it might not be wholly desirable for whistleblowing to be stimulated by thoughts of personal gain, it has to be asked whether the public interest is served by denying such whistleblowers legal protection. Practices for encouraging whistleblowing are followed when rewards are offered for information leading to the successful prosecution of criminals in cases of robbery, murder, hijacking and so on, and nothing is judged to be untoward in these circumstances. One must ask what the distinctions are that make whistleblowers of organisational malpractices less valued by society than whistleblowers of other crimes.

The 'crime' of revealing corporate malpractices is sometimes seen as greater than the corporate malpractices themselves. Whilst offering rewards for the capture of, say, criminals who have robbed a bank is acceptable, normal practice even, the offering of rewards for evidence against companies that have 'robbed' shareholders and employees is somehow seen in a different light.

Whistleblowing: a positive or negative force in society?

The tragedies referred to earlier in the chapter might suggest that organisations would be wise to institute internal whistleblowing procedures to allow employees to raise their concerns and thus create early warning systems upon which the employing organisations could act. Indeed, internal whistleblowing structures can be seen as essential to good corporate governance. So is whistleblowing a characteristic of a healthy, self-aware and self-critical society, with those who reveal organisational malpractices regarded as performing positive civic acts? The evidence would suggest that as a society we are some way away from such a position, although Borrie (1996) observed that the development of organisations such as Childline might be heralding a changing view in relation to those who reveal evidence of abuse, recklessness and disregard for the integrity and sanctity of fellow human beings.

Sternberg (1996) argued that companies should look upon whistleblowing processes as critical elements within good corporate governance practice, and Borrie and Dehn (2002: 5) have also discussed the development of a whistleblowing culture in which the whistleblower would be seen 'as a witness, not as a complainant'. They argued that, thirty years ago, it was rare to find a company seeking the views of its customers about the quality of the company's products or services. Now it is regarded as central to staying competitive. Borrie and Dehn suggested that, maybe, in thirty years' time, whistleblowing processes will not merely be the norm, but be seen as essential elements of a corporation's information-gathering processes. Whilst a Kantian perspective would see the instrumental rationale implicit in such a development as reducing its ethical integrity, prospective whistleblowers might just be grateful for the development. A more serious concern for the development of supportive whistleblowing cultures is that if their justification is based upon economic rather than ethical grounds, then if the economic justification ceases to exist (i.e. the costs of operating a whistleblowing process are judged to outweigh the benefits being derived), then whistleblowers will once again be seen as impediments to organisational competitiveness.

As mentioned earlier, incidents such as the Lyme Bay canoeing disaster and the *Herald of Free Enterprise* disaster created the social and political conditions that allowed the Public Interest Disclosure Act to become law, but history is replete with examples of individuals who have revealed organisational malpractices, invariably to their own personal cost. Peter Drucker (quoted in Borrie 1996: 9) referred to whistleblowers as informers and likened societies that encouraged whistleblowing as bearing some of the characteristics of tyrannies such as those of Tiberius and Nero in Rome, the Spanish Inquisition, and the French Terror (cited in Borrie, 1996). Others see the acts of whistleblowers as equivalent to referees who maintain 'the rules of the game'. However, the analogy of the whistleblower as a referee in a sporting contest is flawed and a closer examination of the acts of whistleblowing within the context of a sporting event goes some way to explaining the antipathy that some feel towards whistleblowing and whistleblowers.

A whistleblower in a sporting event would not be the referee, but a member of one of the opposing sides who, upon seeing an infringement by one of his own side, stops the game and calls the referee's and the crowd's attention to the incident. This would be referred to as displaying a Corinthian spirit, i.e. placing the ideals and integrity of the sport above the mere winning of the immediate contest. Whether the supporters and fellow team members would see the incident in exactly the same light is debatable.

The sporting analogy should not be taken too far, because whistleblowing cases involve far greater consequences than the result of a game. The point of the analogy is that whistleblowers are not the appointed referees of organisational affairs. Neither do they claim to be. They are usually unfortunate individuals who become ensnared in the maelstrom of a situation, which for a variety of reasons becomes irresolvable, at least to their satisfaction. They are then faced with the predicament of either allowing their concerns to subside and 'keeping their heads below the parapet', or seeking to get the issue resolved by revealing their concerns to either an internal or external audience. Some have described whistleblowing acts as heroic acts, because the outcomes for many whistleblowers tend to be so negative. But why are whistleblowers so often maligned and cast as the wrongdoers, in situations where others have created great potential harm?

Besides potentially suffering the unpleasantness of being seen as a 'snitch' or informer, the prospective whistleblower has to weigh the implications for an organisation of news reaching its critical markets about the practices in question. These markets include both product markets and securities markets. In competitive markets, ground lost to rival organisations can be difficult to make up, and confidence lost by investors in the organisation difficult to restore. The threat of lost jobs can mean that even long-term colleagues may not support the whistleblower.

The following example, which is taken from a study conducted by the authors (Fisher and Lovell, 2000), indicates that such bad practices are not confined to small, back-street operators who exploit the vulnerability of a low-skilled workforce. The company concerned was a large, internationally known engineering organisation.

CASE STUDY 6.1

The engineering company and its overseas markets

This company operated in a range of domestic (UK) and overseas markets. In at least one of the overseas markets 'arrangements' sometimes had to be negotiated with overseas agents that involved exported goods being artificially reclassified to reduce the level of import duties in the overseas country. For example, a £1m order for engineered products would be reclassified for invoice purposes as £700K engineered products and £300K consultancy services. In this particular overseas country consultancy services (and many other service industry 'products') were not subject to import duty.

Case study 6.1 continued

The engineering company did not suffer as a result of the reclassification, and the importing agents acquired the goods at a lower cost (taking import taxes into account) than they would otherwise have had to pay. The only losers were the governments of the countries concerned. When these situations arose, the unofficial, but well-understood, procedure within the engineering company was for the requested 'arrangement' to be passed directly to the sales director and managing director of the engineering company. This ultimate decision-making unit would then weigh the risks, the returns and the implications of the decision and then decree whether the proposed deal with the agent would be sanctioned. Clearly this act was illegal, yet it was argued that such behaviour was necessary in order to stay in the markets concerned and to protect jobs in the UK. It was claimed that other operators in these markets offered similar 'arrangements'. Here the consequentialist argument that all the implications of a decision should be weighed in order to identify the decision that offers the greatest good to the greatest number might be tabled. The waters became further muddied when the management of the engineering company argued that the government of the overseas country operated a repressive regime, employing punitive import taxes in order to shore up excessive government expenditure on military equipment and government largesse.

None of the claims about the foreign government could be validated, but if they were true, what did the actions of the senior management of the company say to the employees of the engineering company? Whatever the rights and wrongs of the situation the engineering company was employing criteria and a decision process that sanctioned law-breaking activity.

If the argument is raised that business is not a precise and neat ethical practice and that one has to accept that in certain cases ends justify the means, one is accepting a situation where different rules are known to apply in different contexts. No part of a code of behaviour can be seen to be inviolate and every organisational value has its price. This is not to suggest that all laws have to be respected, however repressive and immoral, but the behaviour of the engineering executives was not law breaking born of high ideals, but law breaking born of motives of organisational or personal gain and/or prejudice.

An interesting development to this case was that the practice involving the reclassification of exported products had come to the attention of an overseas government and the major operators in this market (including the UK engineering company) were making provisions for substantial repayments of undeclared import taxes. There was also the possibility that a number of the operators could be barred from selling in the overseas market in the future. This development does not suddenly make the decision-making procedures employed invalid, when previously they could be justified on an ends-means basis. An action does not acquire the status of being ethical or unethical merely on the grounds that its existence is either publicly known or unknown.

An obvious question regarding the engineering company is why the employees we interviewed tolerated their organisational environment. The answer to this question is not explained by one single factor, but it did appear that the most senior management of the organisation were implicated in the practices. Fear that any form of dissent would be quickly suppressed and would impair future promotional prospects was the overriding reason offered by the interviewees for their muteness. There were no whistleblowers within this organisation. Was this a state of affairs to be applauded or encouraged, and how and why can middle and senior managers possess such feelings of organisational impotence?

Within the engineering company many understood the practices, but no one possessed the courage, the will or the independence (as a result of the need to retain their employment) to raise their concerns, either within the organisations or to external agencies. The extent of the malpractices acted like a cancer, corrupting others who might otherwise have exercised moral judgement. There appeared to be view amongst certain middle and junior management levels of 'what is sauce for the goose (senior management) is sauce for the gander (themselves)'.

The engineering company might seem an extreme example of modern organisational life. However, the continuing evidence of unacceptable organisational practices and whistleblowing cases (*see*, for example, Hartley, 1993; Hunt, 1995, 1998), and the work of organisations such as Public Concern at Work and Freedom to Care, do not provide much support for benign assumptions about respect for the moral agency of individual employees.

Suppressed whistleblowing

For the concerned employee, there are not only potential costs associated with revealing organisational malpractices, there are also costs associated with suppressing whistleblowing. The latter costs tend to be emotional and psychological and are associated with a loss of self-esteem. This is illustrated in Figure 6.1. A fuller account of the issues relating to this framework is given in Lovell (2002).

The framework possesses two layers. The first of them is concerned with two non-organisational factors that are significant in shaping the third element, that of the individual's personal autonomy. The three elements of layer 1 are:

Layer 2	Intensity of problem	Organisational values/ strength of practices	Support of others
Layer 1	Personal values	Personal autonomy	Societal values

Figure 6.1 Elements of ethical complexity

- The individual's personal value system, born of past experiences, including family values and perspectives (both nature and nurture are included).
- Broader societal values, which are unlikely to be homogenous or consistent.
- The feeling of personal autonomy held by the individual.

Layer 2 also possesses three elements, which are context specific. These are:

- Values derived from within the organisation.
- The ethical intensity of a situation or problem felt by the concerned employee.
- The support from others (normally organisational colleagues, both peers and hierarchical superiors; family; but also support groups, professional associations, etc.).

In Figure 6.1 the six cells are shown as the same size. However the figure can be used to describe the relative importance of the six elements in different potential whistleblowing situations. The relative size of the cells is contingent on the specifics of each case.

The emboldened part of Figure 6.1 represents an inflexible organisational boundary. If an ethically charged situation develops in which the position of the troubled employee is at loggerheads with the senior management, it is likely that the organisational mores/strength of practices will flex and grow in scale. With the boundaries of Figure 6.1 fixed, either one or more of the other elements has to shrink, or a fracture in the boundary will occur. If this happens, then confinement of the problem within the organisation will have ceased and an external whistleblowing situation could follow.

If the troubled employee wishes to retain employment within the organisation, but retains a belief that the organisational practice is wrong, then their personal autonomy will need to shrink to accommodate organisational/managerial interests. As a consequence of this diminution of personal autonomy, the ability to exercise moral agency is driven out.

Effectively an individual's personal autonomy acts as a type of shock absorber, allowing confinement of the issue within the organisational boundary. As a consequence, however, the confidence of the suppressed whistleblower can be severely affected. This was particularly so with respect to the individual who was central to revealing the practices outlined in Case study 6.1. The shrinking of personal autonomy was also significant in Case study 6.2.

CASE STUDY 6.2

VAT and the charitable organisation

G possessed a strong religious faith, which reflected his family upbringing. He worked for an internationally known charitable organisation, whose *raison d'être* was love, understanding, tolerance and forgiveness. During our initial interview with him G revealed that he had an interesting example of principle that was live at the time of the interview. Having recently attended a seminar on value added tax (VAT), G had realised that a practice operated by the charity was liable to VAT, but the practice had never been declared for VAT purposes. On returning from the seminar G brought the matter to the attention of the directors, believing that the correct

Case study 6.2 continued

approach would be to notify Customs and Excise and to discuss the issue with them. G was very aware that the charity could not afford to repay the sums that were now clearly owing to Customs and Excise, but G believed that Customs and Excise would agree that the VAT rules were never intended to apply to charities like his own, and at worst the charity would need to lobby Parliament and the Treasury to get the rules changed retrospectively. As the charity was internationally known and attracted widespread public support, G believed this would be possible.

At a subsequent meeting with G, he was clearly less buoyant than at our first meeting. He described how the charity's solicitors had been contacted to obtain a legal ruling on the practice in question and they had confirmed G's assessment. However, the attitude of the senior management towards G was not one of gratitude, but rather coolness, even a degree of wariness. At our third meeting with G, he revealed that the affair had been a sickening experience for him. The legal advice had been that the practice should be terminated immediately, but that no mention should be made to Customs and Excise. The belief was that Customs and Excise would demand a refund of the unpaid taxes and that the probability of the Treasury seeking a change to taxation legislation to exclude the charity from future liability was low, with no chance of retrospective legislation. G's wishes to be honest and 'come clean' with Customs and Excise were dismissed as naive. What particularly vexed and troubled him was that he was now, in his own words, 'perceived as a potential whistleblower'. His relationship with members of the charity's Board of Directors had changed from a close and friendly one, to one characterised by considerable wariness and mistrust. He had no intention of whistleblowing (out of loyalty to the organisation, not to the senior management), but it hurt greatly to come face to face with his organisational impotency, when he had thought that he and his work were highly valued.

At the start of his ethical dilemma G carried with him a set of values that he argued reflected a strong commitment to notions of fairness, equity and justice. These underpinned his initial reasoning of the problem. These were values that he believed corresponded with those of the broader society and the charity in question. G enjoyed a quite senior position within the charity. A quiet and softly spoken man, G considered his individual autonomy to be high. He was confident of his (moral) position and his arguments. In this case G could and did cite the 'Golden Rule', in his words, 'treat others as you would want to be treated yourself'.

For G, the intensity of the problem was initially high, but he quickly realised that the support of others did not exist, particularly at a very senior level. This mix of Kohlberg's Stage 2 elements (high problem intensity; total resistance from senior management; and low support from others), transformed the issue from one (in G's eyes) capable of resolution within notions of justice and equity, to an ethical dilemma. G's preference to discuss the issue with Customs and Excise put him at variance with the charity's board of directors. G became isolated and was seen as a deviant. He had a loyalty both to the organisation, whose values and mission he wholeheartedly believed in, and to his fellow employees, whose livelihoods would certainly be affected if the tax authorities did demand a repayment of back taxes.

G expressed the view that if he really believed that Customs and Excise would be successful in demanding repayment of back taxes, he too would support concealment, as the work of the charity would be affected to the point of ruin. However, he simply could not accept that this would be the ultimate outcome. He believed that the Board of Directors did not wish to be seen as having made a serious error in the decisions they had taken over the configuration of the organisation that had led to the practice in question attracting VAT liability, a ramification they had overlooked.

G's apparent willingness to 'break the law' is not necessarily a reprehensible position to hold. In G's view the particular VAT law in question represented a failing in the legislation's drafting. It was 'bad law', and could be corrected once its failings were brought to the attention of the relevant authorities. This form of reasoning would normally be considered to reflect high levels of moral reasoning, that is Stage five, possibly even Stage six, within Kohlberg's hierarchy (*see* p. 174), depending upon how far G was prepared to fight for his convictions. However, G considered the concealment, decided upon by the directors, reflected an avoidance of pain motive on their part, the very lowest stage of reasoning within Kohlberg's hierarchy. The values imposed upon the situation by the Board of Directors effectively challenged G. He either stayed, and kept quiet, or he left. Due to family commitments and a strong belief in the work of the charity G stayed, but his personal autonomy was severely diminished and he viewed the future with sadness and apprehension. Figure 6.2 reflects an application of the elements of ethical complexity to the case.

Layer 2	Intensity of problem		Support of others
		Organisational mores/ strength of practices	
Layer 1	Personal values dominated by cynicism		Societal values
		Personal autonomy	

Figure 6.2 Elements of ethical complexity (Case study 6.2)

▨ Whistleblowing as a civic act

If a whistleblower reveals an organisational practice that he or she considers to be against the public interest such a whistleblowing act could be considered a civic act. In the sense used here, civic describes an act that an individual citizen carries out as a member of a community or state. The term citizen is an inclusive term. It locates the individual within a community of others. It stresses relatedness, without the integrity and specialness of the individual being lost in the amorphousness of the crowd. The citizen is both part of a community, but identifiable and separable within it.

There is no suggestion that in such a society every individual is perpetually and desperately seeking to achieve a utopian form of communitarian existence, a form of societal nirvana. What the term civic does describe is a context in which justice and understanding are at the bedrock of social relationships. Thus, when a (potentially) significant injustice is observed, the civic-minded individual does not walk away from his or her civic responsibilities by ignoring the injustice or public hazard. They seek to change the practice, and if this is unsuccessful, they seek to bring the problem to public attention. They act in an autonomous way, i.e. they act as free people. They act with moral agency. This is what many whistleblowers would claim for their acts. This is not an argument for an anarchy that would allow everyone to challenge everything. As with all aspects of human relations rights should normally carry with them responsibilities. As a consequence the right to exercise moral agency requires that individuals also respect the beliefs of others insofar as they represent commonly held views.

The whistleblower can be portrayed as a somewhat heroic figure, and some writers do argue this position. Whilst no attempt will be made to suggest that whistleblowing is a saintly act, there is no doubt that particular whistleblowing cases portray individuals who have displayed personal courage and determination to overcome legal, financial, psychological and physical obstacles to their attempts to stop a particular organisational practice, or to bring it to public attention (*see* Hoffman and Moore, 1990; Hunt, 1995, 1998; Lovell and Robertson, 1994; Matthews, Goodpaster and Nash, 1991; Miceli and Near, 1992 for examples). But, for some, there can be an exhilaration associated with whistleblowing. Van Buitenen was the EU employee whose revelations about the misuse of EU funds contributed to the resignation of the entire European Union Commission in 1999. His autobiography reveals that although his whistleblowing damaged him, he also relished the excitement of the clandestine meetings and the media attention that arose from it (Van Buitenen, 2000).

Returning to our consideration of the societal role and defensibility of whistleblowing, we consider Case study 6.3. This case provides further evidence of the psychological damage that can be inflicted upon an employee who rails against an organisational practice. The person in question occupied a senior position within the organisation concerned, but was judged to pose a threat to certain key individuals within the organisation.

CASE STUDY 6.3 The costs of whistleblowing

W had worked for the organisation concerned for seven years and had risen to a senior position, effectively being the joint deputy head of finance. However, his unease about certain accounting 'adjustments' he was being asked to make and the obstacle that he represented to the advancement of a junior colleague who the chief executive appeared to favour, meant that W suddenly appeared to be a 'persona non grata'. This was surprising to all those who were interviewed because W was held in very high regard by everyone interviewed, barring the chief executive. A decision appeared to have been made that W had to go, and considerable psychological pressure was exerted on W to encourage him to resign. W's last annual appraisal spoke about his failing performance, despite glowing previous appraisals. W finally resigned, although he appeared to have been 'constructively dismissed', and an out-of-court settlement was made to remove the threat of an industrial tribunal hearing for wrongful dismissal. The words of W are illuminating:

Case study 6.3 continued

> they drag you down to such an extent that your confidence is absolutely rock bottom. You have no confidence in your own ability and it takes you a long time to realise that you didn't deserve this. You hadn't done anything wrong . . . in the back of your mind you're thinking, did I do something wrong to deserve this? Until now, I have not said anything about my case . . . You want a career and you're not quite sure what influence they have in the rest of the public sector – I still haven't got a permanent position.

The governance structures of the organisations so far considered were clearly deficient. Whistleblowing was not on the agenda of any of the central characters within the cases, because of fear for their respective employment prospects. Many of those who, in a study of accountants and HR managers (Fisher and Lovell, 2000), expressed disgust over certain organisational practices felt impotent and unable to do anything to put things right.

The words of a hospital's deputy director of finance reveal behaviour that might surprise some.

CASE STUDY 6.4

The hospital case

This case was recounted to the researchers by a range of middle-ranking HR managers and accountants within a hospital, as well as by H, the Deputy Director of Finance. It was a situation that troubled many in the hospital (*see* Case study 2.19 for another interviewee's perspective).

The case relates to the waiting lists initiative instigated by the Department of Health in 1998. The intention of the initiative was to provide additional funds to hospitals to allow them to reduce hospital waiting lists in key areas. This was a manifesto pledge of the incoming Labour government in 1997. The following are the words of the Deputy Director of Finance.

> The government has just put all this money into the waiting list initiative, to treat patients and get them off the waiting list. It's taxpayers' money – the spirit of that money was not to line consultants' pockets. In theory, it's NHS money, health sector money. A number of the specialties reacted as one would hope. However, the ophthalmologists said, 'Yes, we will do this, if you pay me something like £750 per case. We will pay the nurses time and a half. . . . And if you don't pay us that rate we won't do the list.' So ophthalmologists got their way – a very dirty deal – nurses get a bit and porters and cleaners get nothing. The ophthalmologists are getting about £15,000 extra per list.

> In addition to the ophthalmologists, ENT specialists and anaesthetists at this hospital also negotiated their own special deals with regard to the waiting lists initiatives. When asked how particular specialties could drive through such arrangements, the response was, 'They confronted the organisation. The chief executive is frightened of the power of these groups, so he is prepared to do deals, rather than risk not getting patients done.'

Case study 6.4 continued

When asked to describe his own feelings towards this situation, H replied, 'Perhaps I am naive, but I wouldn't have let it happen. I think all staff should be treated equally and I would have waged war with the consultants and said, I am sorry – we are not playing.'

Had H ever been tempted to blow the whistle at any time? The answer was yes, and the above situation was such a time. He had not because, 'I have to respect the chief executive's decision. My loyalty to him, my accountability – I haven't done anything wrong.'

'I haven't done anything wrong.' These are words to ponder.

Justifiable whistleblowing

Using De George's six criteria for justifiable whistleblowing it is possible to argue that H could have responded positively to conditions 1, 2, 4 and 6.

- H would have been acting honourably, assuming he did not sell his story to the press, if he had chosen to go public with his knowledge (condition 6).
- It was disgust with the way senior consultants were using their organisational power to 'line their pockets' with public money that was at the heart of H's angst (condition 1).
- H had also discussed the issue with the finance director (condition 2), although the latter seemed resigned to the realities of organisational power within the hospital.
- H also had the documentary evidence to substantiate his case, had he chosen to use it (condition 4).
- However, H had not taken the matter to the chief executive because the chief executive was a central figure in the affair (condition 3), and
- he doubted whether a whistleblowing act would change much, after the initial furore had died down (condition 5).

Thus, against the six criteria H would have found a degree of support for an act of whistleblowing, although the belief that little if anything would change as a result of a whistleblowing act (condition 5), does provide a justification (within De George's framework) for 'keeping quiet'.

A further consideration was that H feared that the adverse publicity that such a revelation would attract would do the hospital great harm, at a time when hospitals across the UK were under considerable media scrutiny due to revelations about the concealment of negligent practices by clinicians (*see* Case study 2.17). It is not just organisations operating in the profit seeking sectors that can suffer from adverse publicity and falling 'client' confidence. H's concerns over the ramifications for 'his' hospital of any disclosure about the greed of a significant number of consultants were real.

Within this account of H's case, there are a number of issues that need to be explored further. The first is the harm that can be caused by an act of whistleblowing. Notwithstanding the existence of unacceptable organisational practices, or shortcomings in quality and/or safety, the whistleblowing act itself may inflict harm upon individuals and organisations including individuals known personally to the whistleblower. To present whistleblowing situations as always clear-cut, with 'good guys' and 'bad guys' clearly demarcated, and issues neatly packaged with 'right' and 'wrong' labels attached, would be misleading. Life is messy, and organisational life particularly messy on occasions. However, this is not an excuse to do nothing. Judgement has to be a major factor in shaping personal decision making, but when that judgement is constrained by employment fears, moral agency is undermined and impoverished. This takes us to the second point, that of floating responsibility (Bauman, 1994).

Definition

> **Floating responsibility** refers to the situation where all the individuals that were potentially involved or implicated in a particular incident or problem are able to explain that responsibility for the problem was not theirs. Responsibility becomes impossible to pinpoint. It appears to fall between the cracks of job descriptions and roles.

H's closing words, 'I haven't done anything wrong', could be seen as an example of floating responsibility. It becomes an organisational defence against individual conscience. In this way the following of rules and adherence to the commands of superiors make identification of responsibility difficult to isolate. 'I was only following orders', is a plea heard from junior clerks to senior military officers.

The third point to consider is H's expressed loyalty to the chief executive. 'I have to respect the chief executive's decision. My loyalty to him, my accountability.' Besides loyalty to the chief executive, H was also thinking of his other work colleagues. As the case indicates, H was not alone in his knowledge of the affair, yet H indicated that no one else would 'rock the boat'. These others preferred to 'keep their heads down' for fear of the personal consequences. Colleagues, who choose to ignore the implications of a practice, could (with their families) be significantly affected by any revelations. These are heavy considerations to weigh in the decision of whether or not to whistleblow. The vulnerability and loneliness of potential whistleblowers and of those who adopt a 'not my business' stance need reflecting upon. Jos (1988: 323) argued that:

> Modern organisations require workers to do things they might not otherwise do . . . [they] undermine the capacity of workers to make their own judgement about what they should do. By uncritically deferring to others, workers may become party to immoral or illegal activities and policies. In short, it is the worker's autonomy, his status as a chooser that is at stake.

Jos's lament over the demise of moral autonomy needs to be juxtaposed with the celebration of 'the individual' as evidenced in much political and corporate rhetoric. The wishes of the individual consumer are claimed to be sovereign. Citizens charters abound, and organisations, both public and private sector, claim to dance to the tune of consumer preferences. Nisbet (1953), whilst addressing issues of political economy, offered some thoughts that are relevant to this debate.

> The political *enslavement* of man requires the *emancipation* of man from all the authorities and memberships . . . that serve, one degree or another, to insulate the individual from the external political power . . . totalitarian domination of the individual will is not a mysterious process, not a form of sorcery based upon some vast and unknowable irrationalism. It arises and proceeds rationally and

relentlessly through the creation of new functions, statuses and allegiances which, by conferring community, makes the manipulation of the human will scarcely more than an exercise in scientific social psychology . . . there may be left the appearance of individual freedom, provided it is only individual freedom. All of this is unimportant, always subject to guidance and control, if the primary social contexts of belief and opinion are properly organised and managed. What is central is the creation of a network of functions and loyalties reaching down into the most intimate recesses of human life where ideas and beliefs will germinate and develop.

(Nisbet, 1953: 202, 208, emphases in the original)

Thus, Nisbet argued that the freedom inherent within current conceptions of individualism is a particular and partial form of individualism, located precisely in the economic sphere. This ideology has, however, facilitated the neutering of people as political actors. Yet in the economic sphere individualism is again prescribed, with certain forms of action almost proscribed. Sarason (1986) commented on a society in which individuals affected by social dilemmas perceive their dilemmas as their, and only their, responsibility. Paraphrasing Sarason:

If *your* ethical dilemma is *your* responsibility according to *my* morality, this is quite consistent with the increasingly dominant ideology of individual rights, responsibility, choice and freedom. If *I* experience the issue as *yours*, it is because there is nothing in my existence to make it *ours*. And by *ours* I mean a socio-cultural network and traditions which engender an obligation to be part of the problem and possible solution.

(emphases in the original)

What we hope is becoming evident is that whistleblowing is a complex, many-sided debate that cannot be removed from the social, cultural and economic contexts to which it relates.

Whilst individual attitudes might be difficult to change, certainly in the short term, maybe the least that might be expected of a civilised society is that those of its members, who do act in ways that reflect a civic orientation in their whistleblowing, should enjoy the protection of the law. Thus, it is appropriate that we now progress to a consideration of the law relating to whistleblowing in the UK, the Public Interest Disclosure Act 1998.

The Public Interest Disclosure Act 1998

There are two central elements to the Public Interest Disclosure Act 1998 (PIDA) to recognise from the outset. The first is that it does not give a right to an employee to whistleblow. The Act has been constructed upon the premise that confidentiality of corporate information is the primary principle, from which there are few exceptions. It is to these exceptions that the Act speaks. It offers protection to those who speak out (in the parlance of the Act, make a 'disclosure') against specific types of organisational malpractice, as long as certain conditions are met. The construction of the Act encourages disclosure to be kept within the employing organisation's boundaries by increasing the conditions that have to be satisfied if one makes a disclosure outside of the confines of the employing organisation.

The second element that lessens the Act's potential from the perspective of the concerned employee is that the burden of proof is upon the employee to show that a malpractice has occurred, although the burden of proof does vary depending upon to whom a disclosure is made. In circumstances where the work environment is intimidatory and oppressive, obtaining supporting evidence, such as corroboration from current employees, could prove extremely difficult.

The term 'protected disclosure' relates to the type of whistleblowing act that falls within the protection of the Act. The malpractice must normally relate to the employing organisation. However, in certain, restricted, situations a protected disclosure can be made against third party organisations. Interestingly, auditors do not have a duty to report wrongdoing, with the exception of matters relating to terrorism and money laundering, and neither are they protected by the PIDA if they do make such a revelation. It could be argued that this exclusion from protection by the Act and the omission of a duty to report wrongdoing, other than in the two areas mentioned, suits the practising members of the accountancy profession, as it saves them from coming into conflict with their clients. Audit income is but a part of the income that most practising accountancy firms earn from their audit clients. It is not in the interest of practising accountancy firms to be required to play the role of society's watchdog on the activities of their clients.

For a disclosure to fall within the protection of the PIDA, the disclosure itself must relate to a specified set of malpractices. These are:

- A criminal offence.
- A failure to comply with any legal obligation.
- A miscarriage of justice.
- Danger to the health and safety of any individual.
- Damage to the environment.
- Deliberate concealment of any of the above.

To comply with the PIDA (and thus to stay within its protection), an ethically concerned employee must use to the full the organisation's internal procedures for handling such concerns. Such procedures can be avoided only if the following conditions are satisfied.

- At the time the disclosure was made the employee reasonably believed that they would be 'subject to a detriment' by the employer if a disclosure was made to the employer.
- The employee is concerned that evidence relating to the malpractice would be concealed or destroyed by the employer.
- The employee has previously made a disclosure to the employer of substantially the same information.

Detriment is defined in the Act as being penalised by the employer, e.g. being fined, demoted, sacked or denied promotion.

Internal procedures can be sidestepped if they are shown to be seriously flawed, because of legitimate fears of information being confiscated or destroyed. Other fears, such as the existence of an oppressive and threatening employment environment, can be more difficult to substantiate. This is because obtaining corroborating evidence from fellow employees (who are fearful for their own jobs) can be extremely difficult to obtain.

One concern about the Act is that it addresses the circumstances of the employee once that employee has made a disclosure. It is possible that if the concerned employee only makes a *threat* of disclosure, the Act would not protect the employee in the event of the employee being sacked before a full disclosure was made. In addition, whilst expressions of concern by one employee to another employee about a particular organisational (mal)practice might constitute a breach of confidentiality (and thus create the possibility of dismissal), the PIDA would not be available to the sacked employee if they had not raised the issue with the organisation's management.

Whilst the establishment of an internal whistleblowing procedure may, at first sight, be a laudable development by any organisation, in the hands of unscrupulous employers it might merely be a device for complying with the letter of the law but not the spirit. Warren (1993) questioned the rationale of American firms introducing corporate codes of conduct. The same might be said of internal whistleblowing procedures.

There is also the issue of gaining sufficient evidence to give confidence of being able to lodge a concern. Raising a concern within the employing organisation requires that the concerned employee must satisfy two tests. The first is that the employee must 'reasonably believe' that one of the above-mentioned malpractices has occurred. Secondly, the disclosure must be made 'in good faith'. However, the process of gaining evidence, as mentioned in relation to the Maxwell affair, can be a big problem. In such situations, being able to prove that sufficient evidence existed to allow individuals to 'reasonably believe' there were malpractices afoot could be extremely difficult. In addition, the use of internal procedures could prove unattractive to an employee (as in the Maxwell case). This would leave the concerned employee with only external whistleblowing to contemplate. However, the burden of proof required to stay within PIDA protection increases as soon as one raises one's concerns with external third parties. If information is revealed within the firm then the 'reasonably believe' test applies. However, if concerns are expressed to an external third party then the test becomes, 'the employee . . . reasonably believes that the information and any allegation contained in it are *substantially true* [emphasis added]'. Thus the concerned employee must be able to show that there were reasonable grounds for them to believe that the allegation being made was 'substantially true' – a far more rigorous criterion than 'reasonably believe'.

Even if this condition is met, the concerned employee loses protection of the PIDA if the employee is rewarded for disclosing the wrongdoing, if, for example, the employee receives payment from a newspaper. Thus, the motive for the disclosure affects the protection provided by the PIDA. As mentioned earlier, rewards for information (including that provided anonymously), which leads to the successful prosecution of a criminal, are quite acceptable. So why the different treatment of those who report the criminal activity of organisations?

If the internal whistleblowing procedures of an employing organisation are judged to be unsafe by a concerned employee, that employee will normally be expected to use the offices of a 'prescribed body'. Such a prescribed body is likely to be a regulatory body of an industry (e.g. OFWAT for water companies, or the Financial Services Authority for financial services companies). Within the public sector, such prescribed bodies are less likely to exist. It will be important for the concerned employee to establish whether a 'prescribed body' exists to handle the concerns. Failure to follow the required procedures might take the complaint outside of the protection of the PIDA. Notwithstanding this, there exists no requirement for a regulator to act in response to the information supplied by a concerned employee, other than the rules under which the regulator normally acts.

The above uncertainty, over the 'actual' protection afforded by the PIDA, is at the heart of concerns expressed about the Act. The evidence provided by the organisation Freedom To Care on those of its members who have 'blown the whistle' on the malpractices of their former employers is that the PIDA would not have provided the protection they needed to withstand losing their jobs.

Employees working in areas covered by the Official Secrets Act are not protected by the PIDA. There are many examples of classified information within central government and (to a lesser extent) local government that is of dubious sensitivity, yet the information is covered by the Official Secrets Act. A concerned employee needs to check whether any information that relates to the cause of their concern is of a classified nature.

If all the requirements of the PIDA are satisfied (including the requirement that the alleged malpractice be deemed to be a sufficiently serious offence, plus all the other requirements mentioned above), the Act does provide protection that previously did not exist. Two examples of enhanced protection relate to gagging clauses and interim relief.

1 Gagging clauses. These are restrictive clauses in employment contracts that prevent the mentioning of anything of an organisational nature to anyone outside the employing organisation. These were a very real problem for many employees prior to the PIDA, but they appear to be void under the Act – other than those covered by the Official Secrets Act.

Whilst gagging clauses appear to be outlawed by the PIDA, it must still be remembered that an implied term of employment contracts is the duty of confidentiality to the employing organisation on the part of the employee. It is this 'duty of confidentiality' that explains the considerable restrictions that have been placed upon the definition of a 'protected disclosure'. Only when the conditions of the PIDA have been judged to have been complied with, can the 'duty of confidentiality' be usurped by the PIDA in the specified situations identified above.

2 Interim Relief (keeping one's salary if dismissed for whistleblowing). Under section 9, the PIDA extends one of the provisions of the Employment Rights Act (ERA) of 1996. If an employee suffers dismissal as a result of making a 'protected disclosure', they should make representation to an Employment Tribunal within seven days of dismissal. This aspect is known as interim relief. If the Employment Tribunal considers that the disclosure is likely to fall within the definition of a protected disclosure, the Employment Tribunal *may* order the employer to reinstate the employee. If the employer fails to comply with such an order, 'the employee is deemed to remain in employment until the hearing and entitled to continue to be paid as such'.

However, before these conditions are activated on behalf of the employee, three further conditions must be met:

1 The claim for an interim relief must be lodged within seven days of dismissal.
2 The Employment Tribunal must first decide that the employee is likely to be found to have made a protected disclosure (not an obvious decision without studying all the relevant information); and

3 An order must be made to the employing organisation to reinstate the employee (and this ruling happens relatively infrequently).

Thus, an interim order, whilst appearing to be a positive aspect of the PIDA, is likely in practice to be much less frequently activated than it might first appear. For example, in the case, *Bladon* v. *ALM Medical Services ET*, reported by Myers and Dehn (2000), an application for interim relief was rejected by the Chairman of the Employment Tribunal without hearing evidence. The basis for this judgment was that the Tribunal Chairman considered the claimant's (the whistleblower's) case to be 'implausible'. Yet, when the case was finally heard, the whistleblower's actions were upheld and he was awarded damages. However, in the many months between the application for an interim relief and the actual Tribunal hearing, the whistleblower was denied any salary from their former employer.

If an employee's case falls within the protection of the PIDA then:

- The employee will be entitled to a compensation payment if victimisation is experienced as a result of the whistleblowing act (e.g. the employee stays within the employing organisation but suffers demotion). The level of compensation will depend upon the specifics of each case.
- If dismissed, the employee will be entitled to a compensation payment in line with the awards available through Employment Tribunals. These rates change over time.

Myers and Dehn discuss examples of whistleblowers who have successfully employed the PIDA. However, the concerns expressed above about the ability of the PIDA to actually improve the protection available to 'conscientious objectors at work' remain.

Reflections

This chapter has considered various aspects of whistleblowing. Although examples can be cited of revelations of organisational malpractices that have been shown to be both accurate and serious, as well as examples of situations where the concerns of employees have been ignored or 'lost' in managerial structures, and disasters involving loss of life have followed, the prospects for those contemplating whistleblowing remain bleak. Employment law and the PIDA are written with the primary intention of protecting the commercial confidentiality of organisations that operate in legally compliant ways. There is thus a fundamental tension between, on the one hand, the need for employees to feel able to exercise moral agency and raise awareness of issues that have a genuine public interest, and, on the other hand, the need for organisations to protect commercially sensitive information, and be protected from malicious and ill-founded accusations from disgruntled employees. The extent to which the balance between these competing requirements is acceptable and appropriate needs to be revisited regularly.

In modern times strong economies and vibrant business sectors are essential if political and social goals are to be achieved. It is difficult to refute the centrality of a strong economy to many societal aspirations, whether the economy is located in the so-called developing or developed worlds. As a result businesses, and pressure groups representing business interests, act as powerful influences in the creation and maintenance of the legal frameworks that govern business activities. In this context it is perhaps not surprising that the PIDA was framed in the way that it was, if it was to receive sufficient support in the UK Parliament and thereby become law. Yet the very necessity to support and protect business interests creates too many loopholes for unscrupulous organisations to use. In addition there are those situations in which organisations flout the laws that society has passed, and the question then arises as to how and when society should be made aware of these infractions.

There are also questions about the relationships between business, environmental and societal interests (the latter relating as much to future societies as to present ones). It is important that assumptions regarding the roles and power of organisations are challenged, and not taken for granted. Related to, but separate from, these assumptions are the issues relating to notions of individualism and civic perspectives, that have been alluded to in this chapter. These need revisiting on a regular basis to ensure that the issues and debates are themselves comprehended, and not overpowered by the pre-eminence of business interests.

Summary

In this chapter the following key points have been made:

- Whistleblowing includes, but is not limited to, the revelation of an organisational issue to an external party.
- Whistleblowing help-lines can be both important organisational mechanisms for the raising of ethical concerns, and early warning systems of unacceptable practices.
- Protection offered to whistleblowers by the PIDA is particular and limited.
- The pejorative connotation of whistleblowing needs to be reflected upon and understood. Whilst perpetual whistleblowing is an unattractive proposition, the organisational impotence reflected in the case studies cited is equally unpalatable.

Suggested further reading

G. Borrie (1996) 'Business Ethics and Accountability', in M. Brindle and G. Dehn (1996) *Four Windows on Whistleblowing*, pp. 1–23, London: Public Concern at Work, provides a good starting point for studying this subject further. See also G. Borrie and G. Dehn (2002) *Whistleblowing: The New Perspective*, Public Concern website, *www.pcaw.co.uk/policy_pub/newperspective.html*. D.B. Lewis (2000) *Whistleblowing at Work*, London: Athlone Press, is also helpful.

GROUP ACTIVITY 6

Consider the PIDA and make recommendations to change the Act. Your proposals should be able to withstand critical appraisal at both a practical and theoretical level. Divide a sheet of paper into four columns. In the first column list your proposals. In the second column state against each proposal why you believe the amendment is justified. In the third column identify the principal objections or problems associated with your proposal. The final column should reflect your thoughts on the strengths of the objections/problems identified in column three, and whether you believe they are surmountable.

Organisational responses to ethical issues

OBJECTIVES

Having completed this chapter and its associated activities, readers should be able to:

- Discuss the pressures upon organisations to employ codes of practice.

- Differentiate between various types of codes.

- Identify the multiple roles of codes of practice.

- Understand the arguments against the employment of codes of practice within organisations.

- Show an awareness that codes of practice can sometimes conflict with one another, creating organisational tensions.

- Understand the significance and power of organisational culture and unwritten codes of conduct.

Introduction

This chapter considers the developments that have become evident as the attention paid to ethical issues in business has intensified. Broadly speaking, these developments have reflected reactions to one or more problems affecting either a specific firm or an industrial/commercial sector. Sometimes developments can be seen in the form of organisations and/or groups of companies working in tandem, sometimes with governments and/or pressure groups, to draw up codes of practice and conduct.

The International Labour Organisation (ILO) argued that worldwide interest in corporate codes of conduct was initially awakened in the 1980s by scandals in the US defence industry and the overt greed that was displayed on Wall Street. The ILO sees business ethics as a way for companies to promote self-regulation, thereby deterring government intervention and possible regulatory action. Corporate interest quickly led to the institutionalisation of business ethics programmes, consisting largely of codes of conduct, ethics officers and ethics training.

However, Brytting (1997) cited the Zeiss organisation as having a recognisable code of conduct for its employees in 1896, and Mill, writing in 1861 but cited by

Warren (1993: 187), observed that 'it is the business of ethics to tell us what our duties are or by what test we may know them'. It has been argued that the more recent increase in the growth of corporate codes of conduct relates to the potential for such codes to reduce corporate exposure to punitive damages in claims of negligence. As Warren (1993: 109) observed in terms of the situation in the United States,

> The 1984 Sentencing Reform Act and the US Sentencing Commission's 1991 Federal Guidelines for Sentencing Organisations, allow for a fine on a corporation to be reduced by up to 95% if it can show that it has an effective program to prevent and detect violations of law.

Attempts to reduce negligence claims are not the only reason for organisations to be seen to be addressing the ethicality of their practices. Multinational corporations (MNCs) are not only increasingly powerful, but also open to critical scrutiny of any of their practices in all parts of the world. MNCs thus have a vested interest in harmonising and standardising practices throughout their respective organisations in order to minimise the risk of aberrant behaviour. We consider later in this chapter the initiatives being employed by MNCs to address concerns about their practices and those of their supplier networks.

An overview of the pressures upon organisations for ethical development

Figure 7.1 reflects the differing pressures on organisations to institute and formalise their ethical practices.

Of all the connections depicted in Figure 7.1, the only unbroken line is that between '*Governments*' and '*The organisation*'. This reflects the mandatory nature of laws, as opposed to the other relationships that are characterised by frameworks, agreements, codes, understandings, or memoranda, none of which is legally binding. The agreements, or framework documents, between governments and MNCs reflect the dilemma faced by many governments, particularly those of developing countries. The presence of MNCs within the host country can bring the prospect of accelerated economic development, but the support, incentives and conditions that must be agreed to by the host government, in the face of alternative offers by other countries to the MNCs, can weaken the host government's bargaining powers. In such circumstances, legislation is unlikely to be deemed 'appropriate' to control the operations of the MNCs, and more adaptive, negotiable instruments such as framework agreements, or codes, become the norm. The non-legally binding agreements or codes of practice may be developed with or without the involvement of pressure groups and interested charitable bodies.

In turn, non-governmental bodies (NGOs), pressure groups and charitable bodies can exert pressure upon organisations independently of governments by developing their preferred codes of practice for business organisations and then contrasting these codes with the behaviour of specific organisations. These

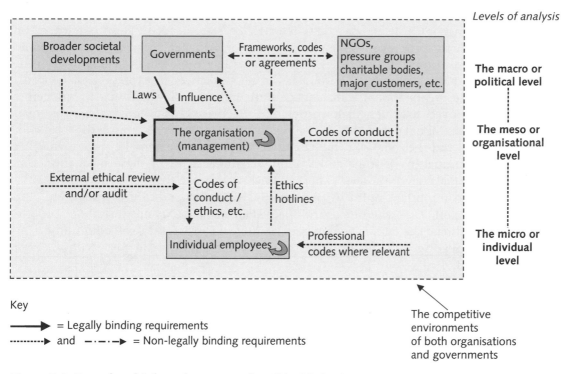

Levels of analysis

Figure 7.1 Formal and informal pressures for ethical behaviour

comparisons can reveal considerable discrepancies between espoused and actual behaviour and, given the glare of national and international publicity, can involve discussions about change. These relationships are reflected in the additional lines emanating from the '*NGO, pressure group*' box and going towards the '*The organisation*' box. Organisations such as Greenpeace, Friends of the Earth and the International Baby Food Action Network (IBFAN) are notable in this field.

Business organisations do not have to wait for external pressure before they act to enhance their own practices and behaviour. We illustrate below examples of ethical initiatives that appear to have come from within organisations, although the initiatives may have been in anticipation of government or pressure group involvement if the organisation did not respond in some way to an ethical issue.

There are examples of co-operation and collaboration between governments and pressure groups, between pressure groups and organisations/industries and between governments, pressure groups and business organisations, that appear to be addressing matters of ethical concern in effective ways. We also highlight, however, examples of apparent 'good' practice that, when carefully scrutinised, are possibly less effective than they might at first appear.

Within Figure 7.1 the introduction of a corporate code of conduct by an employing organisation is shown by the downward-pointing arrow, aimed at '*Individual employees*'. This is because such codes are invariably the result of a 'top-down initiative', with relatively little, or no, involvement from non-senior managerial staff. These codes tend to be statements of how employees are required to behave by the company/senior management. However, companies can also incorporate 'ethics hotlines' to allow those employees with concerns about the ethicality of particular business practices to express their concerns. These organisational vents can be both important mechanisms for concerned employees to express their worries, and effective early warning systems for organisations about potentially damaging practices and behaviour. Both the ethics hotlines and the codes of conduct can be supported by external ethical review, e.g. an annual, or periodic ethics audit, but because all of these mechanisms are optional they are shown as broken lines.

An important point to emphasise is that the 'Codes of conduct, etc.' link between *'The organisation'* and *'Individual employees'* is not just about codes of conduct. The 'etc.' encompasses a range of other ways of communicating, inculcating and nurturing corporate values. McDonald and Nijhof (1999) cited:

- training
- story telling
- reward systems
- monitoring systems
- communication channels
- job design
- ethics officers
- information systems
- recruitment and selection policies and processes, and
- organisational strategies

as further examples of ways in which organisations can influence the values and practices that become accepted as 'the ways things are done around here'. Many of these elements come within what is known as organisational culture. This is a very significant area, upon which many books have been written. A consideration of some of the important issues of organisational culture for values and ethics, and vice versa, is undertaken towards the end of this chapter.

The arrows within *'The organisation'* and *'Individual employee'* boxes that appear to turn on themselves indicate that neither organisations, nor individuals, should expect or passively wait for developments on ethical behaviour to be externally imposed or influenced. If terms such as 'learning organisation' and 'reflective practitioner' are to mean anything, they will need to be evident in the critical reflection of both organisations and individuals on their respective practices. In many respects the integrity with which organisations and individuals reflect upon notions of ethicality are fundamental elements of Figure 7.1. If change is only ever externally stimulated, rather than the result of internal reflection and action, then such change is subject to whims and pressures that will not necessarily be rooted in well-argued principles and values.

The arrow moving from the *'The organisation'* to *'Governments'* acknowledges that business organisations are not passive or disinterested bystanders in the development of laws affecting corporate practice. This arrow acknowledges the quite significant influence that specific organisations and industrial/commercial sectors can have on governments and the laws that are passed. Equally, it must be emphasised that the whole of Figure 7.1 sits within a commercial and competitive environment that bears upon the practices of individuals, organisations and governments.

The levels of analysis

Researchers and organisations that study and work with the many issues that comprise business ethics and values tend to do so from one of three perspectives, as reflected in the column on the right-hand side of Figure 7.1. These levels are the macro-political level, the meso or organisational level and the micro or individual level. Those working at the macro-political level are seeking to understand, and possibly influence, the way that political and particularly economic systems impact upon broad national and societal issues. Examples of interesting monitoring organisations that operate at national and international government levels include Transparency International and One World Trust. Their respective websites are provided in the list of business ethics resources on the World Wide Web at the end of the book.

At the meso, or organisational, level we find pressure groups, professional associations, trade bodies and labour organisations which are working to monitor, analyse, understand, support, defend and develop the ethicality of business practice within organisations. Researchers working at this level study issues such as ethical awareness and training programmes; the development of corporate codes of conduct and/or ethics; and controversies such as those relating to the production, distribution and selling of bananas; the retailing of breastmilk substitutes in developing countries; and sweatshop and child labour issues. In addition to the material on the websites given at the end of the book, there are some interesting ideas and arguments concerning ethical development at the organisational level in Schein (1992); Watson (1994); Fineman and Gabriel (1996); McDonald and Nijhof (1999); Gabriel, Fineman and Sims (2000); and Sternberg (2000).

At the individual level we find debates and research that consider the possibilities for moral agency in organisations. This level is discussed in a number of places in this book, but particularly Chapter 6.

Codes of conduct and codes of ethics

In market contexts where competitive forces are significant, consistency in all aspects of an organisation's operations is imperative. In order to stimulate, foster and maintain consistency in the behaviour of employees, consistency that also reflects the standards of behaviour that an organisation wishes its employees to adopt, organisations often develop codes of conduct and ethics. A distinction can be made between codes of ethics and codes of conduct that is helpful in examining the roles these types of statements perform. Although this distinction is not universally employed, indeed you may find some organisations employing codes of ethics that by our definition would be classed as codes of conduct, it offers some insight into the purpose of such codes. A study by Farrell and Cobbin (1996) discusses variations between codes of conduct and codes of ethics and the findings of this study add support to the distinction. A much higher level of prescription was found in the codes of conduct studied (average number of rules equalled 30.6), as compared to the average number of rules contained in the codes of ethics (16.5).

Definitions

> *Codes of conduct* tend to be instructions, or sets of rules, concerning behaviour. As a result they are likely to be reasonably prescriptive and proscriptive concerning particular aspects of employee behaviour. They identify specific acts that must be either adhered to (prescription), or avoided (proscription). However, the extent to which all possible situations can be addressed within a code of conduct is problematic.
>
> *Codes of ethics* tend to be reasonably general in their tenor, encouraging employees to display particular characteristics such as loyalty, honesty, objectivity, probity and integrity. They do not normally address specific types of decisions, rather they encourage the application of what might be called 'virtues', although, as noted in Chapter 3, what are regarded as virtues can vary over time. Whilst notions of honesty and integrity remain fairly constant over time, concepts such as justice and loyalty are more contentious.

From these definitions it is evident that where all possible scenarios that an employee might face can be predicted with a high degree of confidence, as well all the circumstances relating to those scenarios, then a specific code of conduct might be possible, because ethical judgement becomes redundant. However, where the likely scenarios that an employee might face cannot be predicted in the requisite detail, then reference to general qualities and principles will be preferred, i.e. codes of ethics become more appropriate.

The risk of confusing these two general positions is that if a code of conduct fails to address a particular scenario that an employee actually faces, then the silence of the code on the matter in question might be interpreted by the employee as an indication that the employing organisation is at best indifferent to the ethics of the decision in hand.

In this discussion the employee might be said to be (or be treated as) morally immature, requiring a code of conduct or ethics to act as a reference point in times of need, but that is just what codes imply. By issuing such codes, a company is stating that it does not have sufficient confidence in all of its employees to be able to view a code of conduct or ethics as unnecessary. This is an inference that some, maybe many, employees might find objectionable, but for an organisation that straddles many countries and cultures in its operations, the need for an articulation of expected behaviour and practices throughout its operations can be overwhelming.

The purposes of codes of conduct and ethics

At one level, codes of conduct and ethics can be seen as legitimate and necessary devices for senior management to develop in order to specify expected codes of behaviour of all employees. Each employee of an organisation will be seen as a representative of that organisation by others external to the organisation. Thus, it is important that employees reflect behaviour that is commensurate with the persona and reputation that the organisation wishes to project. In this context some writers see codes of conduct as principally manipulative, control devices to achieve managerial ends. Stevens (1994: 65) argued that 'some ethical codes are little more than legal barriers and self-defence mechanisms; others are intended to influence and shape employee behaviour'. These were observations that had been made earlier by, amongst others, Mathews (1988) and Warren (1993).

Developing and adding to the work of Bowie and Duska (1990), we have listed below eight roles for corporate codes. These are:

- *Damage limitation* – to reduce damages awarded by courts in the event of the company being sued for negligence by one its employees.
- *Guidance* – the 'reference point' role, similar to what Passmore (1984) referred to as 'the reminding role'. An aide-memoire for employees when faced with an ethically complex situation.
- *Regulation* – this is the prescribing and proscribing roles that will stipulate specific qualities that are essential, e.g. independence, objectivity, etc., or acts that are prohibited.
- *Discipline and appeal* – this is the role of a code as a benchmark for an organisation or professional body to decide whether an employee/member has contravened required conduct and what form of punishment might ensue. In addition the code can form the basis of an appeal by the accused.
- *Information* – a code expresses to external audiences standards of behaviour that can be expected of employees/members.
- *Proclamation* – this has echoes of 'information', but it relates more to the role of codes of conduct developed by professional bodies. To achieve 'professional' status trade associations are normally required to assuage public concerns over the granting of monopoly rights to specific areas of commercial/social activity (e.g. auditing, doctoring, etc.). Ethical codes will attempt to reassure that these monopoly powers will not be abused.
- *Negotiation* – this is not dissimilar to *guidance* in that codes can be used as a tool in negotiations and disputes with and between professionals, colleagues, employers, governments, etc.

■ *Stifling* – this is the creation of internal procedures for handling the ethical concerns of employees that are more concerned with management keeping a lid on internal dissent than acting as a conduit for internal debate and examination. Hunt's (1995 and 1998) work on whistleblowing in the health and social services reflects a number of examples of this use of codes of conduct and internal whistleblowing processes.

The attention paid to codes of conduct by both organisations and researchers does presume both that codes are a 'good' thing and that they do have a positive impact upon individual and corporate behaviour. With regard to the latter Mathews (1988) was able to identify only a weak link between the existence of ethical codes and corporate behaviour. This latter point was taken up by Cassell, Johnson and Smith (1997: 1078) who argued that:

> An important, if implicit, assumption of many writings on corporate codes . . . is that such codes do have a 'real' effect upon behaviour. This tends to be something that is taken for granted, but it is not empirically validated by subsequent investigation . . . recipients of the code: those who are required to make sense of it, and respond to it, often as one more instance of managerially-inspired change, amidst a plethora of pre-existing formal and informal control processes within which the impact of the code must be located. As with any example of formal organizational control, the actual, as opposed to the intended effect, may be subject to processes that entail negotiation and bargaining.

Stevens' (1994) observations were that codes were:

■ primarily concerned with employee conduct that might damage the firm, that is, they were thus skewed towards self-protection, and
■ preoccupied with the law.

The legalistic orientation of many codes has been noted by a number of writers, including Farrell and Cobbin (1996). The latter identified differences between American, Australian and UK corporate codes of conduct. They concluded that of the codes they studied, the Australian codes tended to concentrate upon a reiteration of the legal environment within which individuals and organisations operate, emphasising the importance of not doing anything to harm the employing organisation's reputation. American codes included, but went beyond, this orientation, emphasising customers, equal opportunities and insider dealing, whilst the UK codes made more frequent reference to the community, customer welfare and the environment than the Australian or American codes. However, all of these are relative terms, 'the level of specific guidance on ethical content in each country's codes was very low' (1996: 54). As lawyers were identified as the most frequent developers of such codes (30 per cent), a legalistic orientation to the codes was not surprising.

As highlighted in Figure 7.1, the issues relating to the establishment of codes of conduct and agreements between MNCs, national governments and/or pressure groups are particularly interesting. It is to these we now turn.

Codes, agreements and framework documents involving MNCs

Mention was made at the beginning of the chapter of the dilemma that national governments, particularly those of developing countries, sometimes face when wishing to encourage inward investment by MNCs, but also wishing to maintain some form of influence, if not control, over the activities of the MNCs in the host country. Some form of middle ground is often required between the polar extremes of legislation governing particular aspects of economic or corporate activity on the one hand, and a totally laissez-faire approach on the other. Codes of conduct, agreements and framework documents are examples of such 'middle ground'.

If a code of conduct for MNCs has the support of sovereign states, this does not mean the issues encompassed by the code have become international law. Until they do the codes are not legally binding on MNCs. Thus, the obligations cited by a code will be moral, but not legal.

An example of such a code of practice that has received much publicity concerns the selling of breastmilk substitutes in developing countries.

CASE STUDY 7.1

The International Code of Marketing of Breastmilk Substitutes

The International Code of Marketing of Breastmilk Substitutes, the first international code of its kind, was adopted by the World Health Organisation (WHO) in 1981 and by the World Health Assembly (WHA) in 1984. The code was intended to control the practices of those producing and selling breastmilk substitutes and related products (e.g. feeding bottles), particularly in developing countries. These countries tend to have relatively high birth rates but weak economies. It can be argued that expenditure on breastmilk substitutes is a misuse of a nation's resources, when the natural alternative is cost free and more nutritious for the child. However, to the large corporations producing these products the markets of the developing world represent significant profit opportunities. The problem had become so acute in certain African countries that breastfeeding had become almost eradicated. The international code bans free supplies of breastmilk substitutes in hospitals; because once mothers leave hospital the breastmilk substitutes are no longer free. Yet in 1996 Nestlé, a significant producer of breastmilk substitutes, was reported to be providing free and low-cost supplies of infant formula to hospitals in Kunming Province in China. Save the Children reported:

> Nestlé has made Lactogen widely available in six hospitals in Kunming, where it has targeted health professionals with both free and discounted supplies of the formula. This helps to create an incentive for the health workers, not only to use the formula within the hospitals, but also actively to encourage its use among mothers of newborn children. Lactogen has been displayed in some of the hospitals for sale. The report prepared by our China staff and local health workers alleged that there had

Case study 7.1 continued

been an increase in the consumption of Lactogen and that breastfeeding rates had fallen.

Despite getting companies to sign up to the International Association of Infant Food Manufacturers (IFM) and in 1991 pledging to eradicate the supply of free and discounted supplies, a monitoring report entitled 'Breaking the Rules, Stretching the Rules' found that in 19 of 31 countries surveyed contraventions of the pledge were evident. In addition, a study in Pakistan in 1998 found widespread use and distribution of free supplies, with doctors being 'purchased by the companies'.

(*Source*: IBFAN, n.d.)

Even when codes of practice are established, compliance by MNCs is not necessarily automatic, and enforcement can be difficult, as evidenced by the selling of breastmilk substitutes in Malawi.

CASE STUDY 7.2 Breastmilk substitutes in Malawi

In 1994 the Health Ministry of Malawi had discussed with Nestlé the need to have the instructions on their products written in Chichewa, the national language of Malawi, a requirement that was in compliance with Article 9.2 of the International Code of Marketing of Breastmilk Substitutes. Despite these discussions, Nestlé did not respond positively and the instructions remained in English. The level of literacy is not high in Malawi and of those women who could read at the time, it was estimated that only a little over one-half could read English.

Under Article 9.1 of the Code, labels on breastmilk substitutes should not discourage breastfeeding. However, on its Bona infant formula, Nestlé continued to assert in a section headed 'Important Notice', 'Infant formula can be used from birth onwards when breastfeeding is not possible, or as a supplement to breastfeeding'. This statement was retained on the packaging despite there being general recognition that supplementing breastfeeding with breastmilk substitutes brings forward the time when a mother's natural milk dries up, thereby bringing forward the time when breastmilk substitutes will be required as the sole source of infant nutrition.

Humanitarian aid provides another opportunity for breastmilk substitute products to be introduced into vulnerable, but lucrative markets. The International Baby Food Action Network (IBFAN) claims that:

The baby food industry has used emergencies generally to promote its products and used 'humanitarian aid' as a way of entering into the emerging markets of Europe and the former Soviet Union.

(IBFAN, n.d.)

These cases illustrate some of the problems inherent within a 'pledge', 'code' or 'framework agreement' that is not supported by legal or meaningful sanctions.

Another area of contention relates to the use of child labour. Corporate policy statements of MNCs on the use of child labour within its supplier networks tend to reflect one of four options:

1 Stipulate a minimum age for employment by their suppliers.
2 Refer to national laws of the host country regarding minimum age of working.
3 Refer to international standards; or
4 A combination of some or all of the above.

However, some company policy statements that prohibit the use of child labour in the production of their products do not define what they mean by child labour, thus leaving discretion and judgement to local suppliers. This takes us to the issue of the rigour with which codes of practice are implemented and monitored, particularly those relating to overseas suppliers.

▓ Putting MNC codes of practice into effect

Codes of conduct for MNCs can take various forms and the ILO cites three factors that tend to determine the credibility with which codes for MNCs are regarded.

1 The specific governments that have adopted and support the codes, and the particular MNCs that have 'signed up' to the codes.
2 Whether a code actually addresses the critical issues of the business activity being considered.
3 The effectiveness of the monitoring mechanisms employed and the sanctions available.

The International Chamber of Commerce (ICC) is active in pursuing a self-regulatory framework for business operations on the world stage. It sets standards that recognise the tensions inherent within any competitive market setting. The following statement is drawn from one of its publications.

> The globalisation of the world's economies, and the intense competition which ensues therefrom, require the international business community to adopt standard rules. The adoption of these self-disciplinary rules is the best way that business leaders have of demonstrating that they are motivated by a sense of social responsibility, particularly in light of the increased liberalization of markets.
>
> (International Chamber of Commerce, 1997)

A number of initiatives and codes have been developed to address specific global business issues. Examples include the following.

■ The 1990s saw the scope of some agreements expand to take in broader social issues. An example is the Japan Federation of Economic Organisations. Established in 1996, it covered a number of issues including philanthropic activities, resistance against organisations that undermine social cohesion, policies to enrich the lives of employees, safe and comfortable work environments, a respect for individual dignity and 'specialness' and corporate transparency.

■ In 1996 the British Toy and Hobby Association developed a code of practice that forbids the use of forced, indentured or under-age labour in the production of toys. The agreement also speaks to the working and living conditions of employees. An amended form of this code was adopted by the International Council of Toy Industries later in 1996.

- In February 1997, the ILO, the Sialkot Chamber of Commerce (SCCI) in Pakistan and UNICEF formed an agreement to eliminate child labour in the production of footballs by 1999. This specific initiative was the result of world-wide publicity of the use of child labour in the production of footballs, although no other products or industries were specifically targeted. It appears that this initiative has been largely, if not completely, successful. It does appear that high-profile media coverage is conducive to, and possibly necessary for, change to be levered and achieved.

- In the USA similar codes have been developed in relation to other industries, e.g. the Apparel Partnership on Sweatshops and Child Labour which was adopted in 1997.

- The Organisation for Economic Cooperation and Development (OECD) has also produced guidelines for MNCs covering labour relations.

- A variety of organisations have sponsored the Sweatshop and Clean Clothes Codes, which cover labour relations, health and safety issues, freedom of association, wages and benefits and hours of work.

- The Declaration of Principles concerning Multinational Enterprises, developed in 1997 and involving the ILO, is a code that addresses issues such as freedom of association, terms and conditions of work.

- A new international standard has been developed, known as Social Accountability 8000 (SA8000), by the Council on Economic Priorities Accreditation Agency (CEPAA), a not-for-profit organisation now known as Social Accountability International (SAI) – *see* Case study 7.3. It is similar to other standards such as ISO 9000, which deals with quality assurance, and ISO 14000, which concerns environmental standards. The intention is that an organisation's social and ethical practices (including those of its suppliers) could be independently assessed against the published standards and if the organisations passed the scrutiny they would be awarded a certificate or kite mark as evidence that they have reached appropriate standards.

CASE STUDY 7.3 — SA8000

SA8000 is an international standard for corporate behaviour that identifies a range of criteria against which the activities and performance of organisations can be mapped and compared. The intention is that the standard (and the beliefs, values and ethics assumed within it) should be applicable throughout the world, with no exceptions. It is thus an attempt to specify a standard of employment conditions and practices with universal application.

The standard is kept under review and is updated from time to time. Social Accountability International (SAI) invites comments and advice. Indeed, once you have visited the website you may wish to pass on your own thoughts about the standard's comprehensiveness or robustness.

Case study 7.3 continued

The requirements of SA8000

The standard has nine categories. These are:

1 Child Labour
2 Forced Labour
3 Health Safety
4 Freedom of Association and Right to Collective Bargaining
5 Discrimination
6 Disciplinary Practices
7 Working Hours
8 Remuneration
9 Management Systems

Each of the categories has sub-headings. For example, 'Forced Labour' has only one, which effectively states, 'Thou shalt not be engaged in, or associated with, forced labour'. Management Systems', on the other hand, has 14 sub-headings. The standard is not enforced by any national law, but it is hoped that as its use grows as a standard against which corporate practices and behaviours are judged, compliance will become the norm.

SA8000 may be viewed on the website of the Council on Economic Priorities Accreditation Agency (CEPAA): www.ceppaa org.

As the SA8000 standard is a recent development only a small number of companies have been accredited. Although a wide range of companies, governments and NGOs were consulted during the development of the standard some NGOs concerned with international labour standards criticise CEPAA for being too close to the views of industry. Nevertheless the standard is an attempt to formalise universal ethical standards for businesses and organisations.

At first sight the existence of such codes presents a preferable state of affairs to that of no codes at all. However, a closer inspection of such codes poses some uncomfortable challenges to this assumption. For example, within the Sweatshop Code, the wording relating to 'wages and benefits' specifies:

> Employers shall pay employees, as a floor, at least the minimum wage required by local law or the prevailing industry wage, whichever is the higher, and shall provide legally mandated benefits.

This leaves much responsibility with governments to institute laws that enhance working and employment conditions. The lobbying of governments by business organisations, including MNCs, will clearly be listened to in government circles. Those employed in sweatshop conditions are not often well represented at the political negotiating table. In the meantime global organisations and western customers of the manufacturing output of developing countries remain free to exploit the cost differentials of sourcing their production capacity overseas. Indeed the very reason why many western apparel companies have closed their western production capability and transferred production to locations in the

Philippines, India, Honduras, etc., has been to exploit the cost advantages of the developing world, cost advantages that have often involved sweatshop conditions and child labour.

With regard to 'hours of work' the Sweatshop Code states:

> Except in extraordinary business circumstances, employees shall (i) not be required to work more than the lesser of (a) 48 hours per week and 12 hours overtime or (b) the limits on regular and overtime hours allowed by the law of the country of manufacture or, where the laws of such country do not limit the hours of work, the regular work week in such country plus 12 hours overtime and (ii) be entitled to at least one day off in every seven day period.

Thus, unless local laws state otherwise, an employer can require their workers to work 60 hours per week, and stay within the obligations of the code. Employees might be entitled to one day off per week, but whether they will get this is another matter. In addition, when demand is high, the working week can extend beyond the 60 hours. This should be constrained to 'extraordinary business circumstances', but the latter is not defined and less than scrupulous employers will use this as a loophole to work employees for all seven days of the week and exceed the 60 hours per employee. The code could be far more stringent in its demands on behalf of the employees (the majority of whom tend to be women), but of course, the closer wage rates and working conditions are pushed towards western levels, the less the original decision to source production to the developing country makes economic sense.

There are examples of organisations appearing to make serious efforts to put their codes into practice. The ILO reported that Levi-Strauss, for example, conducts annual global training programmes to ensure its audit managers are familiar with their internal code, and has conducted five-day training programmes in the Dominican Republic for 'terms of engagement' auditors. Liz Claiborne (an American retail organisation of women's fashion clothes) has also reported that it had intensified its efforts to identify and remove labour abuses.

An example is provided by McDonald and Nijhof (1999: 140) of an organisation, which employed 6,000 people, and whose CEO sought to roll out an ethics awareness-raising programme across the whole organisation. This involved writing the associated code of conduct in both English and Chinese and then training a series of trainers to deliver the associated workshops. The latter included a video message from the CEO, in which he stated that he would rather the organisation lose a contract than undermine the code. The programme was delivered throughout the company. For the CEO, 'the code needs to come off the pages and into people's lives'. As McDonald and Nijhof report, elements that were not included in the initiative were an annual ethics audit and an ethics hotline. Whether these have since been instituted is unknown.

The rigour with which MNCs police their own codes of conduct (particularly those they apply to their suppliers) does appear to vary. Of the organisation Liz Claiborne, the plant manager of Primo Industries, an apparel contractor based in El Salvador, stated, 'they are the toughest on child labour'. The plant manager told US Department of Labor officials that inspectors from Liz Claiborne visited the plant 'approximately twice a month to check on quality control and see whether rules and regulations are being implemented'. Such vigilance by the

Claiborne organisation must involve costs that some other organisations (maybe its competitors) do not appear to incur, at least not to the same extent. A manager with the Indian company, Zoro Garments, 75 per cent of whose output goes to US markets, is quoted as saying that:

> Representatives of US customers have visited Zoro's factory occasionally for quality control inspections, [but] most of the visits were walk-throughs with some general questions raised about the use of child labour, but no check-list of requirements was administered.

(ILO, n.d.)

A complicating issue occurs where the MNC sources products from a variety of overseas suppliers, with some of these suppliers being in monopsony relationships with the MNC, whilst for other suppliers the MNC in question might be only one amongst a range of customers. Thus, can an MNC be held responsible for the work conditions and labour practices of a supplier from which it sources relatively few orders? Whatever one's position on this question, it has to be taken for granted that for production costs of suppliers in developing countries to be so much lower than those of their western competitors, wage rates and employment conditions cannot be equal. Thus, for MNCs, or any other form of organisation, to feign ignorance of the working conditions of some of its suppliers ignores the logic of the situations. Rather than assuming that all is satisfactory, they must know that the cost differentials between suppliers in developing and developed countries would suggest a default position that all is not satisfactory, and that evidence is required to disprove this assumption.

Establishing a corporate code of conduct is one thing, making it a part of everyday practice is another. Of the 42 apparel companies surveyed by the US Department of Labor in 1996, to establish how many of them had endeavoured to ensure that workers in their overseas suppliers were aware of their code of conduct, 'very few respondents indicated that they had tried'. Only three companies insisted on their codes being posted on their suppliers' notice boards. In a further study reported by the ILO, of 70 supplier companies, 23 (33 per cent) indicated that they were not aware of corporate codes of conduct issued by their US customers.

The US Department of Labor also undertakes company visits and the ILO website gives information on ILO visits to a variety of countries including El Salvador, the Dominican Republic, Honduras, India and the Philippines. In a study of 70 companies, managers at only 47 of these stated an awareness of such codes, and of these only 34 could produce a copy of a code. Thus, less than half of the sites visited could produce a principal customer's code, yet the US retailers refer to their supplier codes as evidence of their (the apparel retailers') commitment to ethical practices at their overseas suppliers.

Awareness of such codes was highest in El Salvador, where managers at six out of the nine companies visited were aware of such codes, whereas in India managers at only two of the seven producer sites visited were aware. Even where awareness was acknowledged, awareness was not the same as accepting the codes and adhering to them. As the ILO observed,

Although a significant number of suppliers knew about the US corporate codes of conduct, meetings with workers and their representatives in the countries visited suggested that relatively few workers were aware of the existence of codes of conduct, and even fewer understood their implications.

Factors that will affect the impact of a code

Cassell *et al.* (1997), combining the work of Hopwood (1974) and Kelman (1961), identified three possible explanations for why individuals might display behaviours that conform with desired organisational behaviours. These are:

1 *Internalisation*, in which the behaviours are accepted by the individual as their own, even though they are set externally. This does suggest, however, that the ethical values displayed will be subject to, and influenced by, further external forces, unless the organisational values are held by the individual at a profound and deep level.

2 *Compliance*, in which the displayed behaviour is associated with the desire to achieve some form of reward, or avoid an identifiable punishment. This form of behaviour will last as long as the punishment or reward is both regarded as significant and realisable by the individual/s concerned, but not beyond. This form of behaviour is thus not ethically based, but instrumental, calculating and unreliable.

3 *Identification*, in which behaviour is shaped by, and mirrors, the behaviours of significant others with whom the individual wishes to identify. Again because of the instrumental and externally located locus of a behaviour's rationale, the reliability of the behaviour in question is problematic.

Of these three possible explanations, only the first holds out the prospect of consistency for the organisations, the other two being unreliable due to external corruption. If this is so then the individual must absorb the organisation's values in a conscious and knowing way because either:

■ The individual's existing values correspond closely with those espoused by the organisation and thus, little change is required to the individual's own ethics, or

■ The individual recognises in the organisation's values a set of principles that transcend their own and to which they wish to aspire.

Alternatively the internalisation is not conscious, but unconscious, achieved by the constant drip-drip of organisational images and rhetoric. This might seem a very distant possibility in the current day and age, but one of the authors is reminded of an ethics workshop he held for a group of managers on a Masters programme. One of the managers worked for a well-known and respected retail organisation, respected amongst other things for the apparently strong employee benefits and care provided by the company. However, during the course of the workshop all the participants reviewed different aspects of their organisation's practices, and this particular manager gradually shifted from a view of his employing organisation's paternalistic care as benign, to one which was more oppressive and manipulative. This change in interpretation came not from questioning by the tutors, but from a series of interactive exercises with other members of the course. The manager in question had worked for the retail organisation for over 15 years and during that time had accepted the organisation's house journal, the management conferences he attended and other practices as evidence of his employer's good intent. His now more critical interpretation did not suddenly make his employers 'bad' employers, when for the previous 15 years they had been 'good' employers. What unsettled him was how uncritical he had been in accepting a particular interpretation of some of the organisation's actions and decisions over the years, some of which did not square with the his original uncritical, 'rose-tinted' description of his organisation.

Using Goffman's (1959) dramaturgical metaphor, individuals can be said to 'act out' their preferred view of themselves on the stage of life. Information likely to enhance others' opinions of oneself is kept 'centre stage' rather than 'in the wings'. The concept of impression management pervades the literature on business ethics, and is particularly apparent in ethnographic accounts of how managers deal with ethical problems (e.g. Jackall, 1988; Schein, 1992; Toffler, 1991; Watson, 1994). Interestingly the 'management' and 'organisational behaviour' literature is a much richer and a more academically robust source of material on this point than much of the business ethics literature.

Jackall (1988) argued that the unethical actions of managers do not result from the individual's moral deficiencies, but rather from the bureaucratic structures of modern organisations that encourage managers to behave unethically. This view has been echoed by others within the literature. For example, Liedtka (1991) concluded that many of the managers in her study found themselves forced to choose between preserving their relationships within the firm (operating within the organisational political model) and following their own values (using a value-driven model). This point is explored further in Chapter 9, so we will conclude our consideration of this issue with a quote from Cassell *et al.* (1997: 1088):

> It is our contention that although individual psychological and demographic factors play a role in influencing behaviour in relation to codes, that role is relatively minor given the significance of the organizational context and culture within which behaviour takes place.

Cassell *et al.* (1997) identified three factors they argued would determine the influence a code would have upon the behaviour of organisational members, namely:

1 The nature of the code, its content and the processes by which it has been designed, developed and implemented.
2 The organisational control mechanisms (both formal and informal). For example, will the employees see the introduction of a (new) code as just another mechanism by which the employing organisation wishes to determine individual behaviour, or a genuine attempt to help employees cope with complex ethical issues that they will face during their day-to-day practice?
3 Individual influences which focus upon perceptual and self-control processes.

Thus, if the individual employee acts in keeping with required organisational behaviour out of either compliance or identification motives, and is sceptical about factors (1) and (2) above, the prospects for a newly introduced code of conduct or practice are likely to be unpredictable and variable throughout an organisation, two outcomes the code was presumably intended to obviate.

Arguments against the employment of codes of conduct and ethics

ACTIVITY 7.1

Although our consideration of codes of conduct and ethics has identified limitations in practice and referred to evidence that casts doubt upon the actual impact of codes 'on the ground', we have not suggested that the development and introduction of a code would be a negative step. There are, however, such arguments, and before discussing these we would like you to think through what these might be.

Identify as many negative aspects as possible associated with the development of a code of conduct or ethics.

Whilst the employment of codes has an intuitive appeal, we can identify five possible objections to their development and employment.

1 Justification

This relates to the lack of any universally accepted set of common principles and ethics. If 'everything is relative' is taken to its logical conclusion and codes can only ever be culturally and socially specific, the notion of universal laws is rejected and with it the argument that a corporation can have a single code of conduct. If a multinational organisation produces a code of conduct that reflects a basic set of values, by definition this implies there are certain basic concepts that it wishes to universalise, at least within its own worldwide operations, but is this possible? The question might become one of distinguishing between negotiable and non-negotiable values – how and when does one balance local customs and traditions with one's own sense of values when the two are in conflict? For example, when is a gift a bribe? We discuss this particular issue in the next chapter.

2 The inability of rules to govern actions

If codes cannot guarantee changes in behaviour, and empirical evidence is very limited with respect to examples of codes shaping behaviour in desired ways, will the negative signals being sent out to employees, that the organisation does not trust them, be the abiding impact of the introduction of a code? If so, then the overall impact of a code is likely to be negative.

3 Support structures

There is a need for, but paucity of, support structures within organisations for employees to feel able to act in accordance with specified codes of behaviour. Where codes of conduct do exist, Warren (1993: 189) argued that:

All too often ethical codes are handed down to employees from the executive above and the importance of trying to create a community or purpose within the company is ignored.

Warren (1993) referred to the field of industrial relations where evidence indicates that rules governing industrial relations need collective agreement if they are to be honoured in the breach as well as the observance (e.g. Terry, 1975). This perspective is supported by Bird and Waters (1989: 83). They argued that just talking about ethical issues is unlikely to enhance the significance of the issues unless mechanisms are found for 'connecting this language with the experiences and expectations of people involved in business'. Taking this argument forward Bird and Waters (1989: 84) argued that.

> Business people will continue to shun open discussions of actual moral issues unless means are provided to allow for legitimate dissent by managers who will not be personally blamed, criticised, ostracised, or punished for their views.

They found that talking to managers individually revealed that the managers had many concerns of an ethical nature. However, when asked if these issues were ever raised amongst managerial colleagues, either formally or informally, the managers replied that they were not. The managers identified a range of explanations for the collective managerial muteness on ethical issues. Such talk was perceived to be a threat to:

- efficiency (i.e. the imposition of rigid rules and regulations);
- the image of power and effectiveness (i.e. previous attempts had resulted in the dissenting manager being shown to be organisationally impotent); and
- organisational harmony (i.e. discussion of moral issues at work was perceived to be dysfunctional).

Thus, the introduction of a code of conduct requires an environment in which expressions of concern over particular practices are not perceived as simplistically 'anti-company', or 'wimpish'. Without such an environment, cynicism is likely to be fuelled, and the overall impact of the code will be negative.

4 The marginality of codes

Codes tend to be treated as 'add-ons', as constraints upon action, and thus act at the margins of corporate activity. To be effective codes need to be at the centre of corporate beliefs, or more particularly, a code becomes redundant if the corporate culture encapsulates those values and beliefs that would be reflected in a corporate code of conduct or ethics. If left at the margins, a code might be interpreted as a necessary accoutrement (garnish) to corporate activities, but one that can be circumvented, or 'negotiated' in certain circumstances. If so, then cynicism about corporate motives would be heightened and the overall effect of the code would be negative.

5 The diminution and ultimate invisibility of individual responsibility

Codes that specify behaviour in particular situations seek to take judgement out of ethically charged situations. Whilst this has the advantage of standardising behaviour throughout an organisation and potentially minimising the risk of behaviour that is unacceptable, there is also the risk of the individual using the 'I was only following orders' defence in the event of an enquiry into a dispute over a particular incident. This shifting of responsibility has been termed by Bauman (1994) as 'floating responsibility' and was discussed in Chapter 6. It becomes an organisational defence against individual conscience. The following of rules and adherence to the commands of superiors makes identification of responsibility difficult to isolate. Identification of responsibility for a particular action or inaction falls between the cracks of job descriptions and responsibilities, and codes of conduct. Morality (or the defining of it) thus becomes someone else's responsibility. The actions of individuals become automatic, with little thought or judgement on the part of the individual required. Whilst actual situations will often present complexities and nuances that take the individual into contexts not addressed adequately by a code, the existence and 'failings' of the code present the individual with an escape route from responsibility. To obey instructions is less demanding and far less risky than exercising moral judgement.

Bauman (1994) identified a second tendency, that of organisational actions being deemed amoral, that is neither good nor bad, only correct or incorrect. In this context codes of conduct can be used to make what could be transparent, opaque. Codes might be expressed, not so much in moral terms, but in technical terms, implying a moral neutrality to the issues being addressed in the code.

When codes of conduct collide

A fundamental problem within many types of organisation, but particularly those in the public and non-proft-seeking sectors, is the issue of the codes of conduct of differing professional groupings and the potential conflicts that the respective codes can create. For example, the role of internal accounting information as a management information support system places the role of accountants within the managerial structures. This does not of itself set accountants and those professionals located within an organisation's managerial structures against those professionals who are outside of those structures, but it creates the possibilities of conflict. One of the six principles upon which the International Federation of Accountants' Code of Ethics is based, and which is reflected in the codes of conduct of all the UK professional accountancy bodies, is that of confidentiality. The duty to protect the confidential nature of corporate information is underscored, even after a contract of employment is terminated.

A consideration of the codes of conduct or ethics within which other professionals must operate indicates the potential for conflict. For example, the United Kingdom Central Council for Nursing, Midwifery and Health Visiting (1996) states that 'each registered nurse, midwife and health visitor shall act, at all times, in such a manner as to safeguard and promote the interests of individual patients and clients'. In an environment that has seen health care be subject to considerable financial strictures over the past twenty years, a number of cases have highlighted the extremely difficult situations health care workers face in delivering effective and appropriate medical care 'that is in the interests of individual patients and clients'. The creation of managerial posts for medical staff such as nurses has only served to emphasise these tensions. Hunt (1995 and 1998) recounted cases in health care and social services where individuals have tried to speak out about their concerns, but found their actions thwarted and future career progression blighted.

The very nature of the codes of conduct of nurses and accountants maps out the territory of potential conflict. Whilst the nursing code requires patient advocacy, the accountants' code reflects an orientation of organisational loyalty. Indeed, in the cases of the codes of conduct developed by the American Institute of Internal Auditors and the (American) Government Finance Officers Association (Harris and Reynolds, 1993), explicit reference is made to loyalty to the employer. Even the human resource managers interviewed in the Fisher–Lovell (2000) study displayed a greater organisational orientation than the stereotypical portrayal of human resource managers might suggest.

The respective codes of conduct under which professional accountants and health care workers must operate are both understandable and defensible when viewed separately. However, when placed within a single organisational context, the potential for conflict is evident.

Even within a code of conduct, tensions often exist. Proctor *et al.* (1993: 166), highlight the contradictory situation that confronts social workers:

> The preamble to the Code itself acknowledges that multiple principles could bear on any practice situation . . . thus, the potential for conflict is inherent in the profession's values and is reflected in its Code of Ethics

At least the code of the social workers' professional body recognises these tensions. For accountants, the needs to both respect the confidentiality of corporate information and to respect the public interest are not usually formally recognised as posing any particular dilemma for accountants.

Interestingly Article IV of the code of conduct of the Project Management Profession (1996: 2) contains the following clause:

> Project management professionals shall protect the safety, health and welfare of the public and **speak out** against abuses in the areas affecting the public interest [emphasis added].

Some would argue that more than a pinch of salt needs to be on hand when considering the pronouncements of aspiring professional associations, but it is quite clear that this aspiring professional body expects its members to take public stands when appropriate. This is an unusually explicit statement from a trade association.

The above discussion has introduced an additional dimension, that of the ethics codes of professional associations. Much has been written on the rise of the professions (*see* Durkheim, 1992; Koehn, 1994; and Larson, 1977, for a discussion of these issues) and the roles of codes of ethics have been influential in this rise. Any trade association that gains the statutory right to control the membership of a particular aspect of human activity (e.g. the British Medical Association and doctoring; the Law Society and particular legal work; and certain professional accountancy bodies and auditing), will possess a code of ethics for its members to follow. The existence of a code of ethics will have been an essential element of the trade association's submission to control the membership of those who wish to practise as specific 'professionals', such as doctors, lawyers and auditors, etc. This is because the trade associations will need to assuage public concern that their state-granted monopolies will not be abused. The 'professional' bodies concerned will commit their members, above all else, to act 'in the public interest' whenever there is a clash of interest.

The 'public interest' is a very slippery concept. It refers to the interests of the public at large, not in a simplistic majority-type way, but rather in terms of what should be in the general interest of civic society if a rational, objective, long-term assessment of a situation is taken. Major scandals involving professional people cast very long shadows over the veracity and intentions of codes of conduct when employed by so-called professional bodies. Examples include the involvement of the international firm of accountants, Arthur Anderson, in the Enron affair, the extent of which is, at the time of writing, just beginning to be revealed; the failure of the accountancy profession to respond in any meaningful way to the travails of its senior members; or the way that doctors appear to have placed the interests of their profession and fellow colleagues' status above that of the public interest in cases such as the Bristol Heart Surgery Unit, or the body-parts shambles (see Case study 2.17). Yet to stay within the membership of a 'profession' the individual member must attempt not to bring the profession into disrepute. As mentioned above, individual professional codes of ethics, whilst defensible when considered on their own, can present a conflict situation when juxtaposed in particular organisational contexts.

In the Fisher–Lovell (2000) study, few of the accountants and HR professionals had studied their respective professional bodies' code of ethics and little weight seemed to be placed on them. In some senses the issue of the codes of ethics of professional associations has diminished in its relevance as an area of interest and study, as the mantle of professional bodies has slipped, and their claims to be acting in the public interest are seen as little more than façades behind which opaqueness is maintained and vested interests concealed.

Given the arguments posed in this section against the use of codes, the question might be asked, 'so do codes have a future?' Judging by the increase in the number of organisational codes in evidence, codes certainly have a present. A survey conducted by Arthur Anderson and London Business School (1999), contrasted the prevalence of codes of conduct in 1996 and 1999. Whereas 59 per cent of companies surveyed in 1996 acknowledged the use of a code of conduct, the figure had grown to 78 per cent by 1999, and 81 per cent of companies surveyed in 1999 had values or mission statements. The question is whether this recent upsurge in interest is anything more than a defensive reaction against potential legal claims, or, as in the case of public sector bodies, merely a necessary response to the outcome of the Nolan Committee reports. Does managerial attention to codes of conduct represent anything more than the latest management fad – after quality circles, business process re-engineering, the balanced scorecard, the learning organisation, etc.?

So far we have focused upon organisational responses to ethical issues by way of the development and employment of a range of different forms of codes of practice. We now move to a consideration of less overt, more subtle, but possibly more effective ways of shaping behaviour within organisations. This is the notion of corporate cultures, either singular or multiple. The development of a particular culture does not preclude the employment of a code of conduct, indeed the unwritten understandings that invariably comprise a particular culture act often as inviolate rules of conduct. All organisations will have 'ways of working', although those ways may be many and varied, with espoused behaviour sometimes deviating from actual behaviour.

Ethical culture and ethos

There are ethical issues about the propriety of using culture as a device for encouraging people to behave in one way rather than another. However, if we assume for the moment that it is acceptable for managers to foster a culture that encourages ethical behaviour, what would such a culture look like? Snell (1993 and 2000) used the term moral ethos, rather than ethical culture, when he discussed this issue. He defined moral ethos as comprising a set of 'force-fields',

> All of which impinge on members' understandings, judgements and decisions concerning good and bad, right and wrong.

(Snell, 2000: 267)

Snell argued that the moral ethos emerges from the interactions of such forces. For example, if the demand for loyalty is low this may encourage openness within an organisation that supports criticism and acting with integrity. Contrarily an organisation's demand for loyalty may inhibit the exercise of integrity. From an organisational perspective, loyalty is possibly the most important behaviour to cultivate amongst employees. Willmott (1998: 83) highlighted the contentious nature of codes of conduct and the implicit role of loyalty within them when he observed:

> the value ascribed to the adoption of codes is made conditional upon their contribution to business objectives. This implies that, in principle, the codes will be refined or discarded according to calculations about their continuing contribution to these objectives.

Integrity is less amenable to codes of conduct. For example, a code or rule to respect the confidentiality of corporate affairs in all circumstances might conflict with a broader social perspective of integrity.

Paralleling Kohlberg's stages of moral reasoning (discussed in Chapter 5), Snell (1993: ch. 6) identified six types of moral ethos that could arise within organisations. They are:

1 *Fear-ridden ethos*. Behaviour that is characterised by coercion, blind obedience and a myopic focus on organisational survival at any cost.
2 *Advantage-driven ethos*. Employees are rewarded for getting the best for the organisation even if this might involve deception, gamesmanship and exploitation of others if necessary. The ethos encourages private alliances, secrecy and personal advantage.
3 *Members-only ethos*. This ethos demands loyalty and a shared concern to present a good image to those outside the organisation. Clever upstarts are to be tamed and brought into the fold. Internally the focus on group membership can encourage paternalism, sexism and racism.

4 *Regulated ethos.* Regulation and accountability are typical of this ethos. Codes of conduct are written and employees are often expected to self-certify that they have obeyed the rules.

5 *Quality-seeking ethos.* This ethos seeks to encourage everyone to work to the highest ethical standards. Training and development encourages debate and argument about what those standards should be. The ethos can create a sense of arrogance and over-commitment.

6 *Soul-searching ethos.* The organisational ethos supports a spiritual learning community that emphasises integrity and an ongoing ethical dialogue.

Given that corporate cultures can be employed in manipulative ways, the issues of ethicality that pervade this area ultimately resolve themselves around

> the process of moral thought and self-scrutiny that precedes it. This understanding of ethics puts weight on the process of thought that precedes action, to qualify behaviour as ethical.
>
> (Sinclair, 1993: 69)

Thus, the ethicality of a decision lies not in the behaviour displayed, or the decision taken, but in the forethought that preceded the behaviour or decision. This suggests that we need think more critically about notions of culture. The 'forces' that Snell referred to can be seen at the visible level (e.g. the behaviour of individuals), or at more subtle, less visible levels (e.g. assumptions and beliefs that inform behaviour). Thus it is argued that culture operates at different levels, with important implications for business ethics.

■ Levels of culture

Schein (1992) offered an analysis that reflects three levels of culture, each with a different level of visibility. The top or first level is the most visible level of culture. Within this category would be included evidence such as signs, symbols, written codes, forms of address (i.e. how seniors, peers and juniors are expected to be addressed), clothing (formal, informal), stories and myths (usually about past leaders), rituals, architecture and décor of the company's premises. These visible signs, practices and images are described as artifacts of culture. Schein argues that whilst these are the most visible evidence of culture they are not always easy to decipher by the external observer. Forms of initiation and 'apprenticeship' are often required before the full significance of these artifacts is revealed.

The second level of culture is represented by the espoused values of a group. These are the beliefs that are articulated, that are audibly expressed. Sometimes these beliefs can be represented by a 'go-get-'em' philosophy, with staff encouraged to 'take the moment', or to 'go for it'. Whether these values are wholeheartedly believed is a matter of question, but if the stated values or beliefs tend to deliver the outcomes sought, then the credibility of the beliefs will grow and become accepted as 'the way things are done around here'. An interesting example of how language is used to create particular attitudes and cultures is reflected in the refusal of one leading security firm to allow its employees to use the term 'failure'. This reflects a refusal by the senior management to accept any level of underachievement by employees, or for the employees to see any demand as unattainable.

Schein referred to the third level as basic assumptions. These are the unspoken beliefs that exist within an organisation. They are the least visible, yet the most pervasive form of culture because they represent deeply embedded ways of thinking about such questions as the nature of human nature, humanity's relationship with environment, the nature of truth and of human activity. The issues explored in Activity 7.1 (see p. 222) are basic assumptions and are difficult to bring to the surface and challenge. Consequently they operate below the level of consciousness and can undermine the idea of moral agency, which requires conscious deliberation. If corporations are capable of subliminal influence on their employees' basic assumptions then this would be a potent threat to moral agency. There is much debate (Smircich 1983), however, about whether top managers do have this power or whether any attempts they make to guide cultures lead only to unanticipated changes. That corporations can shape employees' beliefs is not questioned; whether those influences can be controlled to the organisation's benefit is doubtful, at least in the short term.

How to develop the ethical ethos of organisations leads us to a consideration of ethical leadership.

▦ Ethical leadership

The direction and example presented by senior management in terms of what is considered to be acceptable practice within an organisation must inform and shape the behaviour of others. Most textbooks argue that it is a leader's role to define the vision and core values of an organization. Kanungo and Mendonca (1996) pointed out that employees will not believe leaders who lack ethical integrity and the leaders' values will not be accepted. They suggested that ethical leadership has to be altruistic, putting the well-being of others in the organisation before self-interest. However they noted that western culture was better noted for its emphasis on egoism than on altruism. Blanchard and Peale (1988) argued for a form of virtue ethics, suggesting five 'Ps' – pride, patience, prudence, persistence and perspective – as the cardinal virtues for organisational leaders. The human resource management function has been identified (Connock and Johns, 1995: 159) as the natural repository of organisations' consciences, although a survey found that, in those companies that allocated business ethics to a particular department, responsibility was given to a range of departments (Arthur Andersen and London Business School, 1999: 19).

To suggest that where there is the most virtuous set of senior managers all employees will automatically follow these examples of desired practice would be naive. However negative examples of immoral behaviour by senior executives can act like a cancer on ethical behaviour throughout an organisation, as the example provided in Case study 6.1 illustrated. The organisation in question appeared to harbour unpalatable practices and beliefs at a senior level, which created moral indifference within the headquarters.

A significant problem for any organisation that publicises its commitment to high ethical standards in all its business dealings is that any one single departure from such standards is likely to attract considerable media attention and cast doubt upon the full range of the organisation's activities. If this does happen, the reaction could be both unreasonably harsh (depending of course upon the nature and scale of the alleged infraction), but also a somewhat disingenuous approach to the analysis and reporting of the incident. Even if the infraction in question is finally judged to be an intentional and knowingly unethical act on the part of the individual employee concerned (however senior), the individual transgression might be just that, an individual's error of judgement. It might not be a revelation of institutionally entrenched unethical practices. In such a situation the more telling test of organisational commitment to a broadly accepted notion of corporate ethical behaviour would be how the organisation's senior management respond to the transgression and the steps they take to remedy the problem. In short, no one is perfect, but when errors are made, or mis-judgements are revealed, how do we as individuals and corporations react and respond? The openness of individuals and organisations to acknowledge an error or problem, and the learning that ensues from the incident in question, are more likely to reflect the depth of commitment to ethical practice, than are pious claims to high ethical standards made in mission statements or corporate reports. It is at times of tension or challenge that ethical credentials are more likely to be revealed. Organisational learning is a much vaunted but also a most demanding and challenging notion. The processual model of managing is commensurate with such an approach, and Buchholz and Rosenthal (1998) adopt it to explain their view of moral development within organisations.

> The adjustment between the self and the other is neither assimilation of perspectives, one to the other, nor the fusion of perspectives into an indistinguishable oneness, but can best be understood as an 'accommodating participation' in which each creatively affects and is affected by the other through accepted means of adjudication . . . because of these dynamics, the leader does not 'stand apart' from a following group, nor is the leader an organizer of group ideas, but rather leadership is by its very nature in dynamic interaction with the group, and both are in a process of ongoing transformation because of this interaction.
>
> (Buchholz and Rosenthal, 1998: 418–19)

Such a processual and 'accommodating participatory' approach would represent a fundamental change of perspective for the type of managers represented in the studies reported by Bird and Waters, 1989; and Lovell, 2002. The processual perspective offers, on the one hand, the prospects for moral chaos, but on the other, possibly the best hope for moral agency. The former because the type of leadership implied in the processual model requires a degree of maturity and humility, but also a strength of belief and conviction that might be beyond many managers and leaders. However, if some form of accommodation is achievable in ways that eschew indoctrination, the debates that would be evident might do much to address many of the concerns raised throughout this book.

An important caveat with respect to greater openness and transparency in corporate dealings is the issue of litigation. The greater demands made of public corporations in terms of their various impacts is in many respects a sign of a maturing society. However, there has been an attendant increase in the propensity of members of the public to take legal action against corporations when infractions occur. In such a context it should not be surprising that corporations become very wary of revealing their 'failings' in public for fear of how such information might be employed. These complex issues can only be moved forward by debate and a developing sense of balance between:

- on the one hand, reparation for any 'injuries' experienced as a result of sub-standard performance by an individual or organisation, where culpability is evident; and
- on the other, a recognition that 'things' will and do go less than satisfactorily on occasions and that if the 'failing' was innocent, and all reasonable measures had been taken to avoid its occurrence in the first place, then retribution should be avoided, to encourage and foster learning from the experience.

These words are easy to say and write, but much more difficult to put into practice. Yet this is the challenge facing organisations. No easy compromise or solution is on offer, only the prospect of continued action and attention to the levels of behaviour deemed acceptable within our societies.

Reflections

From the Hobbesian view of human behaviour, that people will not behave morally without the fear of retribution, flows the necessity for rules, of which codes of conduct are an obvious example. Bauman saw rules and codes, based upon reason, as leading to a morality associated with law – the laws of business and bureaucracy. This adherence to procedural rationality requires that

> all other emotions must be toned down or chased out of court . . . the most prominent of the exiled emotions are moral sentiments; that resilient and unruly 'voice of conscience'.
>
> (Bauman, 1994: 8)

Interestingly, Bauman argued that when the term ethics appears in the vocabulary of bureaucracy it is invariably in connection with 'professional ethics'. The latter term is considered to be breached when a member shows disloyalty either to the organisation or to (organisational) colleagues. A qualified notion of honesty thus becomes of critical importance, i.e. the keeping of promises and contractual obligations. This leads to predictability and consistency in organisations, an extremely important managerial need. When this is coupled with the notion of 'floating responsibility', an escape route is provided for those seeking a quiet life in the face of an awkward organisational issue.

People's instrumentalism is seen as something to be encouraged by Clutterbuck (1992: 100–1) as he exhorts organisations to reward exemplary behaviour, possibly with cash payments, and to 'punish breaches of the code publicly; use the key motivators of influence, promotion and access to resources'. This simplistic view of human nature and notions of managing assumes that instrumentalism is the only determinate, or at least the dominant explanation, of human behaviour. From a purely instrumental perspective, it is also an expensive option. In the governing of human relationships, trust is a far less expensive option than contractualism, or financial incentives. But the problem remains of whether trust can be relied upon. When associated with notions of loyalty, it becomes increasingly problematic. For example, in a situation where it has become known to you that a product of your employing organisation poses health risks to consumers, which is paramount, your loyalty to:

- your work colleagues,
- your employing organisation,
- your family (who depend on your income),
- the consumer, or
- the general public?

The converse of the loyalty question is which of these groups has the right to trust you and your actions in such a situation?

Maybe the least that can be said for codes of ethics is that they give the principled employee a reference point should times become ethically challenged and certain organisational practices give rise to serious cause for concern. At its best a code can reflect an honestly expressed expectation about moral conduct within an organisation, with the code probably written in terms of principles rather than in a prescriptive or proscriptive fashion. Employees would be encouraged to act with moral agency and the codes would be supported by mechanisms that would allow concerned employees to raise concerns in a neutral and anonymous forum, preferably using external counsellors.

The roles of codes and agreements relating to the relationships between MNCs, national governments and supplier networks are important and interesting elements in the debates on codes of conduct. At the same time debates relating to codes of ethics and professions, an area of much academic activity at one time, have become less relevant as the compromised positions of many business professions have come to general attention.

Within the complex arenas that are modern business corporations, codes of conduct, codes of ethics and the prevailing culture/s will be important reference points for many of the players involved with, or affected by, the activities of the corporation. At different times the eight roles of codes discussed in this chapter will be seen in operation. Yet if ethics is at the heart of an organisation's practices and its *raison d'être*, embedded within its culture/s, written codes become less important. They become less defensive in terms of their tenor, being essentially codes of ethics.

Summary

In this chapter the following key points have been made:

- Whilst not universally or uniformly recognised, distinctions between codes of conduct and codes of ethics help crystallise the intended purpose of a code.
- Codes of practice can be important mechanisms that allow business corporations to negotiate their position in a society.
- Codes of practice have multiple and not mutually exclusive roles within organisations.

- The development of a code of practice is, at one and the same time, an understandable development by a corporation, but also a reflection of a lack of trust in the integrity and reliability of its employees.
- There are arguments against developing codes of practice that require ethical practice to be at the heart of an organisation's activities and 'ways of working'.
- Organisational cultures are critical to understanding an organisation's actual (as distinct from espoused) values.

Suggested further reading

A useful text is R.A. Buchholz and S.B. Rosenthal (1998) *Business Ethics:The Pragmatic Path Beyond Principles to Process,* London: Prentice Hall. The following articles will be of interest to those who wish to study the topic further: C. Cassell, P. Johnson and K. Smith (1997), 'Opening the Black Box: Corporate codes of ethics in their organisational context', *Journal of Business Ethics*, 16, 1077–93. G. McDonald and A. Nijhof (1999) 'Beyond codes of ethics: an integrated framework for stimulating morally responsible behaviour in organisations', *Leadership & Organisation Development Journal*, 20(3), 133–46. R.C. Warren (1993) 'Codes of ethics: Bricks without straw', *Business Ethics: A European Review*, 2(4), 185–91. *See also* S. Srivastva and D.L. Cooperrider (1988) *Executive Integrity: The Search for High Human Values in Organisational Life*, San Francisco: Jossey-Bass Inc., 1–28.

GROUP ACTIVITY 7

For the purposes of this case, you should assume that most desktop computers are made in a variety of Asian countries. Three parties are in discussions over the development of a code of practice that might cover the activities of the local suppliers to the multinational corporate purchasers of the computers.

The code of practice would cover the operations of the MNCs in **one** of the countries concerned. The three parties are a spokesperson for the Society of Computer Manufacturers and Assemblers, a representative from the host country's ministry for trade and industry and a representative from the pressure group Workers in the Manufacture and Assembly of Computers (WMAC), who is also a local trade union representative.

Divide the seminar group into three sub-groups (one for each of the parties involved). Each sub-group should decide its position, in terms of what is:

(a) morally justifiable, and
(b) likely to be achieved,

on the following issues:

- standard hours of work;
- acceptable overtime working;
- pension rights;
- accident and injury protection and benefits for dependants;

Group Activity 7 continued

- number of continuous working days in normal and abnormal circumstances;
- health and safety standards (equivalent to western standards?);
- employment rights (e.g. period of notice required by both employer and employee);
- minimum employment age;
- social infrastructure support (e.g. support for local schools, sports clubs, youth clubs, medical facilities);
- grievance procedures.

Then, as a complete group, debate the contrasts between the three perspectives.

8

Ethics and values in international business

OBJECTIVES

Having completed the chapter and its associated activities, readers should be able to:

■ Describe how the ethical and business values of countries and societies differ.

■ Argue about the validity of particular values and ethical standards of different countries.

■ Evaluate the options for responding to the ethical issues and dilemmas that arise from international business and globalisation.

■ Relate these issues to the debates about ethical universalism and ethical relativism.

Introduction

Societies and countries may differ in their business ethics and values. They may have, in the high ethics established within their religion, philosophical traditions and literature, different ideals about the conduct of business and organisational life. Cultural tradition in one place might see business growth and profitability as an end in itself; in other places economic ends might be seen as subordinate to other goals. Even if ethics and values are shared, countries and societies may vary in the degree to which they practise them. While two countries might, at a formal level, regard bribery as immoral, one country might conduct its business in line with this standard but the second country might not. These issues are discussed later in the chapter.

Such differences, between and within countries, raise questions that are the subject of this chapter.

■ The first question asks about the similarities and differences between different countries' and societies' ethical principles and practice concerning business.

■ The second question is whether such differences can ever be justified. In ethical terms this question is a particular example of the general debate between ethical relativism and ethical universalism.

■ The third question is whether a worldwide diversity of ethical standards and practices can coexist with the demands of international business, particularly in regard to:

- the increase in international trade,
- the growth of multinational and transnational companies that may be bigger and richer than many nation states, and
- the increasing homogenisation of global brands, products and services.

The concern is that, without universal standards, powerful multinational companies would be able to take advantage of countries with different ethical standards by:

■ employing local labour with inadequate conditions and pay rates,
■ taking advantage of lower standards of health, safety and environmental protection,
■ using their economic power to obtain benefits and privileges from developing countries that are desperate to attract foreign investment.

The case studies provided in Chapter 2 raise many issues of this type. Case study 2.4, for example, deals with the use of child labour, which is seen as acceptable in some countries. The issue is whether universal codes of conduct should be established which carry moral authority, or the sanctions of international law, to prevent companies acting badly in the world market place.

Such universal provisions could be seen as ethically necessary but can also be seen as a form of ethical colonialism in which western multinational companies, and even Non-Governmental Organisations (NGOs), use their economic strength to force societies to accept values and values that are not their own. Apart from any moral objection to such processes Jaeger and Kanungo (1990: 1) expressed a practical criticism:

> uncritical transfer of management theories and techniques based on Western ideologies and value systems has in many ways contributed to organisational inefficiency and ineffectiveness in the developing country context.

Western organisations' concern for equal opportunities in staff selection processes for example might contradict local obligations to support friends, family and relations. Such situations can lead to employees experiencing psychological conflicts between the values of their society and those imposed on them by their western employers (Tripathi (1990), Viswesvaran and Deshpande (1996)). These issues have not arisen only recently, with the expansion of multinational organisations in the world. The dominance of western values has long been recognised and disputed. Vivekenanda, a nineteenth-century Indian nationalist and religious leader, argued:

> I will tell you something for your guidance in life. Everything that comes from India take as true, until you find cogent reasons for disbelieving it. Everything that comes from Europe take as false, until you find cogent reasons for believing it.
>
> (Quoted in Chakraborty, 1999: 4)

A particular form of the tendency of powerful countries and companies to impose their values on weaker societies is sometimes called McDonaldisation.

This is a process by which western brands and organisational methods and structures replace local products and thereby reduce choice and variety.

Definition

> Ritzer (1993) in his book *The McDonaldization of Society* took the global success of McDonald's as an example of the growth of a common, worldwide, mass culture. Ritzer argued that the process of McDonaldisation represents the expansion of instrumental rationality – a drive for efficiency, predictability, calculability and control – with no questioning of the ends being sought. The criticism of mass culture, of which McDonaldisation is a modern example, is that it causes people to be satisfied with a 'vulgar simplicity' (Harrington, 1965: 188). Advertising and sound-bite communications, it is alleged, diminish the masses' ability to exercise moral agency. They lose the ability to distinguish the good from the bad, gourmet cooking from burgers, the noble life from consumerism.

The networks of multinational and transnational companies and organisations and NGOs form the arenas in which such problems may arise and the business cultures of different societies and countries may come into contact with each other. It will be useful to define the differences between the two. Multinational companies have a country that they regard as their home base even though they invest in and organise the production and delivery of services in other countries. Transnational companies are rare and have no specific national identification or base. They are run by international managements and are willing to move their capital and operations to any favourable location (Hirst and Thompson, 1996: 11). This puts them beyond the control of any one nation state.

Most of the examples used in this chapter will focus on a comparison between western and Asian, particularly Indian, business ethics. The chapter cannot, because of limitations of space, give a worldwide review of business values and ethics, but by concentrating on some key regions it can illustrate most of the major themes and issues.

The chapter is divided into three parts that deal with each of the questions raised in the introduction.

- The first part describes the extent to which ethical standards, values and practices of business differ between and within countries. It also discusses attempts to produce universal standards for business ethics.
- The second part offers a normative discussion of whether it matters if different countries have different ethical systems. It raises the philosophical debate between universalists, who believe there can only be one true ethical system, and relativists, who believe that cultural ethical difference is justifiable. It is argued that relativism does not mean that 'anything goes' because there are ways of judging between valid differences in business ethics and invalid ones.
- The third part deals with the question of how multinational and transnational companies should behave in a world in which a universal business ethic is not established and in which countries may have valid differences in their business ethics.

Business and managerial values in different countries and societies

This section of the chapter assesses the extent to which values and ethics are universal in the business and organisational arenas and the extent to which they differ between countries and societies.

■ Universal values?

There are ethical norms and values that are transnational, shared by many countries. Sometimes these reflect common cultures, as in the Islamic countries. Sometimes they are the result of coincidence or a reflection of the commonalities of human nature and condition (Wines and Napier, 1992). There have been attempts to identify such standards, to codify them and publish them as a universal guide.

One important example is the Declaration of Human Rights, which was published by the United Nations in 1948 and subsequently, in 1966, divided into two separate codes, one covering civil and political rights and one, more relevant to our field, covering economic, cultural and social rights.

CASE STUDY 8.1

The Universal Declaration of Human Rights

This includes, inter alia, the rights:

- not to be held in slavery;
- not to be subjected to torture or degrading treatment;
- to equality before the law;
- to a standard of living adequate for the well-being of self and family;
- to work and to just and favourable conditions of work;
- to equal pay for equal work;
- to rest and leisure and periodic holidays with pay.

(*Source*: United Nations, 1948)

Other attempts have focused on standards for international business. Sometimes companies and industries publish codes that they believe should govern their business operations worldwide. This sort of standard has been particularly common in relation to the employment practices used by companies' partners in their international supply chains. There are arguments for saying that the World Trade Organisation (WTO), which was set up in 1995 as a successor to the General Agreement on Tariffs and Trade (GATT), should be the body to take on this ethical responsibility as it is the regulatory body for world trade. In particular Tsogas (1999) argued that it should publish and regulate labour standards across the world. The WTO has not taken on this role.

The Caux Round Table is an international body that, with the involvement of the Minnesota Center for Corporate Responsibility, developed a set of ethical principles for international business. It was founded in 1986 by Olivier Giscard D'Estaing of INSEAD, a French business school, and Frederick Philips, chairman of Philips Electronics. They accepted that law and markets provided insufficient guides for conduct. They therefore defined ethical principles that are based on the Japanese concept of *kyosei* – co-operating to achieve a mutual common prosperity – and human dignity (Caux Round Table 2001).

Implicit agreement on transnational standards, or even formal agreement about universal ethical standards, does not, of course, mean that those standards are implemented. The gap between espoused values and values in practice has been conceptualised by Hofstede (1991: 9) as the difference between the desirable and the desired. The desirable is an ethical norm that states what is right and good, the desired is a description of what people actually seek to achieve. Bribery and corruption is a case in point. Most societies in the world see it as undesirable; but that does not prevent large numbers of people in many societies desiring the benefits it can bring them.

It is worth considering bribery and corruption in more detail. Some types of bribery in particular circumstances might not be immoral. Case study 8.2 suggests a scale of impropriety for the payment of bribes.

CASE STUDY 8.2

A scale of bribery and corruption

- *Gifts* – expressions of friendship and good faith, openly given, of low value and often reciprocated.

- *Tips* – discretionary rewards for good service.

- *'Grease'* (sometimes known as facilitation payments) – small payments on a customary scale to encourage people to do what their job requires them to do. Not a payment to make them do what they should not do. Grease is often a recompense for the very low wages of those accepting the inducement. The Anti-terrorism, Crime and Security Act 2001 made it a crime in the UK for British firms to make such payments (or any other form of bribe) to officials overseas. The UK government did not anticipate that overseas officials extorting such payments in countries in which it was normal would lead to prosecutions in the UK.

- *Commissions* – often large payments for acting as a go-between and facilitating deals. It could be a fair payment for professional services but if the payment is disproportionate it might be a way of delegating responsibility for paying bribes from the principal to an agent.

- *Bribes* – payments to encourage people to do things that they should not.

The following factors should be considered when judging the badness of a bribe.

- It gives the bribe giver an unfair advantage or access to resources or benefits that would not otherwise be available to them.
- The amount of the bribe is greater than is customary.
- The opportunity to offer a bribe is not equally open to all and when different people or groups have to pay different amounts in bribes.
- It is illegal.
- Its cultural impact is to undermine trust and probity in a society.

It can be argued that bribery of a government official is worse than bribery of a company or a private individual. This is because a public body or official has a special obligation to the well-being of the population as a whole that cannot be discharged if that body or official responds to private and sectional interests through bribery. The OECD (2001) published a convention that outlawed the bribing of public officials in international business negotiations. A private individual or company in contrast might be thought to have a responsibility only to themselves, their close associates and their shareholders. In this case the damage caused by the giving or taking of bribes may be less.

Nevertheless most countries formally proscribe the giving and taking of bribes for the reasons outlined above. Yet in many countries corruption is endemic. Transparency International is an NGO that researches the level of perceived bribery and corruption, in terms of both offering and receiving bribes, in a wide range of countries. They produce two indices based on surveys of informed persons. The indices do not measure the actual frequency of corruption but people's opinion of its frequency.

Selections from the 2001 Corruption Perceptions Index are shown in Table 8.1. Ninety-nine countries were analysed in the index but they are not all shown for reasons of space. The complete results can be seen in Transparency International's (2001) website. The Index uses a 0–10 scale in which 0 means highly corrupt and 10 means very honest.

The second index produced by Transparency International, the Bribe Payers Index, is based on a survey of 19 countries. The respondents were asked how likely it was that companies from named countries would pay bribes to win or retain business. The results are shown in Table 8.2. Again an index number of 10 represents a perceived low level of bribery and 0 a high level.

More attempts are being made to produce universal ethical codes for international business. But there is still much work to be done. Even if the difficulties of promulgating codes are overcome the problem of differing degrees of conformance to the codes remains.

■ Relative values?

This section explores the extent to which different societies and cultures have different values and ethical standards in the fields of business and organisational

Table 8.1 The Transparency International Corruption Perceptions Index (CPI) 2001

Country	Rank	CPI score	Country	Rank	CPI score
Finland	1	9.9	Malaysia	36	5.0
Denmark	2	9.5	China	57	3.5
Singapore	4	9.2	Argentina	57	3.5
United Kingdom	13	8.3	India	71	2.7
Hong Kong	14	7.9	Russia	79	2.3
USA	16	7.6	Azerbaijan	84	2.0
Italy	29	5.5	Bangladesh	91	0.4

(*Source*: Transparency International, 2001)

Table 8.2 The Transparency International Bribe Payers Index (BPI) 1999

Country	Rank	BPI score	Country	Rank	BPI score
Sweden	1	8.3	Singapore	11	5.7
Australia	2	8.1	Spain	12	5.3
Canada	3	8.1	France	13	5.2
Austria	4	7.8	Japan	14	5.1
Switzerland	5	7.7	Malaysia	15	3.9
Netherlands	6	7.4	Italy	16	3.7
United Kingdom	7	7.2	Taiwan	17	3.5
Belgium	8	6.8	South Korea	18	3.4
Germany	9	6.2	China & Hong Kong	19	3.1
USA	10	6.2			

(*Source*: Transparency International, 1999)

life. Geert Hofstede (1991 and 2001) carried out the seminal empirical work on national value differences in organisations. He conducted a questionnaire survey of employees in the national subsidiaries of IBM. Responses were obtained from 72 national subsidiaries in 1968 and 1972. The results from the smaller subsidiaries were ignored and so the analysis finally enabled a comparison between the personal values of employees in 53 countries He identified four dimensions along which the values of employees in different countries varied.

- *Power distance* – the extent to which the less powerful members of organisations expect and accept that power is distributed unequally.
- *Individualism* – high in countries in which the ties between individuals are loose and everyone is expected to look out for themselves. It is low in collectivist countries where people are integrated into strong, cohesive groups and are expected to give loyalty to these groups in return for their protection.
- *Masculinity* – high in those countries in which gender roles are distinct and in which men are expected to be assertive, tough and focused on material success and women are supposed to be more modest, tender and concerned with the quality of life. In societies in which masculinity is low the gender roles overlap and both men and women are supposed to be modest, tender and concerned with the quality of life.
- *Uncertainty avoidance* – the extent to which society members feel threatened by uncertain or unknown situations. Societies in which there is low uncertainty avoidance are comfortable with ambiguity; those in which there is high uncertainty avoidance seek to finesse ambiguity away.

Table 8.3 shows the relative positions of the USA, Great Britain and India, and the highest and lowest scoring countries on each index.

Differences in values need not cause ethical difficulties. For example differences in values about uncertainty avoidance or perceptions of time may not raise major ethical problem; but differences in other values do. The identification by Trompenaars and Hampden-Turner (1993: 144–5) of national differences in attitudes towards nature, for example, affects ethical matters such as humanity's use

Table 8.3 Values and rank score for selected countries on four indices of national value differences

Country	Power distance index	Individualism index	Masculinity index	Uncertainty avoidance index
Highest scoring country	Malaysia (104)	USA (91)	Japan (95)	Greece (112)
USA	38/53 (40)	–	15 (62)	43/53 (46)
Great Britain	42/53 (35)	3/53 (89)	9 (66)	47/53 (35)
India	10/53 (77)	21/53 (48)	20 (54)	40/53 (40)
Lowest scoring country	Austria (11)	Guatemala (6)	Sweden (5)	Singapore (8)

(Figures in brackets are the countries' scores on the scales.)
(*Source*: Hofstede, 1991: 26, 53, 84, 113)

or abuse of the physical world. North American culture, which rose historically from a small society that found itself in a huge continent, developed values that emphasised control over one's environment and destiny as the key to success. In a post-Kyoto world these values appear to be a threat to environmental sustainability. Amongst the value dimensions identified by Hofstede, power distance, masculinity and individualism all raise ethical questions about the nature of good and moral relationships between people.

The various approaches to leadership in different countries may be related to their values. Hofstede looked at two dimensions in particular to map these differences and the analysis is shown in Figure 8.1. This shows how four national cultures might be expected to handle conflicts between people in

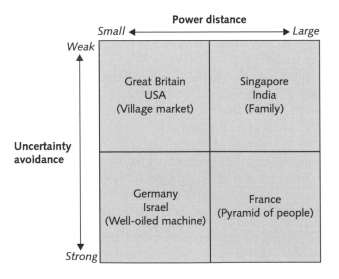

Figure 8.1 The relationship between Hofstede's cultural dimension and national leadership styles
(Source: Hofstede, 2001: 377)

business and organisations. In France, where large power distances are accepted and people are ill-disposed towards uncertainty, it would be done through the chain of command. Those higher in the hierarchy would be expected to resolve disputes between their subordinates. German values also favour order and predictability but have a lower acceptance of large power distances. The German approach to conflict would be to improve procedures that would remove the causes of the conflicts. The British, with their tolerance of ambiguity, but not of big power distances, would prefer to tackle the problems through informal negotiations between the opponents. People would negotiate with each other as if they were farmers haggling in the village market place. Other countries, and India is an example, see relationships in a holistic rather than a functional manner. This can be explained by considering attitudes to friendship. Dewey (1993), who studied British civil servants in India, and their relationship with Indians, in the early twentieth century, discovered they had contradictory views of friendship. The British took their idea of friendship from Oxbridge common rooms and gentlemen's clubs and saw it as a relationship that carried little obligation beyond that of good conversation. The Indians, however, saw friendship as a fundamental bond that carried obligations to sacrifice oneself, if necessary, to support a friend in all their endeavours. Unsurprisingly Dewey found that British officials' attempts to befriend Indians often collapsed in recriminations of faithlessness. The importance Indians place on personal obligations is reflected in Hofstede's suggestion about how managers, in countries like India, might handle conflicts. He argued they would use a metaphor of the family in which problems were resolved by deference to the head of the family or by accepting the demands imposed by a friend.

Hofstede (1991) was concerned that his original IBM survey was conducted using a research questionnaire written from a western cultural perspective. A new survey based on Chinese perspectives was prepared and administered to respondents in 23 countries around the world.

The results from the Chinese Values Survey supported the identification of three of Hofstede's value dimensions. The fourth one, however, uncertainty avoidance, could not be statistically identified in the raw results from the survey. Uncertainty is avoided, Hofstede argued, by establishing the truth. If the Chinese survey did not register this concern then it might be explained by the emphasis in Chinese values on virtue rather than truth. He proposed a fifth value dimension, which he labelled Confucian dynamism. Confucianism, the traditional philosophy of China, is not concerned with establishing religious Truths. Like Hinduism it is more concerned with practice than belief. To follow Confucianism or Hinduism it is not necessary to believe a creed; but it is required to behave in a particular way. This differentiates these religions from Christianity and Islam, which, whilst providing rules for daily life, require commitment to a creed. Confucianism stresses the importance of subordination in five key relationships (ruler–subject, father–son, older brother–younger brother, husband–wife, senior friend–junior friend), virtuous behaviour towards others and the adoption of key virtues such as thrift, hard work and study. Table 8.4 sets outs the Confucian values.

Table 8.4 Confucian values

Long-term Confucian values	Short-term Confucian values
■ Persistence and perseverance	■ Personal steadiness and stability
■ Ordering relationships by status	■ Protecting your 'face'
■ Thrift	■ Respect for tradition, reciprocation of greetings, favour and gifts
■ Having a sense of shame	

(*Source*: Hofstede, 1991: 165–6)

The Confucian dynamism scale effectively measures the extent to which a society values a long-term rather than a short-term orientation. But the acceptance of the whole set of Confucian values marks, according to Hofstede (2001: 363), a major ethical divide between western and eastern ethical approaches. Western ethical approaches are focused on identifying the moral Truth, either by deontological or consequentialist means. The eastern traditions are more concerned with virtuous behaviour, which calls for the development of personal insight and judgement rather than knowledge. As pointed out in Chapter 3, many writers are arguing that a virtue ethics approach would be better suited to western businesses and organisations than that of western moral philosophy.

■ Moveable values

The argument so far has been based on the assumption that countries and societies have definable and discrete ethical beliefs and values. It would be wrong, however, to interpret this as meaning that they have fixed and monolithic ethical systems. Within societies and countries there will be competing interpretations of the shared values, and arguments about how they should change and develop. It is always dangerous therefore to talk about American values, British values or Indian values as if they could be authoritatively and definitively defined.

The development of thinking about management values in India can provide an example of how such debates progress. Much business and management education in India is based on American models. It is unsurprising that Indian managers have acquired through their training an American set of business values. Many Indian academics and business people have seen this as demeaning to an ancient civilisation such as India's and have begun to develop an indigenous approach to management that is based in Indian thought and traditions (Gopinath, 1998). This of course is difficult because India has a rich and varied religious and philosophical history from which values might be drawn. Hinduism is the main strand but Islam, Sikhism, Jainism, Zoroastrianism and others share a significant presence in Indian thought. Zoroastrianism is a particularly important element because it is the religion of the Parsi community from which many important Indian entrepreneurs come. We will concentrate on attempts to build modern business values from Hindu philosophy.

In Hindu thought there are four aims for humanity, *dharma* (righteousness), *artha* (wealth creation), *kama* (pleasure or material needs) and *moksha* (salvation from the transient to the eternal and the infinite). This is normally interpreted as making business and wealth creation an ethical imperative as long as it is circumscribed by a sense of duty and ethics. It is therefore opposed to the Friedmanite version of business ethics that imposes no duty on businesses other than making profits for the shareholders. Chakraborty (1993, 1999) has developed a detailed system of business ethics and values based on the Vedanta and Yoga schools of Hindu philosophy. He has used it as a basis for consultancy and management development in Indian companies. Vedanta is based upon the *Upanishads* which are sacred Hindu scriptures written between the fifth and eighth centuries BC. It is based on the existence of a Supreme Being or absolute called the Brahman. Surprisingly, for those who see Hinduism as a religion with many Gods, Vedanta emphasises a monist belief in a single supreme being. The Brahman is the only reality. The world we perceive through our senses is, more or less depending upon which branch of Vedanta is followed, an illusion. The individual soul, through ignorance of the Brahman, believes in its own independent existence and importance. This sense of ego is the cause of all troubles in life. The end of religious striving is liberation from this false sense of individualism and a practical awareness of oneness with the absolute, with the Brahman. In Yoga this oneness can be expressed by the *purusha–prakriti* pairing. *Purusha* is the worldly and active term and *prakriti* is the still and contemplative term. The aim, according to Aurobindo Ghose, is to create a dual consciousness in which there is 'the one engaged in surface-level activity, caught in obscurity and struggle; the other, behind, remaining calm and strong with effortless insight' (Chakraborty, 1999: 6). It is this sense of oneness that, once achieved, leads to a life of unselfish service that is the basis of Chakraborty's criticism of western management values and ethics. He argued that management development should not emphasise techniques and calculation but should encourage the spiritual development of managers and employees. Only when people have made a personal psychological journey will they be able to make ethical decisions in their jobs. This is an important theme in much Indian management literature. Mahesh (1995) and Diwedi (in Saini and Khan, 2000) stress the importance of ethical leadership and leaders with 'oriental soul'. Chakraborty argued, to take one specific example, that people who have achieved *moksha* would take a different view of change in business to that advocated by western textbooks. He criticised the fashion for constant change in business, in the name of economic growth, that has only led to disharmony between nations and between individuals. He proposed (Chakraborty, 1999: 24) some Vedantic principles that might be applied to organisational change:

- Natural change, that is the cycle of birth growth and death, is good but manmade change often goes against natural change and leads to irreparable harm to the environment and to relations between people.
- For people to develop dual consciousness it is necessary for structures and institutions that have been developed from tradition to remain constant. Constant change of organisational structures and processes distracts people from their psychological development.
- Change in organisation and business often implies exchanging a condition closer to the eternal for a position that is more ephemeral and transient. In particular the tendency for organisations to focus on the measurable, at the expense of that which is not, ethically weakens organisations.

Chakraborty's work is a complex attempt to produce business values that are specific to India and which provide a critique of western and American values. It will be subject to debate and challenge within India if for no other reason than that it is based on one of India's religions and on a particular strand of Hinduism.

Other writers have drawn on different sources in Indian classical literature and identified other schemes of business ethics. One common source is the *Arthashastra* of Kautilya (Rangarajan, 1992), sometimes known as Chanyaka. This is a vast treatise on statecraft probably written in the third century BC and designed as a manual for the guidance of kings. Little is known of the author although there are many legends, and it is not even certain that a single person produced the work. This is a practical rather than a scriptural work and it is often compared with Machiavelli's *The Prince* (*see* p. 173). Most commentators on the work recognise that, like Machiavelli, Kautilya accepts that evil things sometimes have to be done in the best interests of the state. Several writers have argued that the lessons from the *Arthashastra* fit well with the values of modern western strategic thinking. Starzl and Dhir (1986) argued that the modern business world resembles the competing feudal states of India in the third century BC and that there is potential for Kautilya's principles to be applied to strategic planning. Kumar and Rao (1996) interpreted the *Arthashastra* as a recipe for modern value-based management. By this they meant the style of management, advocated by Peters and Waterman (1982), that involves defining corporate values and ensuring that staff are committed to them. They did not see Kautilya as being machiavellian but instead saw his work as a source of 'ethical, moral and value based guidelines . . . which will be useful for present day management and organisations'.

Whether Kautilya, as some argue, is seen as providing unethical but practical advice on statecraft, or, as others argue, is a source of value-based managerial prescriptions, he is still the source of a set of values that are held to be close to those of western management thought. This indigenous approach to management therefore is contrary to Chakraborty's approach, based on Vedanta, which is highly critical of western business values. This contradiction illustrates why it should not be assumed that countries or societies have simple, clear and consensual business ethics.

The discussion so far in this section has focused on the formal and normative literature about what Indian business ethics should be. The business values adopted in India can be seen in the broad sweep of Indian history in the second half of the twentieth century. From Indian independence in 1947 until 1991 public policy focused on economic isolationism and self-sufficiency. As Nehru, the first prime minister of independent India said, 'It is better to have a second-rate thing made in one's own country than a first-rate thing one has to import'. The socialism that predominated in these years also led to the development of a Licence Raj in which there were many bureaucratic controls on business. This approach to economic development also reflected Mahatma Gandhi's moral preference for self-sufficiency. At this period policy reflected Hindu values that refused pre-eminence to economic growth.

In 1991 the government of India changed its policy and started a process of liberalisation. The licensing system was abolished, trade barriers were lowered and foreign investment was made easier. The amount of direct foreign investment rose from virtually nothing to US$2 billion a year. Liberalisation encouraged Indian companies to adopt western business values and Indians working for western multinationals in India exhibited western business values (Singh, 1990: 92). The change in India's business policies may encourage Kautilya's ethics rather than those of Vedanta.

Section summary

Although there are attempts at producing universal ethical standards they have not yet had a major impact on international business. There is evidence that people in different countries have different values that they apply to business. In broad terms there is a conflict between the predominant values of western businesses and cultures and the desire of many in developing countries who wish to see business ethics that reflect their indigenous ethical and religious traditions.

The normative debate about ethical universalism and relativism in the business context

■ The normative implications and arguments

The existence of different ethical standards and values in different societies and countries raises difficulties for normative and philosophical thinking about ethics. If different countries have different customary values that each regards as valid then philosophers' attempts to define what is good and right are undermined. All the multinational company has to do is follow the maxim, 'When in Rome do as the Romans do'. But what if we feel that what is allowed in some countries is wrong? Does a relativist position mean that any practice or value in a society has to be accepted as long as it has a patina of tradition? A number of arguments can be made that constrain the apparent arbitrariness of relativist ethics.

The need for standards is universal

Although societies may have different ethical practices and values they all have a universal requirement to have such norms (Blackburn, 2001: 22). Societies may treat their children differently when they come of age. Some buy them cars and send then as far away as possible to universities, some send them out to find their fortune, some require them to join the family firm and some require them to get married as soon as possible. But all these societies share a need to have some ethical standards about how they treat their new adults. It is a similar situation in organisations. They all need, for example, ethical standards for the treatment of family members working in an organisation. In some cultures they would be seen as an embarrassment and people would feel guilty that they might be seen to be favouring their relatives. In other cultures it would be expected that family members would be favoured. Family members might be less favourably treated in cultures where they are seen as a threat to the status of other family members in the organisation. Yet in all this variety there is an acceptance that there need to be some standards to help people cope with this particular situation. This allows a universal imperative to underlie ethical diversity.

In some cases it really does not matter what the rule is as long as there is one. It is important that all the drivers in a country drive on the right or on the left; but which they choose is of little consequence. Many differences in business and managerial values fall into this category in which value diversity causes no ethical problems. Attitudes to working hours and holidays are an example. Americans generally put more hours into their job than Europeans, and the gap between the two is increasing. Americans also have less entitlement to holidays. The Spanish in contrast to the Americans take two-hour lunch breaks, eat late at night, go to bed late, have lots of public holidays and take extended vacations in July or August (*Director*, 2001: 32). This is often explained by the different cultural values of the Americans and the Europeans. The former value increasing their income over leisure and there is some evidence that the Americans are correct in thinking that extra effort leads to higher income. One study showed that extra effort does result in promotions and pay increases (Koretz, 2001). The Europeans place a premium on leisure. These differences in values may have good and bad economic consequences – the Europeans are poorer than they might be if they had adopted American values – but the differences are ethically neutral. As long as most Europeans are happy with their values, and most Americans happy with theirs, it does not matter ethically which values they choose. It is possible that there is a loss of happiness caused by Americans spending less time with their families but it is by no means certain that the detriment is not counterbalanced by some families being happier when one of their number is at work and by the pleasure they gain from spending the extra money that is earned.

Some value differences between countries do raise ethical problems however. Attitudes towards discrimination at work against certain population groups often differ and they can become points of intercultural conflict. For example, the degree to which discrimination against women is accepted varies between countries. The next section begins to describe a way in which such differences might be evaluated.

A contingency approach

So far it has been argued that the need for some values and standards may be universally present in all societies but that the particular values adopted by different societies may, in practice, vary. This relativism does not mean that anything goes: that because there is no one best scheme of values all contenders may be equally valid. If a system of values is relative it must be relative to something; and if this is so then it must be possible to argue that some sets of ethics are more relevant to the 'thing' than other sets. The difficult question of course is 'what is the thing' to which ethics can be judged relevant. There are several answers. According to situational ethics, which developed from Anglican theology (Fletcher, 1966), that thing is love, the obligation to act lovingly towards others. Another possible answer, which may be of particular use in a business and management context, is the economic and social context people find themselves in. Although it may be possible to argue that a set of ethical standards is more or less suited to particular circumstances, the naturalistic fallacy prevents us from claiming that such standards are true, in the same way that true standards could be derived from the notion of love. This is because it is not possible to derive an 'ought' statement from an 'is' statement. A social and economic account of a society is a descriptive statement and so moral imperatives cannot be derived from it. Love however is a normative, moral concept and can be the basis for a definition of universal values. Nevertheless a contingency approach rescues relativist ethics from being undiscriminating; it does allow some ethical schemes to be judged as better than others.

Definition

> The **naturalistic fallacy** was defined by the philosopher G.E. Moore (1873–1958). Naturalism is the belief that the criterion of right action is some feature of the world that can be described, such as the happiness of people. Moore argued that this was wrong and took an intuitionist view that fundamental moral truths are directly understood by a special faculty of moral knowledge or thinking. Moral thinking, just as mathematical thinking, is a priori and exists independently of our perceptions of the world. The knowledge that one plus one equals two is not based upon experimentation. The good can be explained but it is too simple to be defined. The good can no more be defined than can the colour yellow. In general terms the naturalistic fallacy is taken to mean that a moral statement about what is good or right (i.e. what ought to be) cannot be inferred from any description of how things in the world are. To say, for example, that a particular ethical code adopted in one country makes its citizens prosperous and happy does not imply that those values and standards are moral.

The contingency idea is a common one in management theory. It is the idea that there is no one best way of doing something, no universal answer, but that there will be different best ways for different circumstances. Styles of leadership, organisational structures and cultures and strategic choices may all be contingent upon particular aspects of an organisation's nature and circumstances. This idea might be applied to business ethics.

All societies need a system of ethical values and standards that, with more or less effectiveness, create circumstances in which people feel safe to do business. These values and standards should encourage the trust necessary for people and organisations to work with others; or at least provide remedies and sanctions if trust is broken. But insurance against untrustworthy business contacts can be achieved by various sets of values and norms. In different places at different times this end might be achieved by:

- reliance on contracts and the rule of law;
- relying on family and friendship and by only doing business with those from whom trust can be taken for granted. In China this is known as *Guanxi*, the network of personal and family connections that cement business relationships;
- developing personal and individual relationships with those with whom business is done;
- deal making so that it is in the mutual self-interest of both parties to show trust.

The ethical end of all of these means is the same; but it could be that each would be effective in particular circumstances. The contingency idea provides a possible yardstick against which the relative merit of a set of ethical standards might be judged. So whilst it might not be possible to say that a particular set of values is true and definitive and allows room for no other, it could be argued that one set of values is better suited to the contingent circumstances than another. As Umberto Eco (1992: 52) wrote when discussing the wide range of interpretations one can put on a particular text, 'If there are no rules that help ascertain which interpretations are the "best" ones there is at least a rule for ascertaining which ones are "bad"'.

This idea can be explored by looking at Indian and Chinese overseas businesses operating in the Asian arena. A particular feature of businesses in South-east Asia (Hong Kong, Indonesia, Malaysia, Thailand, Indonesia and the Philippines) is the presence of networks of Chinese and Indian family-based firms. The family businesses that make up these networks are often large conglomerates. Haley and Haley (1998) argued that these networks exist in a different strategic environment to that of most large western companies.

- The Chinese and Indians are mostly ethnically separate from the populations of the countries in which their companies do business. They have the uncertainty of being alien, and in the case of the Indian networks the memory of their community's expulsion from Uganda in 1972 provides a reminder of the risks borne by aliens.
- Governments in the region are often whole or part owners of major companies and this increases the importance to strategic success of contacts with, and access to, ministers and public servants.
- There is in South-east Asia an 'informational void'. Relative to the western economies there is a shortage of objective, statistical, research-based market and business information.
- There are doubts about the extent of the rule of law and, in some cases, about the adequacy of the 'background institutions' that support trust in business transactions.

These features make the strategic environment uncertain and difficult for overseas entrepreneurs. In South-east Asia contract and law were thought to provide a poor source of security for the Indian and Chinese networks. Instead they created the trust they needed by working within their family- or community-based networks where trust is ensured by traditional community values and/or by family relationships. Both the Chinese and Indian networks share a belief in filial loyalty to fathers. Chinese Confucianism identifies this as one of the five relationships that are an ethical duty. The intensity of familial loyalty is as strong amongst the Indian networks. The concept of *dharma* imposes the need to achieve financial success as a duty to the family (Gidoomal and Porter, 1997 and Haley and Haley, 1998: 310). They also pointed out though, that in their dealings with large western corporations, which generate less uncertainty, the overseas Indian networks do view their contractual obligations as ethically binding. The Chinese networks also place importance on developing personal relationships with individuals outside the family.

The existence of the Chinese and Indian networks allows the businesses within them to operate differently from western corporations. They are secretive and keep low public profiles. They use their family-based networks for support, finance and advice. Rather than base decisions on objective research network members often use the subjective judgements and experience of trusted members of the network. The Indian overseas businesses often use their own networks to finance their ventures, thus avoiding the conventional banking system. This is a development of a traditional Indian financial instrument known as the *hoondie*. A *hoondie* is a bill of exchange issued within a network and the system is based upon the honour and reputation of those within it. The reliance on internal network resources, including trusted contacts within regional governments, and on qualitative judgements that can be rapidly collated, allows overseas Indian and Chinese businesses to take decisions and actions very rapidly. Haley and Haley (1998: 314) argued that these Indian and Chinese entrepreneurs take an emergent approach to strategy that responds to knowledge of changes in the business environment that are detected and disseminated by the network. Through their webs of contacts these businesses also seek to influence the regional governments so as to acquire and maintain a favourable business environment and government contracts. The choices of the Indian and Chinese networks to give ethical priority to family and personal relationships rather than to legal or corporate relationships is arguably appropriate for their circumstances.

As shown in Table 8.5, Japanese business values are different from those of the overseas Indian and Chinese business networks. Japanese society values traders whereas the status of merchants in Chinese and Indian cultures is questionable.

Table 8.5 Value attributes of overseas business networks in South-east Asia

Attributes	Chinese	Indian	Japanese
Firm			
Merchants	Reviled	Specialised	Exalted
Primogeniture	None	Very strong	Strong
Firm's lifespan	Short	Medium	Long
Loyalty			
Family definition	Blood	Blood	Role
Focus	Individual	Group	Institution
Intensity	Low	High	High
Filial piety v. patriotism	Opposed	No relationship	Equivalent
Commercial trust			
Ethical foundation	Five relationships and social harmony	Dharma	Mutual self-interest
Ethical focus	The Way	Family	Service to father figure
Expectations of benefits	Immediate and up-front	Immediate and up-front	Delayed

(*Source*: Haley and Haley, 1998)

The importance of primogeniture in Japan means that Japanese family businesses outlive Chinese ones. In Japan's business culture trust is built upon contractual obligations and personal and corporate self-interest whereas the obligations of personal relations are more important in the Chinese and Indian environments. Japanese business people are more likely to take a long-term view whereas the overseas Indian and Chinese business networks expect more immediate returns. Haley and Haley (1998: 307) argued that Japan's different business values were appropriate to their different strategic environments compared with the Chinese and Indian overseas business networks. Whereas the latter, as has already been argued, worked in an informational void and were operating in regional markets in South-east Asia the Japanese companies aimed their exports at North American and European markets. They have not operated in the informational void experienced by the overseas business networks and their emphasis on contractual obligations and mutual self-interest is arguably well suited to dealings with western economies.

This is not to imply that there may not be cultural clashes between Europe and North America on the one hand and Japan on the other. Trompenaars and Hampden-Turner (1993: 196–7) gave an example of how an American's neglect of role and ritual in his dealings with a Japanese company president caused problems in a negotiation. The American was trying to nail down the specifics of a deal and ignored the largely ceremonial role of presidents of Japanese firms. In his frustration at the evasive answers he was receiving in response to detailed questions he absent-mindedly rolled up the president's business card that had been formally presented to him, and scraped his fingernails clean with it. The Japanese president was apparently displeased. Nevertheless the common emphasis of Americans and Japanese on contractual obligations and corporate mutual self-interest as an ethical basis for trust would generally be of benefit to the business relations between the two countries.

A contingent approach to ethics does not mean that circumstances cause the acceptance of particular values or ethical norms. The business conditions found in South-east Asia did not cause the overseas Indian and Chinese business networks to adopt their particular values. These came, as much as from anywhere, from the traditional values of their communities. The fit between their values and the strategic environment did however create an 'evolutionary' pressure that maintained them.

The relationship between situational factors and a society's ethical norms is mediated by people's thinking, debating and power games. People will only begin to change their values if they think there is a misfit between their values and their circumstances. Such awareness does not come easy for an individual and may only have an impact through generational changes. The direction of the influence between situation and ethical norms may also alternate. The situation might influence changes in norms, or norms may encourage changes in the situation. These processes tend to operate over long periods of time. They can be illustrated by the history of Christian and Islamic attitudes towards the payment of interest on loans.

Interest is the money paid for the use of money. It is an essential feature of modern financial systems. The Bible however clearly states that taking interest on a loan is wrong. Usury is the formal term for charging any interest on a loan although it is now only used for extortionate rates of interest. The Old Testament forbade the Israelites to charge each other usury but they were allowed to levy usury on 'foreigners' (Deuteronomy 23: 20). The logic appears to be that in ancient societies most loans were for consumption, to help people survive hard times, rather than to finance entrepreneurial activities. In this circumstance it was wrong to charge interest. The New Testament also finds usury wrong. It is implied that even charging usury to 'foreigners' is wrong. As part of loving one's enemy interest-free loans should be made to any who needed them. In medieval times these Biblical injunctions were taken very seriously. Interest was seen as unjust because it meant charging a continuing rent for the use of money that could only be spent once (Buckley, 1998).

Such an ethical position was not helpful to the growing number of merchants and entrepreneurs who emerged in Europe during the Reformation. Slowly the official position on usury began to change to one that was more conducive to business enterprise. It was recognised that there was a legitimate difference between loans for consumption and loans for investment. The idea developed, for example, that a creditor could receive compensatory payments for the loss of use of their money from the start of the loan and not simply, as was traditional, for failure to pay off the loan at the agreed date. But it was not accepted that the creditor who loaned for entrepreneurial purposes should have a risk-free entitlement to interest whilst the merchant bore all the commercial risk of the enterprise. It was felt that the financier should share the risk in a partnership agreement.

Jean Calvin, who lived in the highly commercial city of Geneva in the sixteenth century, triggered a change in the Christian view of interest although his writings were not a great change on the traditional position. He argued that the poor should still be given loans without interest but that otherwise it was acceptable to charge interest on a loan as long as the rate was reasonable and the security taken was not excessive. He dismissed the Biblical strictures against interest because they were designed for a society very different from the mercantile one in which he lived (Tawney 1966: 115–16). Although Calvin's ethical adjustment was small it led to a widespread acceptance of the justness of interest as long as the rate was fair. The issue moved from the ethics of interest to the ethics of the rate of interest. This example illustrates how ethical norms might change under the influence of new circumstances.

Such changes, however, are not inevitable. Islam, for example, has the same view of interest as that expressed in the Bible. But in Islam, unlike in Christianity, the injunction has survived into modern times so that practising Muslims have developed financial techniques that work without the concept of interest. Interest (*riba*), defined as any risk-free or guaranteed rate of return on a loan or investment, is prohibited. Loans must be made without interest according to Islamic law (*Sharia*) (Failaka International, 2001). Islam defines money as a means of exchange that has no intrinsic value. Value is only generated by the human effort behind exchanges and transactions. It follows that money should not be made from money, because that is the same as receiving something for nothing. Islam is not against entrepreneurial activity but it should properly be conducted through partnership financing (*Mudaraba*) in which the entrepreneur and the financier share profits or losses according to a pre-agreed ratio.

The prohibition against *riba* makes contact with western banks and financial instruments, based as they are on the idea of interest, improper for practising Muslims. Credit cards are a particular problem. Some scholars argue that Muslims can open credit card accounts as long as they always pay off the debt each month and so avoid incurring interest charges. Others (Al Andalusia, 2001) argue that when a credit card account is opened a contract is signed which commits the cardholder to paying interest in certain circumstances. Muslims should not sign such a contract in which they agree, in principle, to sin. However financial techniques can be developed that avoid *riba*. For example the *Bai Muajjal* form of contract is permissible. The bank or provider of capital buys goods or assets on behalf of a business owner. They then sell the goods to the client at an agreed price that involves a percentage for profit. This is proper because, as in Christian thought, it is acceptable to charge a higher price if the payment is to be deferred. At least one bank provides an Islamic credit card based on this form of contract (Failaka International, 2001). Many banks now offer personal and business financing that avoids *riba* (Arif, 1988, Lariba.com, 2001). According to some reports (Anon., 1995) the deposit assets held by Islamic banks increased from $US5 billion in 1985 to over $US60 billion in 1994. The development of Islamic financial instruments is an example of how situations and circumstances can be adapted contingently to a set of ethical principles.

■ A stakeholder approach

In addition to the contingency principle there is another criterion that can be used to judge the relative merits of a system of business ethics and values. It is the question of who benefits from a particular scheme of ethics. This criterion depends upon drawing a stakeholder map of all the groups and constituencies who may be affected by, or have a concern with, an ethical proposition. Identifying who benefits and who suffers from its application can test the validity of the proposition. This can be explained by reference to a Rawlsian perspective, as discussed in Chapter 2. One of the principles Rawls proposed was that social and economic inequalities are to be arranged so that they are both (a) reasonably expected to be to everyone's advantage, and (b) attached to positions and offices open to all. Rawls calls the first part of this statement the difference principle. Different systems of business ethics could be tested against the difference principle and if they do not benefit all the stakeholders involved then they could be judged invalid.

An example can be taken from current Indian recruitment practice. Traditional Indian society was divided into *jati* or castes. These were extended kinship groups that could be classified under four main *varna*, the priestly castes, the warrior castes, the merchants and the farmers. A person's caste no longer determines their occupation but it still carries social and status significance in India. This is particularly so for the groups who are excluded from the caste categories. These are the *dalits*, in traditional terms the untouchables, and people from the tribal areas of India. These groups are normally the most economically and socially excluded groups in India (Dhesi, 1998). Caste discrimination is illegal in India. The government operates a system of positive discrimination in which quotas of jobs in public organisations and nationalised industries and places in colleges and universities are reserved for *dalits* and tribals. How would this policy stand against the difference principle? It clearly benefits a group of people, the *dalits* and the tribals, who would be disadvantaged if the policy were not in place. It could be argued that it is to the advantage of all to overcome discrimination against the worst off in society if for no other reason than to prevent the civil unrest that such discrimination might lead to. However the policy might contravene the second part of Rawls's second principle, that positions should be open to all. Blackburn (2001: 27) suggests that when judging whether a local ethical standard is acceptable it is not enough simply to consider the views of the 'Brahmins, mullahs, priests and elders who hold themselves to be spokesmen for *their* culture'. A wider group of stakeholders need to be considered, especially those who are oppressed or disadvantaged by that ethical standard. A stakeholder analysis based on Rawls's difference principle provides a mechanism for judging the validity of a particular ethical position in business.

Section summary

The diversity of business values and ethics in different societies and countries does not mean that any ethical position can be justified. An acceptance of an ethical relativist position does not imply that any value or practice has to be accepted as long as it can be shown to be indigenous or traditional. In this section a number of tests have been suggested which could be used by managers to decide whether a particular local ethical stance should be regarded as valid or not. It has to be accepted of course that this might not be enough for a convinced ethical universalist who would want to argue that there can only be one true ethical system, and that everyone ought to adopt it.

Globalisation, multinational and transnational companies and business ethics

So far in this chapter we have seen that different countries and societies do have different business standards and that international companies are not ethically obliged to accept those local standards unquestioningly. This section deals with the ethical issues that this situation causes. Imagine the situations experienced by a manager in a multinational organisation who may have been brought up in one country, and internalised its ethical values, who works for an American company that is clear about its own core values and is based in a third country which may have yet another set of local ethical norms. In addition this manager could have come to the view that there ought to be a universal set of ethical principles for the conduct of business that would be different from those of all the particular countries, and which was not directed to the self-interest of the metropolitan country. How ought the manager, and corporately the organisation he or she works for, to respond to this complexity?

It is often argued that these ethical problems have emerged from the process of globalisation. As Petrick (2000: 1) expressed it, the 'high velocity global market place is complex and challenging'. However the ethical issues of globalisation are not new. They could be found in the actions of colonial companies, such as the Dutch and English East India Companies, which were as powerful and globally dominating in the eighteenth and nineteenth centuries as multinationals are today.

Definition

> **Globalisation** is a process which is bringing societies that were previously economically, politically and culturally diverse into convergence. This is being achieved by a combination of the success of capitalism, the growth of a common mass culture (McLuhan and Powers' (1989) 'global village') and the wish of people in all societies, through their rational choices, to choose the same goals.

Although the claims that globalisation has brought new ethical problems need to be seen in historical context, globalisation has increased the velocity and awareness of the ethical problems of worldwide economic integration in relation to the ethical and value diversity of nations. What ethical advice can be given to managers and their organisations? The following guidelines for multinational and transnational organisations, largely based on those developed by De George (1999), are all variations on a famous ethical precept – first of all do no harm.

Definition

> **First, do no harm** is an ancient moral precept. It is often claimed to be taken from the Hippocratic oath that doctors in classical times were required to take. This is not so. The nearest the oath gets to it is in the following statement, 'I will follow that system of regimen which, according to my ability and judgement, I consider for the benefit of my patients, and abstain from all that is deleterious and mischievous'. Today few doctors are required to take the oath.

Good manners

In the face of national diversity of business values managers working with, or in, other countries should show good manners by accepting others' cultures. This does not mean that managers should become promiscuous in the manner in which they take up and put down values. Indeed, Hofstede argued (1991: 237), a person cannot show tolerance of others' values unless they are secure in their own values. Tolerance is necessary, the more so when differences in priorities and practice do not raise serious ethical difficulties. Good manners imply trying to see situations from other people's perspective, empathising with their anxieties and taking what actions you can to put them at ease. There are various disciplines that can be learned for acquiring good manners. One is to recognise that we all possess a wide range of values that we can use to understand others' positions. For example fear of losing 'face' is often cited as a matter of great importance to the Chinese. But there cannot be a western manager who has not also felt shame when she or he made a fool of themselves in front of colleagues or bosses. Recognising the humour in a conflict of values can also aid their reconciliation.

CASE STUDY
8.3

The college principal's new car

One of the authors was once part of a European project team setting up a management college in a state that had once been part of the former Soviet Union. The new college was being developed from a former Soviet institution that had decayed into inactivity. It did, however, retain its former rector who was to be the principal of the new college. He was in his late sixties and was, every inch of his substantial frame, a Soviet *apparatchik*. As part of the package the project delivered two brand-new western-built vehicles to the college. One was a minibus, the other was a good quality car. Both vehicles were, according to the project specification, for the use of the western project team. In practice the minibus was the more useful vehicle because it coped well with the difficult road conditions and could be used to move all the team around, complete with their equipment. The principal began to use the car more and more as if it were his personal vehicle. It was easy for him to do this because both of the drivers were on his staff and took their orders from him. This became an issue because the principal clearly saw the car as his 'commission' for facilitating the project. If the western funding body were to discover this they would think it a misuse of project funds. The issue became a matter of dispute between the principal and the project team. Then one day the team saw some cowboy builders had been brought in and were rapidly constructing a ramshackle garage in the college grounds. The strongest part of the garage was the padlocked steel doors to which only the principal held the key. The project team saw the funny side and could remember occasions when they had tried to guard hard-won privileges and perks that they had won from their organisations. Humour discharged the project team's anger and a compromise deal was made about the use of the car.

■ Responding to the particularness of host countries' ethical standards and values

This guideline goes a little beyond good manners. It suggests that unless there are good ethical reasons for not doing so organisations should learn and respect the values and ethical practices of the host country. This is not an easy thing to achieve. Expatriate staff are often criticised because they try to recreate their pattern of life from their own country rather than learn about and come to terms with the culture of their host country. This has been recognised as a problem for international NGOs. Lewis (2001: 105) has raised the question of defining the management challenges that arise from employing expatriate NGO staff from the northern world to work in partnership with southern-world NGO partners. He asks, but does not answer, the question of whether such staff should be driven by their own values or by the values of their partner organisations.

| CASE STUDY 8.4 | **Testing Maori employees for drugs in a New Zealand company** |

A company that employed Maoris and non-Maoris decided that they wanted to start a programme of testing employees for drug abuse. Their reasons were to improve the safety record at their plant and to fulfil their obligations under New Zealand's health and safety laws. Carrying out drugs testing on employees, however, raised ethical questions about employees' rights to privacy, and the question of the legality of such testing under New Zealand law was uncertain. The Maori employees appeared to be more critical of the proposal than the other staff. A particular point of conflict however was that the company tried to negotiate with employees separately to gain their consent to the testing. Maori culture is collectivist (*see* p. 241) and the staff demanded that the issue between them and the company should be negotiated collectively.

(*Source*: Blackburn, 2000)

■ Doing good in the host country and not taking advantage

As mentioned earlier in the chapter many of the ethical criticisms of multinationals and transnationals arise from their tendency to exploit local conditions for commercial advantage. In practice developing countries may have lower expectations, and weaker laws, concerning acceptable conditions of employment, pollution control, health and safety and many other factors concerning management and business. This guideline proposes that it is wrong to exploit these circumstances to gain a commercial advantage. The application of this guideline is uncontroversial when it would prevent, for example, a company dumping in third world markets a product that has been declared unfit for use or consumption in the country of origin. It is perhaps a little more difficult when applied to companies that move their manufacturing operations to new countries where the cost of labour is much lower. It would be clear that they are taking advantage of the lower wages. The typical corporate response to this charge is that inward investment gives jobs to those who would not otherwise have them. The company is thus doing good by giving people jobs and ought not to be expected to pay them wages above the going rates. Local employers would also object and claim they were being harmed if a multinational started to pay its staff above the labour market rate. Often, however, a form of dual economy emerges in which the multinational companies in a developing country exist in parallel with the local companies but occupy a separate economic 'world', paying higher wages and granting better employment conditions than companies in the local economy. Such a development seems to have happened with the development of the IT industry in India. As the *Economist* (2001) reported most of India's new economy holds aloof from the old Indian economy. Software engineers in Bangalore, the capital of India's IT industry, work in good conditions in state of the art corporate campuses whereas the rest of the economy operates in poor to bad conditions. Such dual economies produce their own ethical problems and critics demand to know why the benefits of inward investment are not being spread more widely in society. Chakraborty (1999: 20) laments the impact of western companies employing Indian MBAs at a salary three times that which an Indian company would pay, but still lower than an equivalent person would be paid in the USA, because of the disaffection produced amongst those not lucky enough to be employed by a multinational.

<table>
<tr><td>CASE STUDY 8.5</td><td>

The Bhopal accident

</td></tr>
</table>

This episode is a tragic and classic case study in business ethics. Union Carbide, an American-owned company, owned 50.9 per cent of a pesticide plant in Bhopal, central India. The government of India had apparently been so keen to receive this inward investment that it had found a way around its own legislation, which at that time allowed overseas companies to own no more than 40 per cent of any Indian company in which they invested. On the night of the 2–3 December 1984, 40 tonnes of poisonous gases were thrown into the air over Bhopal from the plant. The gases burned the eyes and lungs of people on whom it settled and, when it crossed into their blood stream, it damaged many physiological systems. Over 3,000 people died and 20,000 were injured. Large numbers of people still suffer from the consequences.

There appear to have been a number of contributory factors that led to the leakage. They mostly related to a cost-cutting culture in a factory that at that time was making a loss and only working at a third of its capacity. On the night of the disaster six safety measures designed to prevent a leak were inadequate, malfunctioning or switched off. Safety audits had been done that had revealed major safety concerns but no action had been taken. These all raise the question of the extent to which Union Carbide had taken advantage of low levels of safety monitoring and expectations to save costs.

It can be argued that a concern to save costs characterised the company's behaviour during the aftermath of the disaster. On one account the company's legal team arrived in Bhopal days before their medical team (Bhopal.net, 2001). One of the issues after the accident was whether the case should be settled in an American court, as the government of India wanted, or in an Indian court, as the company wished, and as was in fact the case. The company fought liability for the accident and agreed an out-of-court settlement five years later with the government of India for $470m. The families of those who died received an interim payment of $550 per fatality. Had the deaths occurred in the USA the families might have received a hundred times that amount (De George, 1999: 511). Associations of the injured are still fighting for further compensation (Corpwatch, 2001). The Bhopal.com web site (2001), owned by the Union Carbide Corporation, argues that the 1989 settlement has provided sufficient money from its investment to provide the compensation, and that the compensation was much higher than any settlement that would have been payable under Indian law.

■ Contribute to the development of ethical standards of business in the host country and, when standards are unacceptable be prepared to withdraw

Multinational and transnational countries should act as good corporate citizens in the host countries in which they operate. They should play a part in developing the ethical codes, norms and practices of business. This may be particularly important in developing countries which, though lack of resources or of opportunity, have poorly developed legal and voluntary frameworks to encourage ethical business behaviour. The issue facing companies, however, may not just be that the norms of business behaviour are undeveloped. Companies may find themselves in countries where the regimes are commonly regarded as oppressive and human rights are being denied. This situation raises the question of what obligations private companies might have to challenge unethical behaviour by states. Murphy (2001) proposed a theory of benevolence in which people (he was not discussing companies) are not morally obliged to do more to solve the world's problems than would be their portion if everyone else were doing their share. In other words people, and companies, should only do their bit even if others are not doing theirs and so there remains much that the individual or company could do.

Unethical states may, however, seek to influence how international companies conduct their business. If such regimes demand that companies use unacceptable employment practices, for example, or direct their investments in ways that reward their political supporters, then companies may be forced to consider whether it is ethical to remain in that country.

CASE STUDY 8.6

Businesses and South Africa in the apartheid era

In the 1950s the apartheid regime in South Africa was created by a series of laws that enforced racial segregation by restricting the areas in which blacks and coloureds could live and by limiting the jobs they could apply for. There were many foreign-owned companies that had long been present in South Africa. These companies had to obey the apartheid laws. As, by common consensus in the world beyond South Africa, apartheid was evil, and the foreign-owned companies were not in a position to change it, the question arose as to whether in conscience they should disinvest from South Africa. In 1977 Leon Sullivan, a director of General Motors, a company that had a subsidiary in South Africa, proposed a set of principles to govern its business in South Africa (Minnesota Center for Corporate Responsibility, 2001). They amounted to a refusal to obey the apartheid laws. Segregation was not to be practised in its plants and staff were to be paid and promoted according to merit not race. They also imposed an obligation to improve the quality of life in those communities in which companies did business. Many American companies trading in South Africa signed up to the principles. It was hoped that such large numbers would discourage the South African government from prosecuting the companies for breaking the apartheid laws and that their efforts might lead to the collapse of apartheid.

Case study 8.6 continued

However in 1987 Sullivan declared that the experiment was showing no sign of undermining apartheid. He claimed that American companies should withdraw from their South African operations. In that year General Motors sold its holdings in South Africa. In 1991 the South African government began to repeal the apartheid regime. Nelson Mandela was elected President of South Africa in 1994.

Reflections

Corporations may have an ethical responsibility to behave well in their international dealings but it is the individual managers in multinationals, transnationals and international NGOs who exercise that responsibility. In Case study 8.6 it was an individual, Leon Sullivan, who drove forward the response to apartheid. Many of the ethical problems of international business have to be dealt with by people on the ground who stand on the thresholds that separate ethical cultures. It is their ethical reflections and moral agency that determine the behaviour of organisations.

Summary

In this chapter the following key points have been made:

- Universal standards for international business have been written but they are not universally accepted; nor do they cover all the issues.
- Different countries and societies have some ethical standards and values concerning business in common, but they differ on others.
- In some countries there are deliberate efforts to create schemes of business ethics that challenge the predominant American scheme.
- Although extreme universalists and relativists might reject the idea, it is arguable that a contingency approach can be used to distinguish appropriate from inappropriate local ethical standards.
- If this is so then transnational and multinational companies have to make moral judgements about whether they should adopt or challenge the business standards of the countries they are working in.
- In dealing with these matters transnational and multinational organisations need to show:
  – good manners,
  – a willingness to respond to the particularness of the host countries' ethical standards and values,
  – a willingness to do good in the host country and not to take advantage, and to contribute to the development of good business standards in the host country.

Suggested further reading

F. Trompenaars and C. Hampden-Turner (1993) *Riding the Waves of Culture*, 2nd edn, London: Nicholes Brealey, is good on the problems of managing intercultural misunderstandings. Nigel Holden (2002) *Cross Cultural. Management. A Knowledge Management Perspective*, Harlow: Pearson Education, provides an interesting perspective based on the principles of knowledge management. He challenges the common assumption that cultural differences are simply a cause of problems. R.T. De George (1999) *Business Ethics*, 5th edn, Englewood Cliffs, NJ: Prentice-Hall, has very interesting chapters on ethics in international business.

GROUP ACTIVITY 8

Conduct a debate in class on the motion, 'Transnational and multinational organisations are a major force in improving the ethical standards of the global world of business'.

9

Corporate citizenship and social responsibility

OBJECTIVES

Having completed this chapter and its associated activities, readers should be able to:

- Understand the arguments for and against corporations being defined as corporate citizens.

- Be able to reflect more critically upon their own views about the desired relationship between business corporations and the societies in which they operate.

- Be aware of the developing debates relating to corporate manslaughter.

Introduction

As with many of the issues covered within business ethics, the challenges presented by the topics considered in this chapter are not solvable by simple formulae. Whether corporations can assume the status of citizens, and if so, whether such a development is desirable, are issues we will discuss. As the various elements in the debates are considered, each argument which might appear to offer a way forward will also contain the tensions that could seriously undermine such progress. For example, the best-case scenarios for locating corporations within sociopolitical structures contain the elements for the complete subversion of sociopolitical systems by corporate interests. Alternatively, the worst-case scenarios for the domination of sociopolitical systems by corporate interests can also be argued to hold the prospects for more active participation by the citizenry.

Essentially, the relationships between the societal, economic and political dimensions to human existence are dynamic. The role of the individual within these is, at one and the same time, extremely minor, yet also extremely critical. The concept of corporate citizenship will respond to the force of arguments, the actions of individuals and pressure groups and the practices of corporations.

Calls for corporations to behave in more socially responsible ways became increasingly frequent in the 1960s, reflecting the growing recognition of the influence of corporations in general and the antisocial behaviour of a number of specific corporations, e.g. the dumping of toxic waste as in the *Love Canal* case, and the exploitation of national governments by the manipulation of transfer prices by multinational organisations, both reported by Tinker (1985).

The phrase 'corporate social responsibility' became, and remains, central to much of this debate. Recently an additional phrase has entered the vocabulary, that is, corporations should be viewed as, and behave like, 'corporate citizens'. This latter term has taken over from corporate social responsibility, although even corporate citizenship is now being considered by some to be too restrictive. Wood and Logsdon (2001) suggest that the term 'business citizenship' overcomes the more localised and parochial connotations that they argued corporate citizenship implies.

Corporations as corporate citizens

Notions of citizenship

Definition

The term **citizen** normally relates to the relationship between an individual and the political state in which she or he lives. It carries with it notions of rights and responsibilities on the part of the individual and the state. However, this reciprocity (i.e. two-way relationship) is unlikely to be an equal one. Within democratic theories of the state, citizens have ultimate sovereignty over the state, or at least sovereignty over those who represent the citizenry within government. Practice, however, can reflect a quite different balance of power.

Being described as a citizen does not of itself infer much about morality. It is a noun in need of an adjective such as 'good' or 'moral' before it can confer a positive societal influence. Wood and Logsdon (2001: 88) referred to this issue when they observed, in the context of the corporate citizen debate,

> One important debate distinguishes the concept of citizenship-as-legal-status from the concept of citizen-as-desirable-activity. The minimum requirements to be called a citizen are very different from the requirement to be called a 'good citizen'.

The role of the citizen can vary from the active notion of citizenship evident in ancient Greece (for those conferred as free men), to a passive acceptance of governance from a sovereign body (*à la* Hobbes) or from the bureaucratic state (*à la* Weber). Within the corporate citizen debate, the demands made of corporations vary from a minimalist societally neutral influence, to a proactive role. The societally neutral arguments do not, however, reflect a status quo situation, or even a single understanding of what might be meant by societally neutral. For example, would being societally neutral mean that:

- Negative and positive effects of corporate activities could be balanced out (possibly involving an international perspective), or would a corporation's impacts need to harm no one or nothing at any time?
- Acting within legal constraints would be acceptable, even if the law were judged by many to be inadequate (as a result of the political lobbying by corporations)?
- There is a general acceptance that corporations do have social responsibilities?

These debates are still developing and represent just some of the issues that make the general area of business and values both dynamic and vital.

Hobbes (Pojman, 1998) held a pessimistic view of human nature, seeing people as essentially selfish and untrustworthy. Thus, Hobbes deemed that a sovereign power was necessary, to which the people would owe allegiance. The relationship between the sovereign power and the citizen is, in a Hobbesian world, a subjugated one. In this context, being a citizen within a Hobbesian state is quite different to that which would be acceptable in the twenty-first century. However, if the idea of conferring citizenship status upon corporations is one that concerns people, due to their distrust of corporations acting in socially beneficial ways, then a Hobbesian notion of citizenship has some appeal. But much depends upon the constitution and constituent parts of the sovereign power.

As societies have developed and the scope of governments has increased, the lack of possibilities for active participation of citizens has come to be viewed as a weakness of modern conceptions of democratic states. In modern societies political citizenship is increasingly limited to periodic elections of political representatives, and even the relevance of these is being questioned. For example, in the 2001 general election in the UK, only 58 per cent of those eligible to vote did so, the lowest turnout for many years. In the UK, local elections and those for the European Union achieve even lower levels of elector participation. In these elections approximately two out of three people do not vote. Thus, when we, or others, use the term citizen, we need to be clear about the form of citizenship we are discussing.

One of the most widely expressed concerns about modern corporations is that they have relatively unfettered authority, with only limited responsibilities (basically to keep within the laws of the land). However, there is a need to be more specific about the form and level of participation in the operations of the state that are being suggested when the phrase 'corporate citizenship' is employed. Given the significance of business organisations within democratic (as well as undemocratic) states, the presumption must be that the notion of corporate citizenship assumed by its advocates would reflect the acceptance of certain societal responsibilities, although whether an equal bestowal of citizens' rights on corporations is envisaged is far from clear.

■ The early calls for corporate social responsibility

As indicated above, calls for corporate social responsibility (CSR) came before the phrase corporate citizenship gained currency. The desire to encourage, or even require, corporations to assume greater responsibility for their actions can be traced back over many decades, and it reflects growing concerns about the power and influence of corporations over people's lives and even the independence and integrity of governments. For example, Oberman (2000) refers to academic debates over corporate social responsibilities taking place in the 1920s.

As the power and influence of business corporations has grown so too have the calls increased for mechanisms to be put in place that would make corporations more accountable, to be responsible to a wider constituency than just their shareholders. Within this latter aspect of the debate the use of the term *stakeholder* has gained currency in recent years, and it is a subject to which we will return later in this chapter.

The progression from requiring corporations to act in socially responsible ways, to more recent calls for corporations to be seen as corporate citizens, reflects a desire to lock corporations, both formally and possibly legally, into the responsibilities that this status would confer. Two aspects of these calls require consideration.

1 The citizenry currently has little or no access to, and certainly few, if any, rights with respect to, corporations (other than as individual shareholders). With corporations playing an increasingly influential role over many aspects of social and political life, the demands for more accountability and responsibility on the part of corporations are unlikely to diminish, yet it is difficult to see why or how conferring upon corporations the status of corporate citizens will enhance the accountability. Indeed the converse might be true, which leads us to (2).

2 If the theoretical position of the citizen being sovereign to the state is taken at face value, the corporate citizen would be above the state. Is this what is argued for? We think not, but it reflects part of the theoretical weakness in the corporate citizen argument.

To take this debate forward, we will first consider the option of leaving business alone, keeping it clear of political or social interference, to allow it to get on with what it does best. This option follows the dictum that 'the business of business is business' (this phrase is in fact a corruption of a statement made by Calvin Coolidge, during his presidency of the United States, that 'the business of America is business'). To review the arguments in favour of not shackling business with demands for socially responsible actions, we will consider the arguments put forward by Milton Friedman (1970).

■ Friedman's arguments against corporations being charged with social responsibilities

Milton Friedman is a Nobel Prize-winning economist, whose ideas were very influential in America and the UK during the 1980s and 1990s. It is worth reading Friedman's oft-cited article on why the only social responsibility of business is to increase its profits, and not to indulge in social interventions such as sponsorship of community activities, the funding of charities, community activities or other 'good deeds'. Friedman's article appeared in the *New York Times Magazine* in 1970, but it remains the neatest encapsulation of the arguments against corporations being required to act in what is loosely described as 'socially responsible ways'.

Friedman's article was a response to what were becoming increasingly frequent calls for corporations to act in socially responsible ways in the late 1960s and early 1970s. Precisely what was meant by 'socially responsible ways' was often left vague and poorly explained, save for concerns being expressed that corporate power was authority without responsibility. Friedman's criticisms were rehearsed by Wolf (2000) thirty years later when the latter accused those (still) calling for greater corporate social responsibility as not only distorting business activity, but confusing and misunderstanding the rationale of business. 'The role of well run companies is to make profits, not save the planet', Wolf argued.

A phrase currently in vogue is organisations' 'triple bottom line'. This is distinct from the traditional use of the term 'bottom line' to mean simply profit. The triple bottom line encompasses economic, social and environmental concerns, but the articulation and operationalising remains problematic. Explanations of what is meant by 'triple bottom line' do not suggest an equal weighting being given to the three elements. Birch (2001), in reviewing a draft charter of corporate citizenship developed by BP Australia, referred to a statement it contained. Under the heading 'sustainable development' the following statement appeared:

> BP is committed to a socially, environmentally and economically responsible business. This means maximising profit in order to create wealth and sustainable jobs, always intending to have a positive social and environmental impact.
>
> (Birch, 2001: 62)

The reference to maximising profit is interesting. No attempt was made in the draft charter to discuss the tension between this commitment and the commitments made to the social and the environmental issues mentioned elsewhere in the draft charter. However, Birch did refer to earlier discussions with BP Australia during which these issues appeared to have been raised.

> The tensions between capitalism and democracy as currently defined are irreconcilable without serious change. We agreed that we could not achieve long-term sustainability without change. Business needs, therefore, significant policy directions to enable this change to occur, not just within business practices but also within society overall.
>
> (Birch, 2001: 59)

The phrase, 'business needs . . . significant policy directions' refers directly to the need for a 'sovereign power', *à la* Hobbes. There is no suggestion that business can be assumed to resolve these tensions itself. The 'hidden hand' of the market is viewed as too unreliable to be left to its own devices in this context.

Friedman criticised the arguments for corporate social responsibility on three fronts. The first criticism was an economic one, with ethical undertones. If corporations are required to engage in corporate philanthropy, e.g. making a donation to a charity, school or hospital, these acts will distort allocative efficiency (i.e. the efficiency with which capital is employed, the principal concern of capitalists). Friedman argued that corporations are responsible for using shareholders' funds in profitable ways. Worrying about which charity to support, or which good deed/s to perform, merely 'takes management's eye off the ball', the ball being how to increase profits. Thus, the only form of corporate philanthropy that Friedman's argument would accept is where it could be shown that a donation, or good deed, would improve a company's profitability in superior ways to other ways of spending that same sum of money. We can view this as 'prudential altruism'. In such a case the charitable donation would in fact more accurately be described as a commercial investment.

Windsor (2001) reinforced this point with the demand that all business activities, including 'good deeds', should 'add value', or more precisely, 'add shareholder value'. This is most emphatically a Friedmanite position.

The second of Friedman's criticisms drew upon both ethics and political philosophy. It said that it is undemocratic for corporations to use shareholders' funds to support charities or other 'good causes'. Any such donation can only be at the expense of lower dividends, higher prices or lower wages (or a combination of all three). Friedman asked, 'How can it be ethical that a corporation should act first as unpaid tax collector (i.e. levying a tax on the shareholders, customers and/or employees) and then as unaccountable benefactor?' It is either for publicly elected representatives of the people (i.e. national or local politicians) to provide financial support to public services or charities, etc. from public funds, or for individuals to decide to which charities they wish to make private donations.

The third criticism was a philosophical one. It was that corporations cannot possess responsibilities. Corporations are social constructs, i.e. they have been brought into existence by societies passing laws that give legal protection to certain forms of business associations and structures. Without these legal and social devices, corporations could not and would not exist. In Friedman's terms only individuals can have responsibilities, not corporations.

ACTIVITY 9.1

Challenging Friedman

Taking the three criticisms that are raised by Friedman, try to develop arguments that challenge Friedman's claims. It is important that you think through the arguments that Friedman is making, so take your time.

Responses to Friedman's criticisms

From the perspective of advocates of unfettered (or as unfettered as possible) market-based economies, which we referred to in Chapter 1 as the *classical-liberal-economic position*, or simply liberalism, the best hope for the protection of individual freedoms is the maintenance of open markets (i.e. no barriers to trade), and minimum interference in the workings of business by governments. This is the concept of 'negative freedom', as discussed in Chapter 3. Not only is interference by government seen as economically counter-productive in the medium to long run, but it is argued that such interventions are themselves unethical. That is, they impose a big-brother-knows-best mentality over individual preferences, and thus undermine the sovereignty of individual choice. Thus, from the perspective of liberalism the first and second objections raised by Friedman are both strong objections. Non-accountable tax raising, whether by government or corporate leaders, is a distortion of allocative efficiency, injurious to the sovereignty of the individual and undemocratic, and thus to be opposed.

Friedman did not argue that corporations should be above the law, but he did argue that corporations should not be expected to exceed what the law defines as minimum levels of behaviour. It is assumed that laws represent what society deems to be acceptable behaviour (of both individuals and corporations), and only if society increases the burden upon business in terms of legally defined levels of performance (e.g. increased levels of pollution control), should corporations have to raise their performance. This obviously ignores the pressures for increased performance resulting from normal competitive forces, although such pressures will often present countervailing forces to those emanating from environmental concerns.

Supporters of liberalism would accept that considerable negative human consequences sometimes result from economic fluctuations. For example, large-scale redundancies and/or high levels of unemployment can result from significant economic downturns, with resulting impacts upon local infrastructure issues in the form of, say, lower than desired levels of expenditure on education, health care, transport, etc. This would be the economic consequence of lower tax-collection levels and increased social security benefits. These are seen as unfortunate, but unavoidable consequences that society must accept in order to protect the overall integrity of the market system. Yet the increasing impact of what is known as globalisation, and the powerful moves towards full deregulation of markets across the world by the World Trade Organisation (WTO), have raised the political and social stakes in this debate.

Within the arguments presented by Friedman, either the role and impact of business in general must be benign, or, the more traditional argument, the acknowledged inequities and imperfections in market-based systems are more than counterbalanced by the claimed advancements and advantages that everyone ultimately enjoys, as a result of the market dynamic levering change and economic progress. That everyone does not benefit to the same extent as a result of these claimed economic advances is not disputed, but, it is argued, everyone is better off, to some extent, in the long run. You may recognise something of the Rawlsian position (which was discussed in Chapter 3) in this argument, that whilst the poorest of society are indeed relatively poor, they are better off than they would be, or could be, under any other economic system. This claim can be considered at two levels. The first is the empirical level.

Tensions regarding globalisation

Does the evidence we have of the globalising and deregulating effects on world markets display an overall elevation of people's well-being? The available evidence is at best mixed. At worst we are experiencing even greater concentrations of power over resources, which lie outside the political arena, with fundamental questions regarding authority, responsibility and accountability remaining unanswered. The observations of Anita Roddick, founder of the Body Shop organisation, are interesting in this context. She was responding to an article that had appeared in the *Guardian* (on the day before the publication of her letter), by Phillipe Legrain. The latter had made the case that the deregulation of world markets, in line with the actions of the WTO, should be welcomed by all, as ultimately all would benefit (the argument outlined above). Case study 9.1 presents the words of Ms Roddick.

| CASE STUDY 9.1 | **Anita Roddick's views on globalisation** |

I went to Seattle in November 1999 to speak at a teach-in on globalisation and to peacefully protest against the WTO. Probably the only international retailer on the 'wrong' side of the police lines. I was baton-charged and tear-gassed by riot police. It was a frightening experience of what corporate controlled reality might look like. Perhaps it prejudiced me against the WTO, it certainly re-radicalised me. Mr. Legrain trots out the freetraders' familiar falsehood that globalisation is all about making the poor richer. No, Mr. Legrain, its about making the rich even richer . . . I can only presume his travels haven't taken him out of the international conference centres into the slums and shanty towns where the poorest and most exploited people live. How else could he glibly state that seamstresses in Bangladesh are not exploited because 'they earn more than they would as farmers'? I recently visited Nicaragua, a country restructured to comply with the WTO and IMF vision of economic progress. There I met workers from the free trade zone, who are paid less than $5 a day to make jeans and shirts exported to the US and sold at obscene markups. Does their pay afford them [the means] to live decently? Depends if a 10 ft square, dirt floored, shack with no plumbed in water or sanitation is decent.

I also visited a cooperative of peasant farmers who grow sesame seed in a remote part of Nicaragua. The price of sesame crashed in 1993. Working with Christian Aid, Body Shop now community trades with the cooperative, sustaining the farmers' livelihoods and culture. They may not be rich, but they do lead dignified lives off the rollercoaster of the commodity market. When the WTO promotes such fair trade, I may 'dump my prejudices'.

(*Source:* Anita Roddick, Letter to the *Guardian*, 13 July 2001)

It is always possible to highlight acts by individual people or specific corporations that present a poor image of the groups they are said to represent. Proverbially speaking, bad apples do not necessarily tell us much about the rest of the apples in a barrel. However, if one can point to a trend of manipulation of power by large corporations, or groups of corporations, then we might have something more than the odd bad apple. The following case studies present just a selection of possible examples that could be used.

The concealment and misuse of critical information

| CASE STUDY 9.2 | **The tobacco industry** |

For many years, medical research has indicated a clear link between the use of tobacco products and various forms of cancer. These findings have always been contested vigorously by all the tobacco companies, despite their own research, which confirmed the linkages. However, in 2000, the tobacco company Reynolds broke ranks and announced in court that it was accepting liability for certain smokers' ill-health. There is evidence to suggest that the tobacco companies had confirmed the link between their products and cancer-based illnesses many years ago but concealed the evidence. Since sales of tobacco products in most western countries have been either stagnant or in decline since the early 1990s, the tobacco companies have targeted developing countries (and particularly young people) as growth markets for their products.

Case study 9.2 continued

Notwithstanding the many previous denials by the tobacco companies of the link between cigarettes and cancer, it is now clear that such a link is accepted. This is exemplified by the use made of a study commissioned by the multinational tobacco company, Philip Morris. In 2001 the tobacco firm, one of the world's leading producers of tobacco products, and responsible for 80 per cent of the cigarettes sold in the Czech Republic, felt the need to respond to claims that cigarette smoking was costing the Czech economy significant sums by virtue of higher levels of hospitalisation, absenteeism from work and thus lower tax-collection levels caused by smoking-related illnesses. The study commissioned by the tobacco company concluded that rather than impose costs on the Czech economy, cigarettes saved the Czech government over £100m each year. The basis for this assessment was that, because cigarette smokers would be dying earlier than non-smokers, due to smoking-related illnesses, this would save the government hospitalisation costs for elderly people, lower pension costs and lower housing costs.

Collusion between governments and corporations

CASE STUDY 9.3

Genetically modified crops

In many western countries, including the UK, the planting of genetically modified (GM) crops is limited and tightly controlled by governments. A moratorium has been imposed by the UK government on the commercial development of GM crops in the UK. The principal companies concerned have accepted the need to monitor trials and to develop a thorough body of evidence before large-scale, commercial planting can be considered. Yet, at the very same time, in the Indian state of Andhra Pradesh, an area of approximately 150 square kilometres, known as Genome Valley, is to be developed for GM crop production, funded by overseas aid from the UK government. In excess of £50m was allocated to this project by the UK government in 2001. Monsanto, the principal company involved in the controlled trials in the UK, is amongst the companies being invited to participate in the development in Andhra Pradesh. The concerns amongst the farmers in Andhra Pradesh are that development of prairie-style fields will result in the mass migration of millions of small farmers and labourers to the cities in search of work. The Andhra Pradesh project (known as Vision 2020) was the result of a study undertaken by a large American consulting firm, which, critics argue, gave little, if any, consideration to alternative forms of raising agricultural efficiency that utilised local resources more effectively and sensitively. Local farmers in Andhra Pradesh wish to control their own destinies, but the fear is that this scheme, with such influential corporate involvement, involvement that will have secured governmental support before it was officially announced, will lead to a social disaster in the region.

CASE STUDY 9.4

Indonesia

The situation regarding the fate of Indonesia since 1965/6, as documented by Pilger (2001), is one of the most troublesome examples of corporate capital and western governments working in tandem, first to engineer a change in political leadership, and then to dictate both economic policy and the way ownership and control of a nation state's natural resources would be allowed to develop. It involves the overthrow of then leader President Sukarno in 1965/6 by General Suharto, with significant western support. The prize in ousting Sukarno was great. Of Indonesia, Richard Nixon, a former President of the United States said, 'With its 100 million people, and its 300-mile arc of islands containing the region's richest hoard of natural resources, Indonesia is the greatest prize in southeast Asia.'

The UK also had a vested interest in seeing a regime in power that was more friendly to the west than Sukarno and his ruling Communist party. In 1964 the UK Foreign Office produced an analysis of the region and 'called for the "defence" of western interests in south-east Asia, a major producer of essential commodities. The region produces nearly 85% of the world's natural rubber, over 45% of the tin, 65% of the copra and 23% of the chromium ore' (Pilger, 2001: 26).

The complicity of America and the UK in the bloody aftermath of the Suharto takeover (it is claimed that as many as one million have been murdered) appears to have been considerable and is documented by Pilger (2001). The American Central Intelligence Agency (CIA) reported that, 'in terms of the numbers killed the massacres rank as one of the worst mass murders of the 20th century' (Pilger, 2001: 24).

With Suharto in power, a conference took place between corporations, predominantly American, but also including some UK and other European corporations, and the Indonesian government. In Pilger's words, 'the Indonesian economy was carved up, sector by sector. In one room, forests; in another minerals. The Freeport Company got a mountain of copper in West Papua. A US/European consortium got West Papua's nickel. The giant Alcoa company got the biggest slice of Indonesia's bauxite. A group of US, Japanese and French got the tropical forests of Sumatra, West Papua and Kalimantan. In addition a foreign investment law was hurried on to the statute books by Suharto, allowing all profits made by foreign companies to be tax-free for at least the first five years of operations.'

Over the next thirty years the World Bank provided loan finance amounting to £30bn to Indonesia. Of this, it is estimated by the World Bank itself that up to £10bn went into Suharto's own pockets, or those of his family and associates.

'In 1997 an internal World Bank report confirmed that at least 20–30% of the bank's loans [to Indonesia] are diverted through informal payments to GOI [Government of Indonesia] staff and politicians' (Pilger, 2001: 22).

In recent years attention has been drawn to the working conditions (e.g. up to 36-hour shifts) and pay (equivalent to 72p per hour) of factory workers in Indonesia making products for major companies such as Nike, Adidas, Reebok and GAP, and the squalor of the living conditions they endure in the camps located next to the 'economic processing zones' (i.e. the factories). In 1998, following mounting demonstrations in the Indonesian capital of Jakarta by large crowds protesting at their poverty and their desperate living conditions, Suharto left office, taking with him many billions of pounds sterling provided for his country over the years by the

Case study 9.4 continued

World Bank. These are monies that the country is obliged to keep paying the interest on, before it can even start repaying the capital.

The fall of Suharto might have marked the end of Indonesia's plight, but it may not have done. In 2000 the IMF offered the post-Suharto government a 'rescue package' of multi-million-dollar loans. However, there were conditions. These included the elimination of tariffs on staple foods. 'Trade in all qualities of rice has been opened to general importers and exporters' (Pilger, 2001: 24), decreed the IMF's letter of intent. Fertilisers and pesticides lost their 70 per cent subsidy, thereby ending for many farmers the prospect of staying on their land. They too will be forced to try and find work in the cities, which are already overburdened with unemployed 'citizens' looking for work. However, 'it gives the green light to the giant foodgrains corporations to move into Indonesia' (Pilger, 2001: 24).

Although Case study 9.4 is a long case, it is only a cursory summary of what appears to be murky and unsavoury episode in the affairs of governments and business.

Why and when business needs government

The relationship between government and business is, as the above account suggests, complex and in continuous need of scrutiny. It is far more complex than the simplistic call for minimal government, which is heard from free-market fundamentalists, would suggest. In a market system, businesses require the autonomy to respond to market signals and claim the right of freedom from government interference in business decisions. Yet, even the claim that businesses do not require governments is disingenuous. It ignores the role of governments in setting fiscal policies; the management of government borrowing and macro-economic affairs; the support given to businesses during times of local or national recession; the funding provided by governments to support both pure and generic research; as well as the funding of major projects that might be too large for private capital formation.

Business and political processes

In addition, business in general has a vested interest in the maintenance of particular economic and legal conditions. As part of the pluralist political system business organisations lobby governments and parliaments to achieve the conditions and laws that suit them. In the modern era it is argued that pressure groups, and particularly business pressure groups, have a far more significant influence upon the construction of legislation than the polity in general. Here are some recent examples.

■ The significant campaigns (on both sides of the argument) by business pressure groups to try and shape political and public opinion with regard to the UK's possible adoption of the Euro.

■ The initial opposition of business pressure groups such as the Confederation of British Industries (CBI), the Institute of Directors (IoD), and the British

Chambers of Commerce, to the principle of a national minimum wage, and then a campaign to limit the amount of the minimum wage.

■ The use of political leverage by business interests in opaque ways. For example, the incoming Labour Government in 1997 had a manifesto commitment to a total ban on tobacco advertising. No such legislation was every formally debated in Parliament during the 1997–2001 administration. By the time the Labour Party's 2001 manifesto was published, the commitment to a complete ban on tobacco advertising was noticeable by its absence, although in March 2002 the Minister for Health announced legislative plans for an almost complete ban on tobacco advertising and sponsorship, the one exception being motor racing sponsorship. It might be just a coincidence that Bernie Ecclestone, who effectively controls worldwide Grand Prix motor racing, was a significant donor to Labour Party funds in 2001.

■ The Labour Party's commitment, in 1997, to a reform of company law to recognise a stakeholder perspective is also instructive in our consideration of corporate citizenship. Respecting its manifesto commitment to make such a change to company law, upon election, the new Labour government established a committee to consider how the stakeholder commitment could be operationalised. The committee deliberated for nearly two years. An interim report was published, after the first year, which retained an attachment to the notion of pluralism in corporate decision making. The Company Law Reform Committee's interim report included the following statement:

> The principal arguments are that the present scheme of law fails adequately to recognise that businesses best generate wealth where participants operate harmoniously as teams and that managers should recognise the wider interests of the community.

The notion of a pluralist perspective can be seen in the concluding phrase of the quotation.

One year later the committee published its final report, but by now the term pluralism had been lost and in its place appeared the term 'enlightened shareholder value'. The removal of the commitment to pluralism led to the resignation from the committee of the finance director of Body Shop. He described himself as a proponent of social and environmental responsibility, and said he was not prepared to remain a member of the committee once the commitment to enlightened shareholder value had replaced pluralism. Newspaper reports on the outcome of the committee's work talked of frantic lobbying by business interests that ultimately led to not only the retention of the shareholders' interests being the only one formally recognised at law, but also the conversion of the committee's proposals for compulsory statements on corporate issues into proposals that statements would only be voluntary, i.e. at the discretion of directors.

The example of the Company Law Reform Committee's experiences is not cited to illustrate an opportunity missed. For our purposes it illustrates the way the business lobby successfully influenced legislative matters. The lobbying did have a direct impact upon businesses, but the example also illustrates the significant ramifications for social and democratic processes of the lobbying phenomenon. The lobbying on behalf of business interests was by its very nature opaque. An image thus emerges of business interests playing an active, although not always transparent, role in political and social, as well as economic, matters.

■ The actions taken immediately following the inauguration of George W. Bush as President of the United States of America in 2001 raised considerable comment and concern regarding the power of corporations. The following table shows the amount of money donated by leading industrial sectors (the principal corporations within these sectors) to Mr Bush's campaign funds and the actions taken by the President during the first three months following his election.

Table 9.1 Actions taken following President Bush's election

Industry	$m donated	Actions taken following election
Tobacco	7.0	Removal of federal lawsuits against cigarette manufacturers
Timber	3.2	Restrictions on logging roads scrapped
Oil and gas	25.4	Restrictions on CO_2 emissions abandoned; Kyoto agreement scrapped; moves to open Arctic refuge to drilling
Mining	2.6	Scrapping of environmental clean-up rules, e.g. arsenic limits in water supply
Banks and credit card companies	25.6	Bankruptcy Bill making it easier for credit card companies to collect debts from bankrupt customers
Pharmaceuticals	17.8	Medicare (government-supported health insurance) reform removing price controls
Airlines	4.2	Federal barriers to strikes introduced; back-pedalling on antitrust (mergers and monopolies) legislation

(*Source*: *Guardian* G2, 27 April 2001, p. 2. © Guardian Newspapers Ltd., 2001.)

A brief recap

To summarise the argument so far, the harm that corporations can do if they only meet the minimum constraints to their activities specified by law contradicts the difference principle. The examples highlighted above, regarding globalisation and deregulation issues, challenge the claim that the overall effects of liberalism will necessarily be a benefit for all. An application of the Rawlsian original position test might cast doubt upon the efficacy, let alone the ethicality, of the poor being better off as a result of globalisation and the World Trade Organisation's strictures, rather than the employment of other, more culturally and socially sensitive, approaches to economic development. The evidence that corporations lobby for 'business-friendly' conditions reinforces the expectation that corporations should act as citizens within society, rather than apart from society. As governments, in theory at least, are in power to represent the interests of society, governments have the authority and the responsibility to make demands of business to operate in ways that are in the interests of society, not the other way around.

An emerging issue from this discussion is the complex question of how the strengths of market-based systems can be tempered by socially acceptable considerations. Nearly two hundred years ago, David Ricardo (a significant figure in British economic thinking) described profit as 'the lever and the lure'. It is a lure because it is the indicator of how successfully capital has been invested, thereby acting as a lure to new capital investment. The notion of the lever, however, speaks to the social, as well as economic, impact that capital migration can have on whole communities. The migration of capital from one region to another, from one country to another, as it seeks out the most advantageous investment opportunities, can have destabilising impacts upon those areas affected by the capital flows. Whilst Friedman points to the undemocratic nature of corporate social responsibility, the argument to leave business alone ignores the profound influence of corporate decisions, and their impact upon (potentially) millions of lives. Corporate decisions are made by decision makers who are unseen and largely unaccountable, other than to shareholders. Critics of Friedman's 'undemocratic' argument see these issues as far more significant and serious threats to democratic processes, than the objections raised by Friedman himself.

Businesses are social constructs – so what?

Moving to the third of Friedman's criticisms, we find that it is open to challenge at the levels of both principle and empirical evidence. To remind you, the third of Friedman's arguments was that businesses cannot have responsibilities because they are not real people, they are social constructs, i.e. they are artificial entities. Whilst we accept Friedman's argument that a corporation is a social construct, this does not deny the possibility that the passage of time may confer upon business organisations new constraints, attributes, rights or responsibilities. In essence, social constructs can be reconstructed. Therefore, the simple fact that corporations are social constructs does not deny the possibility that the significance of such entities can develop to such an extent that society deems it necessary to place constraints, or responsibilities, upon corporations. There would be nothing philosophically objectionable, or flawed, to such developments. Whether such moves would achieve their desired ends is, however, a quite different question and set of issues.

In addition to challenging the validity of Friedman's third criticism at the level of principle, corporations have themselves undermined the strength of the criticism by their own actions. Corporations in America have challenged the argument that they are not entitled to the protection of the American constitution, the bedrock of American citizenship.

First National Bank of Boston v. *Bellotti*

In this legal case the American Supreme Court ruled that corporations are in fact protected by the First Amendment in the same way as individuals, in terms of freedom of speech. The case is reported in Shaw and Barry (1998) and relates to a referendum that was called in the state of Massachusetts to allow the state legislature to amend the constitution and raise a state income tax. The proposal was rejected but the important point, from our point of view, is that the First National Bank of Boston and four other businesses wanted to spend corporate funds in opposing the referendum. A lawsuit was brought against the five corporations and the way they were using shareholder funds in this action. The ruling of a lower court that heard the case was that the actions of the bank, and the four other businesses, were illegal. It was judged unconstitutional for a corporation to spend corporate funds to publicise political views which did not have a direct bearing upon its operations.

The corporations decided to appeal and the case ultimately went to the Supreme Court (the final arbiter in such matters). The Supreme Court overturned the earlier ruling and ruled that corporations could use the American constitution to defend their freedom of speech, just as individuals can. The Supreme Court was thereby conferring upon these business corporations the same rights that are conferred upon individuals via the American constitution.

The legal position of Case study 9.5 was supported when, in 1996, the US Supreme Court unanimously overturned a Rhode Island law which had stood for forty years. This law had prohibited businesses advertising the price of beers and spirits. Referring to the First Amendment the Supreme Court ruled that corporations could claim the same rights of protection as individuals. Thus, notwithstanding that they are social constructs, the five corporations involved in the Massachusetts case, and the corporations that contested the Rhode Island law, claimed, and were granted, the same rights under the American constitution as those available to individual American citizens. Thus, if corporations can be assigned the rights of citizenship, why should they not be assigned equivalent levels of responsibilities?

◼ Social responsibility and environmental accounting

Initiatives under the banner of social responsibility accounting came principally from academics in the 1960s and 1970s, but in 1975 the UK Accountancy Standards Steering Committee published *The Corporate Report*, which was the response of the professional accountancy bodies to the growing clamour (amongst academics at least) for reporting of corporate activities beyond that which was of concern to shareholders. The environmental accounting movement is of more recent vintage, with the demands relating to information on the impact of organisational activity on the environment. Both of these developments are associated with retrospective reporting. They are not concerned with integrating stakeholder perspectives into decision-making processes, although by increasing the amount of disclosure required of companies in terms of their social and environmental impacts, supporters of these initiatives argue that scrutiny is enhanced and debates better informed. Indeed one the UK professional accountancy bodies (ACCA) makes an annual award for the 'best' environmental report by a company.

Holland and Gibbon (2001) provide an overview of various frameworks for environmental reporting, including those produced by:

- The Chartered Association of Certified Accountants (ACCA), *Making Values Count* (Gonella *et al.*, 1998).
- The Institute of Social and Ethical AccountAbility in 1999 (AccountAbility Standard AA1000).
- A discussion paper on a proposed framework for environmental reporting, from the Fédération des Experts Comptables Européens (FEE), in 1999.
- The Global Reporting Initiative (GRI), of the Coalition for Environmentally Responsible Economies (CERES), also in 1999.
- A set of guidance rules issued by the International Organisation for Standardisation (ISO) known as ISO 14000.

A different perspective

So far we have considered Friedman's arguments in particular, and the general issues surrounding the activities of business corporations, from a broadly consistent, albeit distinct, set of philosophical positions. If you refer back to Chapter 1, you will see that three of the theories of the firm, the classical-liberal-economic, the pluralist (Type A and Type B) and the corporatist each locate the business corporation within a capitalist-driven, market-based economy. Each perspective accepts the need for corporations legitimately to seek out new ways to generate profits on behalf of shareholders, but with other interest groups (employees, customers and suppliers) benefiting in differing ways as a result of these corporate activities. Within these perspectives nature, in all its various forms, is seen as a resource, at the behest of society in general, and corporations in particular, to be employed in whatever ways are deemed socially and legally permissible to facilitate economic activity.

Before these issues are discussed in more detail, we would like you to take a few minutes to undertake the following task.

ACTIVITY 9.2

Subjects and objects

Try to identify a place or an object that has a special significance for you. The place or object might be very commonplace (e.g. a ring, an ornament, a book, a photograph), or it might be a little unusual, a location for example. Whatever it is, for you it is special. If you cannot identify such a place or object, try to identify a place or object that you know to be special to someone else, your mother or father perhaps, or your brother or sister. If you were then asked to place a value on that place or object, how might you express that value as a number, a monetary value?

Prior to Activity 9.2, the perspective that has so far underpinned our discussions in this chapter has been that of a clear distinction between ourselves (subjects) and the world of objects that surround us. We have assumed that we are separate from nature and nature is separate from us. We possess the technologies to control, manipulate and direct nature, and we possess the capabilities, and some would argue the right, to do with nature as we see fit. The law of property rights (another social construct) underpins this belief. Landowners can prohibit access to their lands because laws have been passed that allow such prohibitions. Countries fight over, or at least contest, ownership of areas of land and sea (the Arctic and Antarctic regions for example), because of their mineral deposits and other valued resources. Even the moon is subject to property rights claims, for its mineral deposits. Currently companies are seeking to decode human DNA so that they can patent and thus 'own' the codes. The ability of humanity to benefit from such 'code-breaking' research will then be subject to commercial exploitation of these medical understandings. At one level this is no different to the patent rights and copyright constraints that exist in many areas of organisational activity, but it can be argued that deeper philosophical issues are at play when one considers knowledge breakthroughs that can possibly alleviate great human suffering in the areas of genetically inherited diseases and disabilities.

Practically everything that you see around you, that you can touch, or what you are wearing, represents some form of intervention of human activity on nature. This is not to say that these interventions have been/are bad, or wrong. The question is, how do we view nature, and equally importantly, how do we view ourselves with respect to nature?

Martin Heidegger (1959, 2000) is the person who is most identified with the perspective we are about to discuss. It is known as phenomenology.

Definition

> *Phenomenology* is the belief that the world around us can only be understood through our lived experiences. The world does not exist outside of those experiences. We impose understandings and interpretations on that world, or worlds, based upon the values, perspectives and beliefs we hold. The relationship between nature and ourselves is a symbiotic one (i.e. mutually dependent) and not one of independence.

Whilst Heidegger was not the first to challenge the notion that subjects and objects are distinct and separate entities, his analysis was more radical than that of those who had come before him, for example, Edmund Husserl (1931, 1965), who was Heidegger's teacher. Heidegger died in 1976, so by the standards of notable philosophers, his arguments are quite new.

As the definition above indicates, Heidegger's principal argument was that we cannot understand nature other than how we experience it. Nature does not exist outside of our experiences of it. Those experiences might have come to us via first-hand knowledge, or stories, accounts, films, newspapers, books, the Internet, conversations, whatever. So, when we look at something, or hear something, what we see and hear is filtered through our mental faculties, which in turn process information and understandings through many subtle processes including emotions, memories, existing values, beliefs and understandings – essentially our experiences. For example, when we look at something, say an NHS hospital, what do we see? Some would simply say that they see a place where those who are unwell or injured are taken in order to receive treatment. Others might see the building as representing a symbol of a civilised society that has created facilities to tend to the sick or the injured, irrespective of their ability to pay for their treatment. Others might see the building as representing a bundle of resources, which are outstripped by demand for its services. From the latter perspective, the hospital is a cauldron of ethical dilemmas in terms of the choices over which treatments to prioritise and which to de-prioritise.

The same object can represent different visions to different people. Think back to Activity 9.2. Why was the place or object you selected special? The answer will be related to the history of the place or object. It is likely to hold memories that are important to you. The place or object keeps you in touch with something or someone you want to hold on to. History and context are central to this debate. Were you able to place a monetary value upon your object or place? For some, the importance of the object or the place will be incalculable, because of the memories it reveals, what it represents.

Whilst the argument that different people will have different views about the importance of places and objects is reasonably uncontentious, you might ask, 'are we moving towards a position that simply admits that all we are likely to agree upon is that we are likely to disagree upon the values we are prepared to place upon various objects?' If so, how is this going to help individuals and corporations make choices over the use of natural resources, whether they be tropical rain forests, a local park, playing field or set of allotments, or the survival of a threatened species of animal? Heidegger does not offer a magic formula, but he does offer a way of thinking, a way of seeing that could prove helpful.

Heidegger's concern was with what he described as the 'enframing of technology', or what we might call a technology mentality, i.e. seeing nature as purely instrumental, as simply a means to an end. If nature represents merely the opportunity to make money, if that is all nature means to us then, from a Heideggerian perspective, society has become emotionally and spiritually bankrupt.

Definition

> If an object is viewed in purely **instrumental** terms then it possesses no worth beyond its functional use, that is, what might be obtained for it by either selling it as it is, or converting it into another form of tradable object. It is purely a means to an end. The end in this case is to make money, although this is not the only 'end' that can be considered.

Heidegger was not anti-technology. He recognised the contributions that technological advancements had made, and continued to make, to people's lives. Improvements in sanitation, health care, education, etc. can be seen as benefiting either directly or indirectly from technology. In Heidegger's view, we have a symbiotic relationship with nature. The relationship between humans and nature is one of mutual dependency. As we exploit nature, we cannot avoid, to a greater or lesser extent, having an impact upon ourselves. In this context 'ourselves' is used in a very broad way, reflecting impacts not necessarily upon our own generation, but on those that have yet to come.

The treatment of nature in purely instrumental ways is not limited to profit-seeking organisations. Neither is the 'enframing of technology' limited to capitalist systems. Examples of the destruction of the environment in the name of 'progress' can be seen in many different political and economic contexts. However, in an economic system in which the *raison d'être* (the reason for being) of business enterprises is to make money, the question has to be asked, 'How is it possible for corporations to view nature in anything other than an instrumental fashion?' Whilst we cannot expect everyone to value as highly as we do the objects that we regard as important, and vice versa, how can a corporation place a value upon any object, other than in terms of its instrumental worth to the corporation? How can objects have meaning to a corporation beyond their functional or instrumental worth? Where is a corporation's memory that might allow it to attach feelings to objects that transcend their instrumental worth? What is the market value of the site of the Parthenon of ancient Greece to a property developer; or, for a mining company, a spectacular ravine in a site of special scientific interest that contains valuable mineral deposits?

We are possibly approaching a critical point in our consideration of corporate social responsibility and corporate citizenship, certainly in terms of Heidegger's view of a 'technology mentality'. Asking where a corporation's memory might lie, or whether a corporation can possess feelings towards objects, is attributing human characteristics to business enterprises that many would regard as simply unrealistic, as silly. The technical term is reification, which is giving concrete form to an abstract idea (a corporation). If corporations can only ever view objects in instrumental ways, then society cannot expect corporations to value and to treat nature in ways that it (society) might wish or demand. To repeat, this is not to suggest that all members of society will hold the same views on particular aspects of nature, but at least a debate can ensue between interested parties about the various merits of different choices under debate. And the debate will embrace many value systems that go beyond instrumentality.

Following Heidegger, the fundamental objection is that corporations *cannot* fully act in socially responsible ways because they possess a perspective on nature that is extremely limited. A societal perspective on nature that is compatible with a Heideggerian view is denied to a corporation, as long as corporations are constituted in their current form. Corporations cannot be citizens because their value systems are highly constrained and unable to handle concepts of value beyond instrumentality. A corporation's perspective is 'enframed by technology'. However, this does not dismiss corporations as irrelevancies to modern life. Clearly business, in its many forms, is fundamental to the way we live. In many respects it is the dominant force in modern societies. The central issue concerns the relationship between corporations and society, but citizenship is not a realistic or appropriate concept in this debate. Welford (1995), in discussing issues of sustainable development, referred to this issue when, in the six areas that, it is argued, require shifts of thinking, a key transformation is the move from 'objects to relationships'.

The issues addressed so far in this chapter have been whether corporations can assume the status of citizens, and whether corporations are able to reflect societal preferences over the application of nature. As Heidegger would see it, the answers to these two questions are 'No' and 'No'. Therefore we must debate what the relationship between business and society can be and should be. This is one of Heidegger's principal legacies. He has provided a way of seeing both nature and ourselves. The process allowed for greater clarity in debates about the realistic expectations we should hold for corporations and their treatment of nature, a vital aspect of social responsibility. In addition, we can also consider the relationship between corporations and individuals, whether those individuals are employees, customers, suppliers, or members of other stakeholder groups.

From a Heideggerian perspective the traditional approach of science has been to portray the many aspects of nature (the objects) as quite distinct from people (the subjects). Heidegger sees science's relationship with nature as a dominantly exploitative one. The relationship is exclusively instrumental. If we take this argument a step further, then people are themselves part of the resources at the disposal of corporations, and thus, in this context, merely objects. This might be termed the objectification of man, although Marx referred to it as the commodification of man.

It might be appropriate at this point to offer possible ways forward in terms of the relationship between business corporations and the development of societies, but another important dimension to the corporate citizenship debate must be considered first, that is, the issue of corporate manslaughter.

Corporate manslaughter

The concluding major topic in this chapter continues the theme of attempts to hold corporations to account for their roles in, or impacts upon society. To do this, there is a need to consider both the legal position and the philosophical position of corporations with regard to this issue.

Within the UK the prosecution of corporations, as distinct from individual employees, for claimed acts of wilful neglect of a duty of care has been difficult, at least via criminal law. Actions through the civil courts against corporations have been possible for many years, but the expense and the many years involved in prosecuting such cases make the civil law option one that is rarely taken up by members of the public.

Recent developments, reflected in proposals to change UK criminal law with respect to corporate manslaughter, by possibly bringing it in line with US criminal law, suggest that corporations might, in future, face the prospect of being held to account for criminal neglect of their duty of care.

The first impediment to criminal prosecution for corporate manslaughter has been the argument, with which you will by now be familiar, that corporations do not commit acts, only individuals do. Thus, individual employees can be charged with manslaughter, e.g. a train driver involved in a rail crash, but charging the relevant rail company is a more difficult task. To do so, one has to be able to prove that an individual, who was sufficiently senior in the organisation, and who should have acted in ways that could have prevented the accident occurring, was negligent in his or her duties. This is known in law as the *identification doctrine*, i.e. one has to be able to identify the negligent individual who could be said to represent the failure of the corporation as a whole.

In law, as in many other walks of life, one has to be clear about the precise meaning of words. So, when we use the phrase 'sufficiently senior within the organisation', what do we mean? For the corporation to be charged, the identified individual has to be shown to be the person with overall responsibility for this particular aspect of corporate activity, for example health and safety matters, or rail track inspection. The need for this requirement is that because the law has, to date, only viewed corporations as being answerable via its employees, the employee concerned must be recognised as the person who was 'guiding' this aspect of corporate activity. This is the second legal principle we need to recognise. To be able to prosecute a corporation for corporate manslaughter, the *guiding mind* of the organisation has to be identified, and be shown to be implicated in the negligent act/s. Some real-life examples of this principle will help to illustrate the issues involved.

| CASE STUDY 9.6 | The *Herald of Free Enterprise* |

The case has already been mentioned in Chapter 6. It relates to the capsizing of the P&O ferry *Herald of Free Enterprise* outside Zeebrugge harbour in which 192 people lost their lives. It is possible that the captain of the ferry could have been prosecuted for not fully checking that the bow doors were securely closed before the ferry set sail. However, the fact that crew members had, on five previous occasions, expressed concerns to their seniors about the lack of any warning lights on the bridge relating to the position of the bow doors, was insufficient to bring a prosecution against the P&O corporation. It was not possible to prove that these expressions of concern had reached the top echelons of the P&O corporation, the 'guiding mind'. Although comparative evidence was available concerning the claimed (lack of) commitment of P&O towards safety issues, the prosecution lawyers were refused permission by the trial judge to call captains of the Sealink corporation (at the time of the trial Sealink was a rival ferry company), to contrast the safety practices of P&O ferries with those of other ferry operators. Four years after the capsize of the *Herald of Free Enterprise*, safety issues at P&O were again raised when it was revealed that P&O crew members had to pay for their own basic safety training. One recruit recounted, 'I was sent to a college and given pages of information on things like where lifeboats are kept on a ferry, and how to evacuate in an emergency. But you don't get a chance to practise any of this on a ship. When I worked on a ferry for the first time it was up to me to find out where the evacuation points and passengers lifejackets were' (Crainer, 1993: 67).

Even actions that might have appeared doubtful did not attract the judge's concerns. For example, while the inquests into the deaths of the 192 passengers and crew were still in progress, the *Herald of Free Enterprise*, renamed *Flushing Range* and with its bow doors welded together, was being towed to a scrap yard in Taiwan. Members of the Kent police had to fly to South Africa to intercept and inspect the renamed ship. As Crainer (1993) observes, for many concerned in the case, the vessel was 'regarded as an important piece of evidence in a criminal investigation'.

Case study 9.6 continued

In terms of the 'guiding mind' P&O's marine superintendent admitted that he had misled the original inquiry into the disaster about when he had first heard of a proposal to fit warning lights on ferry bridges. 'It was also revealed that he discounted warnings from one of the company's senior masters about potential dangers because he thought the captains were exaggerating. Sheen (who chaired the initial enquiry) described Develin's [P&O's marine superintendent] responses to the legitimate concerns of the masters as "flippant, facetious and fatuous"' (Crainer, 1993). Yet Develin was not deemed sufficiently senior to be regarded as being (or being part of) P&O's 'guiding mind'.

The chasm that can appear to exist between a corporation's executive and operational management can be seen in other examples. A report in a safety journal during the inquiry into the disaster at Piper Alpha oil rig noted,

> The whole management evidence from Occidental [the owners of the oil rig] paints a picture of complete ignorance of the problems which existed. The senior management provided no support to the platform staff. They provided no training. They provided no guidance. They laid down no procedures. They did not participate in discussions with the operators. They did not seek the views of their employees.
>
> (*Safety Management*, December 1989, reported in Crainer, 1993: 116)

Similarly, King (2001) remarked upon the actions of senior management of the UK rail companies following the 1999 Paddington rail crash.

> It should come as no surprise that soon after the UK suffered its second worse rail disaster of recent times – the 1999 Paddington crash – it was revealed that the rail companies had resisted calls to introduce a confidential reporting procedure, i.e. 'whistleblowing' procedure through which staff could report safety concerns without fear of recrimination.
>
> (King, 2001: 152)

A little over 12 months after the Paddington rail crash, in October 2000, another serious incident occurred involving rail transport when a train was derailed at Hatfield due to faults in the track. This time four people lost their lives and many more were injured. While the official report into the Hatfield crash has still to be published, the early evidence and revelations indicate that management failures, regarding reluctance to heed concerns about the quality of the track and its maintenance, will feature significantly in the final report.

Unlike the situation in the United States, UK courts will not accept the principle of *aggregation*. This relates back to the 'guiding mind' principle. In essence the refusal of UK courts to accept aggregation means that the guiding mind of an organisation needs to be held within a tight area of the corporate structure. However, the US Court of Appeal ruled in 1987 that:

> Corporations compartmentalise knowledge, subdividing the elements of specific duties and operations into small components. The aggregate of those components constitute the corporation's knowledge of a particular operation.
>
> (Crainer, 1993: 122)

The US Court of Appeal thus recognised the complexity of corporate structures, and allowed that if responsibility for a particular facet of corporate activity, such as health and safety, was located in many different parts of a corporation, this was not a defence a corporation (as a totality) could employ to deny responsibility for a failure to adhere to acceptable safety practices. As a result of this approach, all the various parts of a corporation that are responsible for safety can be added (aggregated) together to produce the sum of the corporation's health and safety practices (or lack of them).

During the 1990s the calls for a crime of corporate manslaughter have been growing louder and more frequent in the UK, so much so that in 2000 the UK government, published its own proposals, *Reforming the Law on Involuntary Manslaughter* (Home Office, 2000). The situation in the UK with regard to corporate manslaughter may be about to change.

▤ The UK government's and EU proposals on corporate manslaughter

The government's proposals acknowledge the inadequacies of the current law. Four significant disasters are cited in the report. These are: the capsizing of the *Herald of Free Enterprise*; the King's Cross fire; the Clapham rail crash; and the Southall rail crash. The implicit view in the report is that in each case the law inhibited the successful prosecution of what appeared to be culpability within and of the organisations concerned. The identification doctrine is seen as the principal stumbling-block to successful prosecution of organisations.

The government's proposals (published in 2000 as *Reforming the Law on Involuntary Manslaughter*) are based upon the Law Commission Report No. 237, *Legislating the Criminal Code: Involuntary Manslaughters* (1996). The principal proposals are:

- There should be a special offence of corporate killing, broadly corresponding to the proposed offence of killing by gross carelessness.
- The corporate offence should (like the individual offence) be prosecuted only where the corporation's conduct fell far below what could be reasonably expected.
- The corporate offence should not (unlike the individual offence) require that the risk be obvious or that the defendant be capable of appreciating the risk.
- A death should be regarded as having been caused by the conduct of the corporation if it is caused by a 'management failure', so that the way in which its activities are managed or organised fails to ensure the health and safety of persons employed in or affected by its activities.
- Such a failure will be regarded as a cause of a person's death even if the immediate cause is the act or omission of an individual.
- That individuals within an organisation could still be liable for the offences of reckless killing and killing by gross carelessness, as well as the organisation being liable for the offence of corporate killing.

A different approach has been proposed by the Council of Europe (European Union). This proposal would make organisations responsible for all offences committed by their employees, but corporations would be allowed a due diligence defence, i.e. corporations would be exempted from liability if they could show that every precaution to avoid or minimise the occurrence of such an act had been implemented. In this proposal the conventional approach to law is turned on its head, i.e. the initial presumption is that of guilt on the part of the accused, and it is then the responsibility of the accused (the corporation) to present evidence of its existing practices that would exempt it from liability. Clarkson (1998) has expressed concern at the implications of this proposal in that (from a legal perspective) it would change the offence committed to one of a lesser order than criminal manslaughter. The new offence would be offset by a possible due diligence defence. The result would be the attribution of lesser sanctions than under a criminal prosecution for manslaughter.

The possibilities for the senior management of corporations to deny personal or corporate responsibility for criminal neglect appear to be entering a new era. In 1993, Crainer observed:

> Sadly the failure of the Zeebrugge corporate manslaughter trial seemed to condone an all-too-prevalent attitude among senior managers: 'Don't tell me what is going on because if I know, I might be held accountable'.
>
> (Crainer, 1993: 142)

Clarkson made a similar point when he observed:

> If the company's structures are impenetrable or if its policies are so 'sloppy' that no person has been made responsible for the relevant area of activity, a company can still shield itself from corporate criminal liability. In the P&O case, where there was no safety manager or director, there would be no person whose acts and knowledge could be attributed to the company.
>
> (Clarkson, 1998: 6)

Drawing upon the findings of the Sheen Report into the *Herald of Free Enterprise* disaster, in which the corporation was accused by Sheen of 'being infected with the disease of sloppiness' (Department of Transport, 1987), Clarkson observes, 'the worse the disease of sloppiness, the greater is the immunization against criminal liability'. The inference of Clarkson's comments regarding the 'P&O case' (*Herald of Free Enterprise*) is that the interpretation of the identification principle during the trial was too tight. It is not just the weight of the evidence that determines the outcome of legal prosecutions. The interpretations of law and decisions concerning the admissibility of evidence make the judiciary crucial elements within legal processes.

An example of the power of judges to create legal precedent is exemplified in the ruling relating to *Meridian Global Funds Management Asia Ltd* v. *Securities Commission* (reported in Clarkson, 1998: 3). The presiding judge ruled that the 'directing mind and will' of a company did not have to be a very senior person, if the person committing the act was authorised to undertake the act on the company's behalf. This ruling still leaves identification necessary, at the present time at least, but the clear implication is that the responsible person does not have to be a very senior person in order that a corporation can be held responsible for an act of negligence (Clarkson, 1998: 3).

Twelve years after the *Herald of Free Enterprise* disaster, and following the high-profile rail crashes involving loss of life at Clapham and Southall, two trains collided just outside Paddington Station in 1999, killing 31 people and injuring over 400. In the report published in June 2001 into the causes of the crash, Lord Cullen, the inquiry chairman, condemned the entire rail industry for 'institutional paralysis'. He described the failure of the track operator, Railtrack, to act on previous reported incidents of train drivers passing through red signals as 'lamentable', he was extremely critical of one of the train companies involved, Thames Trains (whose driver passed the red signal), and the company's safety culture which he described as 'slack and less than adequate'. Lord Cullen also spoke of the 'significant failures of communication within the organisation'.

The driver of the train operated by Thames Trains was inexperienced and had not been notified by the company of information that was in its possession that the signal just outside Paddington Station had been passed at danger (i.e. on red) eight times before. The problem appears to have been related to the signal being obscured at certain times of day due to the glare of the sun and/or overhanging foliage. Lord Cullen was also critical of the quality of training given by Railtrack to its signallers, the 'slack and complacent regime at Slough' (the control centre for the signals in question). He was also extremely critical of the railway inspectorate, which he deemed 'lacked resources, acted without vigour and placed too much faith in Railtrack'. These words carry echoes of those used by Sheen, the chairman of the Department of Trade inquiry into the *Herald of Free Enterprise* disaster. Sheen spread the blame far more widely than those directly involved on the night of the disaster. Guilt lay with 'all concerned in management. From top to bottom, the body corporate was infected with the disease of sloppiness.' At the time of writing, consideration is being given to charges of corporate manslaughter being brought against Railtrack and Thames Trains for the crash at Paddington.

The UK government's proposals allow for criminal prosecutions of corporations, as well as individuals, if practices that a reasonable and careful corporation would employ are absent. The speed with which the government's proposals move from discussion paper to actual law will be interesting to observe.

Clarkson offered a further variation on the quest to hold corporations to account, by the application of what he describes as 'corporate *mens rea*'. Clarkson offers his proposal because he fears that the doctrines of 'identification' and 'guiding mind' remain problematic within the government's proposals.

Definition	*Mens rea* is a legal term that means criminal intention, or knowledge that an act is wrong. Thus, corporate *mens rea* refers to an act or set of practices (or lack of them), perpetrated in the name of a corporation, that possess the essence of wrongdoing.

Clarkson argued:

Doctrines – identification, aggregation, etc. – involve fictitious imputations of responsibility. The real question is not whether the question of corporate mens rea involves a fiction, but whether, of all the fictions, it is the one that most closely approximates modern-day corporate reality and perceptions . . . the important point about this approach is that it is not whether any individual within the company would have realised or foreseen the harm occurring but whether in a properly structured and organised, careful company, the risks would have been obvious.

(Clarkson, 1998: 10)

What this argument is saying is, 'Yes, corporate culpability is a fiction, or a problematic concept, but then so are so many of the concepts that are involved in this debate'. Clarkson referred to legal concepts such as identification and aggregation, as equivalent fictions/problematic concepts, but we could just as easily refer to concepts such as citizenship, democracy, property rights, free trade, a living wage. Property rights are entirely socially constructed phenomena, yet this has not prevented hundreds of thousands of lives being lost in their defence over the centuries. It is for society to decide the laws that are appropriate for its own well-being and development. In many respects the fact that some of the laws relate to human beings, whilst others relate to socially constructed beings, is irrelevant.

This still leaves us with the issue of whether corporations can be construed or treated as corporate citizens. From the Heideggerian position corporations cannot be citizens, because the best that can be expected of corporations is that they view nature in exclusively instrumental ways. From a Heideggerian perspective, corporations have to be controlled in ways other than 'wishing' them to act in socially responsible ways. Windsor (2001) supported this view:

The corporate citizenship notion conflates citizen (which a firm cannot be) and person (which a firm can be, but only as a legal fiction). The portrayal is fictional . . . Fictional personhood is not a sound basis for artificial citizenship.

(Windsor, 2001: 41)

The key proposal of the Law Commission report on involuntary manslaughter, which the UK government appears to have accepted, is that management failure to introduce and ensure the application of reasonable safety practices is sufficient to justify the prosecution of corporate manslaughter. This is a fundamental change. Whether it can be cited, retrospectively, against Railtrack and/or Thames Trains is a moot point, but the position of corporations *vis-à-vis* the death of their employees and/or members of the public due to actions or inactions of the corporation is undergoing fundamental scrutiny. As mentioned above, whether any alterations to the law will reflect such a fundamental change remains to be seen.

The rise of the citizen

As has been intimated in this chapter, out of the apparent impotence of the individual citizen might be arising a far more proactive, energised and combative citizenry. Examples are available of pressure groups picketing companies and retail stores, or leading boycotts of particular products in protest at what is considered to be unethical corporate behaviour. In addition to the protests at what is termed global capitalism at various meetings of the political leaders of the G8 countries during 2000 and 2001, more specific and localised examples can be cited. For example:

■ The picketing of Cartier, one of the premier jewellers on New York's Fifth Avenue, by members of the Campaign to Eliminate Conflict Diamonds, in September 2000.

As thousands of potential shoppers filed past, the demonstrators brandished signs depicting children whose hands and feet had been amputated by rebels fighting a brutal war in Sierra Leone. 'Did your diamond do this?' the placards screamed. The protest, which was reinforced later by prime-time television advertising, was aimed at forcing the US diamond industry to support legislation to stem the flow of illegal diamonds, thereby robbing rebels in Sierra Leone and Angola of their main funding source. By linking the diamond industry with such extreme violence, the campaign tried to tarnish the image of diamonds as a sign of love and fidelity . . . NGOs have realised that the quickest way to get the results is to go directly after companies by targeting their customers, their investors, or both.

(Alden, 2001: 11)

■ The picketing of Huntingdon Life Sciences (HLS) is discussed in Chapter 2 (Case study 2.23). In 2002 a number of major clients removed their custom from HLS because of the damage the association was causing the client companies.

■ Mention has already been made of the criticisms levelled at corporations such as Nike for their involvement in Indonesia and other third world countries. In response to adverse publicity and campaigns against their products, some companies, including Nike, have agreed to pay certain non-government organisations (NGOs) to monitor the operations of suppliers to ensure compliance with agreed codes of conduct.

■ The campaign in 2001 against the Exxon Corporation (known as Esso in the UK) urging UK owners of motor cars to boycott Esso petrol stations as a sign of disgust at Esso's alleged part in the removal of the legislation prohibiting the drilling for oil in a wild life sanctuary in the Arctic. The prohibition was lifted in 2001 following the election of President George W. Bush.

It is also argued that the significance of US and UK pension funds, unit trusts and investment trusts has increased the importance of the capital and securities markets as potential points of leverage for NGOs. In July 2001 the *Financial Times* announced the launch of four sets of indices that were designed to reflect the ethicality of corporate practices and activities. An ethical share index was launched. One of the indices relates to companies operating in the UK, one relates to Europe, the third to the USA and the fourth to the whole world. The UK-based index was the first to go 'live' in July 2001.

To be included in the index a company must satisfy a range of criteria including employment issues; type of products produced and/or sold; the human rights records of the countries in which the companies operate; health and safety issues; and community involvement. Of the top 100 UK companies, as measured by the traditional *Financial Times* index, 36 were not included in the first publication of the ethical share index. In some way each of these companies had failed against one or more of the index's criteria.

The Confederation of British Industry (CBI) expressed reservations about the index, fearing that those companies omitted from the index would be perceived as 'bad' companies, whereas any exclusion might reflect merely a difference in terminology or definition. However, pressure groups expressed concern at the inclusion of certain companies in the index. The Free Tibet Campaign, for example, objected to BP's inclusion.

A further development comes from the EU. In 2001 the EU part-financed a business organisation called CSR Europe, which was intended to add impetus to the developments in corporate social responsibility. CSR Europe was charged with promoting corporate social responsibility throughout Europe, culminating with 'European Year on corporate social responsibility in 2004'. Whilst free-market critics accused CSR Europe of being anti-capitalist and anti-market, those on the left have been critical of CSR Europe, seeing it as a 'camouflage', 'allowing big business to claim responsibility without doing anything more than paying its subscriptions. Trade unionists worry that voluntarism cannot provide sufficient protection for workers' (Cowe, 2001).

Those companies initially supporting CSR Europe included Nike, Shell and BP, companies with much adverse publicity to overcome. The reasons for joining CSR Europe are varied but Cowe (2001) observed that, 'while social responsibility is much more than philanthropy, it is about money, not morals'. BT's group personnel director made the following observation, 'It is about doing business in a way that persuades our customers to buy from us, our employees to work hard for us and our communities to accept us'.

The phenomenon of the rise of citizen pressure groups, whether they are human or animal rights based, or associated with environmental issues, is a development that contains the seeds of positive and negative potentialities. The positive aspects relate to the challenging (and sometimes overturning) of unethical corporate practices. Campaigns and protests can reflect active citizen participation in the social, political and economic evolution of nation states and super-nation states. However, there is also the downside potential, the risks associated with these developments. These risks are threefold. The first relates to the ability of the under-represented, the already socially and economically excluded, to be able to articulate their concerns – and be listened to. At least with universal suffrage, each person has only one vote. In pressure group politics, the super-organised, media-wise, politically adept pressure group is likely to have a considerable advantage over less well-organised groups. In the latter scenario, 'might is right' might well prevail, which is hardly an ethically sound approach.

The second concern is that if scarce resources are to be effectively harnessed and utilised (a justifiable ethical concern), decision making in corporations cannot become paralysed by rules, by interminable meetings, or by an inability to achieve consensus on every decision.

The third concern is associated with the way opposition to corporate or government practices is expressed. The violence witnessed at the G8 summits at Genoa, Seattle and London shocked many people. Unintentional violence can be seen as one of the possibilities of democratic expression, but a number of the pressure groups present at these summits were also concerned by the violence, not just because it was never their intention that the demonstrations would develop in the ways they did, but also because the violence detracted from their important messages.

The ways societies evolve to handle these aspects of the corporate citizen relationship is of fundamental importance to societal development.

Reflections

For those who argue for the need to enforce greater responsibilities upon business activity there appear to be one of two options. The first is to lobby for greater legal controls over business. The second is the pressurising of firms to be more socially responsible in their activities, via campaigns and public debate, forcing corporations to take more responsibilities for their actions. These two approaches are distinct but complementary. However, citizenship (corporate or otherwise) is a two-way relationship. Unlike individual citizenship, where a change of allegiance from one nation state to another can be a complex process, with no guarantee of a successful outcome, corporations are far more capricious in their allegiances. Their significance makes them attractive, but not fully reliable 'citizens'. If the demands of 'citizenship' become unacceptable to the multinational corporation then, with little if any national loyalty, capital will migrate towards more seductive locations.

This last point highlights a major tension within the corporate citizenship debates, particularly if economic considerations are to remain the primary organisational determinant of survival. The term 'creative destruction' was coined by Joseph Schumpeter (1976) to describe the dynamic forces within capitalist, market-based systems that ensure that if companies, irrespective of their size and dominance, continue to under-perform, other companies will eventually overtake and possibly crush the once dominant companies. In this respect, the notion of corporate citizenship within a market-based system contains a particular tension. Should society respond positively to pleas from companies that have previously been deemed 'good corporate citizens', but which have subsequently been seen to be less than efficient or innovative compared to their competitors and as a consequence large-scale redundancies appear inevitable? Foster and Kaplan, reported in Brown (2001), claimed that if one were to make a list of the largest global companies at any point in time, then in 25 years, two out of three will no longer exist, and the remaining one-third will be under-performing the stock market, such is the force of creative destruction.

The libertarian position is that corporations *should not* be expected to behave in so-called socially responsible ways, other than operating within legal constraints. A Heideggerian position argues that corporations *cannot* behave in socially responsible ways beyond legal compliance and instrumentality. Arguing from a Heideggerian position, the notion of a corporate citizen is a not only a chimera, but a contradiction in terms (an oxymoron). Thus, the relationship between corporate business and the citizenry has to be one that is marked by consistently reviewed legal parameters, and an active citizenry. The onus in this relationship is not exclusively upon corporations. Far more is required of individual citizens, both in terms of their roles within corporations, but even more so in relation to their roles as members of the citizenry.

From this analysis, three elements to future developments appear to be key:

1 Societies must continuously look at the laws that provide the degrees of freedom and the limits of action of corporate activities to assess their appropriateness and effectiveness;

2 As laws can only provide a broad schema of what is acceptable behaviour (of both individuals and corporations), far greater involvement on the part of individuals is required in shaping the form, structure and details of societies. Notwithstanding the violence that was part of the demonstrations that took place at the G8 summits during 2000 and 2001, the presence of many thousands of people, peacefully demonstrating against what they saw as the inequities and unacceptable behaviour and power of multinational corporations, was an interesting development in terms of the individual citizen. The more localised examples of pressure groups protesting against corporate activities present a counterweight to those who bemoan the power of corporations and the claimed minuscule influence of the individual in the face of global corporate power. The power of concerted and co-ordinated citizen action may yet be an important element in future debates over corporate power.

3 Decisions within corporations are made by individuals, sometimes groups of individuals and sometimes individuals on their own. So the question presents itself as to which guides, rules or codes can be suggested for these people whose actions may have profound implications for many people outside as well as inside a corporation. As the case was made in Chapter 7, there are roles for guides, codes and rules, but these are limited. At the heart of corporate decision making that genuinely seeks to consider the implications of a decision in terms that go beyond mere instrumentality, the non-consequentialist arguments compete for attention. Yet the complexity of many business (and non-business) decisions suggest that personal heuristics will play an important part in explaining the choice of action actually selected.

If corporate citizenship is to mean a range of stakeholder interests being fairly weighed in corporate decision making, there would need to be a paradigm shift from a strictly economic orientation in business decision making, to what we might term *socio-economic rationality*. As a consequence, there would need to be a change in business education, because economic reason dominates decision-making models and approaches. In economics, accounting and management sciences in general, the underlying assumption is that of economic rationality. Yet this key assumption is rarely, if ever, spelled out to students. It creeps into the subconscious unannounced.

Prescribing what business people and prospective business people should do in given situations is not our argument. People must be brought together to discuss ethical issues in business, and not just the grand questions that challenge only the leaders of multinational corporations, but everyday decisions that shape business life. By discussing such issues, each participant might contribute to, but also listen to, the views of others, although the evidence of Bird and Waters (1989) and Lovell (2002) would suggest that much needs to change before such possibilities can become realisable.

Such exposure to debate will not lessen the complexities of many business decisions, but it will at least allow for other factors, besides pure instrumentality, to enter into the thoughts of business decision makers. Such understandings of what the 'good' person would or could do might be more important than a book of rules that attempts to, but never can, accommodate every possible problem that can confront an individual. But decisions have to be made, without the benefit of hindsight, and invariably without the benefit of as rigorous an analysis as might be desired. Time will also inhibit the degree of participation that might be desirable. These are legitimate reasons why decision making can never be perfect, or totally inclusive, and they, along with less legitimate reasons, explain why the first and second elements of this three-pronged strategy are necessary. The first and second elements above provide the bulwarks against instrumentality, let alone dubious or unlawful business practices riding roughshod over more ethical practices. The early years of the twenty-first century may represent an important period in redefining the relationships between corporations, governments and the polity.

Summary

In this chapter the following key points have been made:

- Whilst the criticisms levelled by Friedman at those calling for corporations to act in socially responsible ways can be countered, the concerns of Heidegger raise more difficult challenges.
- Social and environmental accounting initiatives are concerned with expanding the reporting requirements of organisations, but do not address fundamental issues relating to corporate decision making.
- Corporate manslaughter may become easier to prosecute as a criminal offence as a result of possible changes to the law. However, the increasingly litigious nature of society is a double-edged sword with respect to the greater openness and accountability of corporations.
- The relationship between business and society is a dynamic one, although not necessarily one where power is equally divided. The rise of pressure groups to counter and challenge the power of corporations possesses the seeds of both positive and negative possibilities for society.

Suggested further reading

The following three items explore most of the issues raised in this chapter: J. Andriof and M. McIntosh (eds) (2001) *Perspectives on Corporate Citizenship*, Greenleaf Publishing; C.M.V. Clarkson (1998) 'Corporate Culpability', *Web Journal of Legal Issues*, Blackstone Press Ltd, http://webjcli.ncl.uk/1998/issue2/clarkson2.html; and S. Crainer (1993) *Zeebrugge: Learning from Disaster*, London: Herald Charitable Trust.

GROUP ACTIVITY 9

Employing the information provided on the *www.citizen.org/Press/pr-auto7.htm* website debate the arguments that the respective parties might present at a public inquiry held to inquire into the affair. The setting is not a court of law, but rather an inquiry into the justifications of the actions and pronouncements of the respective parties.

- The first student group should represent two factions within the Ford Motor Company – the management and the shareholders.
- The second student group should represent two factions within the Firestone Tire Company – the management and the shareholders.
- The third student group should represent the dealerships in Saudi Arabia and Venezuela that sold the Ford Explorer.
- The fourth student group should represent those who have died or been injured as a result of one the tyres on their Ford Explorer shredding.

Each group should state the principles and arguments that defend or explain their actions. These should be recorded and contrasted at the close of the initial presentations.

The concluding element to this activity is provided by the fifth group, which can be the tutor/s, but preferably should be a fifth student group. This fifth group is required to précis, but also critically evaluate, the arguments presented by the respective groups, identifying what are considered to be strengths of the arguments presented, but also the limitations. These limitations relate both to the philosophical base of the arguments cited, but also to the quality and robustness of the way the groups actually employed the respective arguments they presented.

10 Review

In this final chapter we identify and review the main themes of the book to help you with your revision and reflections.

The morality of business

Throughout the book we have often returned to the question of whether the business system – the free market, capitalist system – is in itself moral. Some argue that free markets, which are based on the exercise of individual choice, are intrinsically good. Some argue the opposite while yet others believe free markets are not inevitably immoral but that they need to be regulated. Some argue that no answer to the question of the morality of business is possible. They claim that business ethics is an impossibility (Parker, 1998b: 294) because every attempt to define what ethical business means draws us into an agony of philosophical debate or accounting casuistry.

If we were to assume pessimistically that the market system were immoral, or that it is impossible to define how it should behave to be moral, does that mean it is impossible to behave ethically within it? Can good deeds be done in a bad world or does accepting one's existence within a bad world taint everything? Such pessimism denies the potential of agency, that is the ability of individuals (and collectives of individuals) to effect change by way of direct action (as evidenced throughout the book, but particularly in Chapter 9); and by indirect action, such as the lobbying of governments to effect greater legal controls over business activity.

Against these successes it is acknowledged that the power exerted by corporate interests within and upon politicians and political systems is significant, and throughout the book we have provided subtle and not-so-subtle examples of such relationships. The increasingly high-profile role of the World Trade Organisation (WTO), with its remit to remove all trade barriers, is a force that appears, too often to many, to put the interests of corporations above the interests of the world market. Similarly, in spite of its commitment to free trade, the American government was not averse to acts of protectionism such as the imposition of import tariffs on steel in 2002.

We believe that markets need regulation to inhibit unethical behaviour by organisations. Such developments will need to take place in something other than

295

piecemeal ways. If not co-ordinated they would be unwelcome to the corporations subject to these changes, which would be placed at a significant cost disadvantage to their competitors which may not be subject to the same strictures. This is not an argument for inertia, but it is an argument that recognises that easing one's conscience by achieving change in corporate practices that have the effect of driving the affected companies out of business due to escalating compliance costs, is a very partial form of morality. The ethical behaviour of consumers becomes important for developing the morality of business. If consumers choose to opt for cheap goods that are known to be cheap only because of the employment conditions experienced by production workers, or the production processes involved are known to have significant, negative environmental impacts, then the societally and environmentally minded corporation will suffer because of the capriciousness of the consumer.

The conflicts between corporate interests and those of the many other societal stakeholder groups will not be resolved by a 'final settlement' that suits all. Therefore perpetual vigilance and involvement by significant societal interests is required. But so too is the belief that morality can be a personal practice, in business as well as non-business contexts.

Awareness of ethical issues in business

Whatever your views on the moral quality of capitalism the public's awareness of businesses' wrongdoing (whether seen as an inevitable consequence of the system or as examples of bad apples) has increased. This may be the result of more people having a stake in business through their investments and pension arrangements. It may also reflect a widening of the agenda for public ethical concern that, fifty years ago, would not have included environmental issues or racial or sexual discrimination at work, for example.

In Chapters 6, 7, 8 and 9 various devices and approaches – whistleblowing, codes of ethics, ethical leadership, charges of corporate manslaughter and so on – have been discussed as means of diminishing the chances of ethical wrongdoing by and within organisations. But corporations tend to respond most purposefully to pressures that threaten economic viability. This is why the role of the consumer is such an important element in the debates about business ethics and values. Paradoxically, while consumerism tends to be associated with the atomisation of the individual and the undermining of the concept of being a 'citizen', consumerism reconstituted as a form of active citizenry could be a powerful force in future business developments which seek to minimise exploitation and corruption.

Labelling to assist consumers in their decision making becomes important, as does the work of agencies monitoring the practices of those involved in multinational companies' supply chains. The possibilities exist for raising notions of morality in business, but not without the support and involvement of individuals, particularly individual consumers. Consumers are often employees themselves, as well as being citizens with the possibilities that this offers. But failure on the part of the public to accept the challenge of active citizenship will leave a moral vacuum that will not remain unfilled for long.

Values and ethics

Most people, in their working lives, do not consciously apply ethical theories and philosophical arguments. Values provide the means for thinking about ethical issues. Values are the commonsense reflections of ethical theories that we accept without argument and use heuristically in our thinking. Plato used the metaphor of the cave to explain how our perceptions are inadequate representations of the true world. Imagine people who live in a cave that they never leave. They are constrained to look only at the back wall of the cave on to which the sun projects the silhouettes of the world beyond the cave. They believe what they see to be the world. The metaphor identifies values as dim reflections of the ethical theories debated in Chapter 3. This does not necessarily make values a source of bias and prejudice. Heuristics, and the heuristic role of values, appear to be effective as well as efficient as a form of thinking. Nevertheless a reflexive person would wish to challenge their values and develop the level of their moral reasoning. Ethics provides a means of questioning the application and appropriateness of our values.

Dilemmas and complexity

There are, no doubt, some ethical issues in business and organisational life that are clear-cut and what it is right to do is unambiguous. Our discussions of cases in this book, and our interviews with managers and employees, indicate that in many matters there are, at the least, contrary views on what is right and wrong and often, in the perceptions of those involved, the issues are seen as dilemmas. The particulars of a case often defy our values and ethical principles because, as Oscar Wilde (1996) quipped, 'generalities in morals mean absolutely nothing'. Our contention is that a better understanding of theories of ethics and moral behaviour, and an encouragement to think more critically about the values that inform our behaviour, will provide each of us with a greater opportunity for reducing the intractability of complex ethical situations.

Dialogue and debate

All of the themes raised so far in this review suggest that questions of business ethics cannot be resolved by promulgating rules and codes. This makes dialogue and debate about business ethics necessary, but here we have a paradox. Whilst the importance of dialogue and debate has been stressed throughout the book, we have also referred to research studies that indicate that moral behaviour is not, in practice, something managers much discuss. The continuing moral muteness of managers is a cause for concern, and a significant impediment to enhancing the prospects for moral agency within business organisations. However, dialogue and debate are, on their own, insufficient to enhance moral agency. They require support structures such as formal mechanisms to raise ethical concerns at work, as well as organisational cultures that are conducive to well-intentioned expressions of concern and the fostering of ethical behaviour. Without these support structures, debate and dialogue become merely additional justifications for cynicism, suspicion and pessimism.

Moral agency

We have placed considerable emphasis upon the notion of moral agency because without this the individual is diminished. Organisations represent the places that the majority of people inhabit for most of their waking lives. If they are unable to exercise moral agency, to follow their consciences, and are required to do things they believe are wrong for fear of reprisals if they do not, then we have created, at best, amoral communities, and at worst immoral communities.

Employing Aristotle's use of the mean to identify a balance of behaviour that avoids the extremes of indulgence or neglect with respect to moral agency we argue for a form of moral agency that recognises and avoids the excesses of priggishness or self-righteousness. We call this mean 'principled judgement'. To see the correction of a 'wrong' as justifiable because it assuages the moralist's conscience, irrespective of the harm that might be caused by righting the wrong, would be an example of moral agency transgressing into the indulgence of self-righteousness. Principled judgement is the mean, or balance, between moral impotence and self-righteousness.

Self-righteousness demands a reflexive wrestling with one's conscience that implies a greater concern for the state of one's soul than for the state of the world. It seems imbalanced to others because

> we feel so extremely uncomfortable in the presence of people who are noted for their special virtuousness, for they radiate an atmosphere of the torture to which they subject themselves.
>
> (Jung, 1953, quoted in Gross, 1987: 196)

Moral impotence, on the other hand, implies a failing that is not necessarily the fault of the individual. Whilst feelings of impotency can be the result of individual failing, they can also be the consequence of factors beyond the control of the individual. In the latter case, an authoritarian regime, coupled with an unsupportive organisational culture, may render the individual employee seemingly helpless in the face of practices with which she or he is uncomfortable. However, much will depend upon the circumstances of individual cases before one can make judgements about the sources of the moral impotency.

Conclusions

A Cambridge academic published in 1908 a tongue-in-cheek guide to university politics. The following quotation from his book may help put the issues in this book into perspective.

> The number of rogues is about equal to the number of men who always act honestly; and it is very small. The majority would sooner behave honestly than not.

The reason why they do not give way to this natural preference of humanity is that they are afraid that others will not; and the others do not because they are afraid that they will not. Thus it comes about that, while behaviour which looks dishonest is fairly common, sincere dishonesty is about as rare as the courage to evoke good faith in your neighbours by shewing that you trust them.

(Cornford in Johnson, 1994: 103)

We share this optimistic view that the world of business and affairs is not necessarily irredeemable. We do not share the pessimists' view that debates about business ethics are hopeless and destined to failure because of the fundamental contradictions within market-based, capitalist relationships (a belief that business ethics is an oxymoron). We do argue that a more proactive citizenry is required to shape business relationships so that citizens and societies exercise greater influence over business behaviour. This reflects a dynamic relationship between business and societies that mirrors the mixture of roles – citizen, employee, supplier, customer, manager, entrepreneur, apologist and critic – that people experience in their own lives. This dynamism is demanding upon individual members of communities, but without active involvement the prophesies of the pessimists are more likely to be realised.

Business ethics resources on the World Wide Web

The World Wide Web is a rich source of information for this subject. Here are some suggested sites. The first two are general guides with many links to other sites.

- **Ethics links**
  http://carbon.cudenver.edu/~jjuhasz/ethiclinks.html#Professional%20Codes%20 of%20Ethics%20and%20Conduct
  This directory is provided as a reference guide for persons concerned about moral problems. It contains a large list of ethics links provided by an independent body with a mission, which is to identify a worldwide consensus on what constitutes right conduct in the age of globalisation.

- **NBS HRM Resources on the Web – Business Ethics**
  www.nbs.ntu.ac.uk/depts/hrm/list/hrbe.htm
  This is a major source provided by the Dept. of HRM at Nottingham Business School. This link takes you straight to its ethics list.

The next sites focus on ethical theories and principles:

- **Ayn Rand's official website**
  www.geocities.com/AthensAegean/1311/rand.html

- **The Bentham project, University College London**
  http://www.ucl.ac.uk/Bentham-Project/index.htm
  Jeremy Bentham's auto icon (his embalmed and preserved body, although the head is waxen, the original having decayed and been ill-treated by students), bequeathed in his will for the inspiration of future generations, can be seen in the south cloisters of the main building of University College. An image of the auto icon can be seen at:
  www.ucl.ac.uk/Bentham-Project/Faqs/auto_where.htm

- **Business open learning archive (The BOLA project), Business ethics resources, Brunel University**
  http://sol.brunel.ac.uk/~jarvis/bola/ethics/index.html
  Brief materials on a wide range of theoretical and applied issues in business ethics. A useful crib and ready reference.

- **Centre for Ethics and Business**
  www.ethicsandbusiness.org/whoweare.htm
  Some useful learning material on this site. If you click on 'toolbox' a cartoon Socrates guides you through some basic ethical concepts. When you click on 'cases and surveys' a cartoon Simone de Beauvoir acts as your mentor on a number of brief cases.

■ **Ethics Updates, edited by L.M. Hinman, The Values Institute, University of San Diego**
http://ethics.acusd.edu/values/index.html
This site provides some helpful materials on all the major ethical theories and perspectives. It is a general ethics site rather than a business ethics site.

The following two websites are concerned with whistleblowing:

■ **Freedom to Care**
www.freedomtocare.org/

■ **Public Concern at Work**
www.pcaw.co.uk/news/press/_14.html

The next two sites are interesting corporate ethics websites:

■ **Lockheed Martin**
www.lockheedmartin.com/about/ethics.html

■ **Texas Instruments**
www.ti.com/corp/docs/company/citizen/ethics/benchmark.shtml

The remaining sites listed cover a number of specialist aspects of business ethics:

■ **AccountAbility – The Institute of Social and Ethical AccountAbility**
www.accountability.org.uk
This institute is focused on making organisations accountable to stakeholders for their ethical, social and environmental performance. It publishes a standard (AA1000) for certificating companies' performance in these fields. The intention of the standard is to improve performance by learning through stakeholder engagement.

■ **Adaptive Behavior and Cognition; the Max Planck Institute for Human Development, Berlin**
www.mpib-berlin.mpg.de/abc
If you click on the 'basic concepts' button you are given an introduction to fast and frugal heuristics.

■ **Banana trade**
www.bananalink.org.uk/atws.htm
This is a site lobbying on many ethical issues that are practised within the international banana trade.

■ **The Bureau for Workers' Activities at The International Labour Office**
www.itcilo.it/english/actrav/telearn/global/ilo/code/main.htm
This is a good website on corporate codes and on the bad behaviour of some multinational corporations.

■ **Centre for Applied Ethics, University of British Columbia**
www.ethics.ubc.ca/resources/business/
This website on business ethics resources on the World Wide Web is very useful. The 'Topics' page links to a wide range of interesting material.

■ **Centre for the Study of Ethics in Professions**
www.iit.edu/departments/csep/PublicWWW/codes/
This is a good place to find copies of professional, governmental and organisational codes of ethics. Particularly fun is the code of ethics for witches (the Covenant of the Goddess). Most of the codes on this site are totally serious.

■ **CEPAA**

www.cepaa.org/sa8000 review.htm

The Council on Economic Priorities Accreditation Agency (CEPAA) which is now known as Social Accountability International (SAI) was set up to address concerns about labour conditions around the world. It has developed a standard for workplace conditions (SA8000). This and other related information is on its website.

■ **The Corporate Citizenship Unit at Warwick Business School**

http://users.wbs.warwick.ac.uk/ccu/

This site provides some useful materials on a range of issues subsumed under the broad heading of corporate citizenship.

■ **Ethical performance. A newsletter for ethically responsible businesses**

www.ethicalperformance.com/

Provides news and debate about issues in the field of socially responsible business, particularly in Europe. It is a commercial site but you can register as a guest.

■ **Institute for Business Ethics**

www.ibe.org.uk/

The institute is based in London. It is a charity with trustees drawn from many large private-sector corporations. It has useful material on writing codes of ethics. It also has connections with the Caux Round Table and with the Global Compact. This is a United Nations platform for the promotion of institutional learning in the areas of corporate social and environmental responsibility.

■ **Institute for Global Ethics**

www.globalethics.org/links.html

This page is a good introductory site with good links to other sites. The Ethical Orientation Questionnaire, which assesses whether you are into care or justice, is also fun.

www.ethicsandbusiness.org/stylequiz.htm

■ **The International Baby Food Action Network**

www.ibfan.org/english/gateenglish.html

This is a site lobbying for the promotion of breast-feeding of infants and against the marketing of breastmilk substitutes to mothers in developing countries in particular.

■ **International Labour Organisation**

www.itcilo.it/english/actrav/telearn/global/ilo/

The ILO was set up in 1919 and is now part of the United Nations system of organisations. Actrav is a bureau within the ILO concerned with globalisation and workers' rights.

■ **The Internet Center for Corruption Research, provided by Goettingen University and Transparency International**

www.gwdg.de/~uwvw/

The key website on the problem of bribery and corruption in business worldwide. For the 2001 Global Corruption report go to:

www.globalcorruptionreport.org

■ **One World Trust**

www.oneworldtrust.org

The One World Trust was formed to promote a greater sense of world community. The Trust believes that sustainable world peace, prosperity and justice will only be achieved when individuals see themselves as world citizens as well as citizens of their own nations.

■ **OECD**

www.oecd.org

The Organisation for Economic Co-operation and Development is an international organisation helping governments to tackle economic, social and governance challenges. Documentation, statistics and news on the key themes addressed by the **OECD** are on its website.

■ **US Department of Labor**

www.dol.gov/

This site deals with many ethical issues relating to employment.

Finally, if you want help on any of the technical terms in ethics, such as the categorical imperative, the use of a search engine will usually throw up some helpful pages.

References

AccountAbility (1999) *AccountAbility Standard AA1000*, London: Institute of Social and Ethical Accountability.

Adair, J. (1980) *Management and Morality. The Problems and Opportunities of Social Capitalism*, Farnborough: Gower.

Al Andalusia, S.C. (2001) *Credit Cards*, World Wide Web, http://www.islamzine.com/carlo/shari33.html. Site visited 20 August 2001.

Alden, E. (2001) 'Brands feel the impact as activists target customers', *Financial Times*, 18 July: 11.

Alvesson, M. and Willmott, H. (1996) *Making Sense of Management. A Critical Introduction*, London: Sage.

Amnesty International (1997) *The 'Enron project' in Maharashtra – protest suppressed in the name of development*, World Wide Web, http://web.amnesty.org/802568F7005C4453/0/73E2D8C20C9F126F8025690000693183?Open&Highlight=2,enron. Site visited 22 January 2002.

Andriof, J. and Mclntosh, M. (eds) (2001) *Perspectives on Corporate Citizenship*, Sheffield: Greenleaf Publishing.

Anon. (1995) *Principles of Islamic Banking*, World Wide Web, http://cwis.usc.edu/deptMSA/economics/nbank1.html. Site visited 20 August 2001.

Anon. (1997) 'Branson to tell EU of "illegal" BA practices', *Financial Times*, 11 November.

Anon. (1999a) 'Brussels gets tough with British Airways', *Financial Times*, 15 July.

Anon. (1999b) 'US judge throws out last Virgin complaint against BA', *Financial Times*, 26 October.

Anon. (2001) 'Cancer research hampered after Alder Hey' *Guardian Unlimited*, 22 May. World Wide Web, www.societyguardian.co.uk/alderhey/story/0,7999,494612,00hl. Site visited 12 July 2001.

Arif, M. (1988) 'Islamic banking' *Asian-Pacific Economic Literature*, 2(2), September, 46–62.

Aristotle (1976) *The Ethics of Aristotle*, trans. J.A.K. Thompson, Harmondsworth: Penguin.

Arthur Anderson and London Business School (1999) *Ethical Concerns and Reputation Risk Management. A Study of Leading UK Companies*, London: Arthur Anderson.

Badaracco, J.L. Jr. (1997) *Defining Moments: When Managers Must Choose Between Right and Right*, Boston: Harvard Business School Press.

Baldwin, S., Godfrey, C. and Propper, C. (eds) (1990) *Quality of Life: Perspectives and Policies*, London: Routledge.

Barlow, T. (2001) 'Body and mind: Treatments that cost an arm and a leg', *Financial Times*, 7 April.

Barr, N. (1985) 'Economic welfare and social justice', *Journal of Society and Politics* 14 (2), 175–87.

Barry, B. (1989) *Theories of Justice: A Treatise on Social Justice*, Hemel Hempstead: Harvester-Wheatsheaf.

Bartlett, R. (2000) *England under the Norman and Angevin Kings, 1075–1225*, Oxford: Clarendon Press.

Bauman, Z. (1994) *Alone Again: Ethics After Certainty*, London: Demos.

BBC News Online (2001a) 'Railtrack reports massive loss', 24 May 2001. Site visited 24 May 2001.

BBC News Online (2001b) 'Ford confirms $2.1 bn. tyre recall', World Wide Web, http://news.bbc.co.uk/hi/english/business/newsid_1345000/1345087.stm. Site visited 24 June 2001.

Beardshaw, V. (1981) *Conscientious Objectors at Work*, London: Social Audit.

Beck, L.W. (1959) *Immanuel Kant: Foundations of the Metaphysics of Morals*, Indianapolis: Bobbs-Merrill Educational Publishing.

Belbin, R.M. (1981) *Management Teams: Why they Succeed or Fail*, London: Heinemann.

Bennett, R. and Voyle, S. (2001) 'Supermarkets facing more scrutiny after election: The relationship between food suppliers and retailers is likely to be probed', *Financial Times*, 11 April.

Bentham, J. (1982) *An Introduction to the Principles of Morals and Legislation*, eds J.H. Burns and H.L.A. Hart, London: Methuen. Original edition 1781.

Bentham, J. (1994) 'The Commonplace Book', in *The Works of Jeremy Bentham*, Vol. X, ed. J. Bowring, Bristol: Thoemnes Press. Original edition (1843) Edinburgh: Tait.

Bhopal.com (2001) *Bhopal incident review and the settlement*, World Wide Web, www.bhopal.com. Site visited 15 October 2001.

Bhopal.net (2001) *The Union Carbide Disaster. Quick Fact Tour*, World Wide Web, www.bhopal.net/intro2.html. Site visited 25 October 2001.

Billig, M. (1996) *Arguing and Thinking: A Rhetorical Approach to Social Psychology*, 2nd edition, Cambridge: Cambridge University Press.

Birch, D. (2001) 'Corporate citizenship: Rethinking business beyond corporate social responsibility', in Andriof, J. and McIntosh, M. (eds), *Perspectives on Corporate Citizenship*, 53–65, Sheffield: Greenleaf Publishing.

Bird, F.B. and Waters, J.A. (1989) 'The moral muteness of managers', *California Management Review*, Fall, 73–88.

Blackburn, M. (2000) 'Managing the cross-cultural aspect of workplace privacy'. Paper presented at *Cross-cultural Business Ethics*, 2nd *International Conference*, 17–19 April, University of Westminster, London.

Blackburn, S. (2001) *Being Good. A Short Introduction to Ethics*, Oxford: Oxford University Press.

Blanchard, K. and Peale, N. (1988) *The Power of Ethical Management*, New York: Fawcett Crest.

Borrie, G. (1996) 'Business ethics and accountability', in Brindle, M. and Dehn, G. *Four Windows on Whistleblowing*, 1–23, London: Public Concern at Work.

Borrie, G. and Dehn, G. (2002) *Whistleblowing: The New Perspective*, London: Public Concern at Work, World Wide Web, www.pcaw.co.uk/policy_pub/newperspective.html.

Boseley, S. (2001a) 'Arrogance of doctors led to organ scandal', *Guardian,* 11 January: 3. *Guardian and the Observer on CD-ROM.*

Boseley, S. (2001b) '50,0000 organs secretly stored in hospitals', *Guardian,* 11 January: 1. *Guardian and the Observer on CD-ROM.*

Bowe, C. (2001) 'Firestone cuts ties with Ford over tyre recall', *Financial Times*, 22 May: 36.

Bowie, N. and Duska, R. (1990) *Business Ethics*, Englewood Cliffs, NJ: Prentice-Hall.

Bowie, N.E. (1999) *Business Ethics: A Kantian Perspective*, Oxford: Blackwell Publishers.

BP (2001) *BP's 2001 Environmental and Social Report*, World Wide Web, www.bp.com/environ_social/review_2001/index.asp. Site visited 28 March 2002.

Bradley, S. (2000) 'Villagers not sweet on 7-day sugar plan', *Bury Free Press*, 30 June.

Brigley, S. and Vass, P. (1997) *Privatised Ethics. The Case of the Regulated Industries*, in Davies, P.W.F. (ed.) *Current Issues in Business Ethics*, London: Routledge.

British Airways (2000) *British Airways Social and Environmental Report 2000*, London: British Airways.

Brown, J.M. (1972) *Gandhi's Rise to Power: Indian Politics 1915–1922*, Cambridge: Cambridge University Press.

Brown, M. (2001) 'Capitalism: Reconstruction theory', *Financial Management*, November, 20.

Brunsson, N. (1986) 'Organising for inconsistencies: On organisational conflict, depression and hypocrisy as substitutes for action', *Scandinavian Journal of Management Studies*, May, 165–85.

Brunsson, N. (1989) *The Organisation of Hypocrisy: Talk, Decisions and Actions in Organisations*, Chichester: John Wiley & Sons.

Brytting, T. (1997) 'Moral support structures in private industry – The Swedish case', *Journal of Business Ethics*, 16, 663–97.

Buchholz, R.A. and Rosenthal, S.B. (1998) *Business Ethics: The Pragmatic Path Beyond Principles to Process*, Harlow: Prentice Hall.

Buckley, S.L. (1998) *Usury Friendly? The Ethics of Moneylending – a Biblical Interpretation*, Cambridge: Grove Books.

Burns, J. and Shrimsley, R. (2000) 'Racism "remains rife" in the Met: Complaints of discrimination at all levels add to ethnic recruitment crisis says report', *Financial Times*, 14 December.

Cabinet Office (n.d.) *The Civil Service Code*, World Wide Web, www.cabinet-office.gov.uk/central/1999/cscode.htm. Site visited 13 March 2002.

Cantor, N., Mischel, W. and Schwartz, J. (1982) 'Social knowledge: Structure, content, use and abuse', in Hastorf, A.H. and Isen, A.M. (eds) *Cognitive Social Psychology*, New York: Elsevier.

Carmarthenshire County Council (2000) *Whistle Blowing Procedure*, World Wide Web, www.carmarthenshire.gov.uk/agendas/eng/OSTD20011218/REP05_4.htm. Site visited 8 February 2002.

Carr, A. Z. (1968) 'Is business bluffing ethical?', *Business and Society Review*, 100(1), 1–7.

Carroll, A.B. (1990) 'Principles of business ethics: Their role in decision making and an initial consensus', *Management Decision*, 28(8), 20–4.

Cassell, C., Johnson, P. and Smith, K. (1997) 'Opening the black box: Corporate codes of ethics in their organisational context', *Journal of Business Ethics*, 16, 1077–93.

Casson, M. (1991) *The Economics of Business Culture: Games Theory, Transaction Costs and Economic Performance*, Oxford: Oxford University Press, Clarendon Paperbacks.

Caux Round Table (2001) *Caux Round Table Principles for Business*, World Wide Web, www.cauxroundtable.org/ENGLISH.HTM. Site visited 26 October 2001.

Center for Public Enquiry (2000) *The Public I: Major tobacco multinational implicated in cigarette smuggling, tax evasion, documents show*, World Wide Web, www.public-i.org/story_01_013100.htm. Site visited 3 June 2000.

CEPAA (1997) *Guidance Document for Social Accountability 8000*, London: CEPAA.

Chakraborty, S.K. (1993) *Managerial Transformations by Values*, New Delhi: Sage.

Chakraborty, S.K. (1999) *Values and Ethics for Organisations. Theory and Practice*. New Delhi: Oxford University Press.

Clark, A. and Borger, J. (2001) 'Cheaper drugs for Africa: Manufacturer to relax its patent on two Aids remedies', *Guardian*, 15 March: 3. *Guardian and Observer on CD-ROM*.

Clarke, K. (2000) 'Dilemma of a cigarette exporter', *Guardian Unlimited*, 3 February, World Wide Web, www.newsunlimited.co.uk/bat/0,2763,131913,00.html. Site visited 12 August 2001.

Clarkson, C.M.V. (1998) 'Corporate culpability', *Web Journal of Legal Issues*, Blackstone Press Ltd., World Wide Web, http://webjcli.ncl.uk/1998/issue2/clarkson2.html.

Clutterbuck D. (1992) *The Role of the Chief Executive in Maintaining an Ethical Climate*, London: Clutterbuck Associates.

Cohen, N. (2002) 'Without prejudice. Back to the bad old days', *Observer*, 20 January: 27.

Company Law Reform Committee (2001) *Modern Company Law for a Competitive Economy: The Final Report*, The Stationery Office, July.

Connock, S. and Johns, T. (1995) *Ethical Leadership*, London: Institute of Personnel and Development.

Corpwatch (2001) *Personal Appeal from Bhopal to Shareholders of Union Carbide: You Can Still End the Disaster in Bhopal.* World Wide Web, www.corpwatc.org/trac/bhopal/shareholder.html. Site visited 25 October 2001.

Covey, S.R. (1992) *The Seven Habits of Highly Effective People. Powerful Lessons in Personal Change*, London: Simon and Schuster.

Cowe, R. (2001) 'Europe rises to social challenge: Corporate citizenship, *Financial Times*, 19 July.

Crainer, S. (1993) *Zeebrugge: Learning from Disaster*, London: Herald Charitable Trust.

Crouch, C. and Marquand, D. (eds) (1993) *Ethics and Markets: Co-operation and Competition within Capitalist Economies*, Oxford: Blackwell Publishers.

Cyert, R.M. and March, J.G. (1992) *A Behavioral Theory of the Firm*, 2nd edition, New Jersey: Blackwell.

Dallas, M. (1996) 'Accountability for performance – Does audit have a role?' in *Adding Value? Audit and Accountability in the Public Services*, Public Finance Foundation and Chartered Institute of Public Finance and Accountancy (CIPFA): London.

Davies, P.W.F. (ed.) (1997) *Current Issues in Business Ethics*, London: Routledge.

De George, R.T. (1999) *Business Ethics*, 5th edition, Englewood Cliffs, NJ: Prentice-Hall.

Denhardt, R.B. (1981), *In the Shadow of Organisation*, Lawrence, Kans: Regents Press.

D'Entreves, A.P. (1965) *Aquinas. Selected Political Writings*, trans. J.G. Dawson, Oxford: Basil Blackwell.

Department of Transport (1987) *MV Herald of Free Enterprise, Formal Investigation by Hon. Mr. Justice Sheen, Wreck Commissioner, Court Report 8074* (The Sheen Report), London: HMSO.

Derrida, J. with Bennington, G. (1989) 'On colleges and philosophy', in Appignanesi, L. (ed.) *Postmodernism. ICA Documents*, London: Free Associates Books.

Dewey, C. (1993) *Anglo-Indian Attitudes: the Mind of the Indian Civil Service*, London: The Hambledon Press.

Dhesi, A.S. (1998) 'Caste, class synergies and discrimination in India', *International Journal of Social Economics*, 25(6,7,8), 1030–48.

Director (2001) 'Spanish Shuffle', *Director*, February: 29.

Donaldson, T. and Preston, L.E. (1995) 'The stakeholder theory of the corporation; Concepts, evidence and implications', *Academy of Management Review*, 22(1), 65–91.

Dugatkin, L. (2000) *Cheating Monkeys and Citizen Bees*, Cambridge, Mass.: Harvard University Press.

Durkheim, E. (1992) *Professional Ethics and Civic Morals*, trans. C. Brookfield, London: Routledge.

Dworkin, R. (1977) *Taking Rights Seriously*, London: Duckworth.

Eastwood, A. and Maynard, A. (1990) 'Treating Aids. Is it ethical to be efficient', in Baldwin, S., Godfrey, C. and Propper, C. (eds) *Quality of Life: Perspectives and Policies*, London: Routledge.

Eco, U. (1985) *Reflections on the Name of the Rose*, London: Secker & Warburg.

Eco, U. with Rorty, R. Culler, J and Brooke-Rose, C., ed. Collini, S. (1992) *Interpretation and Overinterpretation*, Cambridge: Cambridge University Press.

Economist (2001) 'The plot thickens: A survey of India's economy', *Economist*, 2 June.

Eden, C., Jones, S. and Sims, D. (1979) *Thinking in Organisations*, London: Macmillan.

Elkington, J. (1999) 'Triple bottom line reporting: Looking for balance', *Australian CPA*, March, World Wide Web, www.cpaonline.com.au/03_publications/ 02_aust_cpa_magazine/1999/03_mar/3_2_3_31_reporting.asp. Site visited 12 June 2001.

Elshtain, J.B., Aird, E., Etzioni, A., Galston, W., Glendon, M.A., Minow, M., Rossi, A. (n.d.) *The Communitarian Network. A Communitarian Position Paper on the Family*, World Wide Web, www.gwu.edu/~ccps/pop_fam.html. Site visited 15 November 2001.

Etzioni, A. (1988) *The Moral Dimension: Towards a New Economics*, New York: The Free Press.

Etzioni, A. (1993) *The Spirit of Community*, New York: Crown.

Evans, S. (2001) 'McDonald's grilled over "veggie" fries', *BBC News Online,* World Wide Web, http://news.bbc.co.uk. Site visited 24 May 2001.

Failaka International Inc. (2001) *Glossary of Islamic Financial Terms*, World Wide Web, www.failaka.com/Glossary.html. Site visited 20 August 2001.

Farrell, B.J. and Cobbin, D.M. (1996) 'A content analysis of codes of ethics in Australian enterprises', *Journal of Managerial Psychology*, 11(1), 37–55.

Festinger, L. (1957) *A Theory of Cognitive Dissonance*, New York: Row Peterson.

Financial Times (2000) 'Leader article: Spy trap', *Financial Times*, 22 August.

Financial Times (2001) 'Leader article: Changing track', *Financial Times*, 9 May.

Fineman, S. and Gabriel, Y. (1996) *Experiencing Organisations*, London: Sage.

Firestone Tire Resource Center (n.d.) World Wide Web, www.citizen.org/fireuf/ index7.htm. Site visited 22 May 2001.

Fischer, F. (1983) 'Ethical discourse in public administration', *Administration and Society*, 15(1), 5–42.

Fischoff, B., Slovic, P. and Lichtenstein, S. (1977) 'Knowing with certainty: the appropriateness of extreme confidence', *Journal of Experimental Psychology*, 3(4), 552–64.

Fisher, C. and Lovell, A.T.A. (2000) *Accountants' Responses to Ethical Issues at Work*, London: CIMA Publishing.

Fisher, C.M. (1998) *Resource Allocation in the Public Sector: Values, Priorities, and Markets in the Management of Public Services*, London: Routledge.

Fisher, C.M. (1999) 'Ethical stances: The perceptions of accountants and HR specialists of ethical conundrums at work', *Business Ethics: A European Review*, 18(4), 236–48.

Fisher, C.M. (2000a) 'The ethics of inactivity: human resource managers and quietism', *Business and Professional Ethics Journal*, 19, 55–72.

Fisher, C.M. (2000b) *Dilemma: A Diagnostic Inventory of Managers' Ethical Horizons*, World Wide Web, http://socks.ntu.ac.uk/maze/. Site visited 24 June 2001.

Fisher, C.M. (2001) 'Managers' perceptions of ethical codes: Dialectics and dynamics', *Business Ethics: A European Review*, 10(2), 145–57.

Fisher, C.M. and Rice, C. (1999) 'Managing messy moral matters', in Leopold, J., Harris, L. and Watson, T.J. (1999) *Strategic Human Resources. Principles, Perspectives and Practices*, Harlow: Financial Times Prentice Hall.

Fletcher, J. (1966) *Situation Ethics*, London: SCM Press.

Forster, E.M. (1975) *Two Cheers for Democracy*, New York: Holmes & Meier.

Foster, N. (2001) *The Foster Catalogue 2001*, London: Prestel.

Francis, D. and Young, D. (1979) *Improving Work Groups: A Practical Manual for Team Building*, La Jolla, Calif.: University Associates.

Friedman, M. (1970) 'The social responsibility of business is to increase its profits', *New York Times Magazine*, 13 September, 33, 122–26.

Fukuyama, F. (1993) *The End of History and the Last Man*, Harmondsworth: Penguin.

Gabriel, Y., Fineman, S. and Sims, D. (2000) *Organizing and Organizations*, 2nd edition, London: Sage.

Galton, M. and Delafield, A. (1981) 'Expectancy effects in primary classrooms', in Simons, B. and Willcocks, J. (eds) (1981) *Research and Practice in the Primary Classroom*, London: Routledge and Kegan Paul.

Giddens, A. (1985) 'Reason without revolution? Habermas's Theorie des Kommunikativen Handelns', in Bernstein, R.J. (ed.) *Habermas and Modernity*, Cambridge: Polity Press in association with Oxford: Blackwells.

Gidoomal, R. and Porter, D. (1997) *The UK Maharajahs: Inside the South Asian Success Story*, London: Nicholas Brealey.

Gigerenzer, G., Todd, P. and the ABC Research Group (1999) *Simple Heuristics that Make us Smart*, Oxford: Oxford University Press.

Gilligan, C. (1982) *In a Different Voice: Psychological Theory and Women's Development*, Cambridge, Mass.: Harvard University Press,

Goffman, E. (1959) *The Presentation of the Self in Everyday Life*, New York: Doubleday Anchor Books.

Gonella, C., Pilling, A. and Zadek, S. (1998) *Making Values Count*, Research Report No. 57, Association of Chartered Certified Accountants; London: Certified Accountants Educational Trust.

Gopinath, C. (1998) 'Alternative approaches to indigenous management in India', *Management International Review*, 38(3), 257–75.

Greenawalt, K. (1987) *Conflicts of Law and Morality*, Oxford: Oxford University Press.

Griseri, P. (1998) *Managing Values*, London: Palgrave.

Gross, J. (1987) *Oxford Dictionary of Aphorisms*, Oxford: Oxford University Press.

Guardian (1999) Leading article: "Mr Aitken pays the price", *Guardian*, 9 June: 21. *Guardian and the Observer on CD-ROM*.

Gudex, C. (1986) *QALYs and their Use by the Health Service*, Discussion Paper No. 20, Centre for Health Economics; York: Centre for Health Economics, University of York.

Guerrera, F. (2001a) 'Hit squad to tackle animal rights activists', *www.FT.com*, 27 April. Site visited 6 July 2001.

Guerrera, F. (2001b) 'Huntingdon seeks nominee structure to protect holders', *Financial Times*, 12 May.

Haley, G.T. and Haley, U.C.V. (1998) 'Boxing with shadows: Competing effectively with the overseas Chinese and the overseas Indian business networks in the Asian arena', *Journal of Organisational Change Management*, 11(4), 301–20.

Harding, L. (1999) 'The fall of Aitken: from Eton and Oxford to the Ritz and the Old Bailey', *Guardian*, 9 June: 4. *Guardian and the Observer on CD-ROM*.

Harrington, M. (1965) *The Accidental Century*, Harmondsworth: Penguin.

Harris, J.E. and Reynolds, M.A. (1993) 'Formal codes: The delineation of ethical dilemmas', *Advances in Public Interest Accounting*, 5, 107–20.

Harris, L.C and Ogbonna, E. (1999) 'Developing a market oriented culture: A critical evaluation', *Journal of Management Studies*, 36(2), 177–96.

Hartley, R.E. (1993) *Business Ethics: Violations of the Public Trust*, Chichester: John Wiley & Sons.

Harvey, D. (1989) *The Condition of Postmodernity*, Oxford: Blackwell.

Heelas, P. and Morris, P. (eds) (1992) *The Values of the Enterprise Culture: The Moral Debate*, London: Routledge.

Heidegger, M. (1959) *Introduction to Metaphysics*, trans. R. Manheim, Yale: Yale University Press.

Heidegger, M. (2000) *Introduction to Metaphysics*, trans. G. Fried and R. Polt, Yale: Nota Bene.

Held, D. (1987) *Models of Democracy*, Oxford: Polity Press.

Helson, R. and Wink, P. (1992) 'Personality change in women from the early 40s to the early 50s', *Psychology and Ageing*, 7(1), March.

Hirst, P. and Thompson, G. (1996) *Globalisation in Question*, Oxford: Polity Press.

Hobbes, T. (n.d.) *Leviathan or the Matter, Forme and Power of a Commonwealth Ecclesiastical and Civil*, ed. M. Oakeshott, Oxford: Blackwell.

Hoffman, W.M. and Moore, J.M. (1990) *Business Ethics: Readings and Cases in Corporate Morality*, London: McGraw-Hill.

Hofstede, G.H. (1991) *Cultures and Organisations. Software of the Mind*, London: McGraw-Hill.

Hofstede, G.H. (2001) *Culture's Consequences*, 2nd edition, London: Sage.

Hogarth, R. (1980) *Judgement and Choice*, New York: John Wiley & Sons.

Holden, N.J. (2002) *Cross Cultural Management. A Knowledge Management Perspective*, Harlow: Financial Times Prentice Hall.

Holland, L. and Gibbon, J. (2001) 'Processes in social and ethical accountability: External reporting mechanisms', in Andriof, J. and McIntosh, M. (eds) *Perspectives on Corporate Citizenship*, 278–95, Sheffield: Greenleaf Publishing.

Home Office (2000) *Reforming the Law on Involuntary Manslaughter*, London: Home Office.

Hopwood, A. (1974) *Accounting and Human Behaviour*, Hemel Hempstead: Prentice Hall.

Hunt, G. (1995) *Whistleblowing in the Health Service: Accountability, Law & Professional Practice*, London: Edward Arnold.

Hunt, G. (1998) *Whistleblowing in the Social Services: Public Accountability and Professional Practice*, London: Edward Arnold.

Husserl, E. (1931) *Ideas: General Introduction to Pure Phenomenology*, trans. W.R. Boyce-Gibson, London: George Allen & Unwin.

Husserl, E. (1965) *Phenomenology and the Crisis of Philosophy: Philosophy as Religious Science and Philosophy and the Crisis of European Man*, trans. Q. Lauer, New York: Harper Torchbooks, Harper & Row.

IBFAN (International Baby Food Action Network) (n.d.) *How Breast Feeding is Undermined*, World Wide Web, www.ibfan.org/english/issue/bfundermined01.html. Site visited 17 February 2002.

International Chamber of Commerce (ICC) (1997) *International Code of Advertising Practice*, World Wide Web, www.iccwbo.org/home/statements_rules/rules/1997/advercod.asp. Site visited 13 March 2002.

International Labour Organisation (ILO) (n.d.) *Codes of Conduct for Multinationals*, World Wide Web, www.itcilo.it/english/actrav/telearn/global/ilo/guide/main.htm. Site visited 17 February 2002.

Jackall, R. (1988) *Moral Mazes: The World of Corporate Managers*, New York, Oxford University Press.

Jaeger, A.M. and Kanungo, R.N. (eds) (1990) *Management in Developing Countries*, London: Routledge.

John Paul II (1991) *Centesimus Annus: Encyclical Letter of the Supreme Pontiff John Paul II on the One Hundredth Anniversary of Rerum Novarum*. World Wide Web, http://listserv.american.edu/catholic/church/papal/jp.ii/jp2hundr.txt. Site visited 11 June 2001.

Johnson, G. (1994) *University Politics. F.M. Cornford's Cambridge and his advice to the young academic politician, containing the complete text of 'Microcosmographia Academica'*, Cambridge: Cambridge University Press.

Jones, J.E. and Pfeiffer, J.W. (eds) (1974) *The 1974 Handbook for Group Facilitators*, Iowa City: University Associates.

Jos, P.H. (1988), 'Moral autonomy and the modern organisation', *Polity: The Journal of the North-Eastern Political Science Association*, XXI(2), Winter.

Jung, C.G. (1953) *Psychological Reflections, An Anthology of the Writings of C. G. Jung*, J. Jacobi (ed.), London: Kegan Paul.

Kahneman, D., Slovic, P. and Tversky, A. (eds) (1982) *Judgement under Uncertainty: Heuristics and Biases*, Cambridge: Cambridge University Press.

Kaler, J. (1999) 'What's the good of ethical theory?', *Business Ethics – A European Review*, 8(4), 206–13.

Kanungo, R.N. and Mendonca, M. (1996) *Ethical Dimensions of Leadership*, London: Sage.

Kärreman, D. and Alvesson, M. (1999) 'Ethical closure in organisational settings – the case of media organisations'. Paper presented at the 15th EGOS Colloquium, *Organisations in a Challenging World: Theories, Practices and Societies*, University of Warwick, 4–6 July.

Keats, R. (1993) 'The moral boundaries of the market', in Crouch, C. and Marquand, D. (eds) *Ethics and Markets: Co-operation and Competition within Capitalist Economies*, 6–20, Oxford: Blackwell Publishers.

Kelman, H. (1961) 'The process of opinion change', *Public Opinion*, 25, 57–78.

Kemm, J.R. (1985) 'Ethics of food policy', *Community Medicine*, 7, 289–94.

King, C. (2001) 'Providing Advice on Whistleblowing', in Lewis, D.B. (ed.) *Whistleblowing at Work*, London: The Athlone Press.

Kirchenbaum, H. (1977) *Advanced Value Clarification*, La Jolla, Calif.: University Associates.

Kirkpatrick, J. (1994) *In Defense of Advertising: Arguments from Reason, Ethical Egoism and Laissez-Faire Capitalism*, Westport: Greenwood.

Kjonstad, B. and Willmott, H. (1995) 'Business ethics: Restrictive or empowering', *Journal of Business Ethics*, 14, 445–64.

Knights, D. and Willmott, H. (1999), *Management Lives: Power and Identity in Work Organizations*, London: Sage.

Koehn, D. (1994) *The Ground of Professional Ethics*, London: Routledge.

Kohlberg, L. (1969) *Stages in the Development of Moral Thought and Action*, New York: Holt Rinehart and Winston.

Kohlberg, L. (1984) *Essays in Moral Development, Volume 2, The Psychology of Moral Development*, New York: Harper and Row.

Koretz, G. (2001) 'Why Americans work so hard. How pay inequality galvanizes effort', *Business Week*, issue 3736, 6 November 2001.

KPMG (2002) *KPMG Survey Reveals Workplace Misconduct as a Widespread Problem*, World Wide Web, www.us.kpmg.com/search/index.asp?cid = 563. Site visited 22 January 2002.

Kumar, N.S. and Rao, U.S. (1996) 'Guidelines for value based management in Kautilya's Arthashastra', *Journal of Business Ethics*, 15(4), 415.

Lariba.com (2001) *Lariba Concept*, World Wide Web, www.lariba.com/concepts.shtn. Site visited 20 August 2001.

Larson, M.S. (1977) *The Rise of Professionalism: A Sociological Analysis*, Berkeley Calif.: University of California Press.

Law Commission (1996) *Legislating the Criminal Code*: *Involuntary Manslaughters*, Report No. 237, London: Law Commission.

Legge, K. (1995) *Human Resource Management: Rhetoric and Realities*, London: Macmillan.

Legge, K. (1998) 'Is HRM ethical? Can HRM be ethical?' in Parker, M. (ed.) *Ethics and Organisations*, 150–72, London: Sage.

Lewis, D. (2001) *The Management of Non-Governmental Development Organisations*, London: Routledge.

Lewis, D.B. (2000) *Whistleblowing at Work*, London: Athlone Press.

Liedtka, J. (1991) 'Organisational value contention and managerial mindsets', *Journal of Business Ethics*, 10, 543–57.

Lovell, A.T.A. (2002) 'The vulnerability of autonomy that denies the exercise of moral agency', *Business Ethics: A European Review*, 11(1), 62–76.

Lovell, A.T.A. and Robertson, C. (1994), 'Charles Robertson: In the eye of the storm', in Vinten, G. (ed.) *Whistleblowers*, 146–73, London: Chapman Hall.

Lyons, D. (1984) *Ethics and the Rule of Law*, Cambridge: Cambridge University Press.

Lyotard, J.-F. (1988) *Le Postmodernisme Expliqué aux Enfants, Correspondance 1982–85*, Paris: Editions Galilée.

Mabbott, J.D. (1967) *The State and the Citizen*, 2nd edition, London: Hutchinson and Co.

Machiavelli, N. (1950) *The Prince and the Discourses*, introd. M. Lerner, New York: Modern Library.

MacIntyre, A. (1967) *A Short History of Ethics: A History of Moral Philosophy from the Homeric Age to the Twentieth Century*, London: Routledge.

MacIntyre, A. (1987) *After Virtue: A Study in Moral Theory*: London, Duckworth.

Mackie, J.L. (1990) *Ethics: Inventing Right and Wrong*, Harmondsworth: Penguin.

Maclagan, P. (1996) 'The organisational context for moral development: questions of power and access', *Journal of Business Ethics*, 15(6), 645–54.

Maclagan, P. (1998) *Management & Morality*, London: Sage.

Maclagan, P. and Snell, R. (1992) 'Some implications for management development of research into managers' moral dilemmas', *British Journal of Management*, 3, 157–68.

Maguire, K. (2000) 'Clarke admits BAT link to smuggling', *Guardian Unlimited*, 3 February, World Wide Web, www.newsunlimited.co.uk/bat/article/0,2763,131957,00.html. Site visited 24 August 2001.

Mahesh, V.S. (1995) *Thresholds of Motivation*, New Delhi: Tata McGraw-Hill.

Marcuse, H. (1991) *One-Dimensional Man*, 2nd edition, London: Routledge.

Marx, K. and Engels, F. (1962) 'Critique of the Gotha Programme', in *Selected Works*, vol. II. Moscow: Progress Publishers.

Maslow, A.H. (1987), *Motivation and Personality*, 3rd edition, New York: Harper Collins.

Mathews, M.C. (1988) *Strategic Intervention in Organizations*, Sage Library of Social Research No. 169, London: Sage.

Matthews, J.B., Goodpaster, K.E. and Nash, L.I. (1991) *Policies and Person: A Casebook in Business Ethics*, 2nd edition, London: McGraw-Hill.

McDonald, G. and Nijhof, A. (1999) 'Beyond codes of ethics: an integrated framework for stimulating morally responsible behaviour in organisations', *Leadership & Organisation Development Journal*, 20(3), 133–46.

McGreal, C. (2001) 'Crucial drug case opens in Pretoria', *Guardian*, 6 March: 17.

McKinley, A. and Starkey, K. (1998), *Foucault, Management and Organization Theory: From Panopticon to Technologies of Self*, London: Sage.

McLuhan, M. and Powers, B.R. (1989) *The Global Village. Transformations in World Life and Media in the Twentieth Century*, Oxford: Oxford University Press.

McMylor, P. (1994) *Alisdair MacIntyre: Critic of Modernity*, London: Routledge.

Meade, J.E. (1973) *Theory of Economic Externalities: The Control of Environmental Pollution and Similar Social Costs*, Leiden: Sijhoff.

Meikle, J. (2001) 'Professor quits over tobacco firm's £3.8m gift to university', *Guardian*, 18 May: 6.

Miceli, M.P. and Near, J.P. (1992) *Blowing the Whistle: The Organisational & Legal Implications for Companies and Employees*, New York: Lexington Books.

Michaels, A. (2001) 'Inside Track: Big pharma and the golden goose: interview Hank Mckinnell, Pfizer: Cheaper drugs would mean less money to spend on research and innovation, Pfizer's chief tells Adrian Michael', *Financial Times*, 26 April.

Mihil, C. (1990) 'Thatcher shuns out of court deal for haemophiliacs with HIV', *Guardian*, 9 November: 2.

Mill, J.S. (1971) *Utilitarianism*, Harmondsworth: Penguin (reprint of 1861 edition).

Mill, J.S. (1998) *On Liberty and other Essays*, ed. John Gray, Oxford: Oxford University Press.

Milmo, C. (2001) 'Watchdog warns Virgin over misleading adverts', *Independent*, 30 May.

Minnesota Center for Corporate Responsibility (2001) *The Global Sullivan Principles*, World Wide Web, http://tigger.stthomas.edu.mcer/SullivanPrinciples.htm. Site visited 26 October 2001.

Moore, O. (2000) 'Day of peace plea to sugar factory', *Great Yarmouth Mercury*, 7 July.

Mounce, H.O. (1997) *The Two Pragmatisms: from Peirce to Rorty*, London: Routledge.

Murphy, L.B. (2001) *Moral Demands in Non-Ideal Theory*, Oxford: Oxford University Press.

Myers, A. and Dehn, G. (2000) *Whistleblowing: The first cases and practical issues*, World Wide Web, www.pcaw.co.uk/news/press/_14.html. Site visited 17 February 2002.

NICE (National Institute for Clinical Excellence) (2001) *Interferon Beta/glatiramer Speculation*, World Wide Web, www.nice.org.uk/nice-web/rticle.asp?a = 1370. Site visited 23 May 2001.

NICE (National Institute for Clinical Excellence) (2002) *NICE issues guidance on drugs for multiple sclerosis*, World Wide Web, www.nice.org.uk/article.asp?a = 27619. Site visited 7 March 2002.

Nisbet, R.A. (1953) *The Quest for Community*, Oxford: Oxford University Press.

Nolan Committee (1995) *Standards in Public Life, Volume 1. First Report of the Committee on Standards in Public Life*, London: HMSO.

Nozick, R. (1974) *Anarchy, State, and Utopia*, New York: Basic Books.

Oberman, W.D. (2000) Book review of Mitchell: 'The Conspicuous Corporation', (1997) *Business and Society*, 329(2), 239–44.

Observer (2000) Leader article, 'The mob should never rule', *Observer*, 17 September.

OECD (Organisation for Economic Co-operation and Development) (2001) *The OECD Guidelines for Multi-national Enterprises*, World Wide Web, www.oecd.org/EN/document/0, EN-document-93-3-no-6-18925-93,00.html. Site visited 7 June 2002.

Pagels, E. (1982) *The Gnostic Gospels*, Harmondsworth: Penguin.

Parker, M. (1998a) 'Business ethics and social theory: Postmodernizing the ethical', *British Journal of Management*, 9, September, 27–36.

Parker, M. (1998b) 'Against ethics', in Parker, M. (ed.) *Ethics and Organisations*, London: Sage.

Passmore, J. (1984) 'Academic ethics', *Journal of Applied Philosophy*, 1(1).

Pateman, C. (1985) *The Problem of Political Obligation: A Critique of Liberal Theory*, New York: John Wiley & Sons.

Pava, M.L. (1999) *The Search for Meaning in Organisations: Seven Practical Questions for Ethical Managers*, Westport, Conn.: Quorum Books.

Pereira, J. (1989) *What does Equity in Health Mean?*, Centre for Health Economics, Discussion Paper No. 61, York: Centre for Health Economics.

Peters, T.J. and Waterman Jnr., R. (1982) *In Search of Excellence*, New York: Harper and Row.

Petrick, J.A. (2000) 'Global human resource management competence and judgement integrity: towards a human centred organisation', paper presented at Third Conference on Ethics and Human Resource Management, Towards a Human Centred Organisation, Imperial College, London, 7 June.

Petrick, J.A. and Quinn, J.F. (1997) *Management Ethics. Integrity at Work*, London: Sage.

Pilger, J. (2001) 'Spoils of a massacre', *Guardian Weekend*, 14 July, 18–29

Pilling, D. and Timmins, N. (2000) 'Medicines arbiter delays decision on beta-interferon clinical excellence. Multiple Sclerosis Society angry that drug ruling is only likely after election', *Financial Times*, 23 December.

Plant, R. (1992) 'Enterprise in its place: the moral limits of markets', in Heelas, P. and Morris, P. (eds) *The Values of the Enterprise Culture: The Moral Debate*, London: Routledge, 85–99.

Pojman, L.P. (1998) *Classics of Philosophy*, Oxford: Oxford University Press.

Pollitt, M. and Ashworth, H. (2000) 'Beet lorry victory for villages', *Eastern Daily Press*, 21 July: 63–77.

Proctor, E.K., Morrow-Howell, N. and Lott, C.L. (1993) 'Classification and correlates of ethical dilemmas in hospital social work', *Social Work*, 38(2), 166–77.

Project Management Profession (1996) *Code of Ethics for the Project Management Profession*, www.pmi.orh/pmi/mem_info/pmpcode.htm. Site visited 9 March 2001.

Pusey, M. (1987) *Jürgen Habermas*, London: Routledge.

Rangarajan, L.N. (ed.) (1992) *Kautilya: The Arthashastra*, New Delhi: Penguin Books India.

Raphael, D.D. (1970) *Problems of Political Philosophy*, London: Methuen.

Rawls, J. (1971) *A Theory of Justice*, Cambridge, Mass.: Harvard University Press.

Rawls, J. (1999) *A Theory of Justice* (revised edition), Cambridge, Mass.: Harvard University Press.

Redfern Report (2001) *The Royal Liverpool Children's Hospital Report*, House of Commons Parliamentary Papers, World Wide Web, www.rlcinquiry.org.uk/. Site visited 9 March 2001.

Riddall, J.G. (1991) *Jurisprudence*, London: Butterworths.

Ritzer, G. (1993) *The McDonaldization of Society*, California: Sage.

Rokeach, M. (1973) *The Nature of Human Values*, New York: The Free Press.

Rorty, R. (1985) 'Habermas and Lyotard on postmodernity', in Bernstein, R. (ed.) *Habermas and Modernity*, Cambridge: Cambridge University Press.

Rorty, R. (1989) *Contingency, Irony and Solidarity*, Cambridge: Cambridge University Press.

Rorty, R. (1990) *Philosophy and the Mirror of Nature*, Oxford: Blackwell.

Rorty, R. (1992) 'The pragmatist's progress', in Eco, U. with Rorty, R., Culler, J. and Brooke-Rose, C. ed. Collini, S. (1992) *Interpretation and Overinterpretation*, Cambridge: Cambridge University Press.

Ross, W.D. (1930) *The Right and the Good*, Oxford: Oxford University Press.

Rotter, J.B. (1966) 'General expectancies for internal versus external control of reinforcement', *Psychological Monographs; General and Applied*, 80, 1–28.

Russell, J.B. (1985) *The Devil in the Middle Ages*, Cornell: Cornell University Press.

Saini, D.S. and Khan, S.A. (eds) (2000) *Human Resource Management: Perspectives for the New Era*, New Delhi: Sage.

Sarason, S.B. (1986) 'And what is the public interest?', *American Psychologist*, August.

Schein, E. (1992) *Organizational Culture and Leadership*, San Francisco: Jossey-Bass.

Schreier, M. and Groeben, N. (1996) 'Ethical guidelines for the conduct in argumentative discussions: An exploratory study', *Human Relations*, 49(1), 123–32.

Schumpeter, J.A. (1976) *Capitalism, Socialism and Democracy*, London: George Allen & Unwin.

Scruton, R. (2000) *Animal Rights and Wrongs*, 3rd edition, London: Metro.

Seedhouse, D. (1988) *Ethics: The Heart of Healthcare*, London: John Wiley & Sons.

Senge, P.M. (1990) *The Fifth Discipline. The Art and Practice of the Learning Organisation*, London: Century.

Shaw, W.H. and Barry, V. (1998) *Moral Issues in Business*, 7th edition, Belmont, Calif.: Wadsworth Publishing Company.

Simon, H.A. (1952) 'Comments on the theory of organizations', *American Political Science Review*, 46, 1130–39.

Simon, H.A. (1953) 'Notes on the observation and measurement of political power', *Journal of Politics*, 15, 500–16.

Simon, H.A. (1955) 'A behavioural model of rational choice', *Quarterly Journal of Economics*, 69, 99–118.

Simon, H.A. (1983) *Reason in Human Affairs*, Oxford: Basil Blackwell.

Sinclair, A. (1993) 'Approaches to organisational culture and ethics', *Journal of Business Ethics*, 12, 63–73.

Singer, P. (1983) *Hegel*, Oxford: Oxford University Press.

Singer, P. (1997) *How We Choose to Live. Ethics in an Age of Self-Interest*, Oxford: Oxford University Press.

Singh, J.P. (1990) 'Managerial culture and work-related values in India', *Organisation Studies*, 11(1), 75–101.

Skapinker, M. (1998) 'BA says sorry to Branson', *Financial Times*, 17 May.

Skapinker, M. (2001) 'Michael Skapinker examines the issues raised by Luc Vandevelde's recent decision to turn down a generous pay bonus', *www.FT.com*, 4 May 2001.

Smircich, L. (1983) 'Concepts of culture and organisational analysis', *Administrative Science Quarterly*, 28, 339–58.

Smith, M. (1977) *A Practical Guide to Value Clarification*, La Jolla, Calif.: University Associates.

Snell, R.S. (1993) *Developing Skills for Ethical Management*, London: Chapman & Hall.

Snell, R.S. (2000) 'Studying moral ethos using an adapted Kohlbergian model', *Organisation Studies*, 21(1), 267–95.

Soeken, K. and Soeken, D. (1987) *A Survey of Whistleblowers: Their Stresses and Coping Strategies*, Laurel Md.: Association of Mental Health Specialties.

Solomon, R.C. (1993) *Ethics and Excellence: Cooperation and Integrity in Business*, Oxford: Oxford University Press.

Spaemann, R. (1989) *Basic Moral Concepts*, trans. Armstrong, T.J., London: Routledge.

Srivastva, S. and Cooperrider, D.L. (1988) 'The urgency for executive integrity', in Srivastva, S. (ed.) *Executive Integrity: The Search for High Human Values in Organisational Life*, 1–28, San Francisco: Jossey-Bass.

Starzl, T.W. and Dhir, K.S. (1986) 'Strategic planning 2000 years ago – The strategy of Kautilya', *Management International Review*, 26(4), 70–8.

Sternberg, E. (1996) 'A vindication of whistleblowing in business', in Brindle, M. and Dehn, G. (1996) *Four Windows on Whistleblowing*, 24–39, London: Public Concern at Work.

Sternberg, E. (2000) *Just Business: Business Ethics in Action*, 2nd edition, Oxford: Oxford University Press.

Stevens, B. (1994) 'An analysis of corporate ethical code studies; "Where do we go from here?"', *Journal of Business Ethics*, 13, 63–9.

Stewart, D.W. (1984) 'Managing competing claims: An ethical framework for human resource decision making', *Public Administration Review*, 44(1), January/February, 14–22.

Stokes, E. (1959) *The English Utilitarians and India*, Oxford: The Clarendon Press.

Tawney, R.H. (1966) *Religion and the Rise of Capitalism*, Harmondsworth: Penguin.

Taylor, C. (2001) 'How to be diverse. The need for a "looser" us to accommodate "them"', *Times Literary Supplement*, No. 5116, 20 April: 4.

Terry, M. (1975) 'The inevitable growth of informality', *British Journal of Industrial Relations*, 1(3), 76–90.

Tester, K. (1991) *Animals and Society: The Humanity of Animal Rights*, London: Routledge.

Texas Instruments (1999) *Ethics in the Global Market*, World Wide Web, www.ti.com/corp/docs/company/citizen/ethics/market.shtn. Site visited 12 November 1999.

Texas Instruments (2001) *The TI Ethics Quick Test*, World Wide Web, www.ti.com/corp/docs/company/citizen/ethics/quicktest.shtml. Site visited 19 November 2001.

Thomson, A. (1999) *Critical Reasoning in Ethics. A Practical Introduction*, London: Routledge.

Tinker, T. (1985) *Paper Prophets*, Eastbourne: Holt, Rinehart and Winston.

Titmuss, R.M. (1970) *The Gift Relationship: From Human Blood to Social Policy*, London: Allen & Unwin.

Toffler, B.L. (1991) *Managers Talk Ethics: Making Tough Choices in a Competitive World*, New York: John Wiley & Sons.

Transparency International (1999) *1999 Bribe Payers Index*, World Wide Web, www.transparency.de/documents/cpi/index.html. Site visited 9 July 2000.

Transparency International (2001) *The 2001 Corruption Perceptions Index*, World Wide Web, www.gwdg.de/~uwvw/2001Data.html. Site visited 20 September 2001.

Trevino, L.K. (1986) 'Ethical decision making in organisations: A person-situation interactionist model', *Academy of Management Review*, 11(3), 601–17.

Trevino, L.K. and Youngblood, S.A. (1990) 'Bad apple in bad barrels: A causal analysis of ethical decision-making behaviour', *Journal of Applied Psychology*, 75(4), 378–85.

Tripathi, R.C. (1990) 'Interplay of values in the functioning of Indian organisations', *International Journal of Psychology*, 25, 715–34.

Trompenaars, F. and Hampden-Turner, C. (1993) *Riding the Waves of Culture. Understanding Cultural Diversity in Business*, 2nd edition, London: Nicholas Brealey.

Tsogas, G. (1999) 'Labour standards in international trade agreements: A critical assessment of the arguments', *International Journal of Human Resource Management*, 10(2), April, 351–75.

Turner, C.T. (2001) *The Real Root Cause of the Ford-Firestone Tragedy: Why the Public is Still at Risk*, Public Citizen and safetyforum.com. World Wide Web, www.citizen.org/fireweb/index7.htm. Site visited 3 June 2001.

United Kingdom Central Council for Nursing, Midwifery and Health Visiting (UKCC) (1996) *Code of Professional Conduct*, World Wide Web, www.ukcc.org.uk/codecon.html. Site visited 8 May 2000.

United Kingdom, Government (2000) *Reforming the Law on Involuntary Manslaughter: The Government's Proposals*, London: Home Office.

United Nations (1948) *Universal Declaration of Human Rights*, World Wide Web, www.un.org/Overview/rights.html. Site visited 8 February 2002.

United Nations (1989) *Convention on the Rights of the Child*, World Wide Web, www.unicef.org/crc/crc.htm. Site visited 30 March 2002.

Van Buitenen (2000) *Blowing the Whistle. One Man's Fight Against Fraud in the European Commission*, London: Politico's Publishing.

Vardy, P. and Grosch, P. (1999) *The Puzzle of Ethics*, revised edition, London: Fount.

Verbeke, W., Ouwerkerk, C. and Peelen, E. (1996) 'Exploring the contextual and individual factors on ethical decision making of salespeople', *Journal of Business Ethics*, 15, 1175–87.

Viswesvaran, C. and Deshpande, S.P. (1996) 'Ethics, success and job satisfaction: A test of dissonance theory in India', *Journal of Business Ethics*, 15(10), 1065–69.

Vroom, V.H. (1964) *Work and Motivation*, New York: Wiley.

Walzer, M. (1983) *Spheres of Justice: A Defence of Pluralism and Equality*, Oxford: Martin Robertson.

Warren R.C. (1993) 'Codes of Ethics: Bricks without Straw', *Business Ethics: A European Review*, 2(4), 185–91.

Watson, T.J. (1994) *In Search of Management*, London: Routledge.

Watson, T.J. (1998) 'Ethical codes and moral communities: The Gunlaw Temptation, the Simon Solution and the David Dilemma', in Parker, M. (ed) *Ethics and Organisations*, 253–69, London: Sage.

Watson, T.J. (2002) *Organising and Managing Work. Organisational, Managerial and Strategic Behaviour in Theory and Practice*, Harlow: Financial Times Prentice Hall.

Welford, R. (1995) *Environmental Strategy and Sustainable Development: The Corporate Challenge for the Twenty-first Century*, London: Routledge.

Whysall, P. (2000) 'Addressing the issues in retailing: A stakeholder perspective', *International Review of Retail, Distribution and Consumer Research*, 10(3), 305–18.

Wilde, O. (1996) *A Woman of No Importance*, Harmondsworth: Penguin.

Willmott, H. (1998) 'Towards a new ethics? The contributions of poststructuralism and posthumanism,' in Parker, M. (ed.) *Ethics and Organisations*, London: Sage.

Wilson, J. (1999) 'Aitken "will not be a priest"', *Guardian*, 10 June: 10.

Windsor, D. (2001) 'Corporate citizenship, evolution and interpretation', in Andriof, J. and McIntosh, M. (eds) *Perspectives on Corporate Citizenship*, 39–52, Sheffield: Greenleaf Publishing.

Wines, A.W. and Napier, N.K. (1992) 'Towards an understanding of cross-cultural ethics: A tentative model', *Journal of Business Ethics*, 11, 831–41.

Winfield, M. (1990) *Minding Your Own Business: Self-Regulation and Whistleblowing in British Companies*, London: Social Audit.

Winstanley, D. and Woodall, J. (eds) (2000) *Ethical Issues in Contemporary Human Resource Management*, London: Macmillan.

Winstanley, D., Clark, J. and Leeson, H. (2001) 'Approaches to child labour in the supply chain'. Paper presented at *4th Conference on Ethics and Human Resource Management: Professional Development and Practice*. Middlesex University Business School, 20 April.

Winter, R. (1989) *Learning from Experience. Principles and Practice in Action Research*, Lewes: Falmer.

Wolf, M. (2000) 'Sleepwalking with the enemy: Corporate social responsibility distorts the market by deflecting business from its primary role of profit generation', *Financial Times*, 16 May: 21.

Wood, D.J. and Logsdon, J.M. (2001) 'Theorising business citizenship', in Andriof, J. and McIntosh, M. (eds), *Perspectives on Corporate Citizenship*, 83–103, Sheffield: Greenleaf Publishing.

Woodall, J. and Douglas, D. (1999) 'Ethical issues in contemporary human resource development,' *Business Ethics: A European Review*, 8(4), October, 249–61.

Woodcock, M. (1979) *The Team Development Manual*, Aldershot: Gower Press.

Woodcock, M. (1989) *50 Activities for Team Building*, Aldershot: Gower.

Young, K. (1977) 'Values in the policy process', *Policy and Politics*, 5, 1–22.

Index

Class: 174 FIS

Title: Business Ethics & Values

Author: _____

**7 DAY
BOOK**